Best of British

Cinema and Society 1930—1970

Jeffrey Richards and Anthony Aldgate

BASIL BLACKWELL

For Richard Taylor
and Jane Aldgate

First published 1983
Basil Blackwell Publisher Limited
108 Cowley Road, Oxford OX4 1JF, England

British Library Cataloguing in Publication Data

Richards, Jeffrey
    Best of British: cinema and society 1930—1970.
    1. Moving pictures in historiography
    I. Title   II. Aldgate, Anthony
    907   D16
    ISBN 0-631-13018-7

Typesetting in 11/13 pt Vladimir by Pioneer, East Sussex
Printed in Great Britain by T. J. Press, Padstow

Contents

Acknowledgements

Although this book was conceived as a unity and written according to a set of agreed principles, chapters 1, 2, 4, 7, 8 and 11 were the work of Jeffrey Richards, and chapters 3, 5, 6, 9 and 10 were the work of Anthony Aldgate. The authors would like to thank the following for advice, assistance and information: Paul Berry, Roy Boulting, Elaine Burrows, Stephen Constantine, James Ferman, John MacKenzie, Michelle Snapes, John Trevelyan, and Alexander Walker. Thanks are also due to the ever-helpful Stills and Viewing Departments of the National Film Archive and the Library Services of the British Film Institute, to the British Board of Film Censors and to Pendennis Films Ltd. The stills reproduced in the book are from films originally distributed by the following companies to whom thanks are due: United Artists, GFD, British Lion, Rank, Eagle—Lion, Pathé, and Paramount.

1

Feature Films and the Historian

From the 1920s to the 1950s cinema-going was the principal leisure activity of a large proportion of the British people. The cinema attracted members of all classes, though in particular the working class. It appealed to both sexes and to all age groups, though least of all to the elderly. It occupied a place in people's lives which since the 1950s has been taken over by television, though some of the films that draw today's television audience are the ones that were seen and enjoyed by their parents and grandparents on their regular weekly visits to the cinema.

The cinema was an integral and important part of the mass media, closely associated with newspapers, wireless, pulp fiction and, latterly, television. Its influence was fully recognized in its heyday and was reflected in the regular parliamentary debates on matters cinematographic, in the creation of film propaganda organizations, particularly by the Conservative Party, and in the large number of local and national inquiries, conferences, commissions and investigative studies into the effect of cinema on its audience. The prevalent view was succinctly summarized by the 1936 Moyne Committee Report into the working of the Cinematograph Films Act:

> The cinematograph film is today one of the most widely used means for the amusement of the public at large. It is also undoubtedly a most important factor in the education of all classes of the community, in the spread of national culture and in presenting national ideas and customs to the world. Its potentialities moreover in shaping the idea of the very large numbers to whom it appeals are almost unlimited. The propaganda value of the film cannot be overemphasized.[1]

Broadly speaking, the cinema operates in two ways — to reflect and highlight popular attitudes, ideas and preoccupations, and to generate and inculcate views and opinions deemed desirable by film-makers. Film-makers select in the first case material which they know will appeal to their audience and in the second material with which they can manipulate their audience and shape its perceptions. It may well be that a film will aim to do both things at once; perhaps the greatest problem with films is to distinguish deliberate propaganda from what Arthur Marwick has called '"unwitting" testimony, the hidden assumptions and attitudes, rather than the conscious,

1

and often biased, message'.[2] Marwick argues strongly for the particular value of this aspect of feature films for the historian:

> The more one makes a comparative study of films, the more one becomes aware that, however exceptional within the context of its own country, every film is in fact a product of its own culture. No film-maker, it becomes clear and clearer, can really go beyond certain assumptions accepted within his own country. . . . Over and over again, it has been pointed out to me at seminars and conferences that films are made by members of the upper and more prosperous segments of society. That I would never deny; but I am far more interested in the fact that . . . films . . . were seen by large audiences. There *is* a law of the market; the bigger its commercial success, the more a film is likely to tell us about the unvoiced assumptions of the people who watched it. It is the tedious documentary, or the film financed by political subscription, which tells us least.[3]

But the cinema can also act as a potent means of social control, transmitting the dominant ideology of society and creating for it a consensus of support.[4] First, films provide images of the lives, attitudes and values of various groups in society, created from recognizable but carefully selected facets of such groups. This is important because, as Hortense Powdermaker discovered, film audiences have a tendency to regard as accurate depictions of places, attitudes and lifestyles of which they themselves have no first-hand knowledge.[5] Thus, for instance, a working-class audience may well accept as authentic a cinematic depiction of upper-class life, however inaccurate, while it would reject an inaccurate depiction of its own circumstances.

Second, films provide images of society as a whole, again constructed of selected elements and aspects of everyday life, which are organized into a coherent pattern governed by a set of underlying presuppositions. The process of selection confers status on certain issues, institutions and individuals — say, for instance, the police or the monarchy — which regularly appear in a favourable light.

Third, what J. S. R. Goodlad says of popular drama is equally applicable to popular film: 'It may serve as the vehicle by which a community expresses its beliefs about what is right and wrong; indeed it may function instrumentally as a medium through which a community repeatedly instructs its members in correct behaviour.'[6] Popular films, and in particular *genre* films such as crime dramas, horror pictures or westerns, which regularly use the same elements, characters and situations, function as rituals, cementing the beliefs and ideals of society, enforcing social norms and exposing and isolating deviants.

Last, there is a tendency for the mass media to promote conformity not only of dress, hairstyle and vocabulary but also, and more subtly, of attitudes and world-view. It is therefore of central importance to discover who controls the production of films and what attitudes and ideas they are disseminating through them.

But the relationship between film and audience is reciprocal. An audience does not accept passively every message that is put across in a film. For one thing, it can choose which films to see and which to avoid. Even within films it can accept elements that it likes and reject unpalatable ones. In the last resort it is positive audience approval, expressed via the box office, that ensures whether a film succeeds or fails financially. So producers' calculations of what will appeal to their audiences inevitably influence what goes into a film. Direct propaganda rarely works, as the Nazis discovered in Germany. Their first three feature film exercises in promoting the Nazi Party, *SA Mann Brand*, *Hitlerjunge Quex* and *Hans Westmar*, were such disasters at the box office that Propaganda Minister Goebbels ordered that direct propaganda be confined in future to the newsreels, and he sought to work more covertly on audiences by inserting propaganda elements into 'straight' entertainment films.[7] Audiences the world over go to the cinema primarily to be entertained, not to be instructed. They go for relaxation, diversion and ready-made dreams. As Raymond Durgnat points out:

> For the masses, the cinema is dreams and nightmares, or it is nothing. It is an alternative life, experience freed from the tyranny of that 'old devil consequences', from the limitation of having only one life to live. One's favourite films are one's unlived lives, one's hopes, fears, libido. They constitute a magic mirror, their shadowy forms are woven from one's shadowy selves, one's limbo loves.[8]

The content of these dreams and nightmares and how they are arrived at are matters that historians cannot afford to neglect. Yet historians have been reluctant to quarry feature films for evidence of the social history of this century. As the eminent American historian Arthur M. Schlesinger Jr has written:

> Historians are professionally a conservative lot. Movies have had status problems ever since they emerged three-quarters of a century ago as a dubious entertainment purveyed by immigrant hustlers to a working-class clientele in storefront holes-in-the-wall scattered through the poorer sections of the individual city. Conventional history has recorded the motion picture as a phenomenon but ignored it as a source. Social and intellectual historians draw freely on fiction, drama, painting, hardly ever on movies. Yet the very nature of film as a supremely popular art guarantees that it is the carrier of deep if enigmatic truth.[9]

When in the 1960s historians began to admit the use of film to their deliberations, it was to newsreel and documentary that they turned. They were reassured by the presence of real people and real locations that they were somehow viewing 'reality'. But they were mistaken. Newsreels and documentaries no more presented 'reality' than did feature films, which told stories, used actors and were often made entirely in studios. In the case of the documentary and the newsreel what was seen on the screen was selected, shaped and placed there in pursuit of certain predetermined policies. Newsreel-makers and documentarists worked under the same constraints as feature film-makers, subject to interference from censors, sponsors and outside pressure groups. Admittedly, such films provide first-hand visual evidence of clothing, housing and transportation, just as photographs do. But beyond that surface 'reality', newsreels and documentaries were far from being objective. They were, in fact, highly selective and strictly controlled. As one newsreel chief put it in 1938: 'The newsreel companies were always ready to give, and in fact frequently gave, assistance to the government in portraying matters which were deemed to be in the public interest.'[10]

An extravagant mythology has grown up around the British documentary movement, which is often depicted, on the basis of a handful of genuinely moving films like *Housing Problems*, as the sole repository of realism and radicalism in a predominantly conservative industry. Raymond Durgnat, in a few deft and perceptive pages of analysis, has set the movement as a whole, particularly during 'the heroic age of Grierson', in its proper perspective. He concludes: 'Far from being progressive, these films are, in spirit, just what they were intended to be: literally speaking, commercials for the EMB or the GPO or any other part of the Establishment, and therefore for the *status quo* of — of all periods — the Thirties.'[11]

More seriously, perhaps, documentaries were not on the whole seen by the mass cinema-going public. Gaumont British took a package of six, the so-called 'Imperial Six', and released them as supporting films. However, they were given new musical soundtracks and portentous commentaries and anyway dealt with such romantic subjects as lumberjacking and salmon fishing, topics far from the reality of the life of the urban masses. But the Gaumont British experiment was not repeated. For exhibitors were extremely reluctant to show documentaries, regarding them as box-office disasters. As Mr W. R. Fuller, General Secretary of the Cinematograph Exhibitors Association, speaking in 1936 of exhibitors' failure to interest the public in the EMB documentaries said acidly: 'No documentary . . . has ever set the Thames afire.'[12] Documentaries, then, can really tell us only about the aims and attitudes of their sponsors and their producers. The real value of the documentary movement of the 1930s was to act as a training ground for those directors who went into feature film-making during the war and brought a new patina of realism to fictional films. The idea that documentaries embodied a purer, higher truth is a dangerous fallacy.

It was feature films that were seen and enjoyed by the bulk of the cinema-goers, and it is feature films which have received least attention from historians. There are some signs that this is beginning to change. There have been several attempts in recent years to come to terms with the feature film as a source of historical evidence, and it is on these beginnings that we must build.[13] But among historians an attitude of Puritanical snobbery still prevails, inherited from the indigenous British film culture that emerged in the 1920s and 1930s. Its reaction to the popularity in Britain of Hollywood films has been acutely analysed by Peter Stead.[14] He defines this British film culture as consisting of 'a national film institute, a network of film societies, a number of intellectual film journals, a whole tradition of documentary film-making and close links between those interested in film and educationalists, especially those engaged in adult education'.[15] This resulted in a strong preference for art over entertainment, for Continental (particularly Russian, French and German) films over British and American, for documentary over feature film and for programmes to 'improve' and to 'educate' audiences. Although the film culture modified its approach, particularly after World War II, when journals like *Sequence* and, later, *Movie* came to appreciate the merits of Hollywood and British feature films, historians as a whole remained locked into the old perceptions. They have shied away from feature films because they were produced to entertain the masses and to make money.

Admittedly, film analysis poses a fundamental problem in that, unlike the painting or the novel, film is a collaborative rather than an individual art. Films are produced by a conveyor-belt, mass-production process. They are the end-product of collaboration between director, writer, cameraman, composer and actors and may often represent considered decisions made by men not actually involved in translating the script into visual images. These are the men with the final say, the producers and production supervisors, the men with logistic, financial and sometimes even overall artistic control. In acknowledgement of an understandable desire to confer artistic respectability on the cinema, the *auteur* theory of the 1960s argued for a single artistic vision in film-making and assigned this to the director. There can be no denying that the cinema has produced a high proportion of works of art and that a Hitchcock or a Hawks film, a Ford or a Sternberg, is as recognizable thematically and stylistically as a Dickens novel or a Velasquez painting. But the bulk of films are not so much personal works of art as, to use the term employed in the television industry, 'product'. They are not art but artefacts for instant consumption and discard. They cannot be understood in terms of artistic vision, but they can be seen as a direct response to the era which has produced them. For every Hawks and Hitchcock, for every Ford and Sternberg, there are a dozen Alfred E. Greens and Albert S. Rogells, directors who were merely proficient craftsmen, the servants of mass culture, taking their cue from current preoccupations rather than from timeless individual vision. For historians it is often the work of these journeymen rather than the work of the great artists that is interesting, just as popular novels, picture postcards and wall posters, designed for the moment and reflecting that moment, are interesting. Indeed, as they are collaborative, films are more likely to reflect, and respond to, the marketplace and thus the audience. The top box-office films have rarely been great works of art. A great work of art anyway usually tells us more about the artist than the society that produced him. So the films of Gracie Fields, for instance, are likely to be more valuable to the social historian than the poems of W. H. Auden or the novels of Virginia Woolf.

Nothing demonstrates the collaborative nature of film-making more clearly than the exemplary Wisconsin series of screenplays of key Warner Brothers films from the heyday of that company. Each script is accompanied by a meticulously documented essay, which traces the film's production, detailing its development stage by stage. To take just one example, Rudy Behlmer's essay on the classic swashbuckler *The Sea Hawk* (1940) begins in 1935, when Warner Brothers decided upon Rafael Sabatini's novel as a follow-up to its successful *Captain Blood,* which had launched Errol Flynn as a major star.[16] Behlmer shows how the book passed through the hands of four successive screenwriters, moving further and further from Sabatini's original novel until nothing but the title remained. The film was directed by Michael Curtiz, but it is clear that the Warner production chief, Hal B. Wallis, was deeply involved in every aspect of filming. We see him intervening constantly, ordering the testing of Dennis Morgan for the leading role in case the tempestuous Errol Flynn had to be replaced, seeking to curb Curtiz's desire to alter the script while on the set and insisting that it be shot exactly as written, restraining Curtiz from injecting too much brutality and violence in order to avoid the wrath of the censors, making constructive suggestions about the lighting and staging of individual sequences and tackling the problem of shooting the final duel raised by the total inability of the villain, Henry Daniell, to handle a sword. His mark remains on the finished film, though he actually made none of it himself. Apart from this, there were the contributions of the production designers, costumiers, composers and photographers who gave Warner Brothers films their distinctive look and feel. This kind of documentation is invaluable in assessing the true nature of film-making at the height of the great studio era, which coincided with the period of the cinema's greatest popularity.

There is a further factor which may have frightened off historians latterly, and that is the state of film criticism and film history in general. For much of the 1970s it was in serious disarray, wracked and scorched by controversy. Structuralism and semiology became the fashionable and dominant concepts in a new critical approach that involved the minute dissection of films according to strict, almost mathematical, formulae. Because of the convoluted and jargon-ridden texts which this school of criticism produced, its general accessibility was minimal and its application limited to the elect, the initiates of an intellectual mystery, whose cult words — 'syntagma', 'phoneme', 'signifying construct' — identified members readily to each other and just as readily excluded the outsider. The high priests of this new critical religion, drawn largely from the avant-garde of Eng. Lit., looked to France for their inspiration, to Marxism for their ideology and to linguistics and psychoanalysis for their conceptual models.

But this critical approach has come under increasing attack for its narrowness and intolerance, its intellectual arrogance and its deliberate obscurantism, and it is now losing ground. Our intention is not to enter into a debate about the pros and cons of this approach but to draw attention to a new development which seems to us to offer a challenging, productive and accessible way forward. This development comes not from France but from the United States of America, finding its inspiration and methodology in history. It deals not in pure speculation but in solid research, the assembling, evaluation and interpretation of facts, the relating of films to the world, the search for an understanding through the medium of popular films of the changing social and sexual roles of men and women, the concepts of work and leisure, class and race, peace and war, the real determinants of change and continuity in the real world.

This approach can best be called 'contextual cinematic history', for it places particular emphasis on the exploration of the context within which a film was produced. It has already resulted in two authoritative and stimulating general social histories of the American cinema: Robert Sklar's *Movie-Made America* and Garth Jowett's *Film: the Democratic Art*.[17] It has produced also Lary May's *Screening Out the Past,* subtitled *The Birth of Mass Culture and the Motion Picture Industry*.[18] This bold, absorbing, infectiously readable book takes as its subject the American cinema's formative period, 1890— 1929, and, by examining its development in the context of the age, produces what the French would call *une histoire de mentalité*. May sees the cinema as a key element in the development of a new urban culture, concentrating on the issues at the heart of change and contributing to the transition in America from what, for simplicity's sake, he calls the 'Victorian Age' to the 'Modern Age'. He demonstrates quite convincingly that in the first decades of the twentieth century the film industry was the focal point of a revolution in morals, expectations and attitudes in American society and that the films themselves reflected, highlighted and advanced the change in the relationship between work and leisure, men and women, and in the promotion of a new success ethic and dominant lifestyle.

His method — and the value of his book lies almost as much in this as in its conclusions — is to analyse the content and structure of groups of films, box-office trends, star personalities and their appeal, contemporary reviews and reactions, staging, lighting and action styles, the role of fan magazines, censorship and picture palaces, and to locate all these elements firmly in the political, social and cultural context. In relation to the products of a mass popular culture, this is surely the right way forward, for it extends our understanding and appreciation of films and their world and, above all, illuminates their place in culture and society.

Another recent and admirable book, *American History/American Film,* subtitled *Interpreting the Hollywood Image,* edited by John E. O'Connor and Martin A. Jackson, takes the contextual approach a stage further and applies it to individual films.[19] It contains fourteen essays with such titles as 'The Great War viewed from the Twenties: *The Big Parade* (1925)', 'Our Awkward Ally: *Mission to Moscow* (1943)' and 'An American Cold Warrior: *Viva Zapata* (1952)'. The essays are bound together by two threads: they all attempt to explain both the way in which the film in question documents American social history and captures the state of mind of the American people at the time it was released, and the way in which it illustrates the development of the American film industry.

What we would like to see is the application of this technique to the British cinema. Although there are highly competent general surveys of British film history, useful biographies and autobiographies of producers and directors and pretty well exhaustive studies of the documentary movement, the British feature film industry remains virtually virgin territory as far as contextual history is concerned. An honourable exception is Charles Barr's indispensable book *Ealing Studios.*[20] He has revealed the multi-layered richness of Ealing's films by relating them to their background. He demonstrates their key role in the dramatization of World War II as the 'People's War', the struggle to maintain consensus and at the same time to highlight and defuse social discontents during the period of the post-war Labour Government and, finally, the drift to conservatism and the complacency which followed the return to power of the Tories in 1951. He relates the films to the structure and nature of the studio itself, to the character and attitudes of the personnel involved and to the rise of a middle-class radicalism among the generation that voted Labour for the first time in 1945 and then retreated towards Conservatism in the 1950s. He uncovers the debates and dichotomies between age and youth, tradition and change, subversion and conformity. This study gives an entirely new range of meaning to films like *Passport to Pimlico, Kind Hearts and Coronets* and *The Titfield Thunderbolt,* a depth of interpretation which can be understood only in context. But his book remains a solitary beacon in the darkness. What of other British film companies — Rank, Gainsborough, Associated British, Hammer, for instance? What of the social history of censorship and the social role of cinema-going? What part did reviewing play in the film culture? The materials exist for such studies, but, except for a few pioneering articles, they lie unused.[21]

What of British film stars? How did Gracie Fields, Googie Withers and Anna Neagle, for instance, relate to the roles and aspirations of women in British society? What of male stars like Robert Donat, Jack Warner and Jack Hawkins? What did they embody? What audience needs did they fulfil? What too of the changing style in film heroes from, say, Kenneth More to Albert Finney? What does this tell us of the changing nature of the film industry, of British society, of popular fashions and mores?

For the American cinema in its first decades Lary May has asked these questions and has provided answers. It remains for scholars in this country to start asking similar questions. We hope to help the process along by applying the technique of contextual history to ten British films. They are not (repeat *not*) the ten best British films of all time, but they would probably figure somewhere in the top hundred. They are certainly representative of the subjects and eras which can be illuminated by the use of film.

In examining each of them in turn we have borne in mind three main concerns. The first is the need to analyse what the film is saying, and that involves looking at the structure and meaning of the film, as conveyed by script, visuals, acting, direction, photography and music. Second, we attempt to put it in context with respect to both the film industry itself and the political and social situation which produced it. Third, we try to find out how the films were received and what audience reaction to them was. To some extent all three strands are interwoven, for popular cinema has an organic relationship with the rest of popular culture, and popular culture as a whole plays a part in the social and political history of its time. Many films were based on books, for instance, and were not so much original cinematic creations as 'cinematizations' (as the industry called them) of literary properties, whose success with the public in their original form led producers to assume a guaranteed audience. Also many films were based on plays, and the stage provided (much more in Britain than in America) not only material but also performers — music-hall artists, musical comedy stars and dramatic actors — who became film stars.

We try to elucidate the production histories of the films and the intentions of the film-makers to see who was responsible for what is actually on the screen. Occasionally such information can be gleaned from interviews conducted either at the time and recorded in magazines and newspapers or in later years. But the oral history method presents grave problems, for quite apart from faulty memories, some directors may seek to mislead or may revamp facts to fit their legends. Ford and Von Sternberg, for example, took pleasure in mystifying, confusing and sending up interviewers, while others, like Douglas Sirk on his period in Nazi Germany, could be understandably evasive.

We have already noted that it may not be the director who is ultimately responsible for what is on the screen. The guiding intelligence behind the productions of London Films, whoever may have been directing officially, was usually that of producer Alexander Korda, while Michael Balcon, as production chief at Gaumont British in the 1930s, has the final say on almost every aspect of production. He left people in no doubt as to who was the dominant creative force at GB when he defined the role of the producer in 1933:

> The work of the film producer is to determine the choice of subjects, of directors and of artistes for every picture and to decide the cost to be borne. Under his supervision director, scenario editor and unit executives prepare the script, the plans of sets and the time schedule for each production. When the film is in the making its daily progress is reported to him. He is the sponsor, and the guide, and the ultimate court of appeal. . . . the kind of energy which the producer must stimulate and direct is based upon the creative and artistic impulses of directors, writers, cameramen and artistes. Such impulses are so personal that they constantly require the close attention of one directing mind to blend them into the harmonious

unity which is essential for any successful achievement in a form of entertainment which depends upon the specialized work of many different hands.[22]

Another element which must not be overlooked is the role and iconography of the stars. It was the stars, after all, whom the public went to see: successive surveys revealed that the stars and the story were what attracted the mass audience to the cinema. Fan magazines and fan clubs charted their doings and their lifestyles. The stars set the fashions in clothes, hairstyles, speech, deportment, even lovemaking. As Andrew Tudor observes: 'The basic psychological machinery through which most people relate to films involves some combination of identification and projection'[23] and what audiences identified with and projected themselves on to was the stars. This inevitably had an influence on films and on the roles that were chosen and shaped to highlight the qualities and characteristics of a particular star. As Raymond Durgnat notes: 'The star is a reflection in which the public studies and adjusts its own image of itself . . . the social history of a nation can be written in terms of its film stars.'[24]

Beyond the immediate production context there are further constraints to be considered. In wartime propaganda objectives had to be met, and the Ministry of Information provided detailed guidelines for the content of feature films. But in peacetime there was a continuing framework within which film-makers operated — the censorship system. It is impossible to understand the development and nature of the British cinema without a full appreciation of the work and influence of the censors. Unlike that of other countries, censorship in Britain was not state-controlled. The British Board of Film Censors was set up by the industry itself as an act of self-preservation in 1912. The 1909 Cinematograph Act had given local authorities the right to license buildings used as cinemas. The intention was for them to concern themselves with fire precautions, but the wording of the Act was loose enough to be interpreted as conferring powers of censorship. The possibility that the licensing authorities, estimated at 700 in 1932, might give different verdicts on the suitability of films obviously constituted a threat to the industry's commercial viability, so central self-censorship by the industry was deemed necessary. Its stated aim was 'to create a purely independent and impartial body whose duty it will be to induce confidence in the minds of the licensing authorities and of those who will have in their charge the moral welfare of the community generally'.[25] The basic censorship rules were drawn up by the Board's second President, T. P. O'Connor, and known as 'O'Connor's 43'. The censors were, he said, 'guided by the main principle that nothing should be passed which is calculated to demoralize an audience, that can teach methods of or extenuate crime, that can undermine the teachings of morality, that tends to bring the institution of marriage into contempt or lower the sacredness of family ties'.[26] In fact, their aim was to maintain the moral, political, social and economic status quo and to avoid anything that smacked of controversy. The censors' favourite term of approval was 'harmless', which indicated the negative way in which they viewed the cinema. Their hold on the industry grew during the 1930s as the scope of their activities extended from the vetting of completed films to the inspection of scripts prior to shooting. The rules were relaxed over the years, though always in response to perceived changes in public tolerance of matters like sex and violence. This was particularly true in the 1960s, but by then the cinema was ceasing to be a mass entertainment medium and becoming a sectional and minority one.[27]

The great imponderable in all this is always how the audience reacted. The old hypodermic idea that the audience as a whole was directly injected with the message of a film has long since been discredited. The idea that the entire film output of a country directly reflects the collective psyche of that country has also been seriously questioned. These approaches, seen now as too mechanistic, underlay the pioneering work of Siegfried Kracauer, who saw the whole of German cinema as foreshadowing the rise of Hitler in his classic but now controversial work *From Caligari to Hitler*.[28] The relationship between film-maker, film and audience is now seen to be more sophisticated, a two-way process operating in areas of shared experience and shared perception.[29]

It is reasonable to assume that an audience's reaction depends ultimately on the age, sex, class, health, intelligence and preoccupations of that audience, both as individuals and as a group. Some general evidence exists in the form of box-office returns, where available, and in the record of reissues, which usually signalled a film's success at the box office. The popularity of stars can be gleaned from the polls taken, particularly the influential annual poll in the *Motion Picture Herald* which lists stars according to their box-office draw. But one little-used source of contemporary evidence is newspaper reviews. Allowance has to be made for the attitude and readership of the various newspapers, but the critics were writing with the tastes and interests of their readers in mind. What they wrote was heeded. As Winifred Holmes testified in a contemporary study of film-going in an unnamed Southern town in the 1930s: 'Newspaper reviews of films are read with interest and play a large part in influencing people of all classes in an appreciation of the films shown'.[30]

When all this evidence has been taken into account, we hope to show how feature films can be used to illuminate the history of this century at various key points. It is our hope that it will encourage both those who teach and those who research our recent history to make greater use of feature film evidence. The Open University already does so, and the growth of video equipment and video tape puts feature film evidence within the range of everyone who is interested.

The ten films selected for this study were chosen to represent subjects important to contemporary historians (politics, society, education, industrial relations, etc.) and to illustrate the preoccupations of the decades between 1929, when sound films were introduced to Britain, and 1970, when the British film industry virtually collapsed. From the 1930s we chose *Sanders of the River* (1935) for its discussion of the British Empire and *South Riding* (1938) for its examination of Britain's domestic problems. Both films were based on best-selling books. The war represented a watershed in the history of the British film industry and presented special problems for film-makers. We sought to illustrate these by choosing a film about 'why we fight', *A Canterbury Tale* (1944), and a film about 'how we fight', *The Life and Death of Colonel Blimp* (1943). Coincidentally both films are the work of Michael Powell and Emeric Pressburger, whom many consider to be Britain's greatest film-makers. The post-war period, which arguably saw British film-making at its creative peak and British society in the throes of far-reaching changes, gave us *Fame is the Spur* (1947), a rare film about Labour Party politics, and

The Guinea Pig (1948), which looks at the role of the public schools in a changing society. For British society in the 1950s we turned to a classic Ealing comedy, The Ladykillers (1955), and for industrial relations in that decade we selected a classic Boulting Brothers comedy, I'm All Right, Jack (1959). Both films feature one of Britain's greatest comic actors, Peter Sellers. For the 'Swinging Sixties', we highlight contemporary mores and attitudes by looking at a film from the beginning of the decade, Saturday Night and Sunday Morning (1960), and one from the end, If . . . (1968). If nothing else, these films demonstrate the richness and breadth of the British cinema over the years, and this examination of them will, we trust, inspire others to delve into this largely unexplored mine of information about British culture and society.

Notes

1 Cinematograph Act 1927: Report of a Committee appointed by the Board of Trade, Cmd 5320, London, 1936, p. 4.
2 Arthur Marwick, Class: Image and Reality, London, 1980, p. 22.
3 ibid.
4 See Stuart Hall, 'Culture, the media and the "Ideological Effect"', in James Curran, Michael Gurevitch and Janet Woollacott (eds.), Mass Communication and Society, London, 1979, pp. 315—48, for a good outline of the means of social control.
5 Hortense Powdermaker, Hollywood the Dream Factory, London, 1951, p. 13.
6 J. S. R. Goodlad, A Sociology of Popular Drama, London, 1971, p. 7.
7 Richard Taylor, Film Propaganda: Soviet Russia and Nazi Germany, London, 1979, pp. 161—3.
8 Raymond Durgnat, Films and Feelings, London, 1967, p. 135.
9 John E. O'Connor and Martin A. Jackson (eds.), American History/American Film, New York, 1979, p. ix.
10 Anthony Aldgate, Cinema and History, London, 1979, p. 193.
11 Raymond Durgnat, A Mirror for England, London, 1970, p. 119; cf. pp. 117—29.
12 Board of Trade: Minutes of Evidence taken before the Departmental Committee on Cinematograph Films, 1936, p. 89.
13 See in particular Paul Smith (ed.), The Historian and Film, Cambridge, 1976; K. R. M. Short (ed.), Feature Films as History, London, 1981; Pierre Sorlin, The Film in History, Oxford, 1980. Feature films are also used to elucidate the subjects of war, empire and class in Leif Furhammar and Folke Isaksson, Politics and Film, London, 1971; Jeffrey Richards, Visions of Yesterday, London, 1973, and Arthur Marwick, Class: Image and Reality, London, 1980. The Historical Journal of Film, Radio and Television has since 1981 provided a continuing forum for such research.
14 Peter Stead, 'Hollywood's Message to the World', Historical Journal of Film, Radio and Television, 1, 1981, pp. 19—32.
15 ibid, p. 27.
16 Rudy Behlmer (ed.) The Sea Hawk, Wisconsin/Warner Bros. Screenplay series, Madison and London, 1982. Seventeen other screenplays are currently in print, and more are planned.
17 Robert Sklar, Movie-Made America, London, 1978; Garth Jowett, Film: the Democratic Art, Boston, 1976.
18 Lary May, Screening Out the Past, Oxford and New York, 1980.

19 John E. O'Connor and Martin A. Jackson (eds.), *American History/American Film,* New York, 1979.

20 Charles Barr, *Ealing Studios,* London, 1977.

21 The first steps towards an analysis of the social role of Gainsborough films have been taken in Sue Aspinall and Robert Murphy (eds.), *Gainsborough Melodrama,* BFI Dossier 18, London, 1983. On the role of cinema-going in working-class life in the 1930s, see Peter Stead, 'The People and the Pictures', in Nicholas Pronay and D. W. Spring (eds.), *Propaganda, Politics and Film 1918—45,* pp. 77—97. On the ethos and standards of film reviewers in the 1940s, see John Ellis, 'Art, Culture and Quality', *Screen,* Autumn 1978, pp. 9—49. For the British cinema between 1945 and 1958 Durgnat, *A Mirror for England,* idiosyncratic, sometimes inaccurate, often impenetrable, remains indispensable.

22 Michael Balcon, 'The Function of the Producer', *Cinema Quarterly,* 2, Autumn 1933, pp. 5—7.

23 Andrew Tudor, *Image and Influence,* London, 1974, p. 76.

24 Durgnat, *Films and Feelings,* p. 138. On the phenomenon of stars, see Richard Dyer, *Stars,* London, 1979; Edgar Morin, *The Stars,* London, 1960; and Alexander Walker, *Stardom,* Harmondsworth, 1974.

25 *Bioscope,* 21 November 1912.

26 *BBFC Annual Report, 1919,* p. 3.

27 On censorship and its role, see in particular Neville March Hunnings, *Film Censors and the Law,* London, 1967; Nicholas Pronay, 'The First Reality: Film Censorship in Liberal England', in Short, *Feature Films as History,* pp. 113—37; Dorothy Knowles, *The Censor, the Drama and the Film,* London, 1934; John Trevelyan, *What the Censor Saw,* London, 1973; Guy Phelps, *Film Censorship,* London, 1975; Jeffrey Richards, 'The British Board of Film Censors and Content Control in the 1930s', *Historical Journal of Film, Radio and Television,* 1, 1981, pp. 95—116; 2, 1982, pp. 39—48.

28 Siegfried Kracauer, *From Caligari to Hitler,* Princeton, 1947.

29 Tudor, *Image and Influence,* p. 28.

30 *World Film News,* December 1936, p. 4.

2

The Sun Never Sets
Sanders of the River

It is often said that the masses were indifferent to the British Empire during the inter-war years. But this is an oversimplification. To begin with, it, mistakenly, equates Empire with expansion, militarism and jingoism, which are only phases of the imperial experience. Admittedly, there was no 'mafficking' and no public demonstrations over *causes célèbres* like the plight of Gordon in Khartoum. Emigration to the colonies was declining. Dreams of military glory, so prominent in pre-war literature and thought, had faded in the cold light of the bloody slaughter in the trenches and no-man's-land. Pacifism had gained in strength and standing; in 1933 the Oxford University Union passed the celebrated motion that 'This house will in no circumstances fight for its King and Country', and an anti-war candidate won the East Fulham by-election. But the Empire, which had passed from its aggressive, expansive phase to a period of administration and consolidation that was bound to be quieter, was seen and depicted now as a force for peace, stability and democracy. As Professor Reginald Coupland wrote in 1935: 'Surely this is a time when a world society such as ours, dedicated to freedom, yet knowing it can only be preserved or rightly used in unity, should stand firm for the defence of civilization as we understand it.'[1] 'Civilization as we understand it' was generally seen to comprise parliamentary democracy, the rule of law and the enlightened and equitable administration of colonies and protectorates. If the Empire is seen in this light, then James Morris is surely right when he notes: 'Most Britons still considered it, all in all, as a force for good in the world, and only a minority could conceive of its actually coming to an end.'[2] The fact that none of the major political parties even contemplated its dissolution suggests that such a policy would have commanded little electoral support.

There were prominent and vocal critics of the Empire, but they were on the whole drawn from the left-wing intelligentsia, which is almost always unrepresentative of national opinion as a whole. Just as 'serious literature' in the inter-war years was almost uniformly hostile to the public schools, so too was it critical of the imperial mentality. But for most people — those for whom literature meant Edgar Wallace, Warwick Deeping and P. C. Wren — the public schools were not represented by those tormented, repressed public school boys who figure in the works of Graham Greene and E. M.

13

Forster. They looked instead to the idealized Greyfriars of Frank Richards or James Hilton's Brookfield, to the world of Harry Wharton, Billy Bunter and Mr Chips. Similarly, the Empire was not the arrogant, hollow, hypocritical sham of George Orwell. It was the mythic landscape of romance and adventure; it was that quarter of the globe that was coloured red and included 'darkest Africa' and 'the mysterious East'; it was 'ours'. It may have been true, as H. G. Wells claimed, that nineteen Englishmen out of twenty knew as much about the British Empire as they did about the Italian Renaissance,[3] but most people were not bothered about actual conditions in the Empire. It was the imagery that they absorbed and endorsed, and that imagery was romantic, adventurous and exotic. It was the rich variety of produce and artefacts on show at the Empire Exhibitions and at the Imperial Institute. It was the Prince of Wales's tours of the Empire, so widely publicized in the newspapers and the newsreels. It was the popular novels about derring-do on the North-West Frontier of India or in the jungles of Africa. It was the colourful scenes depicted on picture postcards and cigarette cards. It was an image inculcated at school via lessons about the history and geography of the Empire, via the annual celebration of Empire Day, with its religious services and imperial displays, and via the popular boys' books like those of G. A. Henty and F. S. Brereton, which continued to fill school library shelves, to be awarded as prizes and to be much sought after as Christmas and birthday presents. This image stayed with schoolchildren as they grew into adulthood and was confirmed by all the popular media, including films.[4]

If we take the evidence of popularity at the box-office as 'unwitting testimony' of popular attitudes and preconceptions, then the flourishing cycle of imperial films in the 1930s in both Britain and the USA speaks volumes for the continued attachment of audiences to the concept of Empire,[5] for all these films depicted it as beneficent and necessary. It is on the face of it rather curious that the United States, which still retained strong traditions of both isolationism and anglophobia, should have celebrated the Empire from which it had successfully seceded in 1776, but from *Lives of a Bengal Lancer* (1935) through to *Sundown* (1940) such films were popular with audiences on both sides of the Atlantic. The reason for their popularity was given by Margaret Farrand Thorp in her study of the American film industry, published in 1939:

> The immediate explanation of this burst of British propaganda is a very simple one. As continental audiences dwindled, Britain, which had always stood high, became an even more important section of the American movies' foreign public. It was highly desirable to please Great Britain if possible, and it could be done without sacrifice, for the American public, too, seemed to be stirred with admiration for British Empire ideals. Loyalty as the supreme virtue no matter to what you are loyal, courage, hard work, a creed in which *noblesse oblige* is the most intellectual conception; those ideas are easier to dramatize on the screen than social responsibility, the relation of the individual to the state, the necessity for a pacifist to fight tyranny, the nature of democracy, and the similar problems with which the intellectuals want the movies to deal.[6]

What the Empire stood for was distilled by Hollywood screenwriters from the works of Kipling and his imitators, either directly or indirectly. The extent of the pro-British propaganda that they therefore contained is evidenced by the banning in Mussolini's Italy of the Hollywood films *Lives of a Bengal Lancer, Charge of the Light Brigade, Clive of India* and *Lloyds of London*, specifically because of their pro-British slant.[7]

In Britain Alexander Korda, the producer who had singlehandedly put British films on the world map with the phenomenal success of his *Private Life of Henry VIII* (1933), produced a trilogy of imperial epics.[8] He spared no expense, seeking always to make films which would equal Hollywood's in their polish and appeal. Two weeks after the opening of *Henry VIII* in August 1933 the director Zoltan Korda, brother of producer Alexander, left London for Africa with two film units, one to shoot location footage in East Africa and the other in West Africa. They seem to have had no script but to have been aware that the intention was to produce a film based on Edgar Wallace's popular *Sanders of the River* stories. They returned with many reels of African flora and fauna and of tribal ceremonies and dances. Thereupon Alexander Korda, in script conferences with the writer Jeffrey Dell and Lajos Biro, his regular script editor, worked out a narrative involving the characters, locale and situations from the Wallace stories to fit the location material. An African village was built at Denham Studios under the direction of Major Claude Wallace (no relation of Edgar), an old Africa hand, and peopled with black dockers imported from Cardiff, Liverpool, Glasgow and London. The script was completed and shooting began in the autumn of 1934, with Leslie Banks playing Sanders and the popular black American singing stars Paul Robeson and Nina Mae McKinney in the roles of Bosambo and Lilongo. None of the stars actually went to Africa. The finished film was released on 5 April 1935.[9]

The film fulfils a distinct ideological purpose, presenting a selectively constructed but positive view of British colonial administration in Africa and of the nature and capabilities of the African. The plot is straightforward. The film opens with Commissioner Sanders firmly in control of the River Territories of West Africa. We see him laying down the law to King Mofalaba and appointing Bosambo as chief of the Ochori. For five years the natives enjoy peace and order under the just and watchful eye of Sanders. But then he goes on leave, and Commissioner Ferguson takes his place. The gun runners Farini and Smith spread the rumour that Sanders is dead, and the tribes rise in revolt. Ferguson goes alone to the Old King's country and is murdered. Bosambo stays loyal to Sanders, but his wife Lilongo is kidnapped by the Old King's men. When he goes after her Bosambo too is captured. Sanders returns hurriedly from leave, sails upriver in his steamer, the *Zaire*, and arrives in time to rescue the captives. The Old King is killed and Bosambo is installed in his place. Peace and order are restored.

The tone and theme of *Sanders of the River* are set by the prologue: 'Sailors, soldiers and merchant adventurers were the pioneers who laid the foundations of the British Empire. Today their work is carried on by the civil servants — the Keepers of the King's Peace.' Peace is a recurrent theme. War is repeatedly denounced, and King Mofalaba himself confirms the Empire's commitment to peace when he declares cynically: 'It is easy to lie to the English. They want peace. If you say you want peace, they will believe you.' Then over a map of Africa is superimposed the legend: 'Africa — tens of millions of natives, each tribe under its own chieftain, guarded and protected by a handful of white men, whose work is an unsung saga of courage and efficiency.'

The film's central figure, Commissioner Sanders, is seen as the ideal colonial administrator, and the film is constructed to demonstrate his attributes. Quiet, pipe-smoking, good-humoured and authoritative, Sanders has virtually single-handedly brought law and order to the River Territories over the previous ten years. He has banned slavery and the running of gin and guns, 'the most dangerous gifts of civilization to the natives'. Having brought peace and order, he now seeks to maintain it, a direct reflection of the situation in the contemporary British Empire.

Backed as he is by only a handful of white officers and a single regiment of native troops, he rules by force of personality. The key sequences in the film are predicated on Sanders's charismatic strength. When he summons the troublesome King Mofalaba to palaver, Mofalaba comes with his warriors, who outnumber the British forces by ten to one. Yet Sanders curtly reads the riot act to the king, warning him to behave, and then dismisses him with an abrupt: 'The palaver is finished.' Mofalaba and his men could easily have fallen on to the British and slaughtered them. Instead they go home obediently. The rapid crumbling of the situation when Sanders goes on leave and war and revolt flare up indicates just how essential the personal charisma of Sanders is to the government. The missionary priest Father O'Leary cables the Colonial Office: 'Send four batallions or Sanders.' Sanders returns from leave, descending godlike from a plane, and puts down the unrest. But he expects no thanks. He does the job out of a sense of duty, telling Lieutenant Tibbetts at the start that he is in for 'tramping through swamps and jungles, your only decoration — mosquito bites'. It should, however, be noted that although it is never mentioned, this moral authority is underpinned by Western technology in the form of an airplane, a paddle steamer and machine guns.

The characteristics that Sanders embodies are entirely in line with the criteria actually employed to select colonial administrators. The selection was virtually controlled from 1910 to 1948 (with the exception of the World War I period) by one man — Sir Ralph Furse. Furse selected his men specifically on the basis of character and recruited them mainly from the public schools. He wrote: 'We could not have run the show without them. In England, universities train the mind; the public schools train character and teach leadership.'[10] The public schools taught duty and responsibility, a sense of fair play, qualities of leadership, above all a benevolent paternalism. Experience as a public school prefect and thus an exemplar of these virtues Furse regarded as an ideal training for colonial government. After a prefectship the next best qualification was a university rugger blue, preferably a captaincy. Indeed, the Sudan was described as 'a country of blacks run by blues'. Lord Plumer put it well, if cryptically, when he said in 1916: 'We are often told that they taught us nothing at Eton. It may well be so, but I think they taught it well.'[11] In other words they supplied training rather than an education. Robert Heussler, in his book on the Colonial Service, gathered together some of the testimonial letters used to make selections, which include such statements as: 'He would be capable of dealing with men. His mind is well-balanced, his manner agreeable and in every respect he is a perfect gentleman' and 'He would maintain the best traditions of English government over subject races. . . . He is a gentleman, a man of character.'[12] These could well be descriptions of Sanders. For Wallace had indeed created his hero as 'a mixture of Harry Johnston and the other West African

Commissioners of whom he had heard such romantic and bloodcurdling tales'.[13] It is worth noting that not only did the film distil the essence of the ideal District Officer but it also influenced others to follow it. As a former District Officer told Charles Allen: 'Most of us had seen a film called *Sanders of the River* before we went out, and suddenly here was this thing, and it was real; one was walking behind a long line of porters — and it was just like the film.' Another talks of the *'Sanders of the River* touch' in describing his conduct of affairs.[14] Thus nature imitates art.

The film is a celebration of that 'character and spirit' which, according to his biographer Karol Kulik, Alexander Korda so much admired in the British and which Sanders embodies. His character is the justification of British rule. There is no complex ideology, no constitutional justification for Empire. The man is the message. Korda's films offer no concrete political, economic or constitutional justification for the Empire's existence; nor is there any indication of the state of flux in which the empire actually found itself during the inter-war years, when it seemed to be evolving into something rather different — the Commonwealth. The Empire is justified by the apparent moral superiority of the British, as demonstrated by their adherence to the code of gentlemanly conduct and the maintenance of a disinterested system of law, order and justice. As Lord Curzon put it in 1923:

> We have endeavoured to exercise a steadying and moderating influence on the politics of the world, and I think and hope that we have conveyed not merely the impression but the conviction that whatever other countries or governments may do, the British government is never untrue to its word and is never disloyal to its colleagues or its allies, never does anything underhand or mean; and if this conviction is widespread, as I believe it to be — that is the real basis of the moral authority which the British Empire has long exerted and I believe will continue to exert in the affairs of mankind.[15]

As long as this lofty view of Britain's world role persisted, as long as Britain regarded it as her God-given duty to ensure fair play for all the world, the maintenance of the Empire was inescapable. It was this lofty view that the Korda films projected, seeing British rule as timeless and eternal. The inevitable result was to foster what Francis Hutchins called 'the illusion of permanence' — the idea that whatever they might say about progress towards ultimate independence, the British in fact expected and believed that their Empire would last for a thousand years.[16]

The message of *Sanders* is reinforced by the other two main characters, the archetypes of the 'Good African' and the 'Bad African', their responses to British rule determining their relative goodness and badness. The British govern the River Territories through nominated chieftains, an accurate dramatization of the policy of 'indirect rule', operated in West Africa. Sanders's particular favourite is Bosambo, chief of the Ochori. Their relationship is established from the outset when Bosambo, in reality a Liberian convict, passes himself off as the legitimate chief of the tribe. Sanders confronts him with the truth; Bosambo shamefacedly admits to it and is rewarded with the chieftainship. Appropriately enough, they meet over Sanders's desk, Sanders seated and Bosambo standing. Reprimanding a naughty child and then rewarding it with responsibility is a classic technique for winning loyalty, and in Bosambo's case it works. The headmaster—pupil nature of the relationship is thus clearly established. It is confirmed in the song that Bosambo sings in praise of his master:

> Sandi the strong, Sandi the wise,
> Righter of wrong, hater of lies,
> Laughed as he fought, worked as he played,
> As he has taught, let it be made.

Bosambo is conceived entirely in Western terms as an archetype well established in imperial fiction: a combination of doglike devotion, boastful sexuality and childish naughtiness. Similarly, his relationship with his wife Lilongo is seen in strictly European terms. They love each other. She bosses him about. He risks his life to rescue her. Yet, as Boris Gussman has written: 'The main difference between African and European marriage is that the idea of romantic love does not occur among Africans.'[17] There is equally little appreciation of the African character judged in African terms. Gussman also writes: 'To these Europeans, because they failed to understand the motives that prompted him or the bonds that held him in check, he was seen as superstitious, irrational, lazy, immoral and of a childish or at least adolescent mentality.'[18] The father—child relationship between Sanders and the natives is repeatedly commented upon by characters in the film — the missionary, the gun runners, Captain Hamilton.

The 'Bad African' of the film is King Mofalaba, who is sly, cruel and overbearing. He murders Commissioner Ferguson, kidnaps Lilongo and conducts slaving raids against neighbouring tribes. Where Bosambo loyally serves the British, Mofalaba plots against them. But he does so not in the interests of the Africans, of freedom or principle: he seeks to get rid of the British because they prevent him from tyrannizing the people. They stand between him and the despotic exercise of power that he seeks. At the end of the film he is killed and replaced by Bosambo, who will rule under the British in peace and justice and will not seek to destroy his people with war or tyranny.

The film gives every indication that the tribes will carry on as they always have under British protection — 'at peace in their primitive paradise', as the film puts it. The consent of the governed is implied by the scene in which Sanders, about to go on leave, asks Bosambo if he will still be a popular chieftain when Sanders returns. Bosambo replies: 'I have learned the secret of good government from your lordship. It is this, that a king should not be feared but loved by his people.' 'That,' replies Sanders with a knowing smile 'is the secret of the British.' The inescapable conclusion is that British rule is changeless and unchanging.

There is an implicit subtext in the apparent fragility of British rule, given that it collapses the moment Sanders leaves the scene. One of the great paradoxes of British imperial history was the simultaneous dominance of twin emotions, confidence and fear — confidence in the rightness of the British presence in far-off lands and fear that British rule would be violently overthrown. There was ample justification for such fear. Imperial rule in Africa had been established only in the face of a succession of revolts (the Matabele War, the Ashanti War, the Zulu Revolt, the Mad Mullah's Revolt in Somaliland). The British in India never quite got over the shock of the Mutiny and always secretly dreaded the possibility of another. The plots of all three films in the Korda trilogy are strikingly similar in outline and almost give the impression of having been constructed to exorcise this fear. Just as in *Sanders of the River* Commissioner Sanders puts down a native uprising in Africa and rescues his ally, Chief Bosambo, from the evil King Mofalaba, so in *The Drum* Captain Carruthers joins forces with the Indian boy prince Azim to put down an uprising on the North-West Frontier led by his uncle, the wicked Ghul Khan, and in *The Four Feathers* a disgraced British officer Captain Harry Faversham redeems his honour, assisted by the pro-British chieftain Karaga Pasha, by helping to put down the Khalifa's Revolt in the Sudan. In each film the exercise of power by the British is supported by the consent of the governed and defined by the opposition of self-seeking despots who, if left alone, would prey unmercifully on their own people.

On the surface *Sanders* would seem to be a rather uneasy blend of travelogue, with its sequences of animals and native dances, and drama, with the narrative sequences filmed in Britain. But the mixture is sweetened by the four songs written for Robeson and based on native melodies recorded on location. They are superbly sung and bind the film together, serving to reinforce the central message by supplementing the imagery and the ideology. The African flora and fauna and dancing natives support the contemporary view of the 'Dark Continent' as a place of exotic mystery and beauty, while the songs both hymn the virtues of Sanders and confirm the primitive savagery of the natives, in the words of the 'Killing Song':

> On, on into battle, make the wardrums rattle,
> Mow them down like cattle,
> On and on, on into battle, stamp them into the dust, into the dust,
> Charge, kill, shoot, spill, and smash, smite, slash, fight and slay!

The sequences of bare-breasted native girls were a positive attraction, drawing a horde of appreciative adolescents. But they too embodied a racist attitude, for no white woman would ever have been permitted to appear bare-breasted on the screen. The natives, however, being considered inferior, counted as ethnic curiosities.

Leslie Banks, who was offered the role of Sanders after Raymond Massey and Ralph Richardson had turned it down, effectively projects the authority and dependability of the District Commissioner. As Bosambo Paul Robeson gives a performance that is virile, charismatic and enormously engaging. He shows no sign of the embarrassment that he claims to have suffered over the part. There is also a memorably malignant performance from Tony Wane as King Mofalaba.

Zoltan Korda directs efficiently, using the conventional narrative form of long shots for action, punctuated by close-ups for emphasis. It is a style dictated by the need to blend the documentary location sequences with the studio scenes. At one point his meshing of the film's two elements creates a memorable piece of montage, as he dissolves from a shot of two vultures feeding on a corpse to scenes of the tribal uprising following Sanders's departure, thus wordlessly making the point. But, more important, he renders the narrative as a series of vivid and memorable images which remain in the mind long after the detail of the story has faded, and this is the enduring strength of popular film. These images are Sanders with a handful of Houssas defying the numerically superior might of the Old King and dismissing him with a curt 'The palaver is finished'; Sanders, riddled with malaria, ordering his ancient steamer upriver on a journey never before undertaken;

Sanders of the River

Sanders of the River established the classic archetype of the British District Officer (Leslie Banks), who is head-masterly (1) and authoritative (2). It also created two archetypes of the natives under his control: the Good Native, the faithful pro-British Bosambo (Paul Robeson) (3), and the Bad Native, the tyrannical old King Mofalaba (Tony Wayne) (4).

When the King stirs up trouble the British rapidly restore order (5), and the renegade white men who have been supplying the natives with guns and gin are killed (6).

Sanders and his men racing ashore amidst bursts of machine-gun fire to rescue Bosambo and his wife in the nick of time; and the finale with Sanders, pipe in mouth, leaning on the rail of the boat, the Union Jack fluttering over his head and Bosambo with his warriors hymning his virtues from their canoes. In these images is contained the essence of the message.

Who was responsible for this message, and what motivated him? The film was produced by Alexander Korda, the dynamic head of London Films, and it is clear that his was the decisive voice in the film's creation. He chose the subject, sat in on the script conferences and, when it came to disagreements, imposed his view on the director, his brother Zoltan.

Why did Alexander Korda settle on a film of Empire and, in particular, *Sanders*? First, to remain in business he obviously needed to make financially successful films. He had a policy of acquiring the rights to best-selling books. Edgar Wallace was a phenomenon, a massively popular, astonishingly prolific and consistently best-selling writer. His 'Sanders' stories had first appeared in a weekly magazine in 1909, and since then he had written 102 of them, which had appeared in eight successive hardback collections. They had been continuously in print since their first appearance, and Wallace himself was the most filmed British author of the 1930s. Thirty-three of this plays and stories had been made into films in Britain and America by 1940. There was obviously a ready-made audience.

Second, Korda wanted to capture a larger share of the Empire market and believed that films set and partly filmed in the Empire would contribute to that. In January 1935, three months before the release of *Sanders*, a reporter who had discussed Korda's plans with him noted: 'Korda, having become horizon-conscious, is going out for Empire markets in a big way. He intends to make pictures with specific appeal to different parts of the Empire.'[19]

Third, there was a personal and political reason for Korda's choice. Korda wanted to stress the virtues of the British imperial system, the doctrines of fair play and moral authority at a time when the rise of Fascism was threatening these ideas and offering a different sort of world. Karol Kulik has written: 'He was a confirmed Anglophile who saw the Empire-builders as the embodiment of all the most noble traits in the English character and spirit.'[20] His predilection for imperial settings is demonstrated by the fact that he produced not only the imperial trilogy (*Sanders of the River, The Drum* and *The Four Feathers*) but also films of two of Kipling's classic children's stories of India 'Toomai of the Elephants' (filmed as *Elephant Boy*) and *The Jungle Book.*

But there may have been more than just a personal motive at work. Korda had close links with the Conservative Party, which he advised on film propaganda throughout the 1930s.[21] There was considerable pressure both inside and outside the Government for the production of feature films promoting the imperial idea. There were calls at successive imperial conferences for such films. Sir Philip Cunliffe-Lister, President of the Board of Trade, called in the Commons in 1927 for more use of the cinema to promote imperial unity, saying, 'The cinema is today the most universal means through which national ideas and national atmosphere can be spread.'[22] This statement was quoted as summarizing current British Government thinking on the subject in 1936.[23] Sir Stephen Tallents, Secretary of the Empire Marketing Board, called for the positive projection of Britain:

In the discharge of our great responsibilities to the other countries of the Commonwealth, we must master the art of national projection and must set ourselves to throw a fitting projection of England upon the world's screens. The English people must be seen for what it is — a great nation still anxious to serve the world and secure the world's peace.[24]

Winifred Holmes wrote in *Sight and Sound* in 1936:

It is essential for the continued unity and good will of the Empire that more and better British films should be distributed everywhere and that these films should add to England's prestige and show more of her ideals and epic qualities than before.[25]

But the government was reluctant to spend its own money and preferred to work indirectly by encouraging friendly producers. In a memorandum of notes and suggestions about propaganda sent in April 1934 to Neville Chamberlain by Joseph Ball, Deputy Director of the National Publicity Bureau, he suggested:

The cinema trade as a whole parades the fact that it is opposed to political propaganda in cinema theatres, but much has nevertheless been done without protest from the public by means of the 'newsreels'. Here again, as in the case of the press, an obvious line of approach is to bring influence to bear on the proprietors of the various cinema news organizations. . . . It should also be possible to ensure the adoption by some of the more enlightened producers of scenarios dealing with e.g. historical or imperial subjects in such a way as to enlist the sympathies of audiences on the side of the present government.[26]

There can be little doubt that Korda was one of these 'enlightened producers'. For in 1938 Ball was reporting to Chamberlain: 'I have cultivated close links with the "leaders" of the British film industry and I am satisfied that I can count upon most of them for their full support to any reasonable degree.'[27] He specifically mentions Korda in this context. It could well be, then, that a hint was dropped to Korda that the Government would not be averse to an imperial epic, something that coincided with his own film-making aims. Certainly, Korda's film units received full co-operation from the colonial authorities in Africa, and he acknowledged in particular Sir Bernard Bourdillon, Governor of Uganda, in a foreword to the film.

Whether or not he was directly inspired by sources close to the Government, Korda was determined to make a film that would glorify British colonial administration, and this brought him into conflict with his brother, the director Zoltan. Karol Kulik records that they disagreed about the emphasis of the film.[28] Zoltan wanted to make maximum use of his location footage to depict African tribal life and customs; Alexander wanted to stress the imperial administration aspect. 'My father loved Africa; he loved the black man,' Zoltan's son David told Karol Kulik. This love was movingly and sincerely expressed in Zoltan's film of Alan Paton's classic novel *Cry the Beloved Country* (1952), but it did not mean that he was hostile to a favourable depiction of the District Commissioner. For, returning from Africa, he had written in a magazine article:

The white government of Africa is one of the wonders of the world. No doubt there are some commissioners who are inefficient, but I did not meet any. Those with whom I came into contact combined the patience of

Job with the wisdom of Solomon, and were completely representative of the great traditions that has made us regard them as quite unequal to their work unless they perform miracles. It is to these men that my film is dedicated.[29]

Zoltan did manage to get several of his location sequences highlighted in the film, and he did win a dispute with Alexander about whether or not Sanders and Bosambo should shake hands when Sanders went on leave. (Alexander seems to have felt that the implication of equality might offend white audiences.) On the whole, however, the conception and message must be seen to be Alexander's. That conclusion is confirmed by the reaction to the film of its star, Paul Robeson. Robeson, a communist and tireless campaigner for Negro rights, had come to live in London, where he found less discrimination than in America. Having seen the African location footage, he had signed to play Bosambo, believing that the film would accurately depict African culture. But when he saw the complete film at the premiere, he walked out, claiming that he had been tricked and swore never to work for Korda again.[30] He insisted thereafter on inserting in his contracts a clause giving him approval of the final cut of the films in which he appeared. Interviewed by a black American journalist in 1936, Robeson was told:

> This picture . . . was a slanderous attack on African natives who were pictured as being satisfied with the "benevolent" oppression of English imperialism. You yourself played the role of selling the natives out to the imperialists. Such a role is inconsistent with your professed love for the Soviet Union and what that country represents. . . . You became the tool of British imperialism and must be attacked and exposed whenever you act in such pictures or plays.

Robeson replied: 'You're right, and I think all the attacks against me and the film were correct.'[31] Ironically, it is Robeson's robust and attractive performance that is one of the film's enduring strengths.

The final question we must ask is how was the film received. The critics took the message of the film clearly enough. The right-wing critics exulted. Sydney Carroll in the *Sunday Times* declared delightedly:

> The films are always providing surprises. The latest cause for astonishment is that they have given us the felicity and success with which foreigners, folk who can have no claims, by birth, origin or association with our Empire, can yet evolve moving pictures which voice far more eloquently than we can ourselves the better purposes of our imperial aspiration. These aliens have shown a truer, sounder British nationalism that we ourselves appear capable of displaying. We have lately seen Americans, with the aid of Hollywood's international resources, producing a *Cavalcade* completely in tune with Noel Coward's conception, a *Clive of India* stirringly patriotic and British. Now comes Alexander Korda and his brother Zoltan, two Hungarians, revealing in *Sanders of the River* a sympathy with our ideals of colonial administration, giving us a grand insight into our special English difficulties in the governing of savage races, and providing us with a documentary film of East African nature in its raw state, a picture which could not be improved upon for the respect it displays to British sensibilities and ambitions. *Sanders of the River* owes a tremendous lot to Zoltan Korda. He has directed it brilliantly. He has made it part travelogue, part romance, part thriller. It is crowded with the excitements of life on the Congo. He has displayed the native ceremonials,

the delirious and ecstatic dances, the tribal rhythms of African negroes, the apprehension of giraffe, hippo, crocodile and bird shot from an aeroplane, the terrors and delights of contact and conjunction between civilization and savagery, the white man's burden and the Englishman's rule.[32]

The *Sunday Express* was less fulsome but none the less approving:

> There's marvellous stuff in this picture but it is a film of brilliant fragments rather than good entertainment all along the line. It is big in scale and thrilling in theme — the theme of the white man fighting a lonely battle in the African jungle and trying to establish law among the tribes. Much more might have been made of that. One cannot be modest about an Empire.[33]

The left-wing critic and film-maker Paul Rotha, writing in *Cinema Quarterly*, poured scorn on the film:

> So this is Africa, ladies and gentlemen, wild, untamed Africa before your very eyes, where the White Man rules by kindness and the Union Jack means peace! . . . You may, like me, feel embarrassed for Robeson. To portray on the public screen one of your own people . . . as toady to the White Man is no small feat. For the others, they do not matter. Just one moment in this film lives. Those aeroplane scenes of galloping herds across the Attic Plains. It is important to remember that the multitudes of *this* country who see Africa in this film are being encouraged to believe this fudge is real. It is a disturbing thought.[34]

It was a view shared by the Nigerian scholar Dr Nnamdi Azikwe, who wrote in 1937:

> Whoever sees this picture will be shocked at the exaggeration of African mentality, so far as superstitious beliefs are concerned, not to speak of the knavery and chicanery of some African chiefs. I feel that what is being paraded in the world today as art or literature is nothing short of propaganda.[35]

As to how the British public reacted, there is less clear-cut evidence. But it all points to their approving of both the film and its message. It was so successful when shown in 1935 that it was reissued in 1938, 1943 and 1947. It inspired a stage version, *The Sun Never Sets,* which also starred Leslie Banks and featured songs by Cole Porter. Paul Robeson's recording of the 'Canoe Song' became a hit. *Kinematograph Weekly,* the usually perceptive trade paper whose business it was to assess a film's potential selling points, described it as 'a fine tribute to British rule in Africa' and said:

> Not only is the film a glorious piece of clean, engrossing entertainment, but it has in its title, cast and ready-made public, represented by the popularity of the author's work, unprecedented box-office credentials.[36]

The box-office success of *Sanders* was such as to inspire Korda to produce *The Drum* (1938), set in India, and *The Four Feathers* (1939), set in the Sudan, both in the then comparatively rare Technicolor. As Paul Holt wrote in the *Daily Express* in 1938:

> Mr Korda plans to make a lot of films about the Empire in future. That is good news for this newspaper. It is also good business for Mr Korda. He knows that films about the Empire make money. He knows that films of

his like *Sanders of the River* and *Elephant Boy* and *The Drum* have been far more successful at the box offices of this country than any equal amount of sophisticated sex nonsense. . . . Patriotism goes with profit.[37]

It might be argued that the public went to the film not because it was about the Empire but because they wanted to hear Robeson singing or to see African wildlife or bare-breasted native dancers. But they would not be able to avoid the adventure story anchored within a framework of beliefs in which the chief characters embodied clearly defined ideals and attitudes to life. Given the election and re-election of a predominantly Conservative National Government, the fervent national celebrations of King George V's Silver Jubilee, the immense popularity of the 'Sanders' stories with the reading public, the evidence of 'unwitting testimony' would be that the film genuinely reflected widely held beliefs about the role and function of the British Empire.

There is an interesting footnote to the story, which shows that the life of a film far exceeds its decade. In 1957 *Sanders* was shown for the first time on television, by ATV, as part of the season of Korda classics. *The Times* reported that the Nigerian High Commissioner, Mr M. T. Mbu, had protested to the television company about the showing, saying that it was 'damaging to Nigeria and brought disgrace and disrepute to Nigerians'.[38] The Commissioner regretted that ATV should show a film 'portraying Nigeria as a country of half-naked barbarians still living in caves without any contact with the outside world'. He thought that it would create ill-feeling against Nigerians living in Britain. The *Guardian* carried the same story, with an additional note from its Lagos correspondent observing that the film was very popular in Nigeria and had been showing to packed houses at three Lagos cinemas during that very week.[39]

Notes

1 Reginald Coupland, *The Empire in These Days,* London, 1935, p. 5.
2 James Morris, *Farewell the Trumpets,* London and Boston, 1978, pp. 315−16.
3 ibid., p. 299.
4 This argument is developed at length in John MacKenzie, *Propaganda and Empire,* Manchester, forthcoming.
5 On the cinema of Empire, see Jeffrey Richards, *Visions of Yesterday,* London, 1973.
6 Margaret Farrand Thorp, *America at the Movies,* New Haven, 1939, pp. 294−5.
7 Colin Shindler, *Hollywood Goes to War,* London, 1979, p. 2.
8 On the Korda imperial trilogy, see Jeffrey Richards, 'Korda's Empire', *Australian Journal of Screen Theory,* 5−6, 1979, pp. 122−37; Jeffrey Richards, 'Patriotism with Profit: British Imperial Cinema in the 1930s', in V. Porter and J. Curran (eds.), *British Cinema History,* London, 1983.
9 Production details of *Sanders* can be found in Karol Kulik, *Alexander Korda,* London, 1975, pp. 135−7.
10 Robert Heussler, *Yesterday's Rulers,* Oxford, 1963, p. 82.
11 Jonathan Gathorne-Hardy, *The Public School Phenomenon,* Harmondsworth, 1979, p. 151.
12 Heussler, *Yesterday's Rulers,* pp. 19−20.
13 Margaret Lane, *Edgar Wallace,* London, 1939, p. 225.

14   Charles Allen, *Tales from the Dark Continent,* London, 1979, pp. 79—80.
15   Correlli Barnett, *The Collapse of British Power,* London, 1972, p. 241.
16   Francis Hutchins, *The Illusion of Permanence,* Princeton, 1967.
17   Boris Gussman, *Out in the Midday Sun,* London, 1962, p. 82.
18   ibid., p. 64.
19   Unidentified newspaper clipping, BFI *Alexander Korda* microfiche.
20   Kulik, *Alexander Korda,* p. 135.
21   T. J. Hollins, 'The Conservative Party and Film Propaganda between the Wars', *English Historical Review,* 96, April 1981, pp. 359—69.
22   *House of Commons Debates,* vol. 23, col. 2039.
23   Board of Trade, Minutes of evidence taken before the Departmental Committee on Cinematograph Films, 1936, p. 14.
24   S. G. Tallents, *The Projection of England,* London, 1932, pp. 39—40.
25   *Sight and Sound,* 5, Autumn 1936, p. 74.
26   Neville Chamberlain Papers, NC 8/21/9, 14 April 1934. I am indebted to Dr Stephen Constantine for this reference.
27   ibid., NC 8/21/9 June 1938.
28   Kulik, *Alexander Korda,* p. 136.
29   Unidentified clipping, BFI *Sanders of the River* microfiche.
30   Marie Seton, *Paul Robeson,* London, 1958, pp. 77—9,96.
31   P. Foner (ed.), *Paul Robeson Speaks,* London, 1979, pp. 107—8.
32   *Sunday Times,* 7 April 1935.
33   *Sunday Express,* 7 April 1935.
34   Paul Rotha, *Rotha on Film,* London, 1958, pp. 139—40.
35   Dr Nnamdi Azikwe, *Renascent Africa,* Lagos, 1968 (reprint), pp. 153—5.
36   *Kinematograph Weekly,* 4 April 1935.
37   *Daily Express,* 9 July 1938.
38   *The Times,* 22 November 1957.
39   *Guardian,* 22 November 1957.

3

The Age of Consensus

South Riding

The mainstream British cinema of the 1930s has invariably been characterized in simple terms. It was a 'dream factory', and for the many millions who frequented the cinemas week after week it offered 'an escape from reality into a fantasy world'.[1] Thereafter, we are told, British films were traditionally, in Dilys Powell's words, 'an inferior substitute for the American-made film'. The Americans 'colonized' the British cinema during this period; there was no tradition of British films and scant evidence of a 'national' cinema, and in consequence British films had no important part to play in the 'national life' until the advent of World War II.[2]

The film producer Michael Balcon endorsed many of these arguments in his autobiography, which was published in 1969. There he lamented the absence of any 'social reality' in the mainstream British films of the 1930s. Not one of his own films, he readily admitted, 'in any way reflected the despair of the times in which we were living'. Indeed, 'Hardly a single film of the period reflects the urgency of these times', he commented and added, 'On my bookshelves to this day I find *The Town that was Murdered* by Ellen Wilkinson, and all the other Left Book Club publications, but little of their influence is reflected in the films we were making.'[3]

This passing reference by Balcon to the Left Book Club started by Victor Gollancz in 1936, to its publications and to Ellen Wilkinson's 1939 account of the plight of Jarrow is particularly interesting, for it bears witness to the enduring impression which such 'dole literature' made and to the vision which it projected of the 1930s. Similarly, Balcon's references to the 'despair' and 'urgency' of the times testify to the image which has been set for the 1930s in general. For Balcon, as for many other commentators, the vision of the cinema as a 'dream factory' was predicated upon this image of the period.

For many people then, as now, the 1930s were the 'devil's decade'. They symbolized economic disaster, social deprivation and political discontent; it was an era of mass unemployment, hunger marches, Fascist demonstrations and appeasement. The country was beset by innumerable crises both at home and abroad, and inevitably, so the argument goes, both the crises and the solutions which were adopted to tackle them simply conspired to produce a Britain so divided along social and political lines that the very stability of the country was threatened.

Despite the gravity of Britain's situation during that period, however, some historians have argued that its actual effects upon the country remain open to question, and recently more emphasis has been placed upon the idea of an inherently stable country. One historian commented in 1975, for example, that 'for all the divisions in its social structure', on the eve of World War II Britain remained 'a small and closely knit community, insular, and bound together by strong patriotic or perhaps nationalistic feelings which no historian has yet fully documented'.[4]

In 1977 John Stevenson and Chris Cook set out to document those feelings in part, while at the same time addressing the larger question of the 'myths and realities' of Britain in the 1930s. With regard to unemployment, for instance, they argue that while one must not underestimate its disastrous effects — with rarely less than 1.5 million out of work and at one stage as many as 2.75 million, and with great hardship and personal suffering alleviated only occasionally by the existence of the dole — none the less 'There were never less than three-quarters of the population in work during the 1930s and for most of the period considerably more.' By the middle and late 1930s unemployment had become a regional problem once again, and 'alongside the pictures of the dole queues and hunger marches must also be placed those of another Britain, of new industries, prosperous suburbs and a rising standard of living.' 'For those in work,' the authors believe, 'the 1930s were a period of rising living standards and new levels of consumption, upon which a considerable degree of industrial growth was based.'[5]

On a wider front they argue that 'the economic and social climate for political extremism during the inter-war period was much less favourable than has often been depicted.'[6] The Communist Party and the Fascists never enjoyed widespread support. 'Crucially,' Stevenson and Cook continue, 'the existing political parties do not appear to have been discredited by the depression for more than a minority',[7] and consequently there was no major swing either to the left or to the right. The leadership of the Labour Party and the Trades Union Congress was, for its part, committed to a moderate line and there again 'Violence . . . like political extremism, was a minority response in the thirties to the impact of mass unemployment.'[8]

Their research leads them far and wide, but throughout they talk of factors such as the 'conservatism' and the 'more fundamental unifying aspects of British society'. They quote, approvingly, George Orwell's references to the 'emotional unity' that he felt was evident in the country and, more significant, 'the considerable agreement that does unfortunately exist between the leaders and the led'. All of which prompts them to conclude that 'Even in the face of the slump, Britain remained a relatively cohesive and insular society in which there were still a large number of shared assumptions.'[9]

But what of the British cinema in the midst of this historical revision of British society during the 1930s? Is there any reason to believe that it too is in need of some revision? Certainly, one commentator at least would seem to think that the notion of the mainstream cinema as a mere provider of escapist entertainment merits closer scrutiny. In his *Critical History of British Cinema* Roy Armes makes the following comments:

> The characteristic works of 1930s cinema do not therefore lay bare social

contradictions. . . . They are rather films which organize the audience's experiences in the sense of fostering social integration and the acceptance of social constraints. Emotional problems are shown to find an easy solution in matrimony, and potentially explosive political or legal issues are defused by being turned into mere clashes of character. It is simplistic to treat such a form of cinema as merely harmless — or even harmful — escapist entertainment. The Odeons of the late 1930s did not offer oblivion on the lines of the gin palaces of Victorian times. Instead they consistently gave their audiences a deeper reassurance through a facsimile world where existing values were invariably validated by events in the film and where all discord could be turned to harmony by an acceptance of the status quo.[10]

Clearly, Armes credits the British cinema with having played a far greater role than Balcon and other commentators have suggested. It fulfilled an ideological role, he is arguing, and projected a vision of the world which underpinned the social and political structures of British society at the time.

Indeed, one could go further to argue that the British cinema had both a 'reflective' function, in that it reflected the cohesive society which some historians tell us was in fact prevalent at the time, and a 'generative' function, in that it sought to encourage the assumption that society should continue to cohere and unite as it passed through the changing circumstances of the 1930s. To that extent it may be said that the British cinema had a positive and purposeful part to play in shaping the 'national life' because it helped (along with many other factors, of course) to achieve that high degree of consensus which seemingly characterized British society during the 1930s.

There are several ways in which one might set about exploring this revised picture of the British cinema. One might examine the reasons for Government intervention in the affairs of the British film industry in order to point out the cultural objectives which lay at the heart of the 1927 and 1938 Films Acts.[11] One might consider the purpose and process of the censorship imposed by the British Board of Film Censors in order to look at the subjects that were precluded by that body and to highlight the values that it sought to inculcate.[12] Alternatively, one might utilize the evidence that is available regarding the relative 'popularity' of British films with British audiences to suggest that they were far more popular, in many senses, than they are often given credit for being and to argue that the 'Americanization' thesis must be greatly qualified, at least for the 1930s.[13]

All of these avenues could and should be followed up by any comprehensive survey of the British cinema during the period of the 1930s. Here, though, the intention is to look at the characteristic forms rather than the institutions of British cinema and, in particular, to single out *South Riding* for scrutiny in order to outline the projection of Britain that it depicted and the consensus that it sought to evoke.

Such a course of action is clearly open to the criticism that one film is hardly representative of the mainstream British cinema of the day, which is usually divided into the large 'prestigious' productions (Korda's epics and the like, into which category *South Riding* falls) and the so-called 'provincial' comedies (from George Formby, Gracie Fields, Will Hay and others). The former strain generally receives attention; the latter rarely does and is often dismissed in the same curt tone that was employed by critical commentators on first viewing the films. However, the division is arbitrary. The comedies merit equal attention, certainly, and they can be a rich historical source, as I have sought to show elsewhere.[14] Ultimately they differ little, if at all, in intent from their supposedly 'prestigious' counterparts, and the intent of a film such as *South Riding* can be taken as symptomatic of the mainstream British cinema generally.

The film of *South Riding* was based upon Winifred Holtby's novel, which was published in February 1936. Within a month the book had sold 25,000 copies and was acclaimed Book of the Month. By the end of 1936 it had gone through eight impressions. It was obviously a success and, like all literary successes, was therefore likely to attract the attention of many a film producer. Victor Saville was quick to snap it up. On 25 March 1936 he bought the film rights and paid £3,000 for them to Holtby's estate (she died in September 1935) through the person of Vera Brittain, the literary executor of Holtby's will and her close friend over many years.

Saville determined to make a 'film of quality' out of the novel, a film with literary pretensions and aspirations to do more than simply entertain.[15] There was to be extensive exterior shooting; an international cinematographer of repute, Harry Stradling, was engaged, along with a noted scriptwriter, Ian Dalrymple, and art director, Lazare Meerson; and a large cast was headed by some accomplished British actors. Robert Donat was sought for the leading role, but he fell ill, and it was subsequently offered to Ralph Richardson.

The film was released early in 1938. It turned out, Saville thought, to be his best film. 'They're real people,' he commented later, in interview, of the characters whom he had created on the screen.[16] Vera Brittain recorded in her autobiography that she had reservations about the film, though she conceded, 'According to the standards then expected by film-goers, Victor Saville had made a memorable picture.'[17] In fact, the film found favour with the cinema-going public (it was re-released, though in edited form, in 1943 and 1946) and the critics alike. And in general the critics greeted the film on its release in much the same terms that Saville later used.

'Here is an English picture which is really English,' commented the *Daily Telegraph*. The *Daily Mirror* believed the film provided a 'scrupulous, authentic picture of English life for the first time on any screen', and the *Sunday Pictorial* praised its 'wonderfully authentic settings'. Even the more 'informed' sources of criticism considered that the film was for the most part 'realistic'. 'Well worth seeing as a well acted, well produced story of the realities of English life', commented the *Monthly Film Bulletin* of the British Film Institute, and the *New Statesman* added on 8 January 1938: 'For a time we sit ecstatic upon our plush, unable to believe our eyes and ears — something positively real is unrolling before us', though both these latter sources also subscribed to the opinion that the climax of the film was a 'major blunder', ending 'regrettably, in sheer bathos'.[18]

The plot of the film is simple enough. Squire Carne (Ralph Richardson), the MFH, is increasingly burdened by financial problems. His wife Madge (Ann Todd) is in an expensive mental home, and he lives alone at Maythorpe Hall with his daughter Midge (Glynis Johns). He is the only member of the South Riding County Council who objects to a new housing scheme which would abolish a ramshackle shanty village known as 'The Shacks'. Carne, however, is suspicious of the motives behind the scheme. His suspicions turn out to be well founded. Astell (John Clements), a 'genuine social reformer' as the synopsis describes him,[19] unwittingly accepts the help of two fellow councillors, Snaith (Milton Rosmer) and Huggins (Edmund Gwenn), who promote the scheme but intend to turn it to their own financial advantage.

Carne's finances go from bad to worse, and on the advice of his good friend Alderman Mrs Beddows (Marie Lohr) he decides to send his daughter to the local school. He discusses the matter with its new headmistress Sarah Burton (Edna Best). They begin to meet often and finally fall in love.

Sarah overhears Huggins in a conversation which reveals his duplicity, and she goes straight to Carne. He has been to the mental home where his wife has lapsed into a coma. And when Sarah arrives at Maythorpe Hall, she finds he has gone alone into the woods with a gun. She follows him and stops him from committing suicide. At the Council meeting later that afternoon Snaith and Huggins are exposed, and Carne thereafter decides to back the housing scheme. The new housing estate is opened amid the joyous celebrations of Coronation Day.

But what kind of 'reality' is constructed in the film of *South Riding*? What sort of 'English landscape' does it project, and what 'pictorial impression' does it give of England in the 1930s?

The introductory sequences to the film, which comprise the credits and a prologue, seemingly encapsulate the way in which the drama will unfold. They serve also ostensibly to highlight the issues and to spotlight the protagonists who will dominate the fictional representation that is to follow.

Opening captions pay brief homage to Winifred Holtby and state that she 'realized that local government is not a dry affair of meetings and memoranda, but "the front-line defence thrown up by humanity against its common enemies of sickness, poverty and ignorance"'. Then each of the leading characters makes a brief speech to camera, as follows:

Beddows: Mr Chairman, I stand for the fair administration of the limited funds at our disposal. If we give too much here, another will have to go without there.

Snaith: I take the practical view. I ask myself, is it good business? If it's good business, well, it's right.

Huggins: What I say is, public affairs is a trust from above. We 'ave dedicated ourselves to the service of the people.

Astell: I started life as a socialist. I'm sorry. I'm unrepentant. My ambition is to see the lives of the working masses improved.

Carne: Cheap houses, free education, hospitals and so on, all very excellent. But aren't we teaching people to rely on others, instead of themselves? In which case there's no future for England.

Burton: England's future is in the hands of her children. Give them what they need.[20]

The issues raised in those six statements are socially pertinent and appear to confirm the film's indebtedness to Holtby's novel, in which the chapters are headed 'Education', 'Public Health', 'Housing and Town Planning' and the like. Together the characters making the statements constitute a cross-section of interested informed opinion.

There is the liberally inspired, fair-minded Alderman Mrs Beddows, full of common sense; the practical, down-to-earth businessman Alderman Snaith; Councillor Huggins, the religious zealot, it appears, who believes in a God-given mission; the Labour Councillor Astell, consumptive (he coughs during his speech and continues to cough at appropriate and telling moments elsewhere in the film), yet dedicated to improving the lot of the workers in this world rather than the next; Councillor Carne who trots out the traditional conservative platitudes about self-improvement and the state of the nation; and the visionary Sarah Burton, a schoolteacher, imbued with confidence, optimism and a belief that the youth of today provide hope for the future, given the right sort of start in life. These characters form 'a part of the changing England that is typical of the whole', as another opening caption puts it. Yet it is a society fraught with problems and contradictions, as their statements reveal. The matters that are addressed are of public concern, but the philosophies, as expounded, seem irreconcilable; there is conflict and a difference of opinion.

How, then, does the film effect a resolution of these problems and the conflicting sets of interests?

It does so, to begin with, by personalizing the problems and turning them into clashes of character (an opening caption readily admits that: 'Our story tells how a public life affects the private life, and how a man's personal sufferings make him what he is in public'). Thereafter, the film marginalizes those elements of social commentary which occupied the centre stage in Holtby's original literary narrative and doubtless provided a major source of inspiration for her work, and it moves to the foreground, in their stead, other elements which are determined more by the classic dictates of mainstream narrative cinema than by anything else. Finally, the film achieves its purpose by extirpating the 'evil' and disruptive forces in the society that it creates on screen while negotiating a series of compromise solutions to bring about a consensus of opinion within the remaining 'productive' forces.

Compromise and consensus, in the best interests of society and the nation as a whole, are largely what the film of *South Riding* is about. And the 'moral' of the film, if one chooses to use such terms, is that nobody is above learning how to compromise if important issues are at stake. In this the film is greatly at odds with the novel, which is permeated by an acute sense of loss and unfulfilled promise, though it also concludes with a good deal of sustained emphasis upon the compensations of 'belonging to a community', of being 'one with the people' and of 'national uinity'.

Those characters, like Snaith and Huggins, who are not willing to compromise at all but seek rather to secure their own selfish ends by whatever devious means at their disposal, must be weeded out. Again, this is somewhat different from the novel, in which Snaith is construed as 'subtle as a serpent, yet serving his generation', and Huggins is described simply as having a 'passion for righteousness at war with his appetites'. Neither one is there meted out the retribution that is dispensed in the film. Carne, intransigent and narrow-minded because of his heritage and the personal problems which beset him, must learn to compromise in the face of the changing society around him if he is to survive at all — in the novel he does not do so and he dies. Sarah too must learn to compromise if she is to achieve her goals; but force of circumstance has already taught her, as it has Astell and to some extent Mrs Beddows, something about the need to compromise. (The characters of Sarah and Mrs Beddows are nearest to the novel's original conception of them, though in the novel Sarah does not marry Carne, of course, as she does in the film. Astell's screen persona is ostensibly the complete antithesis of that in the novel. In the latter he finally leaves the South Riding and declares: 'I'm a militant again, thank God, quit of the shame of compromise.')

There are several key sequences that make clear the film's insistence upon the need for compromise in all its forms. In the first one, early in the film, Sarah Burton is interviewed for the post of headmistress at Kiplington High School:

Astell: Why do you want to come here when you've been teaching in London?

Burton: I wanted to come back to Yorkshire.

Beddows: We had a much better vacancy in Flintonbridge last year. Why didn't you apply for that?

Burton: Because I didn't think I would get it.

Beddows: Why not?

Burton: Well, you see, I'm not by birth a lady.

Carne: What do you mean, you're not by birth a lady?

Burton: My father was a blacksmith.

Carne: Well, what part of the Riding do you come from?

Burton: Liptonhunter. My mother was the district nurse.

Carne: Oh, yes, I remember. . . .

Burton: Go on, say it. My father was a drunkard. He drank himself to death. And my mother went to the West Riding and worked herself to the bone to educate me. I'm proud of my mother.

Despite Carne's obvious reservations, Sarah does get the post and, once appointed, she tries to enlist Astell's support for the school:

Burton: The young are important. Oh, you're just yellow.

Astell: Oh no, I'm not. I'm not even pale pink. I'm red. Scarlet. But one thing at a time. It's uphill work. And I'm tired (coughs). You don't know the opposition. I'm worn out with it. And much of it's reasonable, that's the rub. You start by demanding world revolution and end up being satisfied with a sewage farm.

Burton: That reminds me. You haven't seen our cockroaches.

Astell: Oh no, not that. I'm a snob about cockroaches, an absolute Carne.

Subsequently, Sarah catches Midge Carne, newly arrived at the local school because her father cannot afford to send her to a private school, fighting with Lydia Holly, a naturally intelligent girl but born into the poverty and degradation of 'The Shacks'. She takes Lydia aside and counsels her:

Burton: Now then, Lydia, you've got to be kind to Midge Carne.

Lydia: Yes, Miss Burton.

Burton: You don't seem very keen.

Lydia: Miss Burton, I do try, but. . . .

Burton: No, you don't, Lydia.

Lydia: No, Miss Burton.

Burton: You think because she's better off than you, you'll get your own back and take it out of her, don't you?

Lydia: Yes, Miss Burton.

Burton: Well, you're wrong, Lydia. She isn't better off than you. She's unhappy. She's lonely. She's got no brothers and sisters and no mother. You're the lucky one, Lydia, and you're happy. You've got health and strength and brains and everything's fun for you.

Lydia: Yes, Miss Burton, it is. I begin to see what you mean.

South Riding celebrates the social and political consensus that defended British society against the turmoil of the 1930s. Lydia Holly (Joan Ellum), who has grown up in a slum, acquires both a love of Shakespeare (1) and some understanding of tolerance from Sarah Burton (Edna Best) after a fight with Midge Carne (Glynis Johns) (2). Councillor Astell (John Clements), dedicated to improving the worker's lot (3), finally joins forces with Sarah Burton and Squire Carne (Ralph Richardson), a staunch Tory (4). Carne's life is blighted by one woman, his mad wife Madge (Ann Todd), but Sarah Burton restores his happiness (6).

Burton: Life's got such lots in store for you, Lydia, if you'll only work hard. For a start I want you to work for a scholarship. Because of all the girls in this school, you're the one who ought to go to college.

Lydia: Oh, Miss Burton, college, if only I could. It's what I've dreamed about. If you'll help me, I'll mother Midge Carne. I'll, I'll do anything for you. I'll be your slave, I'll. . . . Oh I'm so happy.

But Lydia's mother dies, and there is a threat that Lydia will have to leave school in order to look after the family. So Sarah attempts to secure a boarding scholarship for the girl, with Mrs Beddows's help:

Burton: Mrs Beddows, if the school governors would make a special grant for Lydia to board at school, I'll pay a woman to look after the Hollys.

Beddows: My dear, that's wonderfully generous of you, but it can't be done. You can't afford that sort of thing, and we haven't the power or the means to create a boarding scholarship.

Burton: You're going to allow this to happen?

Beddows: We're hardly to blame for people having families they can't support.

Burton: It's a stupid waste of such an intelligent child.

Beddows: It will make a fine woman of her.

Burton: A fine woman. A drudge.

Beddows: If you consider hard work drudgery, then we're most of us drudges. We do what we can with limited resources. We need patience.

Carne does not so much compromise throughout most of the film as relents, and usually in a reluctant fashion at that. He relents over the appointment of Sarah as headmistress; he relents over sending Midge to the local school; he relents finally about pushing through a scholarship for Lydia to keep her at school. And it is because of his stubbornness that he is driven to desperation and attempted suicide. Yet he does begin at last to learn how to compromise, thanks largely to his blossoming relationship with Sarah. The first signs are evident when he allows Sarah to help him with the delivery of a calf, though initially his response is cold and hostile:

Carne: What the . . . ! How did you get here?

Burton: I heard that awful sound.

Carne: But you can't come here. This is no place for a woman.

Burton: Well, the cow and I are both females.

Carne: Now go away, please.

Burton: I'm going to help.

Carne: What on earth help do you think you'll be?

Burton: Oh, you forget I was brought up to this sort of thing.

Carne: All right. Well, do exactly what I tell you.

Burton: Naturally.

Carne: Yes, well, you won't want that. There's a bucket of water there. Hey, take it easy, take it easy. The beastman's drunk. Now quickly. . . . (Later) . . . Mother and son doing well. I'm awfully grateful. I wouldn't have done it without you.

Burton: Nonsense, I only seemed to get in the way. No vet could teach you anything.

Where though does all this compromise get everybody? What sort of consensus is brought about as a result of it?

The narrative thrust of the screenplay reaches its inevitable conclusion during a confrontation in the council chambers. A council debate reinstates in the foreground the proposal for a housing scheme, always in danger of being lost in the course of the film. Snaith and Huggins are exposed as corrupt and self-interested. Astell is shown to have acted stupidly though with the best intentions. Carne, of course, emerges triumphant. His change of heart and new-found sense of compromise solves all the problems over the housing scheme — he donates his estate to the council for houses and a new school. His wife has died; his private anguish is over; and he has formed a romantic alliance with Sarah, a former antagonist.

Furthermore, the gentleman farmer carries with him another former antagonist, the now repentant socialist Astell, in an alliance that suggests a meeting of the classes for which they stand. The people of the South Riding can only benefit from this symbolic overthrow of social conflicts. Together the paternalistic gentry and the progressive forces in society will forge a new England.

The final scenes show 'the people' gathering together on the Coronation Day of King George and Queen Elizabeth, when the housing estate and high school are to be opened. The camera scans the assembled ranks of firemen and nurses in uniforms, children and rows of people from the community — a representative sample of British society — singling out in the process a small band made up of Astell, Sarah and Carne, happy and smiling. Everybody sings 'Land of Hope and Glory', and the chairman of the council makes a patriotic speech:[21]

> People of the South Riding, today millions of our people line the streets of London and all over the country our townsmen and villagers come together to celebrate the crowning of our new King and Queen. Without boasting and vainglory, we can be proud of our country. Let us remember those who work for the common good, follow their lead and work in our turn for the happiness and the betterment of our people. In this spirit, let us undertake our model coronation housing estate which I now have the honour to inaugurate.

Thus a fitting climax is provided for a film which celebrates essentially a vision of England as one happy, close-knit community, a vision of domestic harmony and national integration to be found most often in British films of the 1930s. And since such films and sentiments were much in evidence, it is little wonder that the British cinema contributed towards the remarkable stability of British society during the period.

Notes

1 George Perry, *The Great British Picture Show,* London, 1975, p. 85. Other standard popular accounts that put forward that argument include, for example, Charles Oakley, *Where We Came In,* London, 1964, and Ernest Betts, *The Film Business,* London, 1973. My own reactions to the argument, and to the arguments for American 'colonization' of the British cinema and against the 'popularity' of British films with British audiences, are charted at greater length in *British Cinema of the 1930s,* Unit 7 of the Open University course *Popular*

Culture, Milton Keynes, 1982. My thanks to the OU for allowing me to use in this chapter some of the material I wrote for that course.

2 Dilys Powell, *Films since 1939,* London, 1947, pp. 64—5. See also A. J. P. Taylor, *English History 1914—1945,* Oxford, 1965, p. 315, where he states that, apart from Korda and Hitchcock, 'the Americans had it all their own way'. The Americanization thesis still holds good in some quarters, as Peter Stead demonstrates in 'The People and the Pictures', in Nicholas Pronay and D. W. Spring (eds.), *Propaganda, Politics and Film, 1918—1945,* London, 1982.

3 Michael Balcon, *Michael Balcon Presents . . . A Lifetime of Films,* London, 1969, pp. 41—2, 90.

4 Paul Addison, *The Road to 1945,* London, 1975, p. 276.

5 John Stevenson and Chris Cook, *The Slump: Society and Politics during the Depression,* London, 1977, pp. 4—5.

6 ibid., p. 30.

7 ibid., p. 142.

8 ibid., p. 193.

9 ibid., p. 276.

10 Roy Armes, *A Critical History of British Cinema,* London, 1978, pp. 113—14. For a more recent assessment, see James Curran and Vincent Porter (eds.), *British Cinema History,* London, 1983.

11 'Should we be content', the President of the Board of Trade asked on the second reading of the Films Bill in 1927, 'if we depended upon foreign literature or upon a foreign press in this country?' The film exhibitors, who did not welcome the Government's interventionist policies, were well aware of that Bill's intentions. One of their organizations commented: 'The object of the Cinematograph Films Bill now before your honourable House has been stated by supporters of the Government to be to promote the making of British films for the purposes of propaganda — commercial, religious, social and political. . . .' In 1936 the Moyne Committee, paving the way for the 1938 Films Act, also asserted that 'The propaganda value of the film cannot be overemphasized' and clearly indicated an acute awareness of film's propaganda potential on the cultural front 'in the spread of national culture and in presenting national ideas and customs to the world'. By contrast, for an interpretation that plays down those cultural objectives, see Peter Stead, 'Hollywood's Message for the World: the British Response in the 1930s', *Historical Journal of Film, Radio and Television,* 1, March 1981.

12 See Jeffrey Richards's two articles, 'The British Board of Film Censors and Content Control in the 1930s', in *Historical Journal of Film, Radio and Television,* 1, October 1981, and 2, March 1982. See also two articles by Nicholas Pronay, 'The First Reality: Film Censorship in Liberal England', in K. R. M. Short (ed.), *Feature Films as History,* London, 1981, and 'The Political Censorship of Films in Britain between the Wars', in Pronay and Spring, *Propaganda, Politics and Film, 1918—1945,* though my own article, 'Comedy, Class and Containment: the Domestic British Cinema of the 1930s', in Curran and Porter, *British Cinema History,* raises some questions regarding the practical effectiveness of the BBFC during the 1930s.

13 See, for example, Simon Rowson's evidence to the Moyne Committee (*Minutes of the Evidence taken before the Departmental Committee on Cinematograph Films,* 1936), where he stated that though there were more American than British films in circulation in Britain between 1933 and 1936, none the less his statistics showed that each British film had been screened on average 6 per cent more frequently than its American counterpart. For the second half of the decade, see the *First Report of the Cinematograph Films Council* which concluded, in 1939, that 'there was an insistent demand by exhibitors for British films which was not limited by the extent of their statutory quotas and

as a result any satisfactory British picture had an eager market in this country.' The slump in British film production in 1938, furthermore, bore little or no relation to the 'popularity' of British films. The plain fact was that no matter how 'popular' a British film might be with British audiences, it could rarely hope to recoup its outlay and make a profit, thereby sustaining film production in this country, simply because of the inadequate system of financing and floating a production and because of the delay in getting films ready for release and subsequently released. Such deficiencies meant, according to Rowson, that making a film in Britain involved the employment of from 70 to 80 per cent more capital than it cost to make a film in America. It was, he concluded, 'a dangerous spiral'.

14 See, for example, the two television programmes made to accompany Unit 7, *British Cinema of the 1930s,* of the Open University course *Popular Culture,* viz., TV 3, *Comedy,* and TV 4 *South Riding.* Both were presented by myself and produced by Susan Boyd-Bowman, and both are broadcast on BBC TV each year throughout the life of the course.

15 Interview conducted with Ian Dalrymple, 12 May 1980.

16 In Cyril B. Rollins and Robert J. Wareing (eds.), *Victor Saville*, London, 1972, p. 12, where Saville also announced, 'I never attacked the establishment in any way.'

17 Vera Brittain, *Testament of Experience,* London, 1979 (reprint), p. 188, where she describes her reaction after attending the first night of the film at the London Pavilion in 1938: 'According to the standards then expected by filmgoers, Victor Saville had made a memorable picture, renewing Winifred's spirit through the candid Yorkshire scenes rather than by an over-romantic treatment of her moving but astringent story. A more realistic film could be made today, showing Sarah Burton and Robert Carne as the star-crossed middle-aged semi-lovers whom Winifred created and depicting Alderman Mrs Beddows as a patriarchal 74 instead of the glamorous 66 presented by the young-looking Marie Lohr.'

Holtby's book was successfully dramatized for a 1974 Yorkshire Television series with Dorothy Tutin, Hermione Baddeley and Nigel Davenport, which won a BAFTA award as best series of the year. And her career and writings have lately been the subject of further scrutiny, which has provided the occasion for a modest revival. See, for example, Stuart Hall *et al., Culture, Media, Language,* London, 1980, pp. 249–56; Mary Stott, 'Winifred Holtby: Cause and Effect', *Guardian,* 18 November 1981; and Joy Holland, 'Rediscovering a Feminist Novelist', *Spare Rib,* 117, April 1982, pp. 17–18. *South Riding* was last reprinted in 1981 by Fontana, and in that same year the Virago Press reprinted Holtby's *Anderby Wold* and *The Crowded Street.*

18 See the microfiche on the film compiled and held by the British Film Institute Library, London.

19 ibid.

20 The BFI Library holds an accurate dialogue continuity script of *South Riding* (6 November 1937). My thanks to Paul Berry, literary executor of the Winifred Holtby Estate, and to Pendennis Films Ltd for allowing me to quote extracts from the script here and elsewhere.

21 The 16 mm print of *South Riding* currently in distribution runs for ninety minutes. The 35 mm print of the film, on its initial release in 1938, ran for ninety-one minutes. An analysis of the film and the dialogue continuity script reveals that the Coronation Day scenes at the climax of the film have been cut slightly. It is clear that originally this sequence began with a short rendering of a few lines from 'Land of Hope and Glory' and was followed by the chairman of the council's speech, and that the whole proceedings were rounded off with everybody launching into the first verse of 'God Save the King'. This is

confirmed by the *New Statesman* review of the film, in which the critic notes that 'there is a macabre fascination in the spectacle of the entire cast singing first "Land of H. and G." and then "God Save the King". "Send him victorious," warbles Miss Best; "Happy and Glorious," counters Mr Richardson; "Long to reign o'er us," adds Mr Clements, sheepishly however, because, you see, he is really a horrid Red.'

We are obviously spared such delights, though if one looks carefully at the three shot of Best, Richardson and Clements in the closing scenes of the film as it presently stands, one can spot a definite lack of synchronization between what they are singing and the sound of 'Land of H. and G.' coming over the soundtrack. This is obviously the point where they should be singing 'God Save the King'. Why, when and where these changes were made is difficult to ascertain. The print of the film in the National Film Archive, London, is of little help on this score, since it is obviously a copy of the re-released, re-edited version of 1943 or 1946. This is shorn of the opening sequences in 'The Shacks' and the closing Coronation Day scenes, an unwitting comment in itself perhaps of the relevance which these particular scenes were felt to have for the 1930s, though not the 1940s.

4

Why We Fight

A Canterbury Tale

At the outbreak of World War II all cinemas in Britain were closed. But their value to the maintenance of morale was soon appreciated, and they were reopened to become one of the principal sources of recreation for the nation at war. Feature films were seen as providing not just escapist entertainment but also instruction and information. So for the duration of the war they operated under the watchful eye of both the British Board of Film Censors and the Ministry of Information. Lord Macmillan, the first wartime Minister of Information, issued a memorandum in 1940 suggesting three themes for propagandist feature films: what Britain was fighting for, how Britain was fighting and the need for sacrifice.[1] The industry responded to these suggestions and, in so doing, experienced perhaps its finest hour. It enjoyed a surge of creativity, an explosion of native talent such as it had not before witnessed. The nature and demands of the situation focused the mind of the film world squarely and continuously on the projection of Britain and the British people, something that had on the whole not occurred in the 1930s.[2]

The earliest British war film, *The Lion Has Wings,* rapidly put together by producer Alexander Korda and on view by November 1939, embodied many of the themes which were to be reworked by later and better films. It established the images of the two sides for the duration by contrasting the goodnatured, decent, hardworking, democratic British, with their sense of humour and their love of sport, and the regimented, fanatical, jackbooted Nazis, marching in faceless formation.

The film looked both to the future and to the past — to the future in the documentary-style reconstruction of wartime operations, and to the past in the staged sequences of the response to the war of a 'typical British couple', the very upper-middle-class Ralph Richardson and Merle Oberon, scenes which evoked the rigidly stratified class system enshrined in the films of the 1930s. Initially the cinema continued to reflect this class-bound 1930s tradition, resolutely middle-class in tone and values and with little realistic evocation of the lives of working-class people. In films like Carol Reed's *Night Train to Munich* (1940) the war was treated as a gentlemanly jape, in which an upper-class hero (Rex Harrison) ran rings around the humourless, ranting, dunderheaded Hun. The apotheosis of the romanticized, class-bound and hopelessly out-of-touch war film was Ealing's *Ships With Wings* (1941), a *Boy's Own Paper* yarn in which a disgraced Fleet Air Arm Officer (John Clements) redeems his honour by undertaking a suicide mission. It received such a hostile press that Michael Balcon, head of Ealing, took the decision to produce essentially realistic stories of Britain at war. He turned therefore to the only group in Britain that was familiar with the evocation of real life — the documentarists. This group, nurtured in the 1930s by John Grierson, was committed to the concept of realism in setting, mood and content and to the dramatization of the everyday experience of ordinary people. Several of them, notably Harry Watt and Alberto Cavalcanti, went to work for Ealing Studios, and from that time on the documentary influence permeated the whole field of feature film production.

The image of a nation divided by class barriers and epitomized by the notorious slogan of the early war years — '*Your* courage, *your* cheerfulness, *your* resolution will bring *us* victory' — was replaced by the concept of the 'People's War', the idea of ordinary people pulling together to defeat a common foe. Ealing's war films exemplify the new image. Typical of them is *San Demetrio—London* (1943), recounting the true story of the salvaging of a Merchant Navy tanker by part of its crew, a cross-section of ordinary chaps, and *The Bells Go Down* (1943), dramatizing the work of the Auxiliary Fire Service in London. Significantly, neither of these films had an officer-and-gentleman hero. Indeed, the lifestyle and rationale of the old-style officer and gentleman was comprehensively demolished in Michael Powell's and Emeric Pressburger's controversial *The Life and Death of Colonel Blimp* (1943).

Comradeship and co-operation, dedication to duty and self-sacrifice, a self-deprecating good humour and unself-conscious modesty characterized the films about the fighting services. The war produced a masterpiece for each. For the Navy there was *In Which We Serve* (1942), written, produced, co-directed and scored by Noel Coward, who also played the leading role. It was based on the true story of the sinking of HMS *Kelly*, the ship commanded by Coward's friend Lord Louis Mountbatten. Carol Reed's *The Way Ahead* (1944), scripted by Peter Ustinov and Eric Ambler, was a semi-documentary account of how a group of conscripts from all walks of life were welded into a disciplined army unit. Anthony Asquith's *The Way to the Stars* (1945), scripted by Terence Rattigan, recalled life on a single RAF station between 1940 and 1944, its joys and losses, its tragedies and camaraderie.

The contribution of women to the war effort was vital, and the cinema's tribute to them reflected the dramatic change in their social role and expectations. Leslie Howard's *The Gentle Sex* (1943) was a female version of *The Way Ahead*, a realistic account of the training of a group of women from all classes and backgrounds in the ATS. Frank Launder's and Sidney Gilliat's moving and memorable *Millions Like Us* (1943) dramatized the experiences of another mixed group of girls drafted to work in an aircraft factory. All these films contained characters and situations that were sympathetically and realistically depicted. They both reflected the shared experience of the audience and promoted that spirit of co-operation and self-sacrifice which was needed to win the war.

Films about *why* Britain was fighting were rarer than films about *how* she was fighting, perhaps because of the difficulty of constructing acceptably entertaining stories around sophisticated ideological and philosophical concepts. Probably the best programmatic account was provided by Michael Powell's and Emeric Pressburger's *49th Parallel* (1941). Financed by the Ministry of Information, it told the gripping story of a stranded crew of a Nazi submarine making their way across Canada towards the neutral United States and encountering en route various representatives of democracy. An uncommitted French Canadian trapper (Laurence Olivier) turns against the Nazis when they maltreat the 'racially inferior' Eskimoes. A democratic Christian community of Hutterite exiles, led by Anton Walbrook, demonstrate the workability of a system of equality, co-operation and Christian love. A donnish aesthete (Leslie Howard) beats one of the Nazis to pulp when they burn his books and pictures. Finally, an ordinary Canadian soldier (Raymond Massey) takes on and defeats the Nazi 'superman' commanding the fugitives (Eric Portman). The Nazis are thus effectively depicted as standing for cruelty, tyranny, arrogance and philistinism.

It was clear what we were fighting against. But what sort of England were we fighting for? The war brought into sharp focus the meaning of England and Englishness. The result was a spate of books analysing and investigating England and the English, books with titles like *The English People* and *The Character of England.* Anthologies of poetry and prose also sought to project an image of England. One such was Collie Knox's *Forever England* (1943). It contains poetry by Shakespeare, Wordsworth, Kipling and Browning apostrophizing England, speeches by Churchill, Asquith and Disraeli eulogizing England, essays on the armed forces, the church, cricket and the public schools, and comments by sympathetic foreigners on what they see as the essence of Englishness. Over and over again, in these and similar works, one finds the ideas that together represent the concept 'England' — a love of tradition, balance and order; a belief in tolerance and humanity; a sense of humour. But also highlighted is that visionary aspect of Englishness, that fey, mystical quality, that striving after the secrets of the eternal that crops up periodically in English history and English thought. It is there in the music of Elgar and Vaughan Williams, in the writings of Kipling and Haggard, in the poetry of Newbolt and Rupert Brooke. It is associated inextricably with war and can be seen in the lifestyles and ideas of a remarkable succession of soldier-mystics who sought out deserts and high places in order to commune with the Almighty — Lawrence of Arabia, Gordon of Khartoum, Younghusband of Tibet and Orde Wingate of the Chindits.[3]

It is deeply Romantic and deeply emotional. But then there is in wartime a heightening of the emotions, a quickening of the pulse. It is a time for poetry and brave words, for sentiments can be uttered and felt and believed that in prosaic peacetime seem inflated, exaggerated, unreal. Feelings come bubbling to the surface in people who face every day the prospect of death, feelings that in ordinary times are buried so deep that their existence may not even be consciously acknowledged. That is why C. A. Lejeune, the influential film critic of the *Observer*, was wrong when, reviewing *The Gentle Sex* in 1943, she wrote:

> It seems tolerably clear by now that the best thing the war is likely to draw out of the cinema is not poetry but prose; no masterpiece but a number of small, candid snapshots of the soul of the people. . . . To create or to savour the larger forms of art requires leisure of mind, and *that* is a thing we have not.[4]

She had reckoned without the mystical vision summoned up by the war in the Romantic Right (Michael Powell and Emeric Pressburger) and the Romantic Left (Humphrey Jennings), whose meditations on England were to produce celluloid poetry of the highest order.

Few film-makers have been as controversial, as innovative, as adventurous or as deeply Romantic as Michael Powell and Emeric Pressburger.[5] Working within mainstream commercial cinema, they produced a succession of films that were both popular entertainment and high art, that were distinctively and recognizably personal, yet said something profound about England and the English. They were without question the most remarkable of several film-making teams that occupied an influential place in British cinema. The others include the Korda Brothers (Alexander, Zoltan and Vincent), the Boulting Brothers (Roy and John), Frank Launder and Sidney Gilliat, Basil Dearden and Michael Relph, and Herbert Wilcox and Anna Neagle. It was Alexander Korda who first teamed Powell and Pressburger to make *The Spy in Black* in 1939. Pressburger, a Hungarian writer and refugee from Nazi Germany, and Powell, the Kentish director who had gained a critical reputation after making *Edge of the World* (1937) on the island of Foula, worked so well together that in 1942 they formed The Archers, one of a number of independent production units working under the overall umbrella of Rank. They signed their films jointly — Produced, directed and written by Michael Powell and Emeric Pressburger — though it was generally recognized that Pressburger provided the script and Powell directed. They were anxious to contribute to the cinema's war effort and made two films on the subject of 'how we fight' (*One of Our Aircraft is Missing* and *The Life and Death of Colonel Blimp*) before turning back to the subject of 'why we fight', first explored in *49th Parallel.* Powell subsequently described *A Canterbury Tale* (1944) as his version of 'why we fight'; it was an exploration of the spiritual values for which England stands, testimony to the belief that the roots of the nation lie in the pastoral and to the idea of England as synonymous with freedom. He also called it a 'crusade against materialism'.[6]

The England evoked by *A Canterbury Tale* is the England of Chaucer and Shakespeare, a rural England of half-timbered cottages and stately country houses, quiet, leafy churchyards and rich hopfields, an England whose spirit resides in Thomas Colpeper, gentleman farmer, magistrate, historian and archaeologist, a man who understands England's nature and seeks to communicate her values. It is a film, on the one hand, of astonishing tranquillity and entrancing visual beauty and, on the other, of riveting power and mystical suggestiveness. Superbly photographed at genuine Kentish locations, it hymns the beauties of the countryside, which are seen as timeless and unchanging. The film recreates the Canterbury pilgrimage for a trio of latter-day visitors in search of spiritual peace. The timelessness is encapsulated at the outset, as Esmond Knight reads the introduction to Chaucer's *Canterbury Tales* in Old English and the camera moves in on a map of medieval England to rest on the road to Canterbury. Then, amid laughter and the jingle of accoutrements, Chaucer and the pilgrims are seen riding along the Pilgrim's Way, the camera picking out individual faces. A falconer unhoods his bird, which flies away; it dissolves into a plane sweeping over the same countryside; the director cuts back to the falconer's face, but it is now the face of a man wearing modern army uniform. The narrator merely underlines what the camera has shown us — the land is still the same and the people are still the same. But there are new pilgrims now — and armoured troop carriers lurch suddenly into view. For all this, the spiritual values are eternal; a return to them will bring peace of mind. It is why we fight.

Much of the action of the film is set in and around a Kentish village, which appears at the outset almost as a spirit village like Brigadoon, emerging from the enveloping mist and from a distant past. It is called Chillingbourne, and with its stationmaster called Duckett, its squire Colpeper, its innkeeper Woodcock and its inn, where Queen Elizabeth I herself is reputed to have slept, the 'Hand of glory', its image and ambiance is purest Elizabethan. It even has a village idiot.

Colpeper (Eric Portman) is first discovered working at his desk in a sixteenth-century panelled office in the town hall. He is shot from a reverential low angle across a wooden beam inscribed with the words 'Honour the Truth'. Later he is seen scything his grass like some stout Tudor yeoman, eliciting from Alison, one of the modern pilgrims, the admiring comment: 'He looks so right.' Colpeper talks of miracles, appears and disappears mysteriously, is seen haloed with light during his lecture in the village hall. Like the village, he seems magical, causing events to happen, manipulating lives like a latter-day Prospero. Magic is an integral part of Powell's vision, evident both in his world-view and in the technical realization of his films, which often amounts to visual wizardry. It is no coincidence that a film of Shakespeare's *The Tempest* is a long-cherished and as yet unfulfilled project of Powell. Spells, prophecies, sorcery and mysticism bind together such apparently disparate films as *The Thief of Bagdad, The Red Shoes, The Elusive Pimpernel, Black Narcissus, Gone to Earth, I Know Where I'm Going* and especially *A Matter of Life and Death,* which Powell himself described as 'a most wonderful conjuring trick'.[7]

The three modern pilgrims on their way to Canterbury are the American Sergeant Bob Johnson (Sergeant John Sweet), the Englishman Sergeant Peter Gibbs (Dennis Price) and the English Land Army girl Alison Smith (Sheila Sim). At the outset they are in the dark — literally — and as the film progresses they find their way towards the light and the truth. They arrive at Chillingbourne in the middle of the night, their faces unseen initially by us or by each other. They set out to walk to the village and are beset by a mysterious attacker in a military overcoat, who pours glue on Alison's hair and flees. They chase him into the fog and lose him, but learn that this is the eleventh such attack by a figure known locally as the 'Glue Man'. They decide to find out who he is. Although there are elements of detective work in the plot, as the three visitors question previous victims, establish the time scale of the attacks and search for evidence of glue purchases, it is obvious from the outset who the 'Glue Man' is, for Colpeper chides himself for not closing the black-out curtains properly, and the camera moves into a bold close-up of his hastily abandoned Home Guard jacket in a cupboard. The question with which the film is really concerned is his motive for making the attacks, and that leads to an exposition of the message of spiritual peace, which changes the lives of the three 'detectives'.

All three are troubled souls. Bob Johnson is worried because he has not heard from his girl and thinks that she has left him. But Bob also serves two other symbolic functions. First and most obviously, he underlines the need for Anglo-American solidarity.[8] The film carefully exposes the locals' patronizing attitude towards this 'Yank': the station master rejects his claim to be a sergeant because his stripes are the wrong way up; the police sergeant retorts, 'This is Chillingbourne, not Chicago' when Bob asks if he is armed; and the fluttering, giggling maid at the inn insists he have early-morning tea rather than his usual coffee. But he is sceptical about the weight of British tradition and cannot understand the telephones, the driving on the wrong side of the road and especially the incessant tea-drinking. But, as Peter points out to him, it is the tea-drinkers of the world — the Soviet Union, China and Britain — who have successfully resisted the onslaught of the Axis powers. Bob is to find that he has much more in common with the English than he had supposed; in particular, his co-operation with the English pilgrims, Alison and Peter, successfully unmasks the 'Glue Man'.

But, more centrally, Bob is spiritually and aesthetically asleep. He has spent all his leaves in the cinema and has not sought out the beauties of the countryside. Even when in Salisbury he noted only its fine cinemas. Colpeper, hearing of this, laments the fact that all Bob has seen of England has been its movie houses and expresses his concern lest people become used to seeing England from their cinema seats. He urges Bob to visit Canterbury Cathedral ('You can't miss it; it is just behind the movie theatre').

The first step towards Bob's spiritual awakening and his appreciation of the English is taken when with Alison he visits the rural wheelwrights, the Hortons, and discusses their craft with them. He wins their admiration through his knowledge of the techniques of wood seasoning and reveals that he comes from an Oregon family of lumberjacks. 'We speak the same language,' says Bob of his encounter with Jim Horton, an encounter which celebrates both the innate virtues of rural craftsmanship and the common bonds of England and America. Alison, baffled by the discussion, replies sadly: 'I'm English, and we don't speak the same language.' This is one of the film's most important themes, reinforced by the character of Peter, that the city dweller, the product of urban culture, has lost touch with his rural roots and the values that they embody. Bob's experiences in Chillingbourne lead him to tell Peter on the Pilgrim's Way that his mind is truly at peace for the first time.

Alison too finds peace. She was a shop assistant in a garden furniture department before the war. She loved the countryside but as a visitor. She never understood it. Now she is mourning the loss of her fiancé, a geologist with the RAF who has been shot down. His father had disapproved of his son's relationship with a shopgirl. 'It would need an earthquake to change his mind,' she says. 'We're having one,' replies Colpeper. But what the film sees as important is that while there may be social change, and the reconciliation of her fiancé's father with Alison acknowledges this, there must be cultural continuity. Alison falls under Colpeper's spell completely. At a lecture in the village hall, attended by soldiers from the local camp, Colpeper talks, with the aid of slides, of the beauties of the countryside and of Old England. His talk is beautifully delivered by Eric Portman in silhouette, with only his eyes visible, until his face is suddenly and dramatically lit up at the climax of the speech. Alison is so entranced that in her mind she hears the clatter of horses' hooves and the merry chatter of the medieval pilgrims. She does so again when she goes walking on the Pilgrim's Way and Colpeper suddenly appears from the long grass to talk to her of miracles.

The third pilgrim, Peter Gibbs, holds out longest. A cynical materialist, he calls on and denounces Colpeper as just another missionary ('The trouble with this country is that every other man has got a bee in his bonnet about something'). He explains to Colpeper that although trained as a church organist, he now plays a cinema organ in the West End for a good wage. He is indifferent to the countryside and admits to spending his Sundays playing cards and waiting for the pubs to open.

The climax of the film comes after they have identified Colpeper as the 'Glue Man', and Gibbs insists that they report him to the police in Canterbury. All three travel to Canterbury with Colpeper, who seeks to explain his motive for the attacks. He had sought for years to spread a knowledge of the country and a love of its beauty, but before the war no one would listen. When the war came an army camp was established at Chillingbourne, and he tried again. But the soldiers were interested only in girls and in going with them to the cinema and dances. So in order to save the village girls from the consequences of these casual liaisons, to protect the wives and sweethearts of the soldiers left behind, and to drum up audiences for his lectures, he launched the 'Glue Man' attacks.

There is a distinct element of misogyny in Colpeper's stance, and the film makes no apology for it. He is a bachelor, living with his mother. He rejects the services of Alison as a land girl on his farm, preferring a male farm worker. At almost his first appearance he demonstrates with approval the use of the ducking stool, for dealing with gossiping women, to Sergeant Johnson. Although he admits later that he has been wrong about Alison, who has come to share his mystic vision, he firmly answers 'No' when she asks if it has ever occurred to him to invite girls to his lectures. He seems to see girls as essentially silly, frivolous and second-rate, weaker vessels who serve only to lead men on and to distract them from their duties to their families and their opportunity to learn about the true meaning of England.

Alison and Bob accept Colpeper's explanation of his behaviour, but Peter is adamant that he must be reported. Colpeper is prepared for whatever may happen, observing serenely: 'There are higher courts than the local bench of magistrates' and gazing out at the Cathedral. They alight from the train and converge, with foreordained inevitability, on the Cathedral. Gibbs learns that the police inspector whom he wishes to see is there. Entering, he picks up a sheet of music that the cathedral organist has providentially dropped and is invited to play. He strikes up with Bach's *Toccata and Fugue,* loses himself in the music and rediscovers his real vocation. Bob, his face transfigured as he recalls that his grandfather built the first Baptist church in Cedar County, Oregon, meets a fellow soldier bearing a sheaf of letters from his girl. She has not forgotten him but is in Australia with the WAACS.

Alison searches for the garage where she has left the caravan that she and her geologist fiancé shared on their holiday there in 1940. The camera tracks her along the bomb-damaged streets, but above the ruins towers the Cathedral, eternal and indestructible. When she eventually finds the caravan it is cobwebbed and moth-eaten and, faced by this symbol of her lost happiness, she bursts into tears. Colpeper appears and talks cryptically of the transitoriness of caravan life and the inevitability of moving on. Suddenly the garage owner arrives with a message from the father of her fiancé, Jeffrey. He has been looking for her to tell her that Jeffrey is alive and at Gibraltar. She turns to tell Colpeper, but he has gone as mysteriously as he

A Canterbury Tale

A Canterbury Tale tells of a wartime pilgrimage by three young people, Sergeant Bob Johnson (Sgt John Sweet), Alison Smith (Sheila Sim) and Sergeant Peter Gibbs (Dennis Price), in search of spiritual peace. Along their way they encounter Thomas Colpeper (Eric Portman) (1). They are led towards an understanding of the spirit of England by Colpeper, a Kentish magistrate (2). By the time they reach Canterbury Cathedral the pilgrims have found their peace (3), having also discovered the beauties of rural England (4), rural crafts (5) and a sense of the living past (6).

appeared. Joyously, she throws open the windows of the caravan.

The film ends with a regiment of soldiers, about to leave for action overseas, processing through the Canterbury streets to the Cathedral, where Peter plays the organ triumphantly. Bob, Alison and Jeffrey's father join the congregation, and Colpeper, unseen, slips in too. All sing 'Onward, Christian Soldiers'; the bells ring; and the last shot is of the Cathedral as seen from the Pilgrim's Way. This final sequence prefigures the inevitable victory for which we fight on behalf of our country, freedom, beauty, tolerance and spirituality.

A Canterbury Tale rejoices in a sense of the living past, in country crafts, rural beauty, the intimacy of man and nature, and this joy is conveyed in passages of pure camera poetry, with much use of point-of-view shots to lead the audience into the countryside and the Cathedral. These sequences do not advance the plot but celebrate the mood and message. There is the soaring evocation of Canterbury Cathedral around which the camera tracks, pans and cranes as the organ music surges. There is the loving depiction of country crafts, which picks out local faces, felled timber and age-old instruments. There is, in particular, the wonderfully shot sequence of a battle between two sets of village boys; one army, on a boat, is tracked along the river bank by the camera and attacked by its rivals in a sequence of staccato cutting and bold close-ups. The leaders of the armies are recruited by Bob to help search for evidence on the 'Glue Man', but the sequence as it stands exists to celebrate boyish high spirits in the pristine heart of the countryside.[9] The cumulative effect of such sequences wholly justifies the decision of Prudence Honeywood, who tells Alison that the only man who ever asked her to marry him wanted to take her away from this to live in the town and she refused him.

The film is constructed like a symphony, orchestrating the themes of the three pilgrims, which merge and mingle with a central and dominant theme (Colpeper and his message) until all blend triumphantly at the climax, with the converging of the characters on the Cathedral, cut to the music. Powell later observed:

> At the time nobody thought that *A Canterbury Tale* worked, but I must say that it contained some of my favourite sequences . . . you take the last three reels of the film when all three pilgrims converge on Canterbury. I thought that had a most wonderful movement.[10]

Powell is, of course, powerfully assisted by Pressburger's script, by Erwin Hillier's camerawork, which was universally praised, and by a strong cast. There was considerable critical praise for Sergeant John Sweet, an American soldier who had previously acted on stage in the all-soldier cast of a production of Maxwell Anderson's *The Eve of St Mark,* put on in London by the Special Service Division of the US War Department. He was not a professional actor and was chosen, according to the film's press book, because he had 'all the attributes of the ordinary young man'.[11] But the film is dominated and held together by the soft-spoken, enigmatic Eric Portman, whose performance as the Nazi submarine commander in Powell's and Pressburger's *49th Parallel* had made him a major star and who was to carve out a career unique in British films by playing a succession of haunted murderers, quirky maniacs and demented millionaires. There was something cold, sinister but compelling about his personality, something out of the ordinary, and Powell utilized that quality here to imbue Colpeper, the self-confessed missionary, with an unearthly yet serene omniscience.

In celebrating the countryside as the source of national strength, Powell was in the mainstream British tradition, which has been so brilliantly expounded (indeed, indicted) by Martin Wiener and which is encapsulated in the words of the popular song of World War II:

> There'll always be an England while there's a country lane
> Wherever there's a cottage small beside a field of grain.

Wiener sees in the glorification of the countryside and all things rural a deliberate rejection of the urban and industrial reality of Britain by a non-industrial, non-innovative and anti-materialist patrician culture. Endorsed by a gentrified bourgeoisie, this attitude led to what Wiener calls 'the cultural containment of industrial capitalism', a process which contributed powerfully to Britain's industrial decline.[12]

The cultural conservatism of the dominant elite determined the prevalent image of England and Englishness. Donald Horne, seeking to understand what made England tick, proposed two rival metaphors for Englishness — the Northern, which was pragmatic, empirical, calculating, Puritan, bourgeois, enterprising, adventurous, scientific, serious and struggle-oriented, and the Southern, romantic, illogical, muddled, lucky, Anglican, aristocratic, traditional and frivolous.[13] Whereas the Northern was urban and industrial, the Southern prevailed because it was rural, because it was able to accommodate the apparently irreconcilable ideals of the Romantic Right (country house, country church, squire, parson and deferential society) and the Romantic Left (folk society, the village, rural crafts and the honest peasantry). *A Canterbury Tale,* deliberately designed as a 'crusade against materialism', provides a perfect visual expression of all these elements.

The myth of England as essentially rural and essentially unchanging appealed across party lines to both conservatives and socialists. Rudyard Kipling turned in later life from celebrating the robust spirit of Empire to hymning the beauties of rural life in Sussex (*Puck of Pook's Hill,* 'Our England is a Garden', etc.), and Sir Henry Newbolt wrote of the magical qualities of the English landscape in *The Old Country.*[14] The distaste for modern industrial society that lay behind such Arcadian exercises was summed up by another right-wing writer, Sir Arthur Bryant, who in a series of talks entitled *The National Character,* first delivered on the wireless and later published in book form, declared:

> The most important thing about our English civilization is that it grew in the country and has only comparatively lately been transported to the town. Half our present troubles can, I believe, be traced to this. Our industrial discontent, the restless, dissatisfied state of our family life, the discomfort, ugliness and overcrowding of our towns, in part spring from the fact that every Englishman is so certain that the only lasting Utopia for him is a rose garden and a cottage in the country that he can never settle down seriously to make himself comfortable in a town. . . . Most of us today are town dwellers, yet there are very few of us whose great-great-great-grandparents were not country folk, and, even if we have no idea who they were or from what shire they hailed, our subconscious selves hark back to their instincts and ways of life. We are shut off from them as it were by a tunnel of two or three generations — lost in the darkness of

the Industrial Revolution — but beyond is the sunlight of the green fields from which we came.[15]

The same feeling animated socialists like William Morris and Robert Blatchford, who propounded the potent myth of a timeless and idealized medieval village and agricultural society. Blatchford's *Merrie England* (1894) was described by G. D. H. Cole as 'the most effective piece of popular socialist propaganda ever written'.[16]

After World War I, perhaps as a result of it, this rural nostalgia intensified. There were novels about the countryside, books about the English heritage and the English character stressing the rural myth. As Sir Denis Brogan wrote in 1943, in a book seeking to explain England to the Americans:

> Most people in England live in large industrial towns; but they are not written about. Millions live in the great urban aggregate that is called London without seeing Piccadilly Circus or St Paul's once a month. Mr Priestley has done a good deal to restore the balance, but no one has done what Arnold Bennett did — given a view of English life outside London and the country that was accepted as a natural literary phenomenon. We have gloomy stories of the depressed area; we have innumerable detective stories. But *Love on the Dole* and *Murder in the Home Counties* do not cover all or nearly all of English life. The English people show that they know this by reading American fiction with avidity, just as American people show their good judgement in preferring their own more lively, human and truthful fiction to the English standard brands. And the great sin of English fiction, English movies, English plays, English public relations in general, is the refusal to admit that the Englishman is a townsman.[17]

This 'sin' was apparent even in a comic novel like A. G. MacDonell's *England, their England,* which had Scot Donald Cameron searching for the meaning of England. He discovers at the end, when he has a mystical vision of a sort of pilgrimage of poets, all wreathed in good humour, as he lies on a perfect summer day in the grass near Winchester Cathedral, that it is to be found in the mingling of the pastoral and the poetic. The vision fades:

> And there was no longer any trace of the passing of that absurd host of kindly, laughter-loving warrior poets but only what they have left behind them — the muted voices of grazing sheep, and the merry click of bat upon ball, and the peaceful green fields of England, and the water meads and the bells of the cathedral.[18]

It is hard to believe that we are not looking here at the seeds of the idea that gave rise to *A Canterbury Tale*.

This vision was shared by the man who epitomized England, if anyone did, in the inter-war years — Stanley Baldwin, three times Prime Minister and the leading figure in the National Government until his retirement in 1937. He consciously projected himself as a country squire. In a celebrated speech he declared:

> To me England is the country and the country is England. . . . The sounds of England, the tinkle of the hammer on the anvil in the country smithy, the corncrake on a dewy morning, the sound of the scythe against the whetstone, and the sight of a plough team coming over the brow of a hill, the sight that has been seen in England since England was a land, and

may be seen in England long after the Empire has perished and every works has ceased to function, for centuries the one eternal sight of England.[19]

It is against this background and that of Horne's Southern metaphor that it is possible to understand the depiction of 'why we fight' in the handful of films that tackle the question. The England we fight for in *A Canterbury Tale* and in its analogues *The Tawny Pipit* (1944) and *The Demi-Paradise* (1943) is essentially rural, timeless and hierarchical. It makes an interesting contrast with the 'how we fight' films, which were at pains to highlight the social change involved in the lowering of class barriers and often featured townsmen. But the Englishman as urban man was really celebrated only in the films of Humphrey Jennings, who provides an interesting comparison with Powell and Pressburger. Jennings, Suffolk-born, Cambridge-educated, was a left-winger, influential in Mass Observation, steeped in Shakespeare, Marlowe, Milton and Blake. His documentaries display the same lambent photography, mystical quality and feel for landscape as do Powell's feature films. But for him the recurrent image is St Paul's Cathedral, the church of the metropolis, and not Canterbury Cathedral, the church of the older, rural England. In films like *Spare Time, London Can Take It, Listen to Britain, Fires Were Started* and *Family Portrait* Jennings showed himself able to come to terms with, to explore and to celebrate the urban England created by the industrial revolution, an event most other film-makers preferred to ignore.

The intention of *A Canterbury Tale* was made quite clear by the film's press book:

> *A Canterbury Tale* is a new story about Britain, her unchanging beauty and traditions, and of the Old Pilgrims and the New. As the last scene of the picture fades away, to those who see it and are British there will come a feeling — just for a moment — of wishing to be silent, as the thoughts flash through one's mind: 'These things I have just seen and heard are all my parents taught me. That is Britain, that is me.'[20]

But the reaction of the critics was on the whole one of puzzlement. Richard Winnington in the *News Chronicle* expressed the prevalent view of the film:

> Because they represent the only consistent unification of script, production and direction in British films, Michael Powell and Emeric Pressburger arouse expectancy and generally arrive at something different and individual. Their besetting weakness — lack of coherent purpose in their stories — is more pronounced than ever in this their latest production. . . . Through the fog of a confused and at times vaguely unpleasant story can be seen a steady if dim flicker of what I think was the main idea of Powell and Pressburger — to endow an accidental wartime excursion to Canterbury with the hushed, bated magic of the Pilgrim's Way, to link in mystic suggestion the past and the present. And in an odd, untidy sort of way they infuse a lyric feeling into the pastoral progression of their film. The quality of poetry is not entirely due to the first-rate and refreshing photographic compositions of the Kentish countryside, or the 'village pageant' sequences of Chaucer's pilgrims, or the reading of part of his prologue with a modern bit added, or, as I have suggested, to the story. It is something to do with Messrs Powell and Pressburger.[21]

The same tone of dissatisfaction ran through the verdicts of the other critics, who praised the photography and the acting, the celebration of the Kent countryside and the visual beauty of the film. But for the most part they found themselves unable to come to grips with the mysticism or the psychology of Colpeper. The *Daily Telegraph* said:

> Michael Powell and Emeric Pressburger have presented the English scene with such artistry and charm, such a wealth of fresh and amusing incident, that if the story had been halfway tolerable this would have been a masterpiece. It isn't and it's not. The story is silly beyond belief. . . . If you can ignore this nonsense, you will enjoy the film for its beauty, for many shrewd and witty touches, and some excellent acting by Sgt John Sweet (US Army), Sheila Sim, Dennis Price and Eric Portman.[22]

The *Manchester Guardian* could not resist the temptation to describe the plot of the film as a 'sticky mess' but added:

> Luckily one can ignore the untidiness and improbabilities and enjoy wholeheartedly the sheer pictorial beauty of Canterbury and the Pilgrim's Way.[23]

The *Sunday Times* called it:

> an elaborate, beautiful and often witty piece of muddle. The story is half highminded fantasy, half schoolboy thriller. . . . The exterior work is enchanting and the pictorial beauty of the sequences in Canterbury Cathedral seem to me beyond praise.[24]

C. A. Lejeune in the *Observer* pronounced the final word:

> *A Canterbury Tale* is a remarkable film, in which Michael Powell, the writer, has given Michael Powell, the director, a pretty shabby story and the second Powell has almost managed to get away with it. *A Canterbury Tale* is about a Kentish JP who believes so deeply in the study of his native soil that he pours glue on girls' heads in the black-out lest they seduce the local soldiery from his archaeological lectures. That's the theme, and to my mind, nothing will make it either a sensible or pleasant one. This fellow may be a mystagogue with the love of England in his blood, but he is plainly a crackpot of a rather unpleasant type, with bees in the bonnet and blue-bottles in the belfry. Only a psychiatrist, I imagine, would be deeply interested in his behaviour. And yet, on this horrid foundation, director Powell has built up a film that is in parts moving and even dignified. A man of Kent himself, he has taken his cameras exulting in the green spring of Kent on a sunny April morning. His Canterbury is a place loved and understood; his dialogue often simple and true. His three young people. . . . who are all in some way influenced by the mystagogue's enthusiasm, have for the most part an unaffected charm, and do suggest pilgrims undergoing an emotional experience. . . . The piece is an odd example, I should say, of a film that might have reached great heights but hasn't.[25]

As so often, Powell and Presburger were ahead of their time. They started with the handicap that mysticism is always silly to the unmystical. But beyond that their adoption of a narrative form that was discursive rather than strictly linear and their use of a 'kinky' hero, neither of which would seem remarkable to today's film-makers or cinema-goers, alienated and mystified critics used to more straightforward and traditional fare. Audiences seem to have responded in the same way, for the film was not a success at the box office. In an attempt to retrieve something for an American release, Powell was prevailed upon to cut it and shoot additional sequences for the US market. It was reduced from 124 minutes to 95, and Powell added a framing story, involving Raymond Massey and Kim Hunter, in which Sergeant Sweet tells the story to his wife in New York. It was released in America in 1949 but without success. A British reissue of the cut version in 1948 also failed. Powell's original was reconstructed by the British Film Institute in 1977 and has won increasing admiration.

How far was *A Canterbury Tale* a reflection of what people really were fighting for, and how far was it a middle-class cultural myth? When he toured England in 1933 J. B. Priestley discovered three Englands. The second was:

> the nineteenth-century England, the industrial England of coal, iron, steel, cotton, wool, railways; of thousands of rows of little houses all alike . . . a cynically devastated countryside, sooty dismal little towns, and still sootier grim fortress-like cities.

This was the England of the Midlands and the North and of Horne's Northern metaphor. The third was:

> the new post-war England, belonging far more to the age itself than this particular island. . . . This is the England of arterial and by-pass roads, of filling stations and factories that look like exhibition buildings, of giant cinemas and dance-halls and cafés, bungalows with tiny garages, cocktail bars, Woolworths, motor-coaches, wireless, hiking, factory girls looking like actresses, grey-hound racing and dirt tracks, swimming pools, and everything given away for cigarette coupons. . . . It is, of course, essentially democratic. After a social revolution, there would, with luck, be more and not less of it. . . . It is a large-scale, mass-production job, with cut prices. You could almost accept Woolworths as its symbol. Its cheapness is both its strength and weakness. It is its strength because, being cheap, it is accessible; it nearly achieves the famous equality of opportunity.

Significantly, Powell and Pressburger turned their backs on these two images in favour of Priestley's first England:

> Old England, the country of the cathedrals and minsters, and manor houses and inns, of Parson and Squire; guide-book and quaint highways and byways England. . . . We all know this England, which at its best cannot be improved upon in this world. That is, as a country to lounge about in; for a tourist who can afford to pay a fairly stiff price for a poorish dinner, an inconvenient bedroom and lukewarm water in a small brass jug. . . . It has long ceased to earn its own living. . . . There are some people who believe that in some mysterious way we can return to this Old England; though nothing is said about killing off nine-tenths of our present population, which would have to be the first step. The same people might consider competing in a race at Brooklands with a horse and trap. The chances are about the same.[26]

It was this same Priestley who expressed succinctly the war aims of the majority in one of his wartime broadcasts. While for Churchill the aim was victory and, beyond victory, the vague generalized belief that the world would move forward into 'broad, sunlit uplands', for Priestley it was what came after the war that was vitally important. We were fighting, he said, 'not so that we can go back to anything. There's nothing that really worked that we can go back to.' So our aim must be 'new and better homes — real homes — a decent chance at last — new life'.[27]

This was what people fought for, and this was what, in the end, they voted for. As A. J. P. Taylor wrote of the 1945 election:

> The electors cheered Churchill and voted against him. They displayed no interest in foreign affairs or imperial might. They cared only for their own future: first housing and then full employment and social security. Here Labour offered a convincing programme. The Conservatives, though offering much the same, managed to give the impression that they did not believe in it.[28]

The result was 393 Labour MPs returned to 213 Conservatives and a reforming government under Clement Attlee which set out to introduce those tangible benefits for which we had fought. The time for mysticism was past.

Notes

1 The memorandum is reproduced in Ian Christie (ed.), *Powell, Pressburger and Others,* London, 1978, pp. 121—4.

2 On the British cinema at war, see in particular Roger Manvell, *Films and the Second World War,* London, 1974, and Charles Barr, *Ealing Studios,* London, 1977.

3 Jeffrey Richards, 'Speaking for England', *Listener,* 14 January 1982, pp. 9—11.

4 C. A. Lejeune, *Chestnuts in her Lap,* London, 1947, p. 95.

5 On Powell and Pressburger, see in particular Christie, *Powell, Pressburger and Others*; John Russell Taylor, 'Michael Powell: Myths and Supermen', *Sight and Sound,* 47, autumn 1978, pp. 226—9; Douglas McVay, 'Cinema of Enchantment: the Films of Michael Powell', *Films and Filming,* 327, December 1981, pp. 14—19; Douglas McVay, 'Michael Powell: Three Neglected Films', *Films and Filming,* 328, January 1982, pp. 18—25.

6 Michael Powell, interview with Gavin Millar on BBC2's *Arena,* transmitted on 17 November 1981. Cf. also Powell's comments in Christie, *Powell, Pressburger and Others,* p. 34; and David Badder, 'Powell and Pressburger: the War Years', *Sight and Sound,* 48, Winter 1978, p. 11.

7 Christie, *Powell, Pressburger and Others,* p. 34.

8 The Anglo-American dimension of the film was introduced deliberately and Powell and Pressburger returned to it in *A Matter of Life and Death* (1946); see Badder, 'Powell and Pressburger: The War Years', p. 11. *A Canterbury Tale* thus also forms one of that group of films that deliberately sought to promote understanding between Britain and America — cf. *Journey Together* (1945) and *The Way to the Stars* (1945).

9 Seeing the film again after its reconstruction by the BFI, Powell remarked: 'It was a failure and hasn't been seen again until recently. Now it looks a wonderful film, I think. I was really thrilled by it. It's got all the things I knew so well. I was born and brought up in and around Canterbury and there's a lot of a little boy growing up in the film. Of course, what I love is this semi-mystical feeling that you get . . . anybody who has lived near Canterbury's old stones must have this feeling.' Badder, 'Powell and Pressburger: the War Years', p. 11.

10 Christie, *Powell, Pressburger and Others,* p. 33.

11 *A Canterbury Tale* press book, BFI microfiche. The *Manchester Guardian* (12 May 1944) thought Sweet had 'a casual attractiveness which predicts Hollywood for him'; in fact, he made no more films.

12 Martin Wiener, *English Culture and the Decline of the Industrial Spirit 1850—1980,* Cambridge, 1981.

13 Donald Horne, *God is an Englishman,* Harmondsworth, 1969, pp. 22—3.

14 John Russell Taylor, 'Michael Powell: Myths and Supermen', p. 227, reveals that *Puck of Pook's Hill* is one of Powell's favourite books.

15 Sir Arthur Bryant, *The National Character,* London, 1934, pp. 22—3.

16 Wiener, *English Culture,* p. 119.

17 D. W. Brogan, *The English People,* London, 1943, pp. 234—5.

18 A. G. MacDonell, *England, Their England,* London, 1941 (reprint), p. 293.

19 Stanley Baldwin, *On England,* London, 1926, p. 7.

20 *A Canterbury Tale* press book, BFI microfiche.

21 Richard Winnington, *Drawn and Quartered,* London, n.d., p. 22.

22 *Daily Telegraph,* 18 April 1944.

23 *Manchester Guardian,* 16 August 1944.

24 *Sunday Times,* 15 April 1944.

25 Lejeune, *Chestnuts in her Lap,* p. 121.

26 J. B. Priestley, *English Journey,* London, 1976 (reprint), pp. 397—9.

27 J. B. Priestley, *All England Listened,* New York, 1967, pp. 54—8.

28 A. J. P. Taylor, *English History 1914—45,* Harmondsworth, 1976, pp. 722.

5

What a Difference a War Makes

The Life and Death of Colonel Blimp

The original screenplay for the film of *Colonel Blimp* was written by Emeric Pressburger early in 1942.[1] In the first instance it was entitled simply *The Life and Death of Sugar Candy,* 'Sugar Candy' being the nickname of Clive Candy, the leading character in the story. The writer-producer-director team of Michael Powell and Emeric Pressburger planned to shoot the film between July and September of 1942. It was at this stage that they hit upon the idea of approaching the cartoonist David Low to see if they could use his figure of Colonel Blimp as the title and inspiration for their film. 'The thought of dramatizing the life of Colonel Blimp appealed enormously,' Powell records, 'because at that time Blimp was a household word.'[2] And their purpose was to show cinematically that 'Colonel Blimp was the symbol of British procrastination and British regard for tradition and all the things which we knew and which were losing the war.'[3]

For his part Low stipulated only that Powell and Pressburger take full responsibility for the production and, most of all, that Blimp be proved a fool in the end.[4] Since this was also what Powell and Pressburger wished to show, agreement was reached, and the title of the film was changed after production had begun. In one very obvious respect, therefore, the film was unlikely to say anything new. After all, the Blimp cartoons had been in existence since 20 April 1934, and the figure of Blimp had consistently been shown to be a fool in the pages of the *Evening Standard,* where he was regularly to be found. But in the changed circumstances of a Britain experiencing the turmoil of total war the prospect of a film that would make obvious allusions to the figure of Colonel Blimp assumed special significance in the eyes of certain members of the Government of the day. In fact, the cartoon of Blimp disappeared with the *Evening Standard* edition of 27 February 1942 (and did not reappear until over a year later, on 25 June 1943).[5] But if Blimp himself was absent temporarily, accusations of 'Blimpery' remained and indeed reached a peak between the spring and autumn of 1942, when the war was going particularly badly for Britain and when Powell and Pressburger embarked upon and completed the production of their film. 'The months from February to November 1942 were politically the most disturbed time of the war', A. J. P. Taylor has remarked.[6] And this, above all, helps to explain the nature of the official reaction to the film of *The Life and Death of Colonel Blimp* and why the film came to be construed as 'negative propaganda'.[7]

By the beginning of February 1942 the state of public morale was in decline, and it was further depressed by events that occurred in the first weeks of the month. On 13 February three German warships, the *Scharnhorst,* the *Gneisenau* and the *Prinz Eugen,* arrived in Germany from Brest, having succesfully evaded the attention of the Royal Navy and the RAF and having navigated the English Channel. Then on the 15 February General Perceval and 60,000 British troops surrendered at Singapore. *The Times* said of the former event that 'Nothing more mortifying to the pride of seapower has happened in home waters since the seventeenth century.'[8] Many thought the latter to be 'the greatest capitulation in British history.'[9] The Home Intelligence Weekly Report, prepared by a department of Brendan Bracken's Ministry of Information and commenting upon public reactions, declared the week of 16—23 February 1942 to be 'the blackest week since Dunkirk'.[10]

Other, seemingly lesser, events also gave cause for concern in that week. On 23 February, for example, Mr F. W. Pethick-Lawrence, the Labour MP for East Edinburgh, spoke about the war effort in a Commons debate. He opened his speech with the following comments:

> We are all familiar with the personality that the foremost cartoonist of our day has created of 'Colonel Blimp'. I suggest that what . . . critics desire to impress on the Government — and I am in full sympathy with them — is that if the Government are to carry the country with them in their war effort, they must set about abolishing 'Blimpery' in all fields of life. What is the essence of 'Blimpery'? It has, no doubt, two main characteristics. In the first place, there is the refusal to entertain new ideas, and in the second place, the determination to keep the bottom dog permanently in his place.[11]

Thereafter Pethick-Lawrence went on to cite certain instances in which he felt such 'Blimpery' might be seen at its worse: in the operations of the Colonial Office, where 'the administration of the Colonies was a scandal' and had been so for several years, as many people had pointed out; over India; and in the case of the coal mines. Despite income tax and the rationing of food, petrol and other articles, he argued, there was still an immense amount of 'luxury expenditure and wasteful self-indulgence'. All sorts of expensive foods could be bought and consumed by persons 'whose wealth remains intact'. And on that issue he maintained:

> Everyone who is in touch with the workers knows how detrimental it is to the vigour of the war effort when they see what is happening among a certain class of people. I say, without any doubt, that 'Blimpery' is still rampant in certain circles, and it is up to the Ministers concerned to put a stop to it.

However, he reserved his most vigorous onslaught for criticism of the Army. There, to begin with, he asserted that:

> The traditional view in the Army of the common soldier is that he is just a common soldier and as such can be equally well employed upon any task which needs to be done at the moment. It may be sweeping floors or handing round Brussel sprouts in the officers mess.

He did not doubt that there were 'wise heads' in the War Office or that there were 'enlightened' commanding officers who knew better, had much better judgement and responded more aptly to the needs of the moment. But 'Blimpery' existed all the same. He quoted damaging passages from a manpower survey prepared by Beveridge for the Ministry of Labour that condemned the Army for its failure to use men with engineering skill according to their worth and recommended that the services generally needed to scrutinize the use of all the manpower available and not just that of skilled men.

Subsequently Pethick-Lawrence cited examples provided by his own constituents to argue that men from the ranks were prevented, as often as not, from proving their worth as officer material. While there was a genuine desire to give commissions to competent men 'who start from humble positions in life', nevertheless in many cases this purpose was frustrated by 'purely financial considerations'. With respect to clothes alone the initial cost of obtaining a commission greatly exceeded the Government allowance for the same, and a man could thus incur debts directly he took a commission. The recurring expenses of keeping up with 'convention and tradition' added to the burden and meant that such a man had 'the greatest difficulty in providing for himself and his family at home'. In all it resulted in the reluctance of many men to take up a commission because they would be considerably worse off than they were by staying in the ranks.

It was a pretty bleak picture that Pethick-Lawrence painted, though not without foundation. Finally, he called upon the new Secretary of State for War to be rid of such 'Blimpery'. Indeed, he reserved some ironic comments for the man who had taken up that position only on 22 February, the day before the debate. Pethick-Lawrence knew him well, believed him to be 'a forcible and fearless man' who would cut through red tape, if anyone would, and possessed 'great courage'. Pethick-Lawrence hoped that he would 'prove equal to the task of getting rid of "Blimpery" wherever it manifests itself in the Army', though he also clearly doubted the wisdom of the appointment. The man in question was Sir James Grigg, who would indeed have a lot to say on the matter of 'Blimpery' and the Army.

However, on the day of the debate in the Commons it was Stafford Cripps, in his first speech as Lord Privy Seal and Leader of the House, who rose to reply to Pethick-Lawrence. He asked the House to wait and see, promised that things would be done and invited one and all to 'the funeral of that person whom I hope we may now describe as the late and not lamented Colonel Blimp'.

Some measures were taken to deal with the matters that Pethick-Lawrence had mentioned. Cripps himself tried, albeit unsuccessfully, to overcome the constitutional deadlock in India. And in March 1942 he announced a new round of cuts in civilian consumption that were greeted as 'real steps towards total war', though Home Intelligence also reported that many people felt that they did not go far enough in meeting the popular demand for 'equality of sacrifice'.[12]

Furthermore, the charge of 'Blimpery' continued unabated and, if anything, gained momentum despite Cripps's burial of the Colonel and his subsequent disappearance from the *Evening Standard.* By the end of March Home Intelligence, once again, pointed out that its regional summaries indicated a distinct swing in public opinion towards what might loosely be called the 'left'. This current of feeling among the population was not necessarily of a political character, nor indeed was it necessarily channelled along Labour Party or socialist lines. But it was 'directed against the Conservative Party' in so far as this represented 'the so-called "Men of Munich", "the old gang", "Colonel Blimp", and similar die-hard types'. It was, first of all, a feeling of revulsion against 'vested interests', 'privilege' and the like, which were also blamed for 'ills of production'; secondly, it amounted to a general agreement that 'things are going to be different after the war.'[13]

With such sentiments much in evidence, not least among the reports produced by one of its own departments, it is perhaps not surprising that the Ministry of Information was not particularly enchanted when Powell and Pressburger came along with a script which overtly sought to capitalize on the name of Colonel Blimp. Blimp was a household word for all the wrong reasons. Bracken and Jack Beddington, Director of the Ministry of Information's Films Division, did not look kindly upon the idea.[14] The script was read and thought 'defeatist'. Laurence Olivier was denied release from the Fleet Air Arm to play the part of Blimp, and official help, by way of the provision of arms, trucks, uniforms and so on, was out of the question. Not that this deterred Powell and Pressburger from proceeding with production of the film: Roger Livesey was engaged for Blimp and various devious means were employed to overcome the other obstacles.

In truth, though, the production did not merit the rough treatment it received at the hands of the Ministry of Information. As the testimony of the script and subsequent film bear witness, *The Life and Death of Colonel Blimp* was not unduly critical, and it removed most, if not all, of the political sting in the tail of Low's original cartoon creation. If anything, the filmic rendition of Colonel Blimp singled the character out as being greatly at odds with the times — one of Low's intentions, of course — but hardly as a representative of any type to be found in the British Army by the advent of World War II.

The script makes that abundantly clear and shows, from the outset, the best of intentions.[15] An opening page declares:

> This film is dedicated to the New Army of Britain, to the new spirit in warfare, to the new toughness in battle, and to the men and women who know what they are fighting for and are fighting this war to win it.

Subsequently, the script devotes considerable care and attention to detail — a feature which is beautifully evident throughout — in order to ensure that the characteristics of Clive Candy (Blimp) are precisely delineated. He is given a credible pedigree, for example, which doubtless owed much to the presence of the military adviser on the film, Lieutenant-General Sir W. Douglas Brownrigg, KCB, DSO. It read:

> Clive ('Sugar') Candy, VC, CB, DSO. Late Wessex Light Infantry; served South African War 1899—1902; European War 1914—1918; Major-General, retired pay, 1935; re-employed Base Sub-Area Commandant in

France, 1939; retired pay, 1940; Zone Commander Home Guard, 1940–
1942.

And in one of the most revealing passages, relating to Candy's position by 1942, the script notes (my emphasis):

> A few words are necessary here to explain Clive's position. He was 26 or thereabouts in 1902, so he would have been over the top age for a major-general in 1939 and far over in 1941. It is essential to retain this basic age of Clive in order to portray him as the kind of old fellow who becomes a Blimp. *But it is equally important not to give the impression that our Armies were commanded in 1939 by men who were old, as well as 'not up to it'.* In fact this was not the case and our generals' ages ranged from 47 to 58. The solution is: Clive was retired in 1935. At the outbreak of war he was one of the first to seek employment and was given a Base Sub-Area to command (probably a coastal town such as Boulogne or Entretat). This would be extremely likely and would fit well into the story. After the collapse and evacuation he would be for a few weeks still on full pay, still active, waiting for another job. But he doesn't get it. He is once more on the retired list and, being as keen as mustard, he is very bitter at first.[16]

Powell's and Pressburger's intentions were obvious. Clive Candy was to be portrayed as Blimp and all he symbolized, but he was not meant to represent the men who commanded Britain's 'New Army', and its character was to remain unimpugned.

How far though were these ambitions realized in the film?

Britain's 'New Army' is personified by Lieutenant 'Spud' Wilson (James McKechnie) and his men. From the start of the film, set in September 1942, it is made clear that he is thoroughly equipped to wage 'total war', and he has prepared his men accordingly. As an Army motorcyclist arrives at their encampment, bringing details of a Home Guard exercise that they are to join, the motorcyclist is knocked to the ground as a result of a precautionary ambush laid by Spud's men. 'What's the ruddy idea?' the motorcyclist demands. 'Total war, isn't it?' Spud's men instinctively reply. Spud has instilled the need for vigilance and alertness, even in the midst of mock manoeuvres. Subsequently Spud himself demonstrates the same qualities and harps upon the theme of the exigencies of total war.

He decides to jump the gun on the Home Guard exercise. 'War' starts at midnight, but he intends to 'make it like the real thing'. The 'biggest toughs' from the platoon are to be recruited for his own exercise: 'We attack before war is declared. . . . Yes, like Pearl Harbor.' He sets off to capture the 'enemy' leaders, including Clive Candy (Roger Livesey), before the exercise proper has swung into motion. He does so, after he has found them lounging in the Turkish baths of the Royal Bathers' Club, Piccadilly (the entrance of which is appropriately bedecked with propaganda posters from the period, including the one with the notorious slogan '*Your* courage, *your* cheerfulness, *your* resolution, will bring *us* victory').

There Spud confronts Candy, and the might which Spud urges in taking control of the club ('All right, boys, this is it. Brute force and ruddy ignorance') is pitted in heated argument against the right of Candy's protests ('But war starts at midnight'). Candy demands to know what authority Spud has for making his pre-emptive strike. Spud curtly replies: 'These guns and these men.' Candy accuses Spud and his men of behaving like a band of 'awful militia gangsters' and insists once again that 'War starts at midnight'. 'You say war starts at midnight,' Spud retorts, but 'How do you know the enemy says so as well?' War is not run according to 'National Sporting Club rules', Spud comments, before attempting to excuse his actions on the grounds that 'In forty years' time, at least I shall be able to say I was a fellow of enterprise.' In a fit of anger at such 'impudence', Candy struggles with Spud. They fall into the baths, and with a neat visual flourish the film goes back in time to Candy's own impetuous youth and begins to recount the highlights of his life story from that point onwards.

It is a classic confrontation of the old and the new, but the contemporary allusions are clear. Candy *is* Blimp; furthermore, he is situated in Blimp's best-known setting of a Turkish bath, and he is made up to look exactly like the cartoon figure. Spud represents the men who command the 'New Army'.

Spud, however, at this early point in the film, is always in danger of being painted as the villain of the piece. His apparent philosophy of 'Might is right', his peremptory commands, his precipitate actions, his harsh demeanour and the accusations levelled against him by Candy all hint of Nazi methods and thuggery. Indeed, in a reprise of the opening scenes later in the film he threatens to teach Candy 'Total war . . . Nazi methods, you know'. But he is soon redeemed. In their punctilious fashion Powell and Pressburger reveal his saving graces. He is an able leader and has a close rapport with his men. In fact, he has come up through the ranks (as his girlfriend makes clear) and speedily at that, doubtless as a result of his skills. One moment he is 'a private in training', the next he is 'getting a commission' (obviously, he suffers none of the setbacks that Pethick-Lawrence outlined in Parliament). He has a warm relationship with his girlfriend, 'Johnny' Cannon (Deborah Kerr), and she, furthermore, is Candy's MTC driver. The closeness of this relationship proves him fallible, since he reveals to her, in advance, his plans to capture Candy, whom she tries to warn of the danger. But it also works in Spud's favour, for Johnny helps to awaken Candy to Spud's attributes. Because of Candy's intervention, no charges are brought against Spud for ruining the Home Guard exercise, and by the end of the film Candy and Johnny stand together, proudly watching 'Spud with his men, marching into London'. In the final analysis Powell and Pressburger paint a sympathetic portrait of Lieutenant Spud Wilson, 2nd Battalion, the Loamshires — not surprisingly, in view of the dedication in their script.

Most of their sympathy is reserved, however, for the figure of Clive Candy. Gone is the opprobrium which infused Low's depiction of Blimp. Candy is Blimp, certainly, but Powell and Pressburger's Blimp is not scorned nor disdained. He is a more amiable, lovable and generally understandable character. He is proved a fool, to be sure, and out of touch with the immense changes going on around him, but those are his worst sins. He is quite harmless, and Powell and Pressburger show, particularly in the flashback scenes, that he is meant to be construed as a bit of an outsider and loner throughout.

On returning from the Boer War, for instance, where he has won the VC, he sets out for Germany to correct anti-British propaganda. British military intelligence advises him not to go and would rather have a conversation about Arthur Conan Doyle's latest Sherlock Holmes adventure, *The Hound of the Baskervilles*, in the *Strand* magazine. But Candy determines to go on a whim, and merely because his friend's niece's governess's sister wrote suggesting he might be of help. Once in Germany he has second thoughts, and on meeting the lady in question, Edith Hunter (Deborah Kerr), he counsels her in turn to observe good manners in a foreign country. Referring to the war from which he has recently returned, she replies: 'Good manners cost us 6,000 men killed and 20,000 wounded and two years of war, when with a little common sense and bad manners there would have been no war at all.'[17] Whereupon Candy is goaded into action and inadvertently compelled to defend himself in a duel. His opponent is an Uhlan officer, Theo Kretschmar-Schuldorff (Anton Walbrook). Both men are averse to duelling but proceed to inflict minor wounds upon each other and land up in the same nursing home. Clive, of course, befriends Theo, who woos and wins Edith. Clive realizes what Edith means to him only after she has set upon becoming Theo's wife.

By the time of World War I Clive and Theo are engaged in mortal combat. Clive's increasingly outdated principles are coming to the fore. 'We don't use the same methods [as the Germans]', he asserts, but behind his back and without his knowledge a South African working for Candy and the British Army does. He extracts from a group of captured German soldiers the information that Clive wants. When the war is won Clive sees the victory as a vindication of his belief that 'Right is right after all. . . . clean fighting, honest soldiering have won.' Then he seeks out his friend Theo, now a prisoner of war in an English camp, who rebuffs the offer of renewed friendship. Before embarking upon the return trip to a defeated and desolate Germany, however, he apologizes and enjoys dinner with Clive and some of his now eminent colleagues. Once more, Clive proves different. He leads most of them in declaring his belief that 'The reconstruction of Germany is essential to the peace of Europe' and affirms: 'We want to be friends.' But Theo's former camp commandant, also a guest, sits quietly at the end of the table and declines to join in with the spirit of enforced *bonhomie*.

He knows better. So does Theo. On returning to his fellow officer prisoners, Theo tells of his experience: 'They are children, boys playing cricket. They win the shirts off your backs and want to give it back.' 'This childlike stupidity is a raft for us in a sea of despair,' he decides finally. 'We'll soon have Germany on her feet again.'

In the event, by 2 November 1939 Theo is back in England as a refugee from Hitler's Germany. His wife has died; his two boys have become 'good Nazis'; and Theo is being scrutinized under the Aliens' Act by a man who assures him, 'This time we mean business.' He is allowed to stay but not to practise his skills, even in Britain's cause. Circumstances dictate that he is no longer needed in quite the same way as before. By contrast, Clive is back on the active list — but not for long. He is soon dealt a double bow, which curtails his potential contribution as well. Both become outsiders.

The radio talk that Clive is destined to deliver on 16 June 1940, in the *Postscript* series, is dropped at the last moment and J. B. Priestley does one instead.[18] And Clive is put on the retired list once again — 'axed. . . . they don't need me any more.' He is dumbfounded. But his friend Theo, wiser and more experienced, explains the reasons. He reads Clive's talk on the topic 'Dunkirk — Before and After', which was intended as a contribution to a discussion on 'the cause of the retreat and its aspects for the future'. It is clearly defeatist.

'You commented on Nazi methods, foul fighting, bombing refugees and

The Life and Death of Colonel Blimp

The Life and Death of Colonel Blimp reveals that by the early 1940s the world of the Boer War hero Clive Candy (Roger Livesey) has changed (1). The conventions of gentlemanly sportsmanship are no longer appropriate, as Theo (Anton Walbrook) has discovered through Germany's defeat in the Great War (2). Trench warfare distinguishes that war (3).

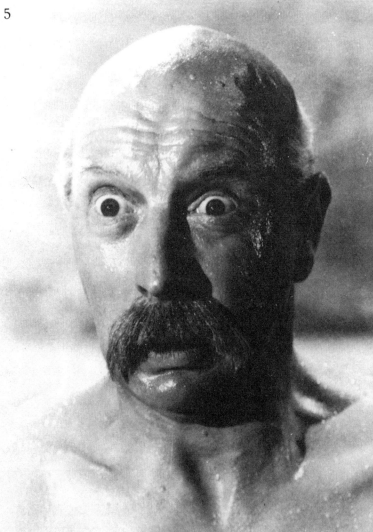

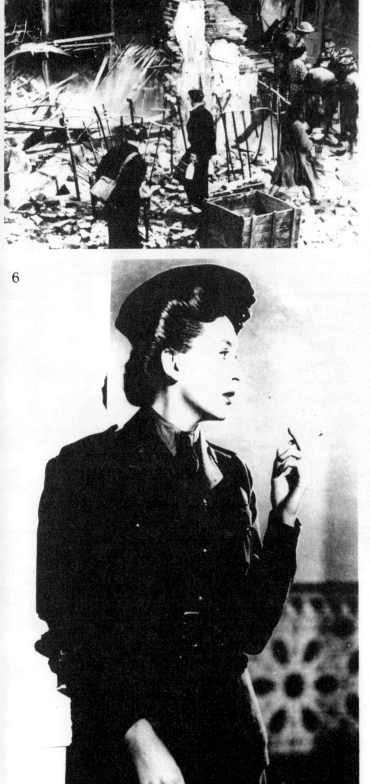

In the Second World War the front line has moved to nearer home (4), and the time has come for the old (5) to be replaced by the new (Deborah Kerr) (6).

so on,' Theo says, 'by saying that you despised them and that you'd sooner accept defeat than victory if it could only be won by these methods.' 'So I would,' replies Clive. But Theo persists: 'You've been educated to be a gentleman and a sportsman. But this is not a gentleman's war. This time you're fighting for your existence against the most devilish idea ever created by the human brain, Nazism, and if you lose, there won't be a return match next year, or for 400 years.' The heart of Theo's message is contained in his statement: 'It's a different knowledge they need now, Clive. The enemy's different, so you have to be different too.' And though initially reluctant to accept the force of these home truths and arguments, even from his close friend, Clive finally faces the inevitable and settles for a role in the Home Guard. He has not changed — far from it: he could never do that — but he is more willing to play the part which circumstances impose upon him.

This, then, is the story which on first reading the Ministry of Information found 'defeatist'. And indeed there are 'defeatist' elements in it, not least in the characterization of Candy, as we have seen. But they are in the script, not of the script. Its purpose was clearly to subject them to scrutiny, if not condemnation, and to suggest that they had been supplanted by new-found values which better served the current situation. For all that they loved him, Powell and Pressburger sought to interpose some distance between their Blimp and the viewer. He was to be sympathized with but not identified with, his sentiments understood but not endorsed. In fact, officialdom obviously grasped many of these nuances, though that did not stop it from damning the venture. But, to repeat, the official reaction owed perhaps as much to factors other than Powell and Pressburger's production.

Before the film had even completed production the official machine rolled into action. It was the Secretary of State for War, James Grigg, doubtless intent upon doing something about the persistent charges of 'Blimpery' in the Army, who sparked the whole thing off.[19] And, frankly, to judge from the documentation in the 'Colonel Blimp File',[20] it is difficult to believe that the film would have caused such a furore without Grigg's initially hostile intervention. For he was dead set against the film from the outset, for reasons which are obvious, and cast it in a sufficiently bad light for Churchill's anger to be aroused in turn.

Grigg's long note to Churchill of 8 September 1942 shows that to be the case. Although the film was well into production, he felt it of the 'utmost importance' to get it stopped. He produced a synopsis of the plot and noted that 'the producer claims that the film is intended as a tribute to the toughness and keenness of the new Army in Britain and shows how far they have progressed from the Blimpery of the pre-war Army.' But 'whatever the film makes of the spirit of the young soldier of today,' Grigg continued, 'the fact remains that it focuses attention on an imaginary type of Army officer who has become an object of ridicule to the general public.' There were other minor objections but clearly the public opinion factor weighed most upon his mind. His claim was that the 'Blimp conception of the Army officer' was 'already dying from inanition' and that the film would give it a 'new lease of life'.

The die was cast. Although nobody had as yet seen the film, since it was still in production, on 10 September 1942 Churchill dubbed it a 'foolish production' and 'propaganda detrimental to the morale of the Army' and asked his Minister of Information to propose measures to stop it 'before it goes any further'. 'Who are the people behind it?' he asked.

Bracken was not daft. He told Churchill who was responsible but said, rightly, 'The Ministry of Information has no power to suppress the film.' The Ministry had tried to discourage its progress 'by withholding Government facilities for its production', but that had not done the trick. And in his eminently sensible reply of 15 September, he pointed out that in order to stop the film 'the Government would need to assume powers of a very far-reaching kind.' For a start, Government would need to be invested with the power to suppress all films if they expressed 'harmful or misguided opinions', and then it would need to insist upon 'a degree of control over films which it does not exercise over other means of expression, such as books or newspaper articles'. In short, such measures would demand nothing less than the 'imposition of a compulsory censorship of opinion upon all means of expression'. Bracken knew full well that such could never be the case. Britain was, after all, a democracy at war. And, as he put it so succinctly and mildly: 'I am certain that this could not be done without provoking infinite protest.'

It was a tactful response. The ball was back in Churchill's court. But Churchill persevered: 'We should not act on the grounds of "expressing harmful or misguided opinions" but on the perfectly precise point of "undermining the discipline of the Army",' he said on 17 September. Impasse was reached. And it was broken only by a War Cabinet minute of 21 September, for that recorded some measure of agreement. When the film had reached 'rough-cut stage' it would be seen by representatives of the War Office and the Ministry of Information. If they took the view that it was 'undesirable', it would be withdrawn by 'friendly arrangement' with the film's backers. The results of that preview were nothing if not revealing. A War Cabinet minute of 10 May 1943 recounts:

> The Secretary of State for War said that the film had now been seen by representatives of the War Office and the Ministry of Information, who took the view that it was unlikely to attract much attention or to have any undesirable consequences on the discipline of the Army. In the circumstances, he had reached the conclusion that the right plan was to allow the film to be shown.

So Grigg withdrew his objections; the War Cabinet endorsed the course of action that he now advocated; and the film was released in Britain.[21] Churchill was adamant, however, that the film should not be allowed to go abroad at least, and he urged Bracken to hold it up 'as long as you possibly can'. This Bracken did, for several months, though he protested that it was an 'illegal ban' and served only to draw attention to the film in a way that they had strenuously sought to avoid. It was a 'wonderful advertisement', and the film was enjoying an extensive run because there were notices 'in all sorts of places' stating, 'See the banned film.' Churchill's views proved vociferous, though (not for the first time) unavailing.[22] By August 1943 approval was secured to release the film overseas.

Why, though, did Grigg of all people change his mind at that crucial meeting in May 1943? Was it just that reports on the completed film compelled him to alter his misguided opinions regarding its intentions? Or was it also that circumstances had changed sufficiently for him to feel confident it could do none of the harm he had originally ascribed to it? The tide of war had, after all, turned in Britain's favour in November 1942. What had been largely a catalogue of military defeats and setbacks by that point changed at last with the Anglo-American landings in North Africa and Montgomery's victory at Alamein. On the home front there was, by the spring of 1943, considerably less talk of 'Blimpery'. And, as Bracken put it in a memorandum to Churchill of 9 July 1943: 'The prestige of the British fighting man stands higher in the world than it has ever done.' Perhaps, then, in the final analysis *The Life and Death of Colonel Blimp* was just another victim of wartime circumstance.

Notes

1 Ian Christie (ed.), *Powell, Pressburger and others,* London, 1978, p. 105.
2 Michael Powell, interviewed by David Badder for 'Powell and Pressburger: the War Years', *Sight and Sound,* 48, Winter 1978, p. 10.
3 Powell, interviewed by Kevin Gough-Yates for the booklet *Michael Powell: in Collaboration with Emeric Pressburger,* London, 1970, p. 8.
4 Lawrence H. Streicher, 'David Low and the Sociology of Caricature', *Comparative Studies in Society and History,* 8, 1965–66, p. 17. See also David Low, *Low's Autobiography,* London, 1956, pp. 273–4.
5 Streicher, 'David Low and the Sociology of Caricature', pp. 13–18.
6 A. J. P. Taylor, *English History 1914–1945,* Oxford, 1965, p. 542.
7 For an overview on the British propaganda effort, see Michael Balfour, *Propaganda in War 1939–1945,* London, 1979, and Nicholas Pronay and D. W. Spring (eds.), *Propaganda, Politics and Film, 1918–1945,* London, 1982.
8 Quoted in Patrick Beesly, *Very Special Intelligence,* London, 1977, p. 123.
9 Taylor, *English History 1914–1945,* p. 540.
10 Quoted in Paul Addison, *The Road to 1945,* London, 1977, p. 198, which provides much of the information used here on Home Intelligence.
11 *House of Comons Debates,* vol. 378, cols. 304–14, 23 February 1942.
12 Addison, *The Road to 1945,* p. 161.
13 ibid., pp. 162–3.
14 See Powell in Badder, 'Powell and Pressburger: the War Years', and Gough-Yates, *Michael Powell.* Bracken and Beddington soon anyway had their own ideas on what might make a 'really good film about the Army', as Vincent Porter and Chaim Litewski demonstrate in 'The Way Ahead: Case History of a Propaganda Film', *Sight and Sound,* 50, Spring 1981, pp. 110–16.
15 See the script of *The Life and Death of Sugar Candy* held in the British Film Institute Library, London (S3034: 1942), Parts I and II.
16 Typewritten addenda to ibid., dated 5 July 1942, p. 5.
17 Though it is not dealt with here, the role of the woman in the film is particularly interesting; see Christie, *Powell, Pressburger and Others,* pp. 117–18, for some astute observations.
18 J. B. Priestley did indeed do a *Postscript* on that date, relating to the Local Defence Volunteers. Two weeks beforehand, on 5 June 1940, he had given the first of what was to become many *Postscripts,* an inspiring and patriotic talk about Dunkirk.
19 As Powell well recognizes in Badder, 'Powell and Pressburger: the War Years', p. 11, where he comments that 'Beddington and Bracken were probably laughing like hell in their offices, but they had to do what they were told and follow the policy of the War Office and the Cabinet.' Powell had, after all, participated in the Ministry of Information's Ideas Committee; see Porter and Litewski, '*The Way Ahead . . .*', p. 110.
20 File PREM 4 14/15, cited in Addison, *The Road to 1945,* and reprinted verbatim in Christie, *Powell, Pressburger and Others,* pp. 106–111.

21 As the BFI microfiche on the film shows, the critical response was divided, though most critics reacted adversely to publicity claims that the film set standards against which 'all entertainment, past, present and future will be judged'. Nor did the critics respond favourably to the film's length, which, at 163 minutes, many felt served only to obscure its message. C. A. Lejeune, writing in the *Observer* of 13 June 1943, thought the film's length 'absurd' and its inevitable fault 'unclarity of purpose', while conceding that it was 'handsome' and 'frequently a moving piece'. The *Evening Standard* of 28 June 1943 found it 'not a great picture' but 'exceptionally good entertainment'. The *Manchester Guardian* said it was a 'consistently entertaining film, nowhere boring and yet hardly anywhere satisfactory as a piece of narrative or a piece of fiction'. Dilys Powell in the *Sunday Times* of 17 September 1943 wrote: 'the Blimp of this intellectually humane film is an honourable man, an incurable dreamer, a soldier holding in the midst of totalitarian war to the rules of a game which to his romantic, if imperceptive, mind was never deplorable'; but, once again, 'the moral of his career is left uncertain; with one voice the film censures his beliefs, with another protests that they are the beliefs of all upright men.'

22 On 17 October 1942, for example, he tried to close down the Army Bureau of Current Affairs and informed the Secretary for War: 'I hope you will wind up this business as quickly and as decently as possible, and set the persons concerned to useful work.' But the attempts proved unsuccessful. See Addison, *The Road to 1945,* pp. 150–1, and Arthur Marwick, *The Home Front: the British and the Second World War,* London, 1976, p. 127.

6

Lest We Forget

Fame is the Spur

The Boulting Brothers' film of Howard Spring's novel *Fame is the Spur* was not a popular success. It took five months to make and cost over £350,000, but, contrary to some critics' confident predictions and unstinting praise, it was not a box-office hit. It was, however, an overtly 'political' film, as was well recognized at the time of its release in 1947. Its historical backdrop was broad, no less a canvas than Britain from the 1870s to the 1930s. Its preoccupations were many — the early days of the Labour movement, the Suffragettes, the first Labour Government, the hunger marches, the National Government and not least one man's rise to fame and fortune as a Labour politician in the midst of it all and his final decline. But despite the film's historical setting and allusions, the Boulting Brothers clearly felt they had a message to impart, in the immediate aftermath of World War II, to a Britain experiencing the Labour Government which came to power in July 1945.

Writing about the film in 1970, Raymond Durgnat noted that the film traced the 'rise and moral fall' of a man whose 'principal motivation was not even the substance of power, but its emptier shadow'. He spotted what many commentators had noted before him (and, indeed, what some had said was plainly evident in Spring's original novel of 1940) — that the character of the aspiring Labour politician, played in the film by Michael Redgrave, was nothing short of a thinly veiled portrait of Ramsay MacDonald. In this regard, he argued, it was a 'tardy broadside'. But Durgnat did not stop there. He proceeded to outline how he thought the film was relevant to post-war Britain. It was, he said, the first film to condemn the Attlee administration; its story 'caught the mood of disappointment and discontent which, despite the introduction of the Welfare State, attended austerity'; and, in all, the Boultings were 'belabouring the Labour Government for its lukewarmness'.[1]

Somebody really should have informed the Labour Government (and the Boultings) of that fact. Attlee, Bevin, Cripps and a number of others from the Cabinet dutifully trooped along to see the film shortly after its release in October 1947, and appear to have missed the point. Certainly, Cripps was heard to remark: 'Every man who sees this picture will want to go away and re-examine himself.'[2] But for the most part everybody seems to have agreed, as *Tribune* reported, that the message of the film was: 'It should not happen again'[3] — an unsurprising opinion, since it clearly accorded with the Boultings' intentions.

Nor did their story seek to capture the 'mood of disappointment and discontent' in the country for the simple reason that by the time Nigel Balchin's screenplay was completed in July 1946,[4] just one year after Labour took office, there was little justification for believing any such mood existed. If it did, it had assuredly not manifested itself, during the course of that first year, in disappointment with the Labour Government. After the 1945 election, as Arthur Marwick points out, 'Labour continued to do well in the country, increasing its majority in the first few by-elections, all in Labour-held seats, and doing very well in the first round of local government elections.'[5] Austerity was bad, of course, and getting worse; rationing, controls and shortages were inevitably unpopular. But, generally speaking, the country accepted the difficult post-war circumstances 'with sense and restraint',[6] and it was some time before the Government was held directly responsible for failing to improve the quality of everyday life and was criticized for it.

There was, it is true, some measure of discontent, at least on the industrial front. Within two months of taking office, for example, the Labour Government was confronted with a wave of unofficial dock strikes, which spread across the country from Merseyside. But Attlee's 'characteristically brisk action', as two commentators have described it, dealt with the immediate problem and kept the nation's food supplies going in October 1945.[7] The Cabinet was called in on 9 October; a decision was taken to put the Army into the docks, and the strike was broken. Of course, as these same two commentators go on to observe, Attlee's response on that occasion very much 'set the pattern for his premiership'. As the 1940s progressed and industrial disputes loomed larger and more protracted, Attlee's pragmatism hardened, and 'by 1948 strike-breaking had become almost second nature to the Cabinet'. But the fact of the matter is that in the first year or two of office Attlee's Government achieved genuine and popular success in the field of industrial relations. His personal standing remained such that even in June 1948 a BBC radio broadcast that he delivered played no small part in helping to bring the then striking dockers back to work.[8]

Furthermore, from the outset the Government had clearly set about fulfilling its election promises. They were by no means effected at once, of course, and some were changed considerably in the process of legislation. But the 'peaceful revolution' which Attlee sought was undoubtedly set in motion.[9] Within the first eighteen months of office alone, the National Insurance Act and the National Health Service Act were passed, though the National Health Service did not come into being until July 1948. The programme of nationalization was embarked upon and took in the Bank of England in May 1946 and the coal mines in January 1947.

In short, then, a good deal was achieved during the opening two years of the Labour Government, when the Boultings' film of *Fame is the Spur* was being scripted and produced. And the Boultings did not seek to use their film to criticize the Labour Government for any supposed lukewarmness on its part during that time, nor indeed generally to condemn it. The film was not 'political' in that sense. What the Boultings consciously sought to do with their film was to highlight what Attlee and many others in the Labour Party described as the 'greatest betrayal in the political history of the country'.[10]

They were interested, quite simply, in writing history of a sort with their film, and their intentions are clarified by a comparison between the completed film and Spring's original novel.

Howard Spring's novel was nothing if not long and ambitious.[11] It centres upon the character of Hamer Shawcross and weaves a fictitious life story around him in the years between 1877, when at the age of 12 he witnesses the funeral of the 'Old Warrior' who has come to occupy the role of grandfather in his family, and 1939, when he is 74 and himself a grandfather. Born illegitimate, he is brought up in a 'respectable' working-class home by his mother and stepfather. But he moves from these humble origins in Ancoats, Manchester, to a position of some power in the Labour Party. His political career flourishes; he enjoys high office and ends up as Viscount Shawcross of Handforth. His career is contrasted with, and regularly crosses, those of his two childhood friends, Arnold Ryerson and Tom Hannaway. Arnold has none of Hamer's learning (albeit self-taught) or skill at political oratory, but he proves to be a gifted and capable Labour Party organizer at the trade union and grass-roots level. Tom's talents lead him in a completely different direction. He turns out a successful businessman, builds up a chain of shops, accumulates considerable wealth and influence, wins a seat as a Conservative and lands a knighthood.

All three men marry, but once again the focus of attention is Hamer and his household. Hamer's wife, Ann Artingstall, is the daughter of a local businessman, who tires of his commitments and lifestyle, comes to prefer more obvious and immediate pleasures and finally sees his business empire largely bought out and supplanted by the enterprising Tom Hannaway's endeavours in that field. Ann greatly aids and abets her husband's progress in his chosen career, but her own powerfully held principles compel her along a path that sets her at odds with her husband. She chooses to support the Suffragette cause and champions votes for women, which Hamer does not condone. Private and public conflicts ensue, and Ann is jailed for engaging in certain 'illegal' protests. Along with other Suffragettes, she is forcibly fed and physically abused, but in Ann's particular case her naturally delicate health deteriorates and she dies while convalescing abroad with Hamer.

In the meantime their son Charles has begun to enjoy many of the benefits which money can buy, such as private schools and a university education, and which Hamer especially sought out for him. His life, however, is blighted by a traumatic wound which he sustains while fighting in the Great War. His path crosses that of Alice, the daughter of Arnold and Pen Muff, who by constrast wins her way to university on a scholarship. She is naturally intelligent and writes well; she is also politically committed. Charles and Alice fall in love, but he feels threatened by her success, and they are estranged, just as Charles in turn is estranged from his father.

Eventually Charles and Ann are reconciled. They set off to join the Republican cause in the Spanish Civil War, but Charles is killed en route. Ann returns to join Hamer and has Charles's baby. Her parents are dead, and she stays with Hamer. Hamer, Ann and the baby are together in 1939 as Europe embarks on another war.

Though concerned in the main with the lives of his fictional characters, Spring also makes reference throughout to historical events and personalities. They are woven into the narrative with fascinating, if sometimes far-fetched, results. Even before we embark upon Hamer's story, for instance, his grandfather recounts the incidents which he witnessed at the Peterloo Massacre in 1819 and bequeathes to the young Hamer a sabre which he took from a dragoon there. (The sabre, in fact, becomes a symbol and an inspiration for Hamer; the three parts of Spring's book are entitled 'Sabre on the Wall', 'Sabre in the Hand', and 'Sabre in Velvet'.) As a young man working in Suddaby's bookshop in Manchester Hamer meets Engels; as an up-and-coming politician he meets Keir Hardie and argues with him. With the outbreak of World War I it is Hamer who suggests that the Labour Party should go in with the Government, and in 1931 it is Hamer who suggests a Coalition Government be formed. Ann becomes involved with the Suffragettes; Arnold leads the hunger marches; and Alice, it transpires, was not only responsible for leaking the Zinoviev Letter but also instrumental in writing it.

Spring was clearly intrigued with historical issues, and doubtless his copious historical allusions helped to make his novel a best-seller. But he was as much intrigued with the difference between the public and private persona. And this is most evident in his treatment of Hamer. For Spring consistently confronts Hamer, and the reader, with the evidence of Hamer's diary. Hamer's actions and statements, particularly in public, are both contradicted and explained by Spring's references to the 'inner man', as gleaned largely from a reading of Hamer's diary. It is a useful and successful literary device, for it enables Spring both to build up a fully rounded picture of Hamer and, at the end of the day, to redeem him in the eyes of the reader. For all Hamer's political compromises and personal failings, he is depicted finally as a sympathetic figure and afforded considerable respect. Indeed, the novel is infused with a sense of forgiveness and redemption at its end, as first Charles and then Alice are reconciled with Hamer. 'Take them by and large,' says Alice, and 'we needn't blush for those who made us.' At the last Alice and her child are left in Hamer's charge.

The film has none of this air of reconciliation and redemption about it — quite the opposite, in fact — and it is also in many other important respects greatly at odds with the spirit and the letter of Spring's novel. The film is concerned rather with betrayal — the acts and consequences of Hamer's betrayal of his political ideals — and that alone.

Given the inordinate length of the novel, the film inevitably compresses a great deal, and many of Spring's characters and incidents are omitted. Hamer (Michael Redgrave), Ann (Rosamund John), Arnold (Hugh Burden) and Tom Hannaway (Bernard Miles) still occupy centre stage, but much else is discarded. Interestingly, the Boultings clearly sought, at least initially, to find a filmic equivalent to Spring's recourse to Hamer's diary as 'historical evidence', and the first 'cut' of their film made extensive use of flashback sequences to achieve this end and to confront the viewer with pictures of Hamer as he was and as he became. But they were compelled to re-edit their film for final release in order to bring it down to a certain length.[12] Consequently, after one early flashback to show the events at Peterloo, the film progresses in a comparatively straightforward chronological fashion, selecting highlights from Hamer's life to show his passage from youth to old age.

Hamer is inspired by the tale of Peterloo (depicted very much as the shooting script intended, so that 'What we see is what the boy sees — a romantic version of the old man's tale')[13] and by the cry of 'Bread and Liberty' which was uttered then and which Hamer hears again as a lad from street-corner speakers in Ancoats in 1870. He treasures the sword which his grandfather has given him and is prone to fantasizing about the power he might also wield as an orator. Already his vanity and visions of grandeur are evident.

As a youth, in Suddaby's bookshop, Hamer reads the works of Owen Meredith, and Jean Jacques Rousseau in the French. He does not meet Engels there, but he does encounter Ann, and he introduces her, in an earnest and pompous manner, to the works of Karl Marx. Hamer's intellect is clearly being developed, thanks largely to his own efforts, but so is his capacity for self-aggrandizement. And when he rekindles his friendship with Arnold, who by now is standing as a Labour candidate for Parliament, Hamer is sufficiently vain as to make the initial mistake of thinking that he is being sounded out as a potential candidate instead of just being recruited by an old friend for a difficult campaign.

For Arnold is standing as Labour candidate in the solidly Tory seat of St Swithin's, where the Earl of Lostwithiel (Sir Seymour Hicks) is in control and is paving and paying the way for his son Lord Liskeard (David Tomlinson) to secure the seat. Arnold, furthermore, is a poor speaker with little obvious charisma, and it is no surprise when he loses. But Hamer, when speaking on Arnold's behalf, demonstrates great prowess on the platform and goes down well with many of the crowds. Even at this early stage, however, the seeds of doubt are sown about Hamer's true intentions. On being told that he has delivered a good speech, Hamer instinctively replies: 'Oh, it was nothing.' 'Maybe,' he is told candidly, 'but it sounded all right.'

Subsequently, when Liskeard goes to the Lords on his father's death, Hamer contests the seat himself. He proves successful and becomes its first Labour MP. He marries Ann, writes a book entitled *Crusade Against Poverty,* and his career really takes off.

From that point on the film pitches Hamer into a series of situations which test his worth and credibility and from which he emerges with increasingly less credit and esteem, even in the eyes of those nearest and dearest to him. He almost loses Ann's affections over his refusal to espouse the Suffragette cause. They are reconciled on her death bed, though not before she has expressed her fears that he may change his mind about 'what needs doing'. And, slowly but surely, he alienates Arnold.

This process begins when he speaks to striking miners in Wales, at Arnold's request once again, and uses his Peterloo sabre to great effect during the course of a passionate and stirring speech, in which he urges: 'I want you to help me convict and punish the murderers. They're still abroad in this land — not killing perhaps with the sword, but with the slower weapons of starvation and cold.' He succeeds in inciting them to riot, which the pacifist Arnold has not wanted to see happen, and as a result one of their number is killed. On being accused by reporters, after the event, that 'The whole thing arose from a speech of yours', Hamer is distinctly worried and asks them to 'nail that lie at once'. 'Is it likely that responsible men like Ryerson and I would advocate useless violence?' he pleads.

Hamer alienates Arnold further when, on the eve of World War I, they discuss the Labour Party's likely position. Arnold says he has been 'preaching non-violence' all his life and would like to see the Party 'stick to our principles'. Hamer too has endorsed those principles and has made speeches on the theme of 'Europe and peace'. But he is all for going in with the Government 'to increase our prestige' and because 'Nobody's such a fool as to let his principles interfere with his practice.' He supports the Government's stand and is increasingly drawn into the parlour politics waged at the parties given by Lady Lettice Lostwithiel (Carla Lehmann). At one such party Hamer is prompted by the Minister of Mines to go back to South Wales and to put an end to a strike of miners who see the war as the 'bosses' war'. But Hamer's credibility with these men has suffered. Arnold is in jail as a pacifist, and this time Hamer is scorned.

Power is what Hamer is after, and power of a sort is what he achieves as Minister of Internal Affairs in the Labour Governments of 1924 and 1929. But it serves only to widen the gap between him and Arnold, to emphasize their points of difference and to epitomize what the Boultings clearly intended to be read as the two major strands in Labour Party thinking during those years. In 1929, for instance, Arnold invites Hamer to speak yet again, this time to the hunger marchers he is leading into London. Hamer declines, claiming in a letter, 'All my experience leads me to deprecate mass action and to favour the constitutional use of the machinery of Government.' Finally, in 1931, on the eve of the formation of a coalition National Government which Hamer has advocated (indeed, instigated), Hamer and Arnold part decisively and go their own ways. Arnold castigates Hamer for his willingness to contemplate a coalition. He believes Hamer has 'sold the unemployed' by accepting a cut in the dole and has reneged upon the principles for which they all fought in the early days. Hamer retorts: 'Arnold, my dear fellow, there's far too much sentimental talk about "the old days" in this Party. We're no longer a little bunch of enthusiasts speaking at street corners. We're the men responsible for the welfare of this country. This isn't a personal affair. It's a matter of finance and high policy.' Once again it becomes a matter of pragmatism versus principles over a question which genuinely did split the Labour Government in its day and is personified by the fictional characters represented on the screen. Hamer offers his hand in friendship, but Arnold declines to take it, stating quite simply: 'No. There's no ground of friendship for us now.'

In the novel the two men shake hands, though they still part as implacable opponents. And it is from this point on that the Boulting Brothers film diverges most noticeably from Spring's novel.

The National Government is formed in August 1931 and goes to the country in October of that year. It wins, of course, and Hamer is returned once again for St Swithin's but this time as a National Labour MP. In the novel Spring makes great play of revealing the results of the election (and, not surprisingly, he is accurate). But for Spring's Hamer there then comes a moment of reckoning. He has already appreciated that 'Clear of all evasion and self-deceiving', what he has wanted is 'nothing more than the fame that now [is] his.' And now he is well aware of the 'savage wounding blows' that he and a few colleagues have dealt out to his Party, for all that he thought it was necessary at the time to help save the country. So he decides he will not serve in any future Cabinet and writes a letter to his Prime Minister stating, 'I have made up my mind not to accept office again.' Thereafter he happily remains a constituency MP and finds the peace and reconciliation with his family of which we have spoken.

But in the Boulting Brothers' film there is no redemption, merely retribution. Their Hamer stays at his Cabinet post in 1931, survives the election but loses popularity in his constituency and is thrown out finally in the election of 1935. Since in the film he has no children, there is no comfort to be found in that quarter. His life ultimately proves barren and fruitless. The letter that Hamer writes to his Prime Minister is therefore that much more poignant:

> Thank you for your most kind letter. I am too old a hand to be disturbed by political defeat. But I am now nearly seventy-five; accordingly, I shall not seek re-election, and the question of finding me a seat does not arise. I am deeply touched by the suggestion in your last paragraph. As you know, I have been in the past an opponent of the system of hereditary titles. But as I have no children, it would perhaps be possible, if His Majesty so pleased to confer such an honour on me, to accept it without sacrifice of principle.

Whereupon his vanity takes the better of him, and he ponders which title would sound best and writes out a list from which to choose.

It is a logical step for a man who has become enamoured of the charmed circles within which the likes of Lady Lettice moves. She is one of the few friends remaining to him, the only source of some joy and comfort. And on a visit to her country mansion, where he was treated as a trespasser in his youth but is now warmly welcomed, he is moved to comment upon the 'grandeur and spirit of England, expressed in wood and stone' and revels in the tranquillity it brings.

Old age has truly caught up with him. The last we see of the film's Hamer is the image of a frail old man, capable only of delivering rambling speeches but intent still upon seeing whether they have been reported in the press. He too is increasingly afflicted by his conscience, and in a final speech, delivered at a Lord Mayor's banquet in the City of London, he is haunted by the visions which are conjured up before him of Arnold and Tom, the two people he has known since childhood. Arnold is a gaunt and haggard spectre, Tom a leering and enticing figure. At home that evening Hamer reminisces. He is prompted to try to wrest the Peterloo sabre from the handsome scabbard to which he consigned it as a showpiece many years before. But he can no longer do so; it has rusted in. A broken man and a pathetic figure, he is helped to bed by his servant.

To the end the Boultings relentlessly hounded their Hamer. Spring allowed his character some respite, and Hamer's son Charles threw the sabre into the sea on his ill-fated voyage to Spain. Its job done, it no longer served a useful purpose. But it served the Boultings' purpose to keep the sabre on view as a haunting symbol of his betrayal and to leave the audience with a visual image of that.

Hamer had, quite simply, been weighed in the balance and found wanting. The film had surveyed his political career and come down resoundingly against him. But in the process of situating this character within a particular context and in comparing him with his fellows the film had also captured many of the nuances and facets of political life. The pictures it drew — of Arnold, the solid, dependable and principled Party worker; of Ann, the thoroughly middle-class and idealistic 'modern' woman; of Tom, the rags-to-

Fame is the Spur is concerned with the betrayal of political ideals. Hamer Radshaw (Michael Redgrave) reads Marx, Meredith and Rousseau (1) and proclaims his principles before the striking miners roused by Arnold Ryerson (Hugh Burden) (2). But the causes of the Suffragettes (Rosamund John and Marjorie Fielding) (3) and of the hunger marchers (4) do not move him because he has learned political expediency and ambition. He degenerates from saviour (5) to charlatan (6).

riches Conservative businessman; and of the Lostwithiels, the traditional yet by no means uncaring Tories — were often treated, like the historical topics and issues that it broached, in a simplistic fashion. Yet the film was convincing for all that and was nothing if not novel in its choice of subject matter.

The Boulting Brothers' film, then, set its face grimly against its principal character of Hamer Radshaw and allowed him no redeeming characteristics. He was not meant to be construed in any sense as the archetypal 'hero'. This hardly made Michael Redgrave's task as an actor very easy, nor indeed was it likely to recommend the film as a commercial proposition. Although there were critics who dearly liked the film, it is perhaps no surprise that there were also critics who, while recognizing its purpose, found the film unremitting and despondent.

A. E. Wilson in the *Star* was typical in this respect. He noted that it was 'a long and worthily intentioned film', but he found it 'very sombre in tone, with hardly a touch of humour and only a hint of sentiment to relieve it'.[14] Harold Conway in the *Evening Standard* thought it a 'penetrating and rather bitter portrait' but doubted whether 'this fine picture, with its atmosphere of drama and grimness, will prove good box office throughout the country'. He did, however, applaud the Boulting Brothers 'for their courage in making it, and doing so with such unswerving integrity'.[15] The *Observer* considered it 'very serious and rather long'.[16] The *News of the World* concurred, but thought the direction 'intelligent' and that overall it amounted to a 'spacious and imaginative production'.[17] The *Daily Telegraph* believed it to be 'as somniferous as a political speech, indeed it is one'.[18] But the *Daily Worker* found the film a political speech to its liking. It was 'magnificent. . . . not a second is wasted' and it urged that 'all Labour leaders should see the film twice'.[19]

Very few critics failed to comment upon the political import of the film. Richard Winnington in the *News Chronicle* thought that the 'MacDonald-esque effigy supplied by Michael Redgrave is the film's central and incurable flaw'.[20] And some, like the *Sunday Times* critic, felt that the arrival of *Fame is the Spur* meant that henceforth films would be judged on 'political rather than on human and artistic grounds'. This would lead to a sorry state of affairs, since films should speak with 'a voice above politics'.[21] For others such as the *Evening News,* though, it meant that the Boultings had broken the age-old maxim 'Keep politics off the screen', and it declared, 'Thank goodness for a movie that has something to say.' 'Although it deals with past events,' the *Evening News* continued, 'its subject is so timely today.'[22] And the *Daily Mail* agreed that the film's theme was 'of permanent interest, perhaps never more so than now'.[23] 'Its controversial appeal is obvious,' concluded the *Daily Mirror.*[24]

In the event, of course, the film turned out to hold little appeal for the mass of cinema-goers. It was relevant, but in box-office terms it proved to be neither remarkable nor rewarding. It was political but not popular. Still, if nothing else the Boultings had succeeded admirably in putting a controversial political subject on the screen, and that, as the *Evening News* critic had suggested, was no small achievement.

During the 1930s, for instance, such a project would not have been entertained. Then politics, and particularly 'references to controversial politics',[25] were quite definitely barred from the screen by the British Board of Film Censors. And in a notable 1936 speech to the Cinematograph Exhibitors Association, the President of the BBFC, Lord Tyrrell, had reiterated the BBFC's belief that subjects dealing with 'political controversy' should not be introduced into the cinema, since 'Nothing would be more calculated to arouse the passions of the British public.'[26]

During World War II a good deal more flexibility and latitude was introduced, of necessity, into the censorship system, which resulted in several films on overtly political themes, such as Thorold Dickinson's *The Prime Minister* (1941) and Carol Reed's *The Young Mr Pitt* (1942), albeit well shrouded in antiquity and hardly of a controversial nature.

But the Boultings were to benefit in the immediate post-war period from the continued display of latitude on the BBFC's part. When in July 1946 they submitted the scenario of *Fame is the Spur* for pre-production scrutiny by the BBFC's readers, it was found that there were no insuperable problems, though it was noted of the 1880s sequences that 'The class differences of the time are shown by the contrast between the Earl of Lostwithiel and Hamer and his friends. The balance is heavily in Hamer's favour — all simple poverty — while the Tory Earl bribes his way into politics. The worst landlord in England, he is a drunkard, a crook and a brute.' Of the Peterloo Massacre the readers said, 'The actual scenes of fighting with the mob must be reduced to the minimum.' The word 'bloody' was to be deleted from the script, and it was thought that the scenes of the rioting Welsh miners 'suggest extremes of violence very reminiscent of the famous montages in the Russian films *Potemkin* and *Odessa* [sic] many shots of which the Board cut'. Finally, they added that 'forcible feeding should not be overstressed as torture' in the scenes of Ann's imprisonment as a Suffragette.[27]

The Boultings succeeded, then, in convincing many people of the worthiness of their political intentions, with the exception, perhaps, of those people who counted most, the bulk of the cinema-going population.

Notes

1 Raymond Durgnat, *A Mirror for England,* London, 1970, pp. 67, 70.
2 Reported by Harold Conway in the *Evening Standard*, 10 October 1947.
3 'Fame is the Spur', *Tribune,* 562, 17 October 1947, p. 1.
4 Two Cities Films Ltd, *Bulletin,* 15 July 1946 (*Fame is the Spur* microfiche, British Film Institute Library, London). The shooting script was by Roy Boulting. My thanks to Roy Boulting for letting me borrow his shooting script of the film and for being so kind and helpful in providing me with information, both in interview (26 February 1982) and by letter (9 February 1982).
5 Arthur Marwick, *British Society since 1945,* Harmondsworth, Middlesex, 1982, p. 103.
6 ibid., p. 110.
7 Peter Hennessy and Keith Jeffery, 'How Attlee stood up to strikers', *The Times,* 21 November 1979. The authors go on to say: 'Attlee enjoyed several advantages over his succesors. He presided over a nation conditioned by the discipline of war, both from forces' life abroad and experiences of the siege economy at home.' Their researches have lately been published in fuller form in *States of Emergency. British Governments and Strikebreaking since 1919,* London, 1983.
8 See Kenneth Harris, *Attlee,* London, 1982, pp. 422–3.
9 Paul Addison, *The Road to 1945,* London, 1977, p. 278.

10 The Boultings proved to be accommodating in other ways. Spring's character was, of course, called Hamer Shawcross, but the name was changed in the film to Hamer Radshaw. It was changed 'very simply', as Roy Boulting puts it, 'on legal advice. The present Lord Shawcross (then Sir Hartley Shawcross) was a member of the Labour Government, and we were told quite forcibly that to keep the original name of the character in Howard Spring's book would almost certainly take us into the law courts' (letter to the author of 9 February 1982). It is also interesting to note (see chapter 9) how apposite Roy Boulting's 1951 film of *High Treason* becomes in the light of the release of Government papers from that period, which show that the Attlee administration was obsessed with the idea of a communist conspiracy and 'attempts to disrupt the nation's economy' in its last year of office.

11 The novel of *Fame is the Spur* has been reprinted regularly since it was first published in 1940. The last occasion was in January 1982, as a tie-in with a BBC dramatization. The television production was poor, but Spring's novel re-entered the 'top ten' paperback lists. Spring served in British Intelligence between 1915 and 1918, and in 1941 he was one of the two writers assigned by Bracken to accompany Churchill and to produce a 'record for posterity' of his signing, with Roosevelt, of the Atlantic Charter.

12 The first 'cut' of the film ran for 2 hours 10 minutes, but the Rank Organization thought it too long and insisted upon the 'very substantial cuts' that were subsequently made to bring it in at an initial release length running to 116 minutes. Roy Boulting recounts, 'The finished film, then, proved a great disappointment to John and myself. So much indicative of the slow and insidious process of corruption had to be removed.' Marion Howard Spring records that she and her husband saw the film and that they too were 'disappointed with the result, it was not a bit like the novel' (*Howard,* London, 1967, p. 176).

13 Both the shooting script and the completed film show how 'romantic' the boy's vision was meant to be: 'with men and women dancing, and a fantastic Sam Bamford with a hat full of leaves and later, dragoons of enormous size, all on grey horses like tin soldiers, and grandfather in shining armour, avenging his sweetheart. . . . The setting is quite unnaturalistic, and belongs to the pages of a child's fairy book.'

14 *Star,* 10 October 1947.

15 *Evening Standard,* 10 October 1947.

16 *Observer,* 12 October 1947.

17 *News of the World,* 12 October 1947.

18 *Daily Telegraph,* 13 October 1947.

19 *Daily Worker,* 11 October 1947.

20 *News Chronicle,* 11 October 1947.

21 *Sunday Times,* 12 October 1947.

22 *Evening News,* 9 October 1947.

23 *Daily Mail,* 10 October 1947.

24 *Daily Mirror,* 10 October 1947.

25 See the list of barred subjects reprinted in Neville March Hunnings, *Film Censors and the Law,* London, 1967, pp. 408—9.

26 Reprinted in the British Board of Film Censors *Annual Report* for 1936 (BFI Library, London).

27 *BBFC Scenario Reports,* 1946—7, pp. 27, 27a (17 and 23 July 1946; bound volume, BFI Library).

7

Old School Ties
The Guinea Pig

It is a commonplace that total institutions — hospitals, prisons, schools — can be used in fiction as microcosms of the nation. Equally it is said that the public school system is the cornerstone of the class structure and of the deep-rooted social divisions which differentiate British society from that of other countries. We might legitimately expect, then, that a film set in a public school would be open to interpretation both as direct comment on the public school system *per se* and, more broadly, as comment on the state of the nation. The British film industry did, in fact, produce films set in public schools at two different and formative periods of change in British society — *The Guinea Pig* in 1948 and *If . . .* in 1968. An examination of these two films is extremely enlightening about the attitudes towards society, class and education that were prevalent in the film industry during the eras which produced them.

The Guinea Pig was the work of the twin Boulting Brothers, Roy directing and John producing the film. The Boulting Brothers were among the more progressive elements in the film industry. Raymond Durgnat classifies them as 'moralists'.[1] Since founding Charter Films in 1937, they had produced and directed a series of films which had thoughtfully examined serious issues and had won them critical acclaim — *Pastor Hall* (1940) (resistance to Nazi tyranny), *Thunder Rock* (1942) (pacifism), *Brighton Rock* (1947) (crime and guilt). They had identified themselves with Labour by producing *Fame is the Spur* (1947). In *The Guinea Pig,* based on a hit play by Warren Chetham Strode, they set out to examine the role of the public school in the post-war world and, in broader terms, the new society for which the Labour Government was striving. Bernard Miles, another progressive film-maker whose *Chance of a Lifetime* (1950), a film about workers taking over the running of a factory, was rejected by both major circuits, contributed to the screenplay and appeared in the film as the 'guinea pig's' father. Interestingly, both the play's author and the film's producer and director were at public schools — Sherborne and Charterhouse respectively.

The play was directly inspired by the recommendations of the Fleming Report. The first steps towards the creation of the welfare state had been taken during the war. The Butler Education Act (1944) provided for secondary education for all up to the age of at least 15, with a change of school at 11. The Act did not specify the nature of this change, but it was understood to involve a process of selection which would separate children into two groups — those who went to grammar schools and those who attended secondary moderns. In 1942 R. A. Butler, President of the Board of Education, set up a committee under Lord Fleming to consider how links between the public school system and the general education system could be improved. The committee's report (1944) concluded that some measure of integration between the two could be achieved by giving up to 25 per cent of places at all public schools to children selected from the state system by the local authorities. The Headmasters' Conference unanimously accepted the recommendation, but the scheme never really took off. The Government would not provide the money for the state pupils, insisting that this was a matter for the local authorities, and the local authorities were reluctant to spend money on the scheme. But the report had the effect of deflecting Labour's opposition to the public schools, despite the commitment to comprehensive education which had become party policy at the 1942 Labour conference.

Chetham Strode's play examined the experiment by following the progress of Cockney council school boy Jack Read through Saintbury School between 1944 and 1948. He is the 'guinea pig' of the title, though the Americans, with characteristic directness, retitled the film *The Outsider* for its US release, giving it a more obvious class resonance. The film version shot exteriors at Haileybury and Mill Hill, and Saintbury was constructed in the studio, its buildings and layout modelled directly on Sherborne's.

The arguments for and against the Fleming experiment are advanced at various stages in the film by the characters who represent progressive and reactionary standpoints. Lloyd Hartley (Cecil Trouncer), the old housemaster, is a dyed-in-the-wool traditionalist. He is opposed to the experiment, believing that the classes cannot mix successfully. Nigel Lorraine (Robert Flemyng), the young housemaster, supports the experiment. He is a meritocrat who has faith in the public school system but wants to open it up to worthy lads who cannot afford the fees. He believes in preserving the best of the past but adapting also to meet the needs of the present. He is a pipesmoking ex-army officer and former Oxford rugger blue who lost a leg in the war. It is perhaps worth noting that another pipesmoking ex-army officer, devoted to his old school (Haileybury), was at the same time heading the post-war Labour Government. The difference of opinion between Hartley and Lorraine becomes so intensive that Lorraine resigns, though he later withdraws his resignation.

The same argument is rehearsed at a higher level in the school when the governors meet to discuss the War Memorial Fund. The bishop wants a new school hall built with the money. But the headmaster, who shares Lorraine's progressive viewpoint, wants to place a commemorative plaque in the chapel and to allocate the rest of the money to scholarships in order to bring poor boys to Saintbury and to send them on to Oxford and Cambridge. The governors object that this influx of poor boys is likely to lower the tone of the school.

Both conflicts, that between Lorraine and Hartley and that between the governors and the headmaster, are resolved by divine revelation of a kind. Hartley, who is retiring because of heart trouble, takes a walk through the school hall and sees the inscription of the sixteenth-century founder's bequest, setting Saintbury up as a grammar school for use by poor boys. He realizes that he has lost sight of the reasons for the existence of the public schools. He intervenes in the debate at the governor's meeting to support the headmaster, and the scholarship proposal is carried. Hartley then asks Lorraine to take over from him as housemaster because he can make the necessary change within continuity which is required. Lorraine agrees, and the reconciliation is cemented by Lorraine's marriage to Hartley's daughter Lynne, who shares his ideas.

Interwoven with the debate about the merits of the experiment is the progress at the school of 'guinea pig', Jack Read. It follows more or less the standard format for the public school story, as summarized by E. C. Mack:

> A boy enters school in fear and trepidation, but usually with ambitions and schemes; suffers mildly or seriously at first from loneliness, the exactions of fag-masters, the discipline of masters and the regimentation of games; then makes a few friends and leads for a year or so a joyful, irresponsible and sometimes rebellious life, eventually learns duty, self-reliance, responsibility and loyalty as a prefect, qualities usually used to put down bullying or overemphasis on athletic prowess; and finally leaves school with regret for a wider world, stamped with the seal of an institution which he has left and devoted to its welfare.[2]

But added to this is a crucial dimension not usually present in this standard format — class.

The film opens with Jack Read (Richard Attenborough), the bright son of lower-middle-class parents who keep a tobacconist's shop in Walthamstow, boarding the train with the new boys headed for Saintbury. Packed into a carriage, the boys talk excitedly of their prep schools and are silenced when Jack reveals that he comes from Middleton Road School, Walthamstow. We see the school through Jack's eyes in an eloquent sequence of point-of-view shots of the stately buildings. Although one boy befriends Jack and shows him the ropes, the others mock his accent and his manners, and his early days are unhappy. His misery culminates in the Founder's Ceremony, when all the new boys have to bow to a statue of King Henry VIII. As he bows, Jack is kicked on the bottom. Asked to bow again, he refuses, gives a two-finger salute to the founder and is dumped in the 'Rubbish Box'. He denounces the ceremony to Hartley as an excuse 'for kicking you up the arse'. A special censors' dispensation had to be obtained for the use of this four-letter word, not hitherto heard on the screen.[3] The Lord Chamberlain had permitted it on the stage, seeing it, apparently, as having the same deliberate shock value as Shaw's 'Not bloody likely' in *Pygmalion* and as an economical and pointed way of demonstrating the gulf between the classes. The Film Censor followed the Lord Chamberlain's lead.

Jack has not understood that the kicking is a ritual initiation ceremony, and he sees it as the last straw. He tries to run away but is dissuaded by Lorraine. Lorraine explains to him the educational, as distinct from the social, advantages of going to Saintbury. He encourages Jack to stand up against what he does not like and tells him that the boys are not snobs — they have just been brought up in a different environment. It is hard to accept Lorraine's explanation of the boy's behaviour, since their attitude to Jack, like Hartley's, is the purest snobbery. But Jack accepts it and agrees to make a go of it. We see him being initiated into the mysteries of fagging, beating, Latin and rugby. At home at Christmas for the holidays, he tells his father that he is unhappy but wants to stick it out. Significantly, he defends the school and its traditions against charges of snobbery, demonstrating that his socialization is well under way.

This socialization continues back at school when he settles a vendetta with another boy, Tracey, in a boxing match fought in the gym instead of in a rough-and-tumble fistfight outside. The two boys end up friends, and the value of rules over anarchy is demonstrated. By the end of the film Jack is the perfect public schoolboy, accent eradicated, manners impeccable. He wants to become a teacher, and Lorraine arranges for him to receive one of the new scholarships to Cambridge.

The standpoint of the film is patently one of consensus, of the modification of existing institutions to accommodate a wider spectrum of the population, of evolutionary rather than revolutionary change. It is an extension of the principle by which the public schools in the nineteenth century had been employed to merge the aspiring upper middle class with the upper class to produce a single ruling elite with a common set of references and a uniform style. Similarly, the franchise had been progressively extended until it had even been granted to women. Now such schools are also to accept the deserving sons of the lower middle class. If the aspirations of dispossessed groups can be accommodated, then there will be no need to abolish or indeed even undermine institutions such as the public schools.

But the consensus is weighted on the side of conservatism, as the film clearly shows in dealing with Jack's family. One of the factors leading to Hartley's conversion is his discovery of a congruence of view with Jack's father (Bernard Miles). The Reads turn up on Commemoration Day, the living embodiment of continuity and tradition. Mr Read is shown round the school by Hartley, and as they talk, Read, a former sergeant-major, indicates that he knows the value of discipline. He thanks Hartley for taking his son on and praises the public school system for providing not just an education but also team spirit, self-confidence and good manners. Seen from the vantage point of today, the Reads look like deferential lower-middle-class Tories with more or less the same views as the old-style High Tory reactionary that Hartley represents. The Reads are totally supportive of Jack, and Mrs Read is prepared to go out to work to earn the money needed to send him to university, with its obvious educational and social advantages. They are not the sort to rock the boat.

Jack himself is transformed so that there is no trace of the original Cockney urchin. 'Gosh, sir, jolly good show,' he declares on learning he has got a scholarship to Cambridge and he leads the cheers for Hartley at his retirement ceremony. There can be little danger to the system if outsiders can become so totally integrated with the traditions. The film aims to show that both sides can learn from each other, a classic consensual stance, but the evidence suggests that it is the poor boys who do most of the learning.

The film does poke a little fun at the stuffiness of the single-sex school. Jack is found whistling at girls from a nearby girls' school, and Hartley asks him severely if he behaves like that at home. Jack replies innocently that he does, and Hartley is outraged. When Jack is seen walking in the woods with a girl, Hartley is furious and denounces and beats him. But Lorraine defends Jack's behaviour as natural. When Tracey tells his mother that he has painted a nude, she is shocked. 'It's a man,' he replies, 'Oh, that's all right,' says mother.

In sanctioning some change and urging the public schools to unbend a little *The Guinea Pig* reflects a considerable advance in the cinema's attitude to the public schools. For the cinema, education meant the public schools. Although the inter-war years were an era of virulent criticism of the public schools in literature, beginning with Alec Waugh's *The Loom of Youth* in 1917, none of this found its way on the screen. Writers like H. G. Wells, George Orwell, E. M. Forster and Graham Greene castigated the public schools, depicting them variously as hotbeds of philistinism, snobbery and homosexuality, as promoters of conformism and authoritarianism or as soulless machines which turned out identikit people ill-equipped emotionally or educationally to deal with the real world. But the cinema's view of the public schools was summed up by the enormously popular *Goodbye, Mr Chips* (1939), James Hilton's gentle and sentimental celebration of the lifetime's teaching career at Brookfield of the venerable Latin master, Mr Chipping (Robert Donat). The same year saw a similar cinematic tribute to another dedicated schoolmaster, Charles Donkin (Otto Kruger), in *Housemaster*, based on the novel and play by Ian Hay. In both films much-loved, slightly eccentric old teachers defended tradition, repelled innovation and preserved continuity.

The importance of the watershed represented by the war is to be seen in a brace of films made after it in which the cosiness of Chips's Brookfield and Charles Donkin's Marbledown is replaced by the bleakness and repression of schools, depicted by Hugh Walpole in *Mr Perrin and Mr Traill* (1948) and Terence Rattigan in *The Browning Version* (1951). The films of these two works can be regarded almost as direct ripostes to *Chips.* Anthony Asquith's *The Browning Version* makes direct reference to *Chips,* and in Lawrence Huntington's *Mr Perrin and Mr Traill,* although the novel was published in 1911 and therefore pre-dated *Chips,* Marius Goring's Vincent Perrin is made up to look very like Robert Donat's Chips. Both Andrew Crocker-Harris (Michael Redgrave) in *The Browning Version* and Vincent Perrin in *Mr Perrin and Mr Traill* are elderly failures, unloved, pedantic disciplinarians with tormented private lives. Their schools are joyless prisons, Perrin's Banfields being described by one character as 'a decaying tooth'. The next stage is the comprehensive criticism of the system in *If . . .* (1968).

It was not until the mid-1950s that the cinema got round to depicting a grammar school, and a co-educational one at that, in Cyril Frankel's *It's Great to be Young* (1956). Scripted by Labour stalwart Ted Willis, it takes that familiar theme of school fiction — the schoolboy rebellion. But the rebellion is merely the desire to play a little jazz in the school orchestra, and the film's moral is the familiar one of the need to compromise between excessive concern for academic achievement and the desire for free expression. The imagery of the film however, is still rooted in the public schools; Angel Hill Grammar School boasts venerable, ivy-covered buildings, masters in gowns and mortar boards and white-flannelled cricketers at play on lazy summer afternoons. The pupils are well scrubbed, well mannered and well spoken middle-class children, their conversation liberally sprinkled with Greyfriars banter ('Keep cave, you chaps', 'Cheese it', 'Good-oh', 'Scrag him', 'Thanks awfully', 'Oh, lor').

It was 1961 before the first serious film to deal with a secondary modern, *Spare the Rod,* appeared. A melodramatic but well meaning British equivalent of the American *Blackboard Jungle* (1955), this film has a

The Guinea Pig

In *The Guinea Pig* the old housemaster (Cecil Trouncer) opposes and the young tutor (Robert Flemyng) supports the experiment of admitting a lower-middle-class council school pupil to exclusive Saintbury School (1). Jack Read (Richard Attenborough), the 'guinea pig' is ragged at first (2), but he learns the meaning of discipline (3) and also the pleasures of public school life (4). The housemaster (Cecil Trouncer) is reconciled to the experiment when he discovers that he and Jack Read's parents (Joan Hickson and Bernard Miles) share a common outlook (5) and when he recalls why Saintbury School was founded in the first place (6).

6

progressive ex-naval man (Max Bygraves) combating bad facilities, poor teachers, parental indifference and the poverty of working-class expectations. Similar problems and conditions occur in the subsequent secondary school dramas, *Term of Trial* (1962) and *To Sir With Love* (1967). It is significant that the cinema should have turned its attention away from the public schools in the 1960s, for that was the decade that was to see the Labour Government implement its policy to introduce comprehensive education as part of the process of achieving a truly egalitarian society. It had been reaffirmed as party policy at the 1959 party conference, and by 1974 two-thirds of all schools had gone comprehensive. The ethos of the 1960s was established by working-class youth, and the cinema was at last to catch up with the literary criticism of the public schools in Lindsay Anderson's *If. . . .*

Back in 1948, however, the critical reactions to a film about the public schools make fascinating reading and are as revealing about the critics and their standpoints as about the film. The communist *Daily Worker* noted:

> There is a positive idea contained in the story — that any boy will make good if given proper scope for his abilities. The trouble is, the film takes for granted the inherent superiority of the public school. . . . While (gently) criticizing snobbery, the film itself reeks of snobbery, and its patronizing attitude to the 'guinea pig' and his parents is as insufferable as it is unintentional. . . . Nevertheless I must admit that the film is capably directed and acted and has many pleasant touches of human observation.[4]

Joan Lestor, writing in the pro-Labour *Reynolds' News,* agreed:

> Where I think the Boulting Brothers have erred is in caricaturing the Walthamstow family in order to emphasize the conflict. Perhaps it is because they shirk the deeper issues involved that they make the boy from Walthamstow . . . incredibly uncouth. It is taking the easy way out to mark your class boundaries by making one side say 'Pleasedtermeetyer' and wear comic hats on festive occasions. . . . Knowing the makers and actors in this picture to have no particle of snobbery or patronage in their make-up, I'm sure offence was not meant. I am fairly sure it will be taken. . . . The solutions are too easy, the superficial boundaries too easily overlooked. The Walthamstow boy's advent has the indirect effect of giving a fillip to the more progressive forces. He himself learns the value of tradition. Is it as simple as that?[5]

The Times, on the other hand, thought it:

> a rational and intelligent film. The author would not pretend that he has vindicated the Fleming Report . . . but at least he sets out to examine the problem as fairly as he can, and if success is snatched from the jaws of failure, and the public school system is vindicated, the uneasiness implicit in the title remains. The school and its life are presented with a fine plausibility, although the supreme importance of house politics is over-looked, and when the false, misleading note rings out, and Saintbury is less Saintbury than Greyfriars, the acting is usually good enough to hush it up quickly. . . . The film picks its way surefootedly among the treacherous cross-currents of English social life and has the courage to recognize that, unfortunate though it may be, class distinctions still exist.[6]

The *Daily Telegraph* agreed that:

> a subject both topical and timeless is tackled with intelligence, sympathy and that rarest of qualities these days good humour.[7]

The *Graphic* felt that the film had been written:

> with great sensitivity and an admirable lack of bias. . . . It will, I am sure, reassure most people that the Fleming recommendations are practical and altogether worthwhile. I am sure, too, that most people will find it as satisfying an entertainment as they have seen for a long time. It is full of warmth and humour and often is extraordinarily moving.[8]

As ever, the Liberal *Manchester Guardian* saw both sides of the argument and came down in the middle:

> This is not, goodness knows, the first film about a British public school, but it is the first of them to be so truthful. . . . Saintbury, one is convinced, might exist and might besides be a fairly sensible educational establishment. And when one hears the film (like the play from which it was adapted) damned both for brandishing the 'old school tie' and for being 'socialist propaganda', then one is inclined to believe that it has, indeed, found the just, truthful, middle way.[9]

But reviewers were divided not just in their attitudes to the treatment of the Fleming recommendations but also according to whether or not they themselves had been to public school, confirming thereby a great divide that still existed in British life.

The *Evening Standard* critic, admitting that his knowledge of public schools was confined to reading the *Magnet* and the *Boy's Own Annual* reported:

> So convincingly has this tale been told that it has left me with a fresh understanding of public school life and these unanswered questions: is it likely that so class-conscious a housemaster would have changed his general views even if he were satisfied with the conduct of one working-class boy? What would such a boy's reactions be to his old environment when he returned with his new accent and new manners? Does the public school system account in any way for Mr Shaw's remark that 'the whole strength of England lies in the fact that the enormous majority of the English people are snobs'? Now any picture that raises problems of this kind should be seen. But *The Guinea Pig* is far more than just a quiz programme. For it has been made with such intelligent tenderness that you will be carried effortlessly and absorbed through an important aspect of British life.[10]

The *Daily Express* critic similarly confessed to not having been to public school:

> I am perhaps over-sceptical of the value of fagging and ragging (and even let me whisper it, cricket) as character-building factors. . . . What becomes of him afterwards, when he has learned not to sop up his gravy, to pick up his aitches and to love the Old Place, is one of the unanswered questions of a well made and notably well acted picture which takes itself a shade too seriously. . . . But overtones of caricature and an underlying acceptance of snobbish values made me uneasy.[11]

The critic of *Time and Tide,* on the other hand, had been to public school:

> The Boultings have put a public school on the screen convincingly enough to put Messrs Chips, Perrin and Traill to shame. It is not flawless in detail. No head ever called the governors 'the school governors' to a housemaster. Above all, no successful housemaster, however reactionary, would have taken on the first experimental schoolboy suggested by the

Fleming Report without telling him even one thing or two. But the general atmosphere, unlike any other in the world, is true and the playing fields, chapel, fagging, prefects' studies, burnt toast and colts' caps are successfully evocative of the enclosed emotions we never find again outside them. If *The Guinea Pig* were just a super-school story there would be small cause for complaint. But there is the socio-educational problem here to give an extra twist to the guinea pig's tail and the film never really grasps the problem at any deeper level than that of *The Bending of the Twig*.[12]

Whatever their political and social standpoints, the critics were in the main united about the excellence of the film as a film. In a controversial piece of casting, Richard Attenborough, then aged 24, was cast as Jack, but most critics found his performance convincing, and the *Sunday Times* thought it 'one of his best performances so far'.[13] But Robert Flemying earned almost equal praise for his performance as Nigel Lorraine; *Time and Tide* observed that he had 'the very rare gift of making an educated Englishman's understatement as natural and telling as it can be in real life'.[14]

The *Sunday Times* effectively summarized the message which this film carried for its time: 'The piece has two morals. The first, that the public schools should unbend a bit. . . . The second moral, that the Common Boy has something to learn even from the nobs.'[15] In other words, there was nothing wrong with the public schools or society at large that a little more tolerance and mutual understanding between the classes would not put right. So, although it was entering an area of potential controversy and, as the *Sunday Times* put it, infusing 'into its story quite a bit of social consciousness', at bottom the film was rejoicing, as the cinema industry in its heyday so often was, in the essential soundness of our institutions.

Notes

1 Raymond Durgnat, *A Mirror for England,* London, 1970, p. 206.
2 E. C. Mack, *Public Schools and British Opinion since 1860,* New York, 1941, p. 201—2.
3 *Evening News,* 21 October 1948.
4 *Daily Worker,* 24 October 1948.
5 *Reynolds' News,* 24 October 1948.
6 *The Times,* 25 October 1948.
7 *Daily Telegraph,* 25 October 1948.
8 *Graphic,* 24 October, 1948.
9 *Manchester Guardian,* 25 October 1948.
12 *Evening Standard,* 21 October 1948.
11 *Daily Express,* 24 October 1948.
12 *Time and Tide,* 30 November 1948. Desmond Coke's *The Bending of a Twig,* a mild satire of public school stories, was published in 1906.
13 *Sunday Times,* 24 October 1948.
14 *Time and Tide,* 30 November 1948.
15 *Sunday Times,* 24 October 1948.

8

Cul-de-Sac England

The Ladykillers

When Ealing Studios were sold to the BBC in 1955, in the very month that *The Ladykillers* was released, a plaque was installed which declared: 'Here during a quarter of a century were made many films projecting Britain and the British character.' It is reasonable to assume, then, that *The Ladykillers* was consciously projecting something distinctively and desirably British. To find out what this was we need to examine the film and to set it in the context both of Ealing films and of contemporary British society.

The projection of Britain was an aim dear to the heart of the studio's dynamic and imaginative production chief, Sir Michael Balcon. One of the greatest of all British film producers, he was responsible for a distinctive body of work which raised not only the quality but also the standing of British films both nationally and internationally. 'My ruling passion has always been the building up of a native [film] industry with its roots firmly planted in the soil of this country,' he wrote in his autobiography.[1] With the onset of World War II he became concerned as much with the social and political role of cinema as with its economic and cultural importance. Abroad, in particular, he saw 'British films, truthfully reflecting the British way of life' as the 'most powerful ambassador we have'. In 1945 he outlined a programmatic schedule for post-war film-making which demonstrates a high level of civic responsibility and patriotic pride:

> Never in any period of its history has the prestige of this country, in the eyes of the rest of the world, mattered so much as it does now. The political intervention of Britain in the affairs of liberated countries colours the attitude not only of Government towards Government, but of people towards people. And to these people German propaganda with the varying degrees of skill has presented the British in many guises: blood-soaked Imperialists, punch-drunk degenerates, betrayers of our Allies, grovelling servants of fabulous Jewish plutocrats — the list is familiar, and laugh at it as we may, let us not delude ourselves that its authors have been entirely ineffectual in their purpose. Clearly the need is great for a projection of the true Briton to the rest of the world. . . . The world, in short, must be presented with a complete picture of Britain . . . Britain as a leader in Social Reform in the defeat of social injustices and a champion of

civil liberties; Britain as a patron and parent of great writing, painting and music; Britain as a questing explorer, adventurer and trader; Britain as the home of great industry and craftsmanship; Britain as a mighty military power standing alone and undaunted against terrifying aggression. We do not set ourselves up as a master race if we remind the world that Britain has this background; we merely seek a place of recognition among nations who have too long been presented only with the debit side of our account.[2]

There is evidence of the partial implementation of this aim at Ealing in the series of films set in the Commonwealth (*The Overlanders, Where no Vultures Fly, West of Zanzibar*), in a Dickens adaptation (*Nicholas Nickleby*), in films dramatizing the work of the police (*The Blue Lamp*), hospitals (*The Feminine Touch*), the Church (*Lease of Life*) and the probation service (*I Believe in You*), in films dealing with problems posed by the post-war reintegration of returning prisoners of war (*The Captive Heart*) and reconciliation with Germany (*Frieda*). However, perhaps it is worth noting that two of the most spectacular of Ealing's films dealt with noble defeats (*Scott of the Antarctic* and *Dunkirk*), suggesting a view of Britain as perennially gallant loser rather than triumphant victor.[3]

But for most people Ealing's post-war output means the celebrated Ealing comedies. There is no doubt what view people have of the Ealing comedies and of the world they project. It is a world that is essentially quaint, cosy, whimsical and backward-looking; it venerates vintage steam trains (*The Titfield Thunderbolt*), old Clyde 'puffers' (*The Maggie*) and run-down seaside piers (*Barnacle Bill*). It is a world that enshrines what are seen as quintessentially English qualities: a stubborn individualism that is heroic to the point of eccentricity ('It's because we're English that we are sticking to our right to be Burgundians,' says a character in *Passport to Pimlico*); a hatred of authoritarianism and bureaucracy coupled with a belief in tolerance and consensus; a philosophy that can be summed up by the slogan 'Small is beautiful; old is good'. It is for all these reasons that the films have been so popular in the United States, whose philosophy is, of course, their antithesis ('Large is beautiful; new is best'), and have helped to shape American attitudes towards Britain. It is also the reason why non-Ealing comedies, admittedly made by ex-Ealing personnel, are often grouped together with the genuine article — films like *Genevieve* (vintage cars) and *The Smallest Show on Earth* (rundown fleapit cinema). That some of the Ealing comedies conform to this image cannot be denied. But it is too sweeping and incomplete a definition of the studio's entire comedy output, and it takes no account of, for instance, the wickedly elegant *Kind Hearts and Coronets,* which is by any reckoning one of the most distinguished Ealing comedies. Nevertheless, Balcon believed that 'the comedies reflected the country's mood, social condition and aspirations.'[4] To test this assertion we must examine the similarities and differences in the comedies and find out what the film-makers thought they were doing and how far audiences agreed with them.

In what circumstances were the films produced, and by whom? In the days when Basil Dean ran Ealing (1931—38), he had had painted on the studio wall the slogan 'The studio with the team spirit'. It was a slogan Balcon tried to live up to after he took over from Dean. There was a permanent staff at Ealing, and Balcon ran the studio by committee, with regular round-table meetings to discuss projects and current productions. If there was a consensus in favour of a particular production, Balcon would back it even if he had misgivings himself. It was Monja Danischewsky, publicity director at Ealing, who coined the much quoted phrase 'Mr Balcon's Academy for Young Gentlemen', and the role of a paternalist headmaster in which he was cast was one that Balcon goodhumouredly accepted in his autobiography.[5] 'Ealing', wrote Danischewsky, 'had the air of a family business, set on the village green of the queen of London suburbs.'[6] If Balcon was the head of this family, it also had a resident nanny in the Brazilian-born director Alberto Cavalcanti, who helped to integrate the documentarists recruited by Balcon into the mainstream of feature film-making.[7] It is perhaps small wonder, then, that Ealing films were often set in tightly knit little communities animated by a spirit of co-operation.

What was the attitude of this community of film-makers? Balcon recalled it in 1974 in an interview with John Ellis:

> We were middle-class people brought up with middle-class backgrounds and rather conventional educations. Though we were radical in our points of view, we did not want to tear down institutions. . . . We were people of the immediate post-war generation and we voted Labour for the first time after the war; this was our mild revolution. We had a great affection for British institutions: the comedies were done with affection. . . . Of course, we wanted to improve them, or, to use the cliché of today, to look for a more just society in the terms that we knew. The comedies were a mild protest, but not protests at anything more sinister than the regimentation of the time. I think we were going through a mildly euphoric period then: believing in ourselves as having some sense of, it sounds awful, national pride.[8]

The period spanned by the Ealing comedies, from *Hue and Cry* (1947) to *Barnacle Bill* (1957), covers the terms of office of both Labour and Conservative Governments. The Attlee Government (1945–51) implemented Labour's plans to create a 'brave new post-war world' with the introduction of the welfare state, the nationalization of key industries and the granting of independence to India. The Labour victory in 1945 had not been exactly a landslide in percentage voting terms: 47.8 per cent of those who actually voted cast their votes for Labour, but 39.8 per cent voted Conservative, and 20 per cent did not vote at all. In the 1950 election 46.1 per cent voted Labour, and 43.5 per cent voted Conservative. In the 1951 election 48.8 per cent voted Labour and 48 per cent voted Conservative, but, as a result of the inequitable British electoral system, the Conservatives won a majority of seats and formed the Government. They were to remain in power for the next thirteen years. It is clear that the country was more or less evenly divided between Labour and Conservative voters. But what matters more than precise voting figures is that great intangible the national mood, and popular culture is a valuable indicator of it. In 1945 there was a desire for change. Labour duly met this desire through the introduction of much needed reforms, but rationing, shortages and restrictions persisted. The generation which had won the war wanted the welfare state, but it also wanted fun and spending money. The Conservatives stayed in office for thirteen years by maintaining the welfare state but dismantling restrictions, ending rationing and promoting affluence. So having veered leftwards and sanctioned major social changes, the country veered rightwards, settling down to enjoy the fruits of peace and turning its back on further change.

The first half of the 1950s was an era of peace, prosperity and order.

The crime rate was falling. There was full employment and rising productivity. The greater availability of consumer durables blunted class antagonisms. The coronation of Queen Elizabeth II in 1953 was seen as ushering in a 'new Elizabethan age', as the Empire was transmuted into the Commonwealth, a worldwide brotherhood of nations, and as Britain continued to notch up memorable achievements: the Hunt expedition's conquest of Everest in 1953, Dr Roger Bannister's first four-minute mile in 1954 and, in 1956, Britain's tenure of all three speed records, air, land and sea. The cinema meanwhile was reliving the epic deeds of World War II with such popular recreations of British gallantry as *The Dam Busters* and *The Battle of the River Plate.*

Critics have seen the period from 1951 to 1958 as one of 'complacency and inertia', as 'extraordinarily dead', a 'doldrums era'.[9] It is a curious fact that the British film industry ran out of steam at about the same time as the Labour Government. Just as World War II had energized British society, so it had revitalized and stimulated the British film industry. This revival continued into the late 1940s, when British cinemas enjoyed their highest-ever attendances and British films their finest artistic flowering. David Lean, Carol Reed, Thorold Dickinson, Michael Powell and Emeric Pressburger, Frank Launder and Sidney Gilliat and the Boulting Brothers were producing their best work. Then in the early 1950s, just as Labour and the enthusiasm for change were fading, these careers either ended or entered periods of stagnation and decline. As Vernon Bogdanor and Robert Skidelsky wrote in 1970:

> Perhaps the period of Conservative rule will be looked back upon as the last period of quiet before the storm, rather like the Edwardian age which in some respects it resembles. In that case its tranquillity may well come to be valued more highly than its omissions.[10]

But tranquillity is rarely the matrix of cultural excitement. As Orson Welles observed in one of the British cinema's post-war masterpieces, *The Third Man*:

> In Italy for thirty years under the Borgias they had warfare, terror, murder, bloodshed — but they produced Michelangelo, Leonardo da Vinci and the Renaissance. In Switzerland, they had brotherly love, 500 years of democracy and peace, and what did that produce? . . . . the cuckoo clock.[11]

The Ealing comedies, then, were produced against a background first of post-war change and later of post-change complacency. What they have in common was isolated by Balcon.[12] They are not vehicles for established comedians. They are in the main original screen stories and not adaptations. They all deal with people in recognizable settings who are plunged into extraordinary situations. They are essentially wish-fulfilment fantasies. This is a view shared by Ealing writer T. E. B. Clarke, who calls them 'what if?' films: what if part of London declared itself independent (*Passport to Pimlico*)? What if a village tried to run its own railway line (*The Titfield Thunderbolt*)? What if someone discovered a foolproof way of smuggling gold out of the country (*The Lavender Hill Mob*)? All Clarke's comedies involve a fantastical premise realistically worked out.[13] There is a dream-like quality to many of the Ealing comedies: William Rose, in fact, dreamed the idea of *The Ladykillers* and *Passport to Pimlico* takes place during a midsummer heatwave which breaks at the end, giving the film something of the quality of a fever-dream.[14]

The important thing to remember about films like the Ealing comedies is that they are susceptible to different interpretations from different angles at the same time. Also the audience may respond to a film in an entirely different way from that which the film-makers expected. John Ellis offers a class interpretation of the films:

> Ealing's comedy does not deal with resentments or guilt so much as with aspirations and Utopian desires. It is not primarily concerned with satire, which can be identified with the playing out of class resentments. . . . Ealing's comedy style was new in that it dealt with the Utopian desires of the lower middle class rather than its resentments.[15]

He sees the comedies as dealing almost exclusively with the lower middle class, as affirmations of the idea of community solidarity denied by the facts of a competitive, status-conscious, middle-class life. This affirmation of community can take two forms, producing both 'progressive' comedies (*Passport to Pimlico, Whisky Galore*), which disrupt the social order to maintain the well-being of the community, and 'reactionary' comedies (*The Titfield Thunderbolt*), which spring from a respect for ideas swept aside by the forces of history. Ellis believes this concentration on the lower middle class to be a reflection of the background of the Ealing personnel and of the radicalization of their generation by the Depression. But it is a limited radicalism, constrained by Balcon's strict moral attitude and national pride. Ellis concludes that 'no real revolution can be advocated and no serious criticism of national institutions of power.'

The changes in the nature of the comedies he sees as a reflection of the changing preoccupations of the petty bourgeoisie. Thus the early Ealing comedies reflect their revolt against post-war restrictions (*Passport to Pimlico, Whisky Galore*) and their aspirations to higher status via class and wealth (*Kind Hearts and Coronets, Lavender Hill Mob*). But the later Ealing comedies, made during the emergence of the consumer society, attack the lack of social conscience reflected in the closing of railway lines (*The Titfield Thunderbolt*) and the rise of the American multinationals (*The Maggie*).[16]

The lower-middle-class bias of the characters in the Ealing comedies is undeniable, with a draper's assistant killing off a ducal family (*Kind Hearts and Coronets*), small shopkeepers declaring UDI in part of London (*Passport to Pimlico*), a bank clerk and a small manufacturer planning the perfect crime (*The Lavender Hill Mob*). But a purely class-based interpretation of the films is too restricted and too restrictive. It makes more sense to consider class as one dimension of a broader socio-political interpretation.

Given the admitted Labour allegiance of the Ealing film-makers, it is arguable that the early Ealing films (1947–51) constitute a programmatic attack on the evils that labour wished to eradicate: entrenched aristocratic privilege (*Kind Hearts and Coronets*), the power of money (*The Lavender Hill Mob*), monopoly capitalism (*The Man in the White Suit*) and colonialism (*Whisky Galore*). *Passport to Pimlico* (1949) is perhaps the arch-Labour film, pointing to the evils of a blanket removal of restrictions and seeking to reconcile the public to its lot.

Dedicated to the memory of rationing, the film is informed by a desire to return to the wartime spirit of unity and co-operation as the best means of facing and overcoming the problems of the post-war world. The first part of *Passport to Pimlico* shows greed and self-interest surfacing in society to submerge the community interest when Pimlico Borough Council throws out greengrocer Arthur Pemberton's scheme for turning a bomb site into a lido for local children and decides instead to sell it for profit (the evils of the unrestrained free market economy). When an unexploded bomb goes off, revealing a Burgundian treasure and a charter of independence, all restrictions and regulations are abolished, and black marketeers flood in. Naked self-interest rules. At this point an enemy appears to unite the people. In 1939 it was Hitler. In 1949 it is Whitehall, which seeks to bludgeon the inhabitants of Pimlico into surrender. Miramont Place, Pimlico, declares itself independent and fights the war again in miniature. In the end the bureaucrats are beaten by communal effort and self-sacrifice. A compromise is agreed by the two sides, and Pimlico re-enters the United Kingdom, to everyone's relief ('You never know when you're well off until you aren't'). The ration books are redistributed, for, as the message clearly states, rationing and restriction are better than the unrestrained growth of free enterprise.[17] The film captures exactly the mood of J. B. Priestley's 1945 novel *Three Men in New Suits,* in which a returning soldier says: 'Instead of guessing and grabbing, we plan. Instead of competing, we co-operate.'[18]

Balcon was giving a too literal and one-dimensional reading of the comedies when he wrote in his autobiography:

> In the immediate post-war years there was as yet no mood of cynicism; the bloodless revolution of 1945 had taken place but I think our first desire was to get rid of as many wartime restrictions as possible and get going. The country was tired of regulations and regimentation, and there was a mild anarchy in the air. In a sense our comedies were reflections of this mood . . . a safety valve for our more anti-social impulses. Who has not wanted to raid a bank (*The Lavender Hill Mob*) as an escape to a life of ease; commit mayhem on a fairly large scale to get rid of tiresome people in the way (*Kind Hearts and Coronets*); make the bureaucrat bite the dust (*Passport to Pimlico* and *The Titfield Thunderbolt*)?[19]

The key phrase here is 'a safety valve for our more anti-social impulses', for the role of the wish-fulfilment fantasy is not just to reflect but also to defuse discontent, producing heady images of the abolition of rationing (*Passport to Pimlico*), as much whisky as you want (*Whisky Galore*) and money unlimited (*The Lavender Hill Mob*) before returning the characters to earth and reality at the end. The fantasy projection purges the resentment and makes people happier with their lot. Significantly, the first Ealing comedy, *Hue and Cry*, premiered at the height of the appalling winter of 1946—47, lit up cinemas with its exuberance and humour and took people's minds off the fuel shortage.[20]

But times change, and if the early Ealing comedies can be seen as an affirmation of Labour's programme, the later ones can be seen as a retreat from it. Interestingly, the early Ealing comedies were more or less remade in the Conservative era (1951—58) and show interesting and instructive changes. *Whisky Galore* (1949), in which a Scottish island community fools and frustrates an English laird in order to keep a cargo of illicit whisky, is reworked as *The Maggie* (1954), in which the crew of an old Scottish 'puffer' fools and frustrates an American laird to keep its ship. *Passport to Pimlico* (1949), in which a small urban community defies the attempts of Whitehall to suppress its independence, becomes *The Titfield Thunderbolt* (1953), in which a small rural community defies the attempts of British Railways to close its branch line. *Kind Hearts and Coronets* (1949), in which a shop assistant wipes out all those who stand between him and a ducal title, becomes *The Ladykillers* (1955), in which a group of criminals fail to wipe out a little old lady and polish off each other instead. The changes in emphasis, locale and personnel are significant. In *Whisky Galore* an entire community undermines the English colonial power; in *The Maggie* the community has shrunk to a crew defending a vintage boat, and the enemy is an American businessman. A full-scale revolt has become the small-scale defence of a relic of the past, a Scottish analogue of *The Titfield Thunderbolt.* In *Passport to Pimlico* a committee of shopkeepers under a democratically elected leader fight the monolithic power of Whitehall over an inner-city area; in *The Titfield Thunderbolt* a semi-feudal rural community, led by its traditional leaders, the vicar and the squire, defends a rural branch line against British Railways, one of the great nationalized industries. In *Kind Hearts and Coronets*, a lower-middle-class murderer successfully eliminates the aristocracy; in *The Ladykillers* a little old middle-class lady successfully survives attempts by a criminal gang to eliminate her. The shift of values and sympathies in every case is clear.

But there is a third approach to the comedies which cuts across this socio-political interpretation — the personal and artistic, which relates to the intentions of individuals within the Ealing organization. On this level the films fall into two distinct groups, which bear no relation to chronology. The dominant strain, which is nostalgic and conformist, is that associated with the scripts of T. E. B. Clarke — *Passport to Pimlico* (1949), *The Lavender Hill Mob* (1951), *The Titfield Thunderbolt* (1953) and *Barnacle Bill* (1957). Significantly, he also wrote the Ealing tribute to the police, *The Blue Lamp* (1950) and is himself an ex-policeman. Clarke's films come closest to the popular image of Ealing and conform with Balcon's stated desire not to attack established institutions too forcefully.

The subversive strain is represented by Robert Hamer and Alexander Mackendrick. Both are significantly un-English figures. Hamer, French-educated and a Francophile, a man who set four of his films in France, brought Gallic sophistication, sensibility, elegance and wit to *Kind Hearts and Coronets* (1949), making it in that sense unique among the Ealing comedies. Mackendrick, American-born and Scottish-educated, made four Ealing comedies and deliberately subverted the essential cosiness of the Ealing archetype. He said in interview in 1968:

> The films that I made there were personal and I wrote the scripts of them with the scenarists. . . . Personally I was always very attracted by comedy, because I believe that it alone can say certain things. It allows you to do things that are too dangerous or that a certain audience cannot accept.[21]

Superficially, *Whisky Galore* is similar to *Passport to Pimlico*; in both a small community unites to defeat an intolerant outside force. But an extra dimension is added by the location (Scotland) and the object of the struggle (whisky). In *Whisky Galore* the enemy is Captain Waggett, a pukka British officer who is effectively administering the natives. But he is completely out of his depth, does not understand their mentality and is constantly outwitted. The Scottish community is devious and ruthless, unlike the open, honest, decent bourgeoisie of Pimlico. Its aim is not a community facility (a lido) but

The Ladykillers

In *The Ladykillers* Mrs Louisa Wilberforce (Katie Johnson) lives in a cosy corner of London, where her local police station is presided over by Jack Warner (1). Her house is shabby-genteel but basically sound, like the fabric of British society (2).

Her tranquil existence is threatened by the presence upstairs of a string quintet, in reality a gang of robbers (Herbert Lom, Danny Green, Cecil Parker, Alec Guinness and Peter Sellers) (3). She discovers their secret as they are about to leave and confronts Danny Green (4).

The gang are subjected to Mrs Wilberforce's tea-party (5). They decide to kill her but succeed only in annihilating each other, so Alec Guinness and Danny Green transport Cecil Parker to his last resting place (6).

instant gratification (whisky). Similarly, *The Man in the White Suit* (1951), one of the few British films to deal with British industry, focuses on the impossibility of reconciling capitalism and progress. It shows unions and management combining to suppress the invention of an indestructible fabric and demonstrates the inability of a sclerotic industrial structure to deal with discovery, change and innovation. If we can see *Whisky Galore,* and to a lesser extent perhaps *The Maggie* (1954), as anti-imperial parables and *The Man in the White Suit* as a critique of the capitalist industrial structure, *The Ladykillers* needs to be examined in the context of Mackendrick's work as a whole as well as in the context of Ealing and of Britain at large.

Scripted by the American William Rose, *The Ladykillers* was directed by Mackendrick shortly before he departed for the United States to direct an acid study of power and corruption in the intense and inbred world of New York press agents and gossip columnists, *The Sweet Smell of Success* (1956). It is hard, in the light of Mackendrick's career, to see *The Ladykillers* as anything other than an irreverent farewell to England — that England of the Conservative mid-1950s that has been characterized by Arthur Marwick as suffering from 'complacency, parochialism, lack of serious, structural change'[22] — and to Ealing, the well-run 'Academy for Young Gentlemen' with its resident nanny. It is a sardonic recognition of the impossibility of change in either institution. But at the same time it meets perfectly the criteria for inclusion within the dominant Ealing strain that preferred the small and the old, a strain which the public identified as the Ealing world. Whether you take the film as a critique or as a celebration of that ethos, however, depends entirely on your point of view.

One thing which can be agreed, though, is that *The Ladykillers* is the last of the great Ealing comedies. Its plot is simply outlined. Mrs Louisa Wilberforce, a widow living alone in a Victorian house in a cul-de-sac near St Pancras Station, rents her upstairs room to a mysterious 'Professor Marcus', who meets with four oddly assorted friends to play chamber music. The musical quintet is, in fact, a cover to their plans to commit a security van robbery at King's Cross Station. They carry out the robbery with Mrs Wilberforce's unwitting help, but as they are about to leave, she discovers the truth. They plot to kill her but cannot bring themselves to do it and succeed only in eliminating each other. The bodies are dumped on to passing coal trucks. Finally only the Professor is left, and then he is struck down by a signal and also ends up in a coal truck. Mrs Wilberforce tries to turn in the money at the police station, but the police, believing it to be a tall story, tell her to keep the money. She trots happily home.

Artistically the film is wholly satisfying. It has all the ritual formality of a time-honoured ceremony and the internal logic of a remembered dream, with the reiterated drawing of straws for the choice of killer, the succession of deaths, the disposal of the bodies over the railway bridge and their transport thither in a wheelbarrow. The murders themselves are all done off-screen so as not to allow real violence to intrude on the cumulative atmosphere of fantasy. The mood is reinforced by the music. Mrs Wilberforce's departure for the police station at the outset of the film is accompanied by a tinkling musical box rendition of 'The Last Rose of Summer'. The supposed string quintet practises the Boccherini minuet, nostalgic, elegant and gentle, which thereafter accompanies Mrs Wilberforce. A sombre hymn-like tune accompanies the disposal of the bodies.

Within the formal framework of action, music and staging the humour derives both from parody of the horror film (the exaggerated Gothic opening when Professor Marcus, accompanied by shadows, thunder and lightning, first arrives at the house) and of the gangster film (the meticulous planning of the robbery, whose execution is jeopardized by Mrs Wilberforce) and from incongruity. Nothing could be more incongruous than the idea of a criminal gang posing as a string quintet. The juxtaposition of their illegal activities and the genteel existence of Mrs Wilberforce, who is constantly interrupting their planning with offers of cups of tea, requests for assistance to recapture her parrot and insistence that they meet her friends, extracts the maximum humour from the situation.

The cast is uniformly excellent, revealing the strength of the corps of British character actors. Katie Johnson, a long-established Ealing small-part player, could not be bettered as the little old lady. Alec Guinness, complete with straggly hair, buck teeth, black-rimmed eyes, long scarf and fluttering tiptoe movements is the very image of the demented intellectual. His gang are superbly characterized by Cecil Parker as the raffish bogus major, Herbert Lom as the grim, gun-toting, lady-hating old gangster Louis, Peter Sellers as the chirpy Cockney teddy-boy Harry and Danny Green as the dumb ox 'One-Round', a lumpen proletarian moron ('Old Queen who?').

The image of England which the film projects is undeniably parochial, backward-looking and complacent. The setting is a small, enclosed urban community in the shadow of St Pancras Station, that symbol of Victorian exuberance and energy. Everyone knows everyone else. As Mrs Wilberforce proceeds to the police station, she greets all the shopkeepers by name. The police station itself is presided over by Jack Warner, already familiar as the benignly paternalist police officer, having played PC George Dixon in *The Blue Lamp* and later immortalizing him in the subsequent long-running television series.

Mrs Wilberforce herself is the spirit of England. She is the living embodiment of the Victorian age, all lavender and old lace and faded gentility. She is sweet, polite, prim, bourgeois, immaculate and patriotic, a perfectly preserved period piece. She is the widow of a Merchant Navy captain who went down with his ship in the China Seas twenty-nine years ago, having first put his parrots in a lifeboat (the English as a nation of pet lovers).

Her house, at the end of a cul-de-sac, is England, stuffed with Victorian bric-à-brac and suffering from wartime subsidence. Mrs Wilberforce lives there with her memories of the past, recalling her twenty-first birthday in Pangbourne in 1901 when news of the Old Queen's death came through, naming her parrots 'General Gordon' and 'Admiral Beatty' and taking tea with her friends, similarly well preserved old ladies. But she is quite without fear. She shows her steel and causes a street riot when she intervenes to stop a barrow boy from ill-treating a horse, laying into the man with her umbrella. When she discovers the crime, she takes charge like a stern nanny, telling the criminals, who shuffle about like sheepish naughty boys caught out in a prank, 'Try to behave like gentlemen for once.' She insists they join her friends for tea rather than create an embarrassing disturbance. Subsequently Marcus tries to persuade her that no one wants the money back and that they stole it only to help unfortunate dependants. However, Mrs Wilberforce's morality is inflexible. She determines to go to the police even if they send her to prison as an accomplice. She cows them so completely that they wipe each other out rather than kill her and she ends up with the money.

Charles Barr has proposed a fascinating reading of the film:

> The gang are the post-war Labour Government; taking over 'the House', they gratify the Conservative incumbent by their civilized behaviour (that nice music) and decide to use at least the façade of respectability for their radical programme of redistributing wealth (humouring Mrs Wilberforce and using her as a front). Their success is undermined by two factors interacting: their own internecine quarrels, and the startling, paralysing charisma of the 'natural' governing class, which effortlessly takes over from them again in time to exploit their gains (like the Conservatives taking over power in 1951, just as the austerity years came to an end). The gang are a social mix like Labour's — a mixture of academic (Alec Guinness), ex-officer (Cecil Parker), manual worker (Danny Green), naive youth (Peter Sellers) and hard-liner (Herbert Lom).[23]

Barr is needlessly diffident about advancing such a detailed political reading of the film. For it makes sense if it is viewed in the context not just of what had happened since 1945 but also of what was about to happen to British society. The years 1956—58 were to represent a cultural watershed, energizing society with a cultural revolt which was to lead in due course to political change and to the end of the long period of Conservative rule. These years saw on the political front the Suez débâcle and the Notting Hill race riots, symptoms of Britain's emergence into a post-imperial, post-Victorian world. But the period also saw the arrival of rock music from the United States, the appearance of the 'angry young men' of literature and the theatre and the first steps towards the development of the distinctive youth culture that was to flower in the 1960s and took the form of protest against established canons of taste, decency and respectability. It was spearheaded by intellectuals and upper-middle-class opinion leaders and rapidly gained a large young working-class following, which in time threw up its own leaders.

Looked at against this background, the gang in *The Ladykillers* represents not only the elements which made up the post-war Labour Party but also those elements in 1950s society that constituted the forces of dissidence around which the youth culture was to coalesce: intellectuals (Guinness), middle-class renegades (Parker), the young (Sellers), the working classes (Green) and criminals (Lom). Just as the Barr interpretation suggests that the gang as Labour Party is contained and suppressed, so the gang as social dissidence is cowed into submission and disposed of. Mrs Wilberforce gets the money and even gives a fiver to the pavement artist whose most prominent creation is a portrait of Churchill. But 1955 is almost the last year in which these dissident elements can be contained, for they are about to burst forth in all directions, and also to penetrate the film industry in the form of the so-called British 'new wave' cinema, which begins with *Room at the Top* (1959).

In locating the ideological position of a film analysing what is not there is just as important as analysing what is there. *The Ladykillers* is marked by a total absence of sexuality and a relative absence of youth. It is, on the contrary, a paean to old age. The absence of sexuality is not in itself remarkable, in that it was usually suppressed in Ealing films, and indeed in British films in general, until the late 1950s. Robert Hamer's films *It Always Rains on Sunday* and *Kind Hearts and Coronets* are notable exceptions within both Ealing and British cinema. The suppression of sexuality is a reflection of the Puritanism of British life. But its counterpart is the penchant which the British have for brisk, no-nonsense old ladies, of whom the archetype is the 'Old Queen' herself and other more recent examples are Dame Margaret Rutherford, Lady Violet Bonham-Carter and Mrs Barbara Woodhouse. The cult of the nanny and the concept of the nanny society is an extension of this. It is perfectly encapsulated in *The Ladykillers*, in which the little old lady reigns supreme, evoking George Orwell's dictum on England: 'It resembles a family, a rather stuffy Victorian family. . . . It is a family in which the young are generally thwarted and most of the power is in the hands of irresponsible uncles and bedridden aunts.'[24]

Youth is represented by Peter Sellers's Harry, who is part of the gang. He, like contemporary youth itself, is emasculated and neutralized in one of the film's key scenes. The gangsters are forced to take part in the old ladies' tea-party. They stand about helplessly, cups of tea and plates of cake in their hands, as they are swamped by the old ladies, and Professor Marcus glumly hammers out on the pianola 'Silver Threads among the Gold'. Similarly, at the start of the film, as Mrs Wilberforce heads for the police station, she pauses to smile at a baby in a pram. Instead of cooing, the baby screams. It is the nascent revolt of extreme youth against a society dominated by extreme old age. Significantly, the cultural revolt of the late 1950s was to be characterized by those elements of sexuality and youth that are suppressed here.

The absence of youth from *The Ladykillers* is particularly striking in view of the close association of Mackendrick with children in films (*Mandy, The Maggie, Sammy Going South, A High Wind in Jamaica*) that express a child's view of the world. In the context of Ealing it is perhaps also significant that while the first great Ealing comedy, *Hue and Cry,* centred on a gang of youngsters foiling a crime ring, the last great Ealing comedy features an old lady foiling a criminal gang.

It is instructive to compare *The Ladykillers* with the American classic black comedy *Arsenic and Old Lace,* memorably filmed by Frank Capra in 1941. It may even have been a memory of this that inspired William Rose, for in a sense *The Ladykillers* is *Arsenic and Old Lace* turned upside-down. In *Arsenic and Old Lace* it is the inhabitants of a venerable nineteenth-century house in Brooklyn, the Brewster family, whose ancestors came over on the *Mayflower*, who are the murderers. Two dear sweet little old ladies, Aunt Abby and Aunt Martha, poison lonely old men because they are sorry for them. The bodies are buried in the cellar by their nephew, who thinks he is Theodore Roosevelt and is digging the Panama Canal beneath the house. They are joined by Cousin Jonathan, a homicidal maniac who looks like Boris Karloff. Eventually the whole family is carted off to an asylum, leaving a sensible, sane, modern young couple (Cary Grant and Priscilla Lane) in charge. The values, then are completely reversed. In America, it is age, tradition and the past that are mad and irrelevant; in Britain they are venerated and triumphant.

The Ladykillers was both a box-office and critical success, winning the British Film Academy award for best screenplay (William Rose) and best actress (Katie Johnson) for 1955. But there is no evidence to suggest that the critics who reviewed it saw it as a critique of England. The reviews concentrated on the acting, which was universally praised, and on the difficulty of making a comedy about murder. Most critics agreed that *The Ladykillers* had succeeded in avoiding the pitfalls triumphantly.] The *Sunday Times* thought it 'captivating'; the *Evening Standard*, 'the most stylish, inventive and funniest British comedy of the year'; the *Daily Telegraph*, 'one of the funniest comedies of the year'; the *Daily Herald*, 'wonderfully funny'; the *Daily Worker*, 'accomplished and polished'.[25] *Tribune* said, 'It made me laugh more frequently and more heartily than any this year', and the *Daily Mirror* said it had 'lots of laughs with a thrill or two'.[26] Rather more substantial comment came from the *Manchester Guardian*, which thought it 'a thoroughly typical Ealing work — except that it is even better than most', and C. A. Lejeune in the *Observer* called it 'an entertaining piece of harmless nonsense'.[27] This suggests that the film was seen as being squarely in the mainstream, whimsical Ealing tradition.[If the cinema-going public reacted in the same way, it seems likely that it took what Mackendrick intended as a satire on the Ealing view of England as a celebration of that view. They identified, in other words, with the old lady and not with the frustrated and exasperated gang who are her victims.] Mrs Wilberforce's world is an apt metaphor for mid-1950s England, a cul-de-sac slumbering peacefully but shortly to be violently awakened.

Notes

1   Michael Balcon, *A Lifetime of Films,* London, 1969, p. 48.
2   *Kinematograph Weeky,* 11, January 1945, p. 163.
3   The best analysis of Ealing Studios and its output is to be found in Charles Barr, *Ealing Studios,* London, 1977.
4   Balcon, *A Lifetime of Films,* p. 158.
5   Monja Danischewsky, *White Russian — Red Face,* London, 1966, p. 127; Balcon, *A Lifetime of Films,* p. 138.
6   Danischewsky, *White Russian — Red Face,* p. 127.
7   ibid., p. 134.
8   John Ellis, 'Made in Ealing', *Screen,* 16, Spring 1975, p. 119.
9   Vernon Bogdanor and Robert Skidelsky (eds.), *The Age of Affluence 1951—64,* London, 1970, p. 12; Charles Barr, 'Projecting Britain and the British Character', *Screen,* 15, Spring 1974, p. 116; Raymond Durgnat, *A Mirror for England,* London 1970, p. 140.
10   Bogdanor and Skidelsky, *The Age of Affluence,* p. 7.
11   John Russell Taylor (ed.), *Masterworks of the British Cinema,* London, 1974, p. 192.
12   Balcon, *A Lifetime of Films,* p. 158.
13   T. E. B. Clarke, *This is Where I Came In,* London, 1974, pp. 159—60.
14   Balcon, *A Lifetime of Films,* p. 167.
15   Ellis, 'Made in Ealing', p. 113.
16   ibid., pp. 113—27.
17   Jeffrey Richards, 'Passport to Pimlico', *The Movie,* 28, 1980, pp. 552—3.
18   Quoted by Arthur Marwick, *Britain in the Century of Total War,* London, 1974, p. 158.
19   Balcon, *A Lifetime of Films,* p. 159.
20   Clarke, *This is Where I Came In,* p. 157.
21   *Positif,* 92, February 1968, p. 41.
22   Arthur Marwick, *British Society since 1945,* Harmondsworth, 1982, p. 111.
23   Barr, *Ealing Studios,* pp. 171—2.

24 George Orwell, *Collected Essays, Journalism and Letters,* vol. 2, Harmondsworth, 1971, p. 88.

25 *Sunday Times,* 11 December 1955; *Daily Telegraph,* 10 December 1955; *Daily Herald,* 9 December 1955; *Daily Worker,* 10 December 1955.

26 *Tribune,* 23 December 1955; *Daily Mirror,* 9 December 1955.

27 *Manchester Guardian,* 10 December 1955; *Observer,* 11 December 1955.

9

Vicious Circles

I'm All Right Jack

Films about industrial relations were few and far between in the mainstream British cinema from the 1930s to the 1950s. It was a vexed and contentious issue, for a start, and rarely free of controversy. As a result, producers and scriptwriters alike were prompted to steer clear of the matter. Doubtless, they anyway saw little in the subject to recommend it as a viable and commercial proposition. Those films that did touch upon the question, however, have inevitably turned out to be of some interest.

In the 1930s, of course, the 'relations of Capital and Labour' was one of those taboo subjects which greatly exercised the collective mind of the British Board of Film Censors. T. P. O'Connor, the second President of the BBFC, had seen fit to include it as a matter for careful consideration on his list of basic censorship rules, which was compiled in 1917.[1] And from the early 1930s, when the BBFC sought to initiate the pre-production scrutiny of synopses, scenarios and scripts, a good deal of attention was given to the depiction of industrial relations. This meant, quite simply, that when a story was deemed likely to transgress the bounds laid down by the BBFC or to emphasize elements which the BBFC might not wish to see emphasized it was very quickly ruled out of court and declared 'not suitable for production'. In the case, for instance, of a synopsis which was submitted in 1932 under the title *Tidal Waters* and which purported to deal with Thames dockland life and a watermen's strike, the BBFC readers were clearly worried that the film might be in danger of stressing the 'differences between capital and labour which led to the strike' and that the strike might be construed as the 'prominent feature of the story'. One of their number felt compelled to remark:

> Our attitude to the subject has always been very definite. Strikes or labour unrest, where the scene is laid in England, have never been shown in any detail. It is impossible to show such strikes without taking a definite side either with or against the strikers and this would at once range the film as political propaganda of a type that we have always held to be unsuitable for production in this country.[2]

But the BBFC did not worry for long; its anxiety was soon assuaged. The film company proved co-operative and duly obliged by dropping the project without a murmur.

For the most part the BBFC had nothing to fear from the makers of feature films during the 1930s. They were naturally inclined, as we have seen, to favour images of national harmony and relative tranquillity on all fronts, including the industrial, whenever they chose to mention it. Strikes were overcome, as in Michael Powell's 1934 film of *Red Ensign*, by the simple expedient of the management's addressing the workers with stirring calls to 'pull together' (thereby winning an approving nod from the BBFC and the comment: 'Quite a good story with a strong patriotic note').[3] When depression threatened, as it did the cotton industry in Basil Dean's 1934 production of *Sing As We Go* (a film which, incidentally, did not come before the BBFC for pre-production scrutiny), it threatened both management and workers alike, and it neither soured nor broke their close relationship. Besides, Gracie Fields, who fancied the boss's son anyway, was there to keep everybody happy with a joyful and optimistic song as she led the people out of work, into unemployment and then back to work again when the times got better, as they invariably did.[4]

The workers, for their part, were a pretty resilient lot. In the case of John Baxter's *The Navvy* (retitled *A Real Bloke* on its 1935 release), the answer to being thrown on the dole after twenty-three years of continuous employment was not to 'whine and whimper' but to 'keep his chin up bravely'.[5] New employment was eventually found for men of such calibre and character. Indeed, even George Formby was lucky enough to find another job, despite the fact that he was initially taken 'off the dole', in the 1935 film of that name, because he displayed few redeeming characteristics and showed little inclination to work at all. In reply, for example, to the accusation levelled by the manager of his employment exchange that he was 'afraid of work', George cheekily retorted, 'Me, afraid of work? I could sleep beside it'; on being told that he has 'got out of the way of work', he replied, 'Well, I've managed it up to now, but it's been a struggle'; and on being asked what his trade was, George responded by saying, 'Selling calendars every leap year.'

By the end of the 1930s these stereotypes and caricatures, both comic and heroic, were well and truly established. The worker, the workplace and labour—management relations had some meaning in the British cinema, albeit on a limited and carefully delineated scale of representation. World War II was to extend that scale and to expand the British cinema's horizons considerably. It is a commonplace that the 'People's War', in which the civilian population was sometimes as much in the front line as were the fighting troops, produced the conditions that enabled the British cinema to flourish, not least in the creative sense; 'ironically, despite all the paraphernalia of official wartime censorship, British film-makers were now able to approach topics which they would have been warned off in the thirties.'[6] And that latitude extended also to the depiction of industrial relations — not surprisingly, since during the war, as two commentators have put it, 'trade unions and employers' associations amalgamated with the Government into what was virtually a "corporate state".'[7]

Of course, the successful prosecution of the war effort was paramount. It overrode the film-makers' other considerations and largely dictated where their priorities would lie. Yet among that admittedly small corpus of films which included the likes of *Love on the Dole* (1941), *Hard Steel* (1942), *The Shipbuilders* (1943) and *Millions Like Us* (1943) it is possible to discern signs of a fresh and more open approach to matters certainly of social and also, on occasion, of industrial interest. Some of these films were inclined to look backwards in time and were, ostensibly, retrospective in their concerns, but their pertinence to Britain in the 1940s was amply demonstrated. *Love on the Dole,* for instance, was set firmly in the 1930s and dealt mainly with a problem which had been overcome, for the most part, with the advent of war and nearly full employment, but for all that it closed with an extract from a speech by A. V. Alexander, Labour MP and a member of the wartime Government, which stated that: 'Our working men and women have responded magnificently to any and every call made upon them. Their reward must be a new Britain. Never again must the unemployed become the forgotten men of peace.'[8]

The story of *The Shipbuilders* also began in the 1930s, though it continued into the first years of the war. As Arthur Marwick has suggested: 'The film quite deliberately shows prosperity brought back to the Glasgow shipyards by conscious Government action in wartime: there is a very definite message on behalf of interventionist, Keynesian, economic policies, as well, of course, as one of the essential unity and involvement of everyone in the all-consuming war effort.'[9]

Unity was the keynote of *Millions Like Us,* with its tale of girls from all social groups coming to live together in happy harmony, in the main, as a result of their work experiences in a munitions factory. And the needs of the war effort doubtless accounted for the injection of a speech as the climax of *Hard Steel,* yet another film to start its plot in the 1930s and finish after the onset of war, in which the protagonist successfully inspires some steelworkers to 'co-operate, that's the word'. 'Can you and me co-operate so the mills can give of their best?' he asks the men. Initially they prove reluctant, since they have grown to dislike his way of running things, but he slowly wins them round, and to their increasing applause he concludes: 'We know this war is a war of steel, and we're going to give the old country the steel she needs, and more steel, and more, and more. . . .'

The propagandist intentions of both films were obvious and, as ever, the issues to which they alluded were greatly personalized. But at the same time they revealed other distinct features. In the case of the former film there was a clear, and by no means unsuccessful, attempt to paint a more faithful picture of life on the factory front, and in the latter instance there was more than a passing hint of the propensity of the industrial workforce, particularly marked during the period of the war, to resort to quick unofficial strikes to achieve its ends. Finally, in common with the other wartime films in the same mould, there was more detailed characterization, especially in the portrayal of the working-class figures.

But, surprisingly, although labour emerged from the war with its status much enhanced and also, of course, with a stronger bargaining power than ever before, the film-makers quickly turned their backs on the subject in the immediate post-war years. Michael Balcon spoke in 1945 of the need 'for a projection of the true Briton to the rest of the world' and included 'Britain as the home of great industry and craftsmanship' among his list of topics to be covered.[10] But little of that was actually shown in British films of the post-war era. And indeed it was not until the early 1950s that a handful of film-makers looked once again to industrial themes for their inspiration, and then with ominous consequences.

In 1950, for example, Bernard Miles's film *Chance of a Lifetime* was released. It was, in truth, rather a benign and pleasant piece, which told of the owner and managing director of a small works manufacturing agricultural machinery, who has trouble with his workers and, in a fit of pique, relinquishes the running of the place to their control. The men take over and achieve some success but find that they cannot really function properly without the skill and expertise of their old boss. He is invited back; he returns; there is a new found and closer understanding all round; and the film ends 'a little tritely', as *The Times* critic put it, 'with the conclusion that, if the management needs the men, the men need the management'.[11]

'There is nothing very revolutionary in all this,' *The Times* went on to say, and indeed there wasn't. Milton Shulman maintained that the film 'dared to discuss a vital and important contemporary problem — worker and management relations',[12] but if it was daring, it was daring in a benevolent and paternalistic fashion. The film was imbued with the spirit of consensus, and the most it advocated was that some attention be paid to the idea of worker participation in management, a matter about which by 1950 even the Trades Union Congress was increasingly lukewarm, except in the case of the nationalized industries.

Yet the film caused a furore and in fact was only assured a release as a result of direct intervention by the President of the Board of Trade, Harold Wilson. None of the major cinema circuits wished to show the film, claiming it was 'propaganda' and not 'entertainment'. And the same feelings were amplified by Ministry of Labour officials, who reportedly called it 'propaganda for communism and workers' control in industry'.[13] Wilson disagreed with the views expressed by the Minister of Labour, George Isaacs, about the film, and the Cabinet was persuaded to let him use his powers to 'direct' one of the three circuits to show the film. It was released finally on the Odeon circuit but flopped badly.

The film was not 'communist propaganda', of course, though the charge stuck to the film as it did the rounds of the cinemas, but it was unfortunate enough to come into the reckoning at a time when there was a good deal of talk about 'communist propaganda' and 'communist-fomented' industrial unrest in the country, not to mention the cold war tension abroad. The Labour Government, and Ernest Bevin in particular, were suspicious that industrial strikes and disputes were being caused by political extremists from the moment they came to power. Increasingly these suspicions fastened upon 'communist subversion' until, in the last year of office, they became an obsession. Scotland Yard repeatedly urged that it could find no evidence of any 'communist influence',[14] but despite such assurances the fear of 'reds under the beds' and the 'communist threat' was felt as powerfully in government circles as it was elsewhere.

Not surprisingly, it was also manifested in the cinema. Roy Boulting's 1951 film *High Treason* has, for example, been described as the 'paranoid counterpart' to *Chance of a Lifetime* for its allusions to 'Communist Party schemes to sabotage British industry'.[15] But in fairness its paranoia, such as it was, was no more acute, as we now know, than that being shown by no less a body that the Government at the very time the film was being made. Close analysis of Roy Boulting's film reveals, furthermore, that while it makes reference to the perpetration of dockland espionage by subversive workers, nevertheless the communist cell (not actually identified as such, but the inference is obvious) masterminding the operation clearly feels that it cannot depend upon 'effective strike action' and the like to achieve its ultimate objective. The motley band of disenchanted workers, idealistic intellectuals and renegade civil servants are compelled finally, once they have donned their duffle coats, to resort to physical violence and the attempted take-over of several key power stations throughout the country as the only means to 'paralyse' British industry.

The fault did not always lie then with the worker, communist or otherwise, and indeed it is clear from another film released in the same year (1951), Alexander Mackendrick's *The Man in the White Suit*, that management was capable of deeds pretty near as dark as anything done by the workers or their representatives. When the dedicated young scientist Sidney Stratton (Alec Guinness) produces a fabric that repels dirt and will seemingly never wear out, his idea is tardily but enthusiastically taken up by the mill-owning Birnley (Cecil Parker), who sees a golden opportunity to scoop the market. But other implications soon loom large. Sidney 'falls victim to the restrictive practices of the place' and, as Charles Barr goes on to put it in his excellent critique of the film:

> Everlasting suits mean fewer new ones to be bought and less work for the factories. (A topical parallel: the manufacturers' cartel against long-life light bulbs, on which the Monopolies Commission reported in 1951, the year of the film's release.) The owners hastily get together, sort Birnley out and combine to suppress the invention.[16]

The film's gibes at myopic management, and its comments upon the perils of monopoly capitalism are evident. But if management bears the brunt of the criticism for instigating the moves towards pernicious restraint, the unions are by no means forgotten or exempt from criticism. They are brought in by the owners to help suppress the invention and give their support. 'Capital and labour are hand in hand in this' is the message which emanates from their meeting together later in the story. Yet it is also obvious from the same scene that if these two generally opposing sides are in agreement on this one issue, they still view each other with suspicion, if not outright contempt.

In all, the film conjured up a bleak vision of industry and industrial relations: capital and labour were out to do the country down. But it was a vision that some felt to be not without substance in a period that was distinguished by the 'gathering cold war which affected British industrial relations, with a snobbish and often uninformed management entrenched on one side, with an immobile, unambitious workforce, deeply attached to its long traditions, on the other'.[17] And it was a vision, furthermore, that had gained considerable credence by the time that the Boulting Brothers' *I'm All Right Jack* came out in 1959.

With a series of films beginning in 1956, the Boultings had seemingly changed tack and had started, less earnestly, to take every opportunity to poke fun at various facets of the British way of life and the nation's institutions. Their first film of the bunch, *Private's Progress,* which utilized what was to become a regular band of actors and sparked off a fruitful relationship with writer Alan Hackney,[18] was actually placed in a wartime army setting. But it was as much an assessment of 'national service drudgeries and idiocies' as anything else,[19] and the Army duly took it as an 'insult'.[20] Thereafter the Boultings turned their attention to the law, with

Brothers In Law (1957), to the universities, with *Lucky Jim* (also in 1957), and to the sillier side of diplomacy, the Foreign Office and colonialism in *Carlton-Browne of the FO* (1959).

The films met with varying degrees of success. *Lucky Jim*, for instance, was a harmless farce. It displayed none of the trenchant wit that is evident in the original novel by Kingsley Amis and it was ultimately little different from the many comedies that seemed to pour out of the British cinema during the 1950s. But the Boultings' other films were distinguished by a marked, if light, satirical touch. And this rich satirical vein was most in evidence when the Boultings set out to tackle *I'm All Right Jack* early in 1959.

I'm All Right Jack was the industrial relations film *par excellence*. It accurately charted the deteriorating state of the 'industrial cold war', to borrow Arthur Marwick's phrase, and reflected the widening gulf between management and the workforce. This gulf had resulted in a perceptible increase in the number of strikes, strikers and working days lost from the mid-1950s onwards. In the ten years before 1955, for instance, there was an annual average of 1,791 strikes, involving 545,000 workers and resulting in 2,073,000 days lost. In the ten years after 1955 there an annual average of 2,521 strikes, involving 1,116,000 workers and resulting in 3,889,000 days lost.[21] But if the growth in the number of strikes signalled the ever-widening gulf between management and workers, there were also signs, in the kind of strikes that ensued, of a gulf developing between trade union leaders and their rank-and-file members. The enhanced status of the unions after the war, their increased bargaining power and full employment all served to stimulate a rise in trade union membership throughout the 1950s. But even during the war itself some workers 'came to feel that their union leaders were no longer fully representing the interests of the rank and file' and 'the estrangement of union leaders from their members stimulated a militant attitude among shop stewards, who frequently arrogated the role of representing labour opinion which union officials seemed to have relinquished.'[22] These rank-and-file frustrations, and the concomitant growth in militancy among shop stewards, were exacerbated in the post-war period[23] and perhaps help to explain why so many of the strikes that ensued during the 1950s were unofficial and not sanctioned by the appropriate union. But whatever the depth of the division between the trade union leadership and the rank-and-file membership by that time, the plain fact of the matter was that the power and prestige of shop stewards had undoubtedly increased in the workplace. And the Boulting Brothers' film of *I'm All Right Jack* had a lot to say on that matter as well.

The film starts with a brief pre-credit sequence which looks back to VE Day in 1945 and sets the irreverent and jocular tone that will dominate throughout. Church bells are ringing; guns are firing; and people are heard celebrating in the streets as Ern, the servant in a London men's club, awakens old Sir John (Peter Sellers) from his slumber to inform him that the war is over. 'That's another one we've come through, Ern,' boasts Sir John. 'That's right, they can't finish us off, can they?' asserts Ern. But Sir John immediately senses the wind of change and orders Ern to close the window: 'It's become damned chilly in here.' And a narrator interjects to tell us: 'Look hard, for this is the last we shall see of Sir John.' He is a 'solid block in the edifice of what seemed to be an ordered and stable society'. And given his impeccable credentials, who would doubt it? He is, after all, a Justice of the

Peace, Chairman of the Wroughton Unionist Association, Vice President of his local British Legion, Honorary Chairman of the Regional Board for the Adjustment of Distressed Gentle Women and sleeping partner in that vast financial complex, the City and Threadneedle Trust. But now he is on his way out, for with victory has come a 'new age' and with that new age a 'new spirit'.

We are treated to a glimpse of what that 'new spirit' entails with a shot of a soldier (Victor Maddern, later seen as a factory workman, Knowles) who is celebrating while perched on top of a lamp-post, and whose two-fingered 'Victory' sign is instantly reversed into its vulgar opposite. Whereupon the film breaks into a similarly jokey credits sequence to the accompaniment of some comic cartoons and a bouncy raucous title song from Al Saxon (so typical of British pop music from the era when the film was made),[24] the first verse of which states:

> I'm all right Jack, I'm okay, that is the message for today
> So, count up your lolly, feather your nest,
> Let someone else worry, boy, I couldn't care less.
> You scratch my back, I'll do the same for you, Jack,
> That's the message for today.

The scene is set, then; we are into the 1950s, and the film proper begins.

'Times have changed,' Stanley Windrush (Ian Carmichael) tells his aged father (Miles Malleson), who has retired to a nudist camp. 'In industry nowadays they're crying out for people like me.' He is a 'university man' and his father would prefer to see him going into one of the learned professions, the Church or the Army. The old man cannot see why anybody 'brought up as a gentleman' should 'choose to go into industry'. But Stanley persists. 'Of course, I shall be an executive,' he insists, and sets out for an interview with the Combined Universities Appointments Board, where he is told that all he needs is 'confidence, intelligence, and enthusiasm. . . . Above all, an air of confidence'.

Stanley's two forays as a management trainee do not work out quite as expected, however, and he is ultimately rejected by Detto, the detergent manufacturers and the makers of Num-Yum bars (both heavily lampooned by the Boultings with the aid of mock advertising jingles, outrageous slogans and all). He is clearly incompetent, and industry can do well enough without him. The Appointments Board, after finding him another nine such posts, all of which prove equally fruitless, despairs of him.

While staying with his amiable and aristocratic Great Aunt Dolly (Margaret Rutherford), Stanley is finally offered a job in industry by his Uncle Bertram (Dennis Price), who is a director of an engineering firm, Missiles Ltd, that has just landed a big armaments contract. He is cajoled into taking it with the help of a mutual friend, Sidney de Vere Cox (Richard Attenborough). Aunt Dolly does not doubt that Stanley will just 'supervise': 'After all, you were at Oxford.' Sidney suggests, however, that he join 'on the other side' and become a worker, 'unskilled, of course'. Aunt Dolly is aghast at the suggestion that a nephew of hers should 'throw in his lot with the working classes'. But Sidney proceeds to spell out the potential advantages to Stanley and Lady Dorothy alike. Stanley, for instance, says that he might expect to start with £8 a week if he went in on the management side. Yet if he went in as unskilled worker, Sidney counters, 'Your union would see you

I'm All Right Jack

I'm All Right Jack charts the deterioration of the industrial cold war of the 1950s. Stanley (Ian Carmichael) is advised by Sidney (Richard Attenborough) to enter the firm of his uncle Bertram (Dennis Price) as one of the workers (1). Stanley falls for Cynthia (Liz Fraser) (2), whose style and preoccupations are quite different from those of his aunt, Lady Dorothy (Margaret Rutherford) (3). He is introduced to political philosophy by Cynthia's father, Fred Kite (Peter Sellers) (4), who later leads his men out on strike after Stanley has caused a change in the work schedules (5).

A country-wide strike and lock-out ensues (6), which foils Bertram's and Sidney's plot to profit from industrial skullduggery.

never get as little as that.' Aunt Dolly still cannot imagine her nephew 'all muscles and sweat'. 'These days it's the management that does all the perspiring,' Sidney replies, choosing his words carefully.

Aunt Dolly fears he might have to join 'one of those horrid unions' with all that 'violence', but Bertie reassures her that 'that doesn't happen nowadays', and Stanley is convinced. He agrees to join the workforce without mentioning that his uncle is on the board of directors, in case it disturbs the 'industrial peace'. But that is precisely what Bertie and Sidney are hoping for. Stanley is part of their scheme to bring Missiles to a standstill (the others include the imposition of a time-and-motion man and a provocative speech to be delivered to the workers on the theme of 'Export or die'). Bertie intends to sell his shares in the company beforehand; the overseas contract will be transferred at a higher price to Sidney's firm; and a hefty profit will be made and divided between them and the representative of the foreign Government, Mr Mohammed (Marne Maitland), who immediately co-operates when he realizes what is in it for him.

Bertie and Sidney are Big Business incarnate and represent its seamier side, though the implication is clearly that much of business management is invested with the same traits. They scheme, manipulate, are totally unscrupulous in their transactions and, though they talk piously about the benefits that are likely to accrue to the country from their endeavours, are really concerned only with promoting their own personal interests (which are by no means even class interests, for though Bertie is definitely meant to be upper-class, Sidney is very much a *nouveau riche* businessman, as his occasional lapses in language and temper suggest). And when Stanley eventually joins Missiles, he soon encounters their equivalents among the ranks of the workers.

The narrator interjects once again to tell us, with more than a hint of irony, that the British worker has responded to the coming of the 'new age' with a 'new sense of the dignity of labour to match his age-old traditions of brotherhood and comradeship'. The irony is compounded by the image of the workforce ambling lazily towards the factory gates until the hooter goes for the start of work, when there is a sudden mad scramble to clock on in sufficient time so as not to lose any pay. Thereafter we are treated to a rich array of practices as restrictive, as devious and as sharp as it is possible to imagine.

The men are reluctant to start work; they skive when they can seize the opportunity; and they down tools at the slightest provocation. Nobody is laid off, and those that are 'what is known as redundant' are kept on in fictitious jobs and spend all their time playing cards. Nobody works harder than is really necessary, and a strict demarcation of jobs is observed. 'They're an absolute shower, a positive shower,' says the personnel manager, Major Hitchcock (Terry-Thomas), who knows of men 'who can break out into a muck sweat merely by standing still'. But his jaundiced views are amply vindicated when workers talk of not having had 'a stoppage for ages, not since the week before last'.

Not surprisingly, Stanley, with his eagerness and enthusiasm, does not fit easily into this set-up. He is dubbed a 'creep' and is given a hostile reception by the workers, who readily and instantly appreciate that he is not one of them and suspect his motives. However, he succeeds in establishing a relationship of sorts with them, especially after he agrees to join the union —

'It's not compulsory, only you've got to join, see.' He is befriended, in particular, by Fred Kite (Peter Sellers), who is the chief shop steward on the works committee, and he takes lodgings at Kite's house after he has taken a fancy to Kite's daughter, Cynthia (Liz Fraser).

Kite is meant to epitomize the archetypal 'bolshy' shop steward and is brilliantly drawn by Sellers, who rightly won the British Film Academy's award as best actor of 1959 for his performance. He has a short cropped haircut and a purposeful stride. He delights in long, convoluted sentences, which sound good and appear to go down well with the workers but are always slightly wrong ('reverberate to the detriment of the workers', 'barefaced provocative of the workers'). He has intellectual pretensions and boasts to Stanley of having gone to Oxford himself, though it quickly transpires that it was only for a short summer school. 'Very nice tea and preserves they give you,' he says, with just the right air of inverted condescension. Kite's library at home is suitably filled with the works of Lenin, books on Lenin and books with titles such as *Decline of the Privileged Classes.* He dreams of going to Russia someday to enjoy 'all them cornfields and bally in the evening'. Yet despite his talk of the equality of man, he is a racist and fears that the 'blacks' might take over his men's jobs.

For all the power he wields at the factory and for all the influence he initially exerts over Stanley, Fred Kite is by no means the master in his home. That is largely the domain of Mrs Kite (Irene Handl), and she runs it most effectively and respectably. Her naturally conservative inclinations are displayed when she slips easily — and, of course, somewhat deferentially — into a friendly chat with Lady Dorothy when the latter arrives unexpectedly. Mrs Kite shows her into the 'front room' and engages in cosy conversation on the subject of good manners, respect and the like. But without her Fred is lost and his male incompetence in practical matters is revealed after she has temporarily deserted him to pursue her own 'strike'. Harmony is restored only at the film's end, when Fred gains in confidence and reasserts his dominance over recalcitrant wife and fun-loving daughter alike.

In the event, though, the relationship between Stanley and Kite is short-lived. Stanley is unwittingly timed working harder than the other men would like; new schedules are introduced; and Kite calls a strike. At first Stanley is merely 'sent to Coventry', but when he insists, at his Aunt's prompting ('Officers don't mutiny,' she says), upon going into work and breaks the picket line, he becomes a 'blackleg' and is totally ostracized. He wins a considerable amount of press and public sympathy, much to Kite's chagrin and his uncle's delight. But his uncle Bertie is also alienated when a sympathy strike closes down Sidney's factory in turn, and their carefully laid plans are scuppered. The strike spreads throughout the country; millions come out; but all that the Minister of Labour can say is, 'I shall act . . . but I shall not interfere', and all that the Trades Union Congress can say is, 'We are not prepared either to endorse the strike officially, nor to condemn it.'

Prevarication rules on those fronts, and it is left to the bosses and the workers to find a solution to the industrial crisis with, as the narrator wryly puts it, 'the traditional respect of the British for the individual, allied to a rare genius for compromise and the unorthodox approach'. The resulting compromise in this instance, however, is a sour one. Bertie, Sidney, Hitchcock and Kite connive to get rid of Stanley. With a bit of luck, not to mention Stanley's inherent naivety and gullibility and the force of the law in the shape of a magistrate (Raymond Huntley) who roundly condemns him and binds him over to keep the peace, Stanley is accused of 'mental instability' and 'ill health brought on by overwork'. The overwork is put down to the new schedules — that was Kite's bright idea — and they will be withdrawn. The strike will end and 'industrial peace' will be restored. Stanley, for his part, is suitably disillusioned, and he retires to join his father in the untroubled retreat of the Sunnyglades nudist camp.

The film finishes on the same pessimistic, if comic, note on which it starts. But it achieves its desired effect, sometimes with broad and exaggerated strokes, always with considerable humour. Visually it is not a particularly exciting film, though that failing does not ultimately detract from its other qualities. The Boultings depended, in the main, upon the benefits to be gained from a sound script, well versed in the nuances and subtleties of British life, and character acting of the sort for which the British cinema is, and always has been, renowned. And there they scored an undoubted success.

The film's triumph was more than reflected by its box-office returns. It was the biggest money-maker in Britain in 1959, ahead of America's *The Big Country,* a lavish western with a large all-star cast, ahead of more traditional British fare, *Carry on Nurse*, and way ahead of the critically acclaimed *Room at the Top.* A British Lion spokesman believed that 'word-of-mouth recommendation' largely turned it into a hit, since the film had not been given an unusual advertising budget, and the only places where it did not go down well was 'in a few cinemas in the Welsh mining districts'.[25] It was still playing to capacity audiences at London's Studio One cinema after seventeen weeks, and more than 2 million people saw it in that time.[26] The film also, incidentally, took more money on its New York run at the Guild Theatre than any film ever shown at that cinema before, and by its fifteenth week was taking an average of about £4,000 a week.[27]

It was clearly popular, but among British critics, at least, it elicited a divided response. The 'quality' press proved to be more than a little bit snooty about it, and damned it in the main, except for honourable mentions of Peter Sellers's performance, while the 'popular' press revelled in it and found it very much to its liking. *The Times,* for instance, found 'its barbs, very fairly divided between Capital and Labour'. It was all right 'for an evening's light entertainment', *The Times* continued, but 'For satire worthy of the name, if it exists at all today, we shall have to look elsewhere.'[28] C. A. Lejeune in the *Observer* thought that it seemed 'bound to be a triumphant popular success' and felt compelled to add: 'I should be the last one to deny that it has the common touch.' But obviously that 'common touch' was really not to her liking — 'A number of the jokes are fairly blue' and 'The tasteless opening in the nudist camp has no real relevance to the film at all.'[29] (In fact, the opening and closing nudist camp scenes caused the film to be threatened with a ban in Eire if the Boultings proved unwilling to cut them out. They chose not to do so.)[30]

David Robinson of the *Financial Times* also thought that the film 'ingeniously echoed the popular audience's narrowest and meanest fears and prejudices'. 'All is defeatist and destructive,' he concluded, 'And the worst of it is that it is rather well done.'[31] Isabel Quigly in the *Spectator* agreed that there was no 'better target for satire at this very moment than our industrial strikes' but found herself totally 'unamused' and thought the film failed because it had 'no central standard from which to judge anything, no central idea or point of view'.[32] Again, the *Manchester Guardian* harped upon the 'topical and sensitive theme' which was 'not so far from the reality as told in the daily news of strikes'. But, virtually alone among the 'quality' press, it decided finally, 'A remarkable film as to its topic and its tone, it has also been made with a wholly satisfactory sense of form.'[33] And Dilys Powell, in the *Sunday Times*, at least considered it 'uproariously funny' and was grateful to the Boultings for 'their nerve in daring to joke about that sacred institution, trade unionism'.[34]

The 'popular' press loved the film, of course, and its feelings towards it are perhaps best summarized by the comments made in the *Sunday Express*, under the headline 'Are we really as mad as this?', which applauded 'this brilliantly made, gloriously funny, magnificently acted film'.[35] And, again not surprisingly, the left-wing press was suitably outraged. The film was 'All *Right* Jack and No *Left*,' said Nell Vyse in the *Daily Worker*, adding that it painted too black a picture of the workers,[36] while Derek Hill of *Tribune* found himself in a real dilemma: 'Peter Sellers's performance is as brilliant as it is contemptible,' he wrote, and 'The film — I hate to admit — is very well made and often extremely funny. I loathed myself for laughing at it.'[37] So, to put the record straight, one week later *Tribune* published a selection of letters which condemned it in no such uncertain terms. Indeed, left-wing outrage at the film continued for many years thereafter. And in April 1979 the *Evening Standard* reported that the film had been dropped from its proposed slot in London Weekend Television's Easter Sunday schedule after a Labour MP had complained about it, on the eve of a by-election, to Transport House, which had complained in turn to the Independent Broadcasting Authority.

Still, as the same article went on to recount, some people had found the film to be of considerable merit, for when the Prime Minister, Harold Macmillan, went to Balmoral in September 1959 to ask for the dissolution of Parliament, the film that the Queen apparently chose for her house guests was none other than *I'm All Right Jack*.[38] Doubtless it entertained them as much as it entertained a good many people elsewhere in the country at the time. Certainly, the country agreed that it had 'never had it so good'. In 1970, furthermore, the film was put to informational and instructional use as an 'object lesson in reality' when it was included, ironically, on the curriculum of management training courses being run in Britain by Unilever.[39]

For anybody who cared to look and listen, then, *I'm All Right Jack* amply demonstrated that it was relevant enough.

Notes

1 Neville March Hunnings, *Film Censors and the Law*, London, 1967, pp. 408–9.
2 Quoted in Jeffrey Richards, 'The British Board of Film Censors and Content Control in the 1930s: Images of Britain', *Historical Journal of Film, Radio and Television*, 1, October 1981, p. 112.

3   *British Board of Film Censors Scenario Reports,* 1933, p. 209 (bound volume; BFI Library, London).

4   This film is discussed further in Tony Aldgate, 'Comedy, Class and Containment', in James Curran and Vincent Porter (eds.), *British Cinema History,* London, 1983.

5   *BBFC Scenario Reports,* 1934, p. 364.

6   Arthur Marwick, 'Print, Pictures and Sound: the Second World War and the British Experience', *Daedalus,* Fall 1982, p. 147. See also James C. Robertson, 'British Film Censorship Goes to War', *Historical Journal of Film, Radio and Television,* 2, March 1982, pp. 49—64.

7   Keith Jeffery and Peter Hennessy, *States of Emergency, British Governments and Strikebreaking since 1919,* London, 1983, p. 145.

8   See also Richards, 'The British Board of Film Censors', pp. 111—12, and Stephen Constantine, '*Love on the Dole* and its Reception in the 1930s', *Literature and History,* 8, Autumn 1982, pp. 244—5.

9   Marwick, 'Print, Pictures and Sound', pp. 147—8.

10 In *Kinematograph Weekly,* 11 January 1945, p. 163.

11 Reprinted in Edgar Anstey (ed.), *Shots in the Dark,* London, 1951, pp. 159—160.

12 ibid., pp. 160—2.

13 Quoted in the *Guardian,* 2 January 1981, on the occasion of the release of the appropriate papers from 1950 to the PRO.

14 See Jeffery and Hennessy, *States of Emergency,* pp. 172, 191, 200.

15 See Raymond Durgnat, *A Mirror for England,* London, 1970, pp. 70—1 and 234—5. Interestingly, Jeffery and Hennessy, *States of Emergency,* p. 217, quote Lord Citrine's fears of August 1950 that 'the Russians regarded our Power Stations as the nerve centre of British industry, and that they had made special efforts to get influence among workers in Power Stations'.

16 Charles Barr, *Ealing Studios,* London, 1977, p. 137.

17 Arthur Marwick, *British Society since 1945,* Harmondsworth, 1982, p. 163.

18 Alan Hackney's book *Private's Progress* came out in 1954 and was reprinted in paperback in 1957. *Private Life* was published in 1958 and republished under the film's title of *I'm All Right Jack* in 1972 (both by Gollancz). In the meantime Hackney's characters of Stanley Windrush and Fred Kite had appeared also in *Keep Religion Out of This* (1963) and were to reappear in *Whatever Turns You On, Jack* (1972).

19 Durgnat, *A Mirror for England,* p. 235.

20 See *Sunday Times,* 16 August 1959.

21 Marwick, *British Society,* p. 165.

22 Jeffery and Hennessy, *States of Emergency,* pp. 145—6.

23 ibid., p. 189.

24 Ironically, Al Saxon scored his first pop chart hit in the month that the film opened, Aguust 1959, with 'Only Sixteen'. It was, almost inevitably, a poor cover version of an excellent American record and was in fact the second such cover version, the other one being by Craig Douglas. Al Saxon's record did not do particularly well, reaching number 17 in the charts.

25 *News Chronicle,* 11 December 1959.

26 *Star,* 11 December 1959.

27 *Daily Telegraph,* 15 August 1960.

28 *The Times,* 17 August 1959.

29 *Observer,* 16 August 1959.

30 *Daily Telegraph,* 31 October 1959.

31 *Financial Times,* 17 August 1959.

32 *Spectator,* 21 August 1959.

33 *Manchester Guardian,* 15 August 1959.

34   *Sunday Times*, 16 August 1959.
35   *Sunday Express*, 16 August 1959.
36   *Daily Worker*, 15 August 1959.
37   *Tribune*, 21 August 1959.
38   *Evening Standard*, 17 April 1979.
39   *Daily Mirror*, 6 January 1970.

10

The Seeds of Further Compromise

Saturday Night and Sunday Morning

The film of *Saturday Night and Sunday Morning* was a huge commercial and artistic success. In its day it was hailed as a beacon of the 'new wave' in the British cinema, that cinematic equivalent of the theatre's vogue for 'kitchen-sink' drama and literature's penchant for the 'angry young man', and was seen as a typical product of the social and cultural revolt of the late 1950s — an age of affluence in which a new morality was rife, ideas were in the melting-pot, a more open and essentially classless society was in the making, the end of ideology was nigh and a cultural revolution was dawning. Inevitably, much of the heady optimism inherent in that era's strain of journalistic clichés has dissipated, and of late the historical contours of the period have been carefully and stringently redrawn.[1] Now is the time to attempt a reassessment of *Saturday Night and Sunday Morning* in particular and, to a lesser extent, the 'new wave' in general.

Some work has already been forthcoming, albeit sporadically, on both these fronts. Raymond Durgnat observes that the 'new wave' derived little, despite the many claims made at the time, from the documentaries of the so called Free Cinema and notes how much it owed to the mainstream cinema's traditional sources of inspiration, proven successes in other media, notably play and novels. 'Far from originating in a new documentary approach,' he comments, 'the British cinema renewed itself, tardily no doubt, by orthodox commercial procedures.'[2] With regard to *Saturday Night and Sunday Morning*, John Russell Taylor feels that the main novelty of the film lay in its 'subject-matter and milieu', and that while the film is undoubtedly imbued with 'an almost classic quality', nevertheless it was 'too unthinkingly taken by critics of the time to herald a new wave of social realist cinema in Britain'.[3] Roy Armes has pointed out how comparatively short-lived was the love affair between the British cinema and its new-found writers, the novelists and playwrights such as Alan Sillitoe and Shelagh Delaney who were brought in to adapt their works for the screen, of whom 'almost all show an increasing indifference to and disillusionment with the cinema'.[4] Much the

131

same happened to the leading actors who came to the fore with the 'new wave', and the likes of Albert Finney and Tom Courtenay returned for the most part to the theatre, taking their immense talents with them and complaining bitterly about how they had been 'used'.

Yet for all the benefits that such hindsight brings, two critics who first welcomed *Saturday Night and Sunday Morning* on its initial release some twenty-odd years ago have recently felt compelled to single the film out for special praise once again. It may have had its faults and shortcomings, they both conclude, but see the film in the context of its time and its saving graces are more than evident. It was 'very much a film of 1960', Nina Hibbin argues, and 'it changed the whole face of British cinema by proving that audiences enjoyed seeing their own lifestyles on the screen, when the film-makers got it right. . . . it was the first British film to present an inside view of working-class life.' 'To gain a proper historical perspective on *Saturday Night and Sunday Morning*,' Alan Lovell writes, 'it should be seen with a film like Ealing's *The Titfield Thunderbolt* (1953), for example.' He elaborates, thus: 'Through its acknowledgement of sexuality and violence, and through its careful observation of a working-class world being trans-formed by increasing wealth, *Saturday Night and Sunday Morning* destroyed the coyness and showed it was possible for the cinema to be responsive to contemporary social developments.'[5]

Lovell's points are well made. By comparison with other British films, those from the 1950s in particular, this film did indeed break new ground with its story of Arthur Seaton (Albert Finney), the immoral and anarchic worker who 'knows his mind' and is 'not afraid to speak it', as the synopsis puts it.[6] 'What I'm out for is a good time' is Arthur's philosophy; 'All the rest is propaganda.' He is tied to a factory lathe throughout the week, but he more than makes up for it at the weekends, when he drinks hard and enjoys an affair with a workmate's wife, Brenda (Rachel Roberts). Their relationship is soured, however, when Brenda becomes pregnant and Arthur turns increasingly to Doreen (Shirley Anne Field), who is young and 'sharp' and would like to get married. Arthur tries to help Brenda secure an abortion by taking her to see his Aunt Ada (Hylda Baker), but her husband Jack (Bryan Pringle) learns of their affair. He sets his soldier brother and a friend on to Arthur, who is badly beaten up. His affair with Brenda ended, Arthur decides to marry Doreen.

The film certainly destroyed much of the 'coyness' that was a prevalent characteristic of the British cinema. What else, though, may be gained by seeking to place *Saturday Night and Sunday Morning* in its 'proper' historical context?

In answer to that question the first words must surely be given to Alan Sillitoe, the author of the original novel and the film's screenplay. Writing in the pages of the *New Left Review* just a few months before the film opened, he commented:

> When I heard that *Saturday Night and Sunday Morning* was to be made into a film, and that I was going to be asked to write the script, I felt I was in for a tough exercise in resurrection. Nevertheless I agreed to it, mainly because I wanted a hand in the kind of film it was going to be. I didn't want Arthur Seaton — the main character — getting transmogrified into a young workman who turns out to be an honest-to-goodness British

individualist — that is, one who triumphs in the end against and at the expense of a communist agitator or the trade unions. I didn't want him to become a tough stereotype with, after all, a heart of moral gold which has in it a love of the monarchy and all that old-fashioned muck. Not that I imagined Woodfall Productions wanting to tamper in any way with what 'ideological content' the story possessed.[7]

The intentions are clear and the ambitions obvious. Thereafter Sillitoe went on to recount how, with the help of director Karel Reisz, he had sought to render his 'episodic' novel into filmic terms. Very many drafts had been required, in part because 'neither of us had been engaged on a feature film up to that time' and not least 'for reasons of censorship'. Indeed, he proved quite scathing on that latter account and went so far as to state: 'It seems to me that censorship in the British film industry is in its own way as hidebound as that of Soviet Russia.' Finally, Sillitoe outlined briefly the content of three 'soliloquy scenes' that had been written for the film, which he felt were important in helping to explain changes in the character of Arthur Seaton and which, clearly, he confidently expected to see included in the final release print of the film.

According to Sillitoe's account, then, the imposition of censorship proved to be the major stumbling block to his and Karel Reisz's efforts to produce a faithful filmic interpretation of the novel. Yet when the completed film of *Saturday Night and Sunday Morning* went before the British Board of Film Censors for review and award of an appropriate certificate — ironically, in the same month, July 1960, that Sillitoe's article appeared — it had been shorn of the final soliloquy scene. The BBFC had certainly not sought the deletion of that particular scene. Nor indeed, to judge from the BBFC's file on the subject of *Saturday Night and Sunday Morning*, is there much evidence of anything other than a comparatively harmonious relationship between the censors and the production company, at least, over the matter of the changes and modifications that were required of the various drafts of the script that were presented for scrutiny before the film went into actual production.[8] If anything, in fact, the file hints at a good deal of active co-operation and at willingness on the part of the film-makers to accede to whatever major requests were made of them. Perhaps, on this occasion, Sillitoe overestimated the part that the BBFC had played and underestimated those elements of negotiation and compromise that were inherent in the film-making process generally. And perhaps it was his gradual realization of the importance of these latter elements which contributed most to his disillusionment with film as a writer's medium.

A scenario treatment of *Saturday Night and Sunday Morning* was first sent to the BBFC in November 1959. In this Sillitoe adhered quite faithfully to his original novel, though there was an inevitable compression in the number of scenes and the number of characters represented. It retained, in particular, reference to an abortion scene in which the married Brenda successfully terminates the unwanted pregnancy resulting from her love affair with Arthur. It also contained, however, a new concluding scene, which Sillitoe wrote especially for the film to complement those scenes that he had drawn directly from his novel, in which Arthur marries Doreen at a registry office wedding.

The scenario obviously did not meet with the wholehearted approval of the BBFC's readers, and one of them commented in a report of 20 November:

> I see from the accompanying compliments slip that this is the company in which John Osborne is involved; we might almost have known it from the language of the script. I imagine that the company will fully expect to have an 'X', and I fully expect that they are right. Quite apart from anything else, the language would not do for an 'A'. Neither would the love scenes, to say nothing of the discussion of abortion and the fact that the abortion is actually carried out (though not seen). As to the quality of the story, the hero is an immoral fellow who would doubtless end up in jail in real life, but I enjoyed him a lot more than the people in *Look Back in Anger* and *A Taste of Honey* (other products of the new school of Young Writers Speaking for the People), because I could believe in him, and even got to like him towards the end, when he began dimly to perceive that it was time he developed a sense of responsibility. I think most of what happens is tolerable for 'X', *but I have strong misgivings about the slap-happy and successful termination of pregnancy,* which seems to be very dangerous stuff for our younger X-cert. customers and moreover is not necessary for the story.

Thereafter the script reader proceeded to elaborate precisely, by reference to pages in the scenario, those incidents and lines of dialogue which gave rise to his concerns. A rich array of specific words was extracted to exemplify his fears about the language used throughout — all of which, it must be said, were in evidence in Sillitoe's original novel:

> I really don't think we can have 'bogger', 'Christ' or 'sod'. They ought to make do with the numerous 'bleddys', 'bloodies', 'bleedings' and 'bastards' which adorn the script.

His remarks on that score came to a temporary halt with the statement:

> I know that 'bugger' is freely used in such places as the public bars of provincial pubs, but I doubt whether the average working man uses it much in his own home in front of his wife, and that ought to be more the standard for us to adopt, even in films obviously designed for the factory-worker section of society. (A great many young married men choose the films *they* want to see; their wives come with them and often don't enjoy the language, or the violence, at all.)

Subsequently, the doubtful love scenes were highlighted for further attention (with comments like: 'They want love making of a *Room at the Top* directness, and should be allowed to have it, but this seems to go a bit too far'); the scenes relating to the abortion were picked out especially ('As I have said, I think this element dangerous stuff'); and, among other things, it was suggested that caution should be observed in the depiction of violence and 'fighting generally', since 'it will be troublesome if shot as scripted.' Problems relating to language came into the reckoning once again when the reader quoted the line 'I'd been knocking on wi' a married woman' and then added plaintively, 'I don't know how obscene this phrase is.' Finally, it was recommended that the script be subjected to further scrutiny, since 'much of the dialogue is of the kind which some of us find more offensive than others, and it is a pity to have to cut things which were in the script.'

In the event a second examiner concluded: 'This is fundamentally an "A" story which gets its "X"-ness from being too outspoken about abortion, too revealing in love scenes and too foul-mouthed.' That examiner also compiled a list of offensive words and cited the violence as a potentially worrying factor.

Both examiners agreed, then, on the actual and likely areas of concern in the treatment presented for their consideration. And John Trevelyan, the secretary of the BBFC, proceeded to summarize their findings, and to add a few more of his own, in the letter he wrote to Harry Saltzman, the film's producer at Woodfall Production, on 24 November 1959. With regard to the language in particular, he asked Saltzman to note:

> This script is peppered with 'language' throughout, and while for the 'X' category we would, I think, accept a reasonable number of words like 'bloody', 'bleddy', 'bleeding' and 'bastard', we would not accept 'Christ', since many perfectly reasonable people take offence at this: we would particularly dislike 'Christ Almighty' and 'Christ-all-bleeding-mighty'. Furthermore, we simply cannot accept the word 'bogger'. We have not yet accepted the use of the word 'bugger' in films and the substitution of the letter 'o' for the letter 'u' makes no significant difference: on the sound-track the word will certainly sound like 'bugger'. I appreciate that words of this kind are normal in the speech of the type of people that the film is about but I have always found, strange though it may seem, that these are the very people who most object to this kind of thing on the screen. I hope, therefore, that this script will be revised and these words omitted.

Clearly, Sillitoe's attempt to capture the sound of the Nottinghamshire pronunciation of the word 'bugger' — a device he employed consistently throughout the novel — was lost on the censors and counted for nothing. A 'bogger' was a 'bugger' for all that and as such was not allowed.

The rest of Trevelyan's letter went on to chart the censor's remaining misgivings about the script. 'A reasonable bed scene' would be permitted but 'it should not go too far' — 'I appreciate that this relationship is entirely physical but there are limits to what we will accept.' An explanation had obviously been forthcoming as to the meaning of the phrase 'knocking on', and it was cited as being 'a bit crude'. 'The fight should not be too brutal', and, of course, doubts were expressed about the abortion scenes:

> This shows a rather casual attitude to abortion and suggests to the young that if they get into difficulties all they need is to find a kind-hearted older woman who has had a lot of children. Provided that it is not too obtrusive it would probably be acceptable, but I must ask you to bear in mind that this film is likely to be seen by a considerable number of young people of 16 to 20 years of age, and to recognize that social responsibility is called for.

In his concluding paragraph Trevelyan explained that he had gone into a fair amount of detail in making his points because 'this is the kind of film which might well give trouble on points of detail when completed.' He reiterated that the major worries were, first, the language and, second, the abortion, and his parting words were: 'If you can tone both of these down, there should be little other trouble.'

The final draft of the shooting script, which Harry Saltzman sent for the BBFC's consideration on 26 January 1960, might be said to have exercised a considerable amount of 'social responsibility'. The worrying elements were toned down all right. They were, quite simply, changed. The infamous 'bogger' gave way to the innocuous 'beggar', and the abortion turned out to be ineffective.[9] The BBFC reader who had most to say on reading the initial scenario now declared, with some evident relief, in a report of 28 January 1960:

> They have not done all we asked, but they have done what we wanted most. They have taken out 'bogger' altogether, putting 'beggar' in its place, but far less frequently. They have removed all 'Christs'. They have also drastically modified the abortion element: we are told that Ada has given Brenda a very hot bath and much gin and it has not worked; later she means to go to a doctor, but decides against it and resolves to have the child after all; her husband later tells Arthur that she is 'all right', but we are left to assume that the pregnancy has been terminated without any outside interference. I am very glad that this change has been made; and their co-operation in this direction has made one hope that we can be reasonably lenient with the film as a whole (which is still a firm 'X', by reason of some very passionate and physical love scenes and the several discussions of abortion).

The day was not completely won, however, and there were certain obstacles yet to be overcome. The love scenes still needed 'care', for instance, and the reader worried about lines like 'What a time we had last night' and 'Get down in bed.' Language remained a problem when there was a dialogue such as 'Make room for a rabbit arse, Jack' and 'A pellet got her right on the arse.' 'Daft sod' was queried. The question was posed whether 'God-all-bleeding-mighty' was really much better than 'Christ', and it was noted that the phrase 'I'd been knocking on wi' a married woman' was still included, though this time the note was accompanied by the comment, 'I don't know if it really matters.'

Furthermore, it was felt that 'the vicious onslaught by the soldiers on Arthur may give trouble even for an "X"; the repeated kicks seem to be excessive.' And last but by no means least, there were fears about the talk of 'a hot bath and gin'. 'I believe the secretary much objects to this,' added the reader, 'but I don't mind, as it fails.'

On 2 February 1960 John Trevelyan wrote one last letter to Saltzman to tell him of the outcome of the BBFC's latest deliberations. To begin with the Board expressed 'appreciation' at the way in which its comments had been taken into account, and then the points of reservation, along with further recommendations, were listed. There were many fewer of them this time, of course, and they were by no means all the ones that their reader had outlined — clearly, some degree of toleration was being exercised by the BBFC in view of the notable advances that had been made — and the process of negotiation continued. It was suggested that the director should still use 'discretion' in shooting the love scenes and the line 'Get down in bed' was though to be 'rather direct'. The word 'sod' might be altered, since it was 'a word we are trying to keep out of films' and the line 'God-all-bleeding-mighty' was better, though 'we still do not like it.' Care should be taken in the fight scenes to avoid 'excessive brutality'. And, once again, it was hoped that the phrase 'knocking on wi' a married woman' might be changed. Indeed, Trevelyan even went so far as to suggest an alternative and wondered whether 'mucking about wi' a married woman' might not be equally good.

To the last the production company sought to reciprocate and to meet the BBFC's needs and requirements. The film went into production with a script that proved to be a characteristic mixture of compromise, outright acceptance of the BBFC's requests and a modest amount of steadfastness. In one respect — the case of the line 'God-all-bleeding-mighty' — the script remained unchanged, but the line 'Get down in bed' was dropped altogether, the word 'sod' was changed to 'nit' and the line 'knocking on wi' a married woman' was altered to 'knocking around wi' a married woman'. The film was completed and presented to the BBFC for a certificate on 20 July 1960. The censors were obviously satisfied with the changes and with the depiction of the love scenes and the violence, and the film was awarded an 'X' certificate.

The film turned out, as we have said, to be an immense success. It has been reported that initially the bookers were positively hostile to the film, that 'not one would agree to show it in a cinema, much less a chain of cinemas' and that it was only by a stroke of luck that the film opened at the Warner Theatre, Leicester Square, on 26 October 1960.[10] But it did exceptional business in its first week's run, and very soon thereafter few people in the film trade remained to be convinced that it would prove a box-office winner. It had cost a little over £100,000 to produce, yet it grossed more than the sum as a result of a three-week release in the London-circuit cinemas alone.[11]

Critically, the film won considerable acclaim. In general, the critics praised the film's faithful evocation of a working-class milieu and applauded its veracity, citing especially those qualities, such as 'authenticity' and 'realism', that have stood the film in good stead ever since. 'It is set squarely among the working classes,' said the *Guardian* critic, and 'this has been done with a most impressively authentic air.'[12] 'Mr Reisz, in fact, has essentially "got it right",' was the conclusion, and the result was 'a genuine human document'. 'Dead accurate in detail as well as atmosphere,' remarked Isabel Quigly in the *Spectator*, and then she repeated the often heard comment that the film 'made *Room at the Top* look like a Sunday school picnic or something of the sort' — in itself, perhaps, an echo of the verdict passed in the *Daily Telegraph* to the effect that so far as the original novels were concerned, Sillitoe's made Braine's 'look like a vicarage tea-party' — before going on to add that 'it was more authentic, without *Room at the Top*'s occasional lapses into social caricature, so you believe it and take it to heart'.[13] 'A true contemporary character' was David Robinson's judgement in the *Financial Times* on the portrayal of Arthur Seaton.[14]

Even the film's harshest critics felt compelled to admit that they had a grudging admiration for it, or at least parts of it. 'This is perhaps the most immoral, amoral film I have ever seen. . . . I wouldn't like my own children to see it,' Donald Gomery wrote in the *Daily Express,* 'but Albert Finney, as the hero of the film, is brilliant.'[15] 'I dislike the film. But I respect it,' was Fred Majdalany's verdict in the *Daily Mail*, adding that it displayed 'a sympathetic authenticity and humour seldom achieved in the commercial British cinema'.[16] 'It is a superb bit of craftsmanship,' Ernest Betts decided on behalf of the *People,* but 'this story, though brilliant, is brutal and depressing.'[17]

And, inevitably, opinions varied as to the film's intent. 'The "message" of this film is that after the Saturday night of near-debauchery comes the Sunday morning of near-repentance,' concluded Gomery in the *Express*, though he felt certain that the character of Arthur Seaton 'is still a rebel, only half-tamed'. Alexander Walker had much the same thing to say in the

Saturday Night and Sunday Morning

6

In *Saturday Night and Sunday Morning* Arthur Seaton (Albert Finney) is tied during the week to a factory lathe (1), a bleak environment (2) and a predictable routine at home (3). But he makes up for this at the weekends, when he enjoys an affair with Brenda (Rachel Roberts) (4), for which he is eventually beaten up (5). He turns instead to Doreen (Shirley Anne Field) (6), whose hopes for marriage and a new house threaten Arthur's freedom.

Evening Standard, in which he commented that the film 'made perceptible the imperceptible way a harum-scarum rebel settles down — but without being tamed'.[18] The *Sunday Telegraph* was adamant on that latter score, arguing vehemently that the film 'shows the workers as neither contented middle-class types, Merrie Englanders, nor sturdy toilers striving for social reform'. 'The hero is a study in frustration, against everything and for nothing . . . and is only too glad to do anything against "them",' it continued and, if anything, the film served as a timely reminder that 'affluence has not diminished the "revolt of the masses".'[19]

Not surprisingly, Nina Hibbin, writing in the pages of the *Daily Worker*, felt somewhat different about the lessons to be learned from the film. She thought that it 'shows uncompromisingly that Arthur's weaknesses — and his developing strength — spring not from selfishness or irresponsibility but from the oppression and sheer frustration of being a worker under the present social set-up'.[20] Like many another critic of the day, she singled out for particular attention the ending of the film, in which Arthur is seen throwing a stone at one of the new council houses that Doreen hopes they will occupy when they are married. He says to her, 'It won't be the last one I'll throw.' For Nina Hibbin that scene was 'provocative' and posed 'the simple challenge: "Fight"'. For others, like the *Daily Telegraph*, the scene was a 'futile gesture against authority and conformity'.[21] 'He will fight and not lie down,' William Whitebait retorted in the *New Statesman*.[22] No, no, he is 'cooling off in the end', replied Dilys Powell in the *Sunday Times*, who believed that Arthur 'reassures himself with defiant gestures. But he will marry the girl, he will settle down.'[23]

In view of this evident divergence of opinion, one might be forgiven for thinking that, as is often the case, the critics quite simply saw the film that they wanted to see and extrapolated those 'messages' from it that they might naturally have been predisposed to extrapolate. Yet it might also be said that the wide variety of critical readings stemmed from the fact that the film of *Saturday Night and Sunday Morning* was not just open-ended — a feature that several critics found to be in its favour — but open to the point of being ambiguous. In certain circumstances, of course, this can be said to indicate a rich and dense artistic text, in short, 'a classic', which is precisely the status that some have accorded to the film of *Saturday Night and Sunday Morning* in the British cinema. And it cannot be denied that the film has many admirable and enduring qualities. But in this case the ambiguities were hardly the result of any creative intent; they arose directly from the contingencies of its production.

It is little wonder, for example, that there was disagreement over the meaning of the film's ending, since Sillitoe and Reisz appear to have disagreed about their final intentions. Sillitoe recounted:

> The most difficult thing of all was in deciding which way to end the film. In the book Arthur Seaton, the amoral, anarchic, sly, cunning, extrovert factory worker — to use but a few cliché-superlatives of the press — is about to get married to Doreen, but his inner cogitations while fishing on the canal bank show that the confused anarchy within him is by no means quelled at this prospect. In the film I tried to illustrate this in several ways. One — soon discarded — was a wedding scene at the registry office which is made into a travesty by Arthur's larking about. But this wasn't in character, since it meant being cruel to the girl he was about to marry —

as would any act of overt protest at this stage. It had to be more subtle; an acceptance of the life instinct in marriage, yet an obvious rejection of the double-faced society that really takes no account of him. Such complexities did not make for easy filming.[24]

Sillitoe and Reisz undoubtedly did the correct thing in rejecting the idea of a wedding scene, which actually appeared in the first draft presented for the BBFC's consideration. For Sillitoe was assuredly right to believe that it would have made the character of Arthur Seaton appear callous and heartless towards his bride. One script direction, for instance, had Arthur's face showing 'disappointment . . . as if he wants to start bargaining about numbers' at the point where the registrar invites them to join in marriage 'for life, to the exclusion of all others'. And the proposed scene, which does not appear in the novel, simply does not read at all convincingly. Even the BBFC reader had been prompted to remark that the scenario 'ends (so abruptly that I wonder if it *is* the end of the script, or if something has been omitted by mistake) on scenes of the wedding before the Registrar of Marriages'.[25]

Thereafter, by Sillitoe's account, he settled upon the idea of concluding the film with a sequence that included the stone-throwing scene and, to round off the film, a final 'soliloquy scene' in which Arthur is once again seen at his lathe, thinking to himself as follows:

> Jack's not all that bad. He's a good bloke in some ways. Let the factory do as it likes with him, though. They've bossed all the guts out of him. If he had any to begin with. There's thousands like him, though: just love to be told what to do. I'll never get like that. Anybody opens their trap too much to me, gets it shut for 'em. Me, I was born fighting. Like I told Bert: you've got to fight in this world. But there's a bit of sweetness sometimes, and I know that much as well.

Sillitoe's purpose, as he put it, was to show both that Arthur had indeed changed since the beginning of the film and that he was in many ways the same person 'to the extent that he is still going into the future as someone with a mind of his own, a mind that can't be so easily got at as most people's seem to be'.[26] Of all the critics' comments upon Arthur Seaton, then, 'half-tamed' would appear to reflect Sillitoe's intentions most appropriately. But in the event, of course, that final soliloquy, the scene which would perhaps have met Sillitoe's needs most aptly, was not used in the release print of the film.

By way of contrast, Karel Reisz is reported to have viewed the ending of the film more as a 'surrender', and in an interview that he gave some years after the film's release he commented:

> In a metaphorical way Arthur embodied what was happening in England: he was a sad person, terribly limited in his sensibilities, narrow in his ambitions and a bloody fool into the bargain. . . . The stone-throwing is a symptom of his impotence, a self-conscious bit, telling the audience over the character's shoulder what I think of him. I wanted to continually contrast the extent to which he is an aggressor with the extent to which he is a victim of the world. I wanted the end to have this feeling of frustration. . . .[27]

In fairness to Reisz it should be said that by the time of the interview he was no longer 'too keen' on the stone-throwing ending to the film. But if it was a 'feeling of frustration' he was looking for as he was directing the film's final scenes, then he had certainly created that and a lot more besides. He had invested them with ambiguity and confusion.

The same might also be said of the scenes detailing the outcome to Brenda's unwanted pregnancy. It was decided, as we have seen, to change Sillitoe's original intention completely here. As a result of the BBFC's intervention urging 'social responsibility' and its full exercise by Sillitoe, Reisz and Saltzman, the attempted abortion was now reported during the course of the film to be a failure. Though Sillitoe railed against the BBFC on this score, in fact he declared that it did have some advantage in that 'in the film the climax centres around a more complex situation than in the book.'[28] Yet the complexities of the situation, as far as the plot was concerned, were hardly resolved. They were dealt with in a vague and muddled fashion. The abortion proves to be a failure, certainly, but what happens after that is anybody's guess.

The BBFC reader, for instance, noted that in the revised script the abortion does not work and assumed that the pregnancy is terminated naturally in the event. The incidents outlined were, furthermore, included in the release print of the film. Brenda tells Arthur that she could not go through with another attempt at abortion and says: 'I've decided to have it and face whatever comes of it'. And, Jack eventually informs Arthur: 'She's okay. She'll be all right with me. I'll look after her. Keep that between me and you though'.

Yet the BBFC reader's assumption was hardly one that was shared by all those who saw the film. Everybody appreciated that the attempted abortion was not a success, of course; there could be no doubt about that. But thereafter opinions differed as to whether the pregnancy was finally terminated or not. Among the critics, for example, Gomery of the *Daily Express,* Walker of the *Evening Standard,* Whitebait of the *New Statesman* and Wells of the *Sunday Express* clearly thought that Brenda 'remains pregnant' and 'will have the baby'. As with the stone-throwing end of the film, the question of Brenda's pregnancy was left unresolved. Sillitoe's original intent was changed, and considerable confusion was generated as a result. In production integrity gave way to expediency, and clarity of purpose was rendered obscure.

Of such compromises was *Saturday Night and Sunday Morning* — like much of the 'new wave' — undoubtedly made.[29] To say that, however, is by no means to denigrate the film's obvious and lasting achievements. It made great advances. The marvellously truculent portrayal of Arthur Seaton by Albert Finney cut through many of the cinema's traditional stereotypes of a working-class character and left them in its wake. Finney invested the part with authority and made Arthur instantly recognizable and identifiable from the outset of the film. His contribution was immense and has been well summarized by Alexander Walker:

> With his wary eye, cocky banter, short neck and jutting chin, Finney possessed the naturalistic vitality of a working-class environment where survival bred swift responses and not too much care for other people's feelings. The Beatles were soon going to turn such an attitude into stock-in-trade. But its novelty was brand-new in *Saturday Night and Sunday Morning,* and to see it welded together into an anti-hero, unrepentantly sexy in a repressive community, sharper than his mates, tougher than the

pub brawlers he worsts, anti-romantic in his view of women as providing a night's pleasure, reconciled to paying the penalty for his pleasure, but resistant to all life could do to him, as well as to the factory foreman: this was a new force, a new surprise in the cinema.[30]

But if Arthur Seaton was a new force, he was also very much an individual one, born largely of youthful rebellion. There was none of the workers' camaraderie, as evinced in *I'm All Right Jack*, for him; he was a loner, 'individualistic and broadly anarchical with a total repudiation of the political system, trade unions and all forms of private and public authority'.[31] Nor, indeed, was Arthur the only character of note in the film. In fact, it sought to embrace a whole gamut of figures, from the amiable Aunt Ada, to whom Arthur turns in a moment of crisis, to the garrulous street-corner gossip Ma Bull (Edna Morris), whom he constantly antagonizes, and the convivial cousin Bert (Norman Rossington), who counsels Arthur and always advises caution. It depicted a wide range of relationships, created a community, and did so in a thoroughly convincing fashion.

Without doubt, *Saturday Night and Sunday Morning* presented a faithful and realistic picture of an industrial working-class environment in a way that had rarely been evident in the British cinema before. It fully acknowledged the presence of sexuality and violence in the world that it depicted and carefully detailed some of the changes that new-found affluence had wrought among the working-class in this country. To its credit, the film did not argue that the working class was thereby becoming more middle-class in its values or cultural behaviour. It was not patronizing in that respect and, if anything, stood out modestly against any kind of simplistic 'embourgeoisement' thesis. The world that it presented was a totally insulated and isolated working-class world without, if the truth were told, any sense or recognizable sign of a 'class enemy'.[32]

In many ways, then, the film was indeed a film of 1960, and it was imbued with much of the spirit and vision that permeated the cultural revolution of its day. The times had changed, and *Saturday Night and Sunday Morning* reflected a good many of the changes and developments. Yet its vision was by no means unbounded or untrammelled; it was appropriately compromised almost from the start — the traditional dictates of the film-making process saw to that. To place the film in its context is to appreciate that in some respects the revolution had only just begun.

Notes

1 See, in particular, Arthur Marwick, *British Society since 1945,* Harmondsworth, 1982.

2 Raymond Durgnat, *A Mirror for England,* London, 1970, p. 129. For a useful introduction to 'free cinema', see Alan Lovell and Jim Hillier, *Studies in Documentary,* London, 1972, pp. 133—59.

3 John Russell Taylor, Introduction to *Masterworks of the British Cinema,* London, 1974, pp. 15—17. This volume contains a 'script' for *Saturday Night and Sunday Morning* but, unfortunately, it is a poor transcription with many obvious errors.

4 Roy Armes, *A Critical History of British Cinema,* London, 1978, p. 269.

5 See *The Movie,* London, 1979, ch. 57, p. 1124 (for Hibbin), and p. 1126 (for Lovell). For their original comments, see, respectively, the *Daily Worker,* 29 October 1960, and the *New Left Review,* no. 7, January—February 1961, pp. 52—3.

6 On the microfiche for the film compiled and held by the British Film Institute Library, London.

7 Alan Sillitoe, 'What Comes on Monday?', *New Left Review,* no. 4, July—August 1960, p. 58. Sillitoe's novel was first published in 1958 by W. H. Allen. It reportedly sold 8,000 copies in hardback before being published in paperback (as a 'tie-in' with the film, of course) by Pan Books in 1960. The first Pan print run was 150,000 copies, and it was expected by August that sales would reach the quarter-million mark 'within a few months'. Yet by October 1960 sales had already topped 300,000 and were described by Pan as 'absolutely phenomenal'. By December some 600,000 copies had been printed. The book has been regularly reprinted ever since.

8 This contains all the readers' reports and correspondence relating to the film. My thanks to James Ferman, the Secretary of the British Board of Film Censors, for making it available to me. The British Film Institute Library, London, holds the scenario treatment of the film (undated; S329), and a post-production script (July 1960; S330), though the latter is by no means always accurate.

9 Sillitoe, 'What Comes on Monday?', p. 59, recounts simply that it was 'thought best, because of possible censorship complications, to make the attempted abortion fail'. Reisz is reported as admitting that he 'never regretted making those changes' to the abortion scene; see the reprint of Boleslaw Sulik's 1961 essay on the film in Taylor, *Masterworks of the British Cinema,* p. 349.

10 Alexander Walker, *Hollywood, England,* London, 1974, p. 88. The film was given a general release date of January 1961.

11 See Walker, *Hollywood, England,* pp. 81, 88, and *Evening News,* 1 March 1961. The *Sunday Express,* 30 October 1960, said the production costs were 'about £120,000'. The film also did considerable business in America where, for instance, it broke box-office records on its New York run.

12 *Guardian,* 29 October 1960.

13 *Spectator,* 4 November 1960.

14 *Financial Times,* 31 October 1960.

15 *Daily Express,* 25 October 1960.

16 *Daily Mail,* 25 October 1960.

17 *People,* 30 October 1960.

18 *Evening Standard,* 27 October 1960.

19 *Sunday Telegraph,* 12 February 1961.

20 *Daily Worker,* 29 October 1960.

21 *Daily Telegraph,* 25 October 1960.

22 *New Statesman,* 29 October 1960.

23 *Sunday Times,* 30 October 1960.

24 Sillitoe, 'What Comes on Monday?', p. 59.

25 BBFC reader's report of 20 November 1959.

26 Sillitoe, 'What Comes on Monday?', p. 59.

27 In Walker, *Hollywood, England,* p. 85.

28 Sillitoe, 'What Comes on Monday?', p. 59.

29 It is interesting to note, for example, that *Room at the Top* (1959, Jack Clayton) — often credited with being the first of the British 'new wave' films — went through a similar process of being 'toned down' on matters of language, sex and violence. The treatment of Alice's death caused particular concern, though again both the film company and the BBFC declared that they were more than satisfied with the final outcome to their negotiations. Jack Clayton wrote in a

letter of 6 November 1958 to John Trevelyan: 'I am happy that we have found a solution to all the original objections which is mutually acceptable.' Once more, the BBFC file on the film repays detailed scrutiny.

30 Walker, *Hollywood, England,* pp. 83—4.
31 Alan Swingewood, *The Myth of Mass Culture,* London, 1977, p. 69.
32 A point well made in Arthur Marwick, *Class: Image and Reality in Britain, France and the USA since 1930,* London, 1981, p. 296.

11

The Revolt of the Young

If . . .

The 1960s saw a full-scale, almost precipitate, retreat from the rigorous social controls imposed during the Victorian era by the forces of evangelical religion. In 1960 gambling was legalized, and this led to a proliferation of betting shops, bingo halls and gaming clubs. Capital punishment was abolished in 1965 and theatrical censorship in 1968. Abortion and homo-sexuality were legalized in 1967. Divorce was made easier by the 1969 Divorce Reform Act. At the same time there was a vast expansion of the welfare state, with massive slum-clearance programmes and the building of huge new housing estates, the extension of benefits and social services, the introduction of comprehensive education and the founding of a host of new universities and colleges. The campaign for women's rights was launched, leading to the Equal Pay Act (1970) and the Equal Opportunities Commis-sion. Liberalization and egalitarianism were the keynotes of public policy. This spilled over into popular culture, which was dominated by the young and the working class and characterized by sexual permissiveness and the free use of drugs.[1]

Many felt, despite all this, that the old elites remained in charge, adapting to, and accommodating, social and cultural change. The public schools were their bastion, and as the public sector of education went steadily comprehensive, the voices raised against the private sector became more strident. Gone was the desire for cautious, evolutionary reform. Now the call was for the total abolition of those centres of privilege, power and class-consciousness. The opponents of the public school received potent ammunition from a film, Lindsay Anderson's *If . . .* (1968).

Amusing and biting by turns, *If . . .* brilliantly recreates the enclosed, all-male world of the public school. It lays bare the process by which the system produces an authoritarian elite to govern the country, deals with dissidents and induces unthinking conformism. The school is a rigidly ordered society with an unshakeable hierarchy, from 'scum' (fags) to 'whips' (prefects). Its exclusivity is reinforced by its arcane and self-perpetuating slang, in which we see a new boy being painstakingly instructed. He is made aware that it is not just content but style that counts here ('You do realize it's not just a matter of knowing the answers. It's how you say it'). Pride in belonging is fostered by compulsory games, with Matron entering into the supporters' bloodlust ('Fight, college, fight, fight, fight!') and with a celebratory 'House Thump' greeting the winning of the cup.

If . . . opens with the start of term, recreating the turmoil and bustle of the return from the holidays and introducing the school through the eyes of a lost, bewildered and diminutive new boy, Jute. Thereafter the background of routine, ritual and discipline is meticulously recreated as the action is played out against an authentic background of chapel, dinner, medical inspection, dormitory inspection, cadet corps exercises and lights out. Significantly, given the traditional public school commitment to character-forming rather than academic attainment, lessons occupy only a small part of the film, and the boys are seen as unresponsive and apathetic during them. The film closes with Founder's Day, in which the time-honoured ceremonial is disrupted by the attack of the rebels.

The school is in effect run by the 'whips', cold, self-possessed, all-powerful figures, with distinctive dress (flowered waistcoats, canes) and privileges (fags, the right to beat). They revel in these privileges, constantly ordering silence or running in the corridor to remind everyone that they are in charge. They discourage initiative. 'It's not up to you to think,' house captain Rowntree tells his fag, Bobby Phillips. They deal with nonconformists summarily, inflicting cold showers and, when those fail, brutal floggings, performed ritually and with the entire house listening in tense silence. They either find outlets for their sexual urges in a light-hearted homosexuality, epitomized by the bantering discussion between Rowntree and the 'whips' about the attractions of various boys, or they sublimate them in sadistic authoritarianism, as Denson does. This elite is characterized by Mick Travis when he insolently tells Rowntree: 'The thing I hate about you, Rowntree, is the way you give Coca-Cola to your scum and your best teddy-bear to Oxfam and expect us to lick your frigid fingers for the rest of your frigid life.'

Rather less important in terms of running the school are the masters, whom the 'whips' control, as is tellingly illustrated when Denson on his night round virtually reprimands the new master, Mr Thomas, for being out late. The masters are almost all eccentrics, perverts or ineffectual nonentities. The history master (Graham Crowden) rides his bicycle through the corridors singing hymns at the top of his voice, opens all the windows and cheerfully confesses to having lost essays in the Mont Blanc Tunnel. The chaplain (Geoffrey Chater) twists the nipples of small boys in his maths class and pruriently asks for details of the 'dirty thoughts' confessed by Stephans. Housemaster Kemp (Arthur Lowe) and the new master Thomas (Ben Aris) are dominated by the 'whips'.

The headmaster (brilliantly played by Peter Jeffrey) is a bland, self-satisfied, platitudinous pseudo-liberal, a caricature of the liberal house tutor, Nigel Lorraine, in *The Guinea Pig* (1948). He strides round the school lecturing the sixth-formers on the modern world:

> College is a symbol of many things: scholarship, integrity in public office, high standards in the television and entertainment worlds, huge sacrifice in Britain's wars. Of course, some of our customs are silly; you could say they were middle-class. But a large part of the population is in the process of becoming middle-class, and many of the middle class's moral values are values that the country cannot do without. We must not expect to be thanked. Education in Britain is a nubile Cinderella, sparsely clad and much interfered with. Britain today is a power-house of ideas, experiments,

imagination, on everything from pop music to pig breeding; from atom power stations to mini-skirts, and that's the challenge we've got to meet.

He takes the sixth form in the trendy subject of 'business management'. His is the voice of consensus, of change within continuity, that *The Guinea Pig* was endorsing, a standpoint *If . . .* decisively rejects.

The boys in the school fulfil several different roles. There are ambitious conformists like Stephans, who runs the dormitory where the three rebels sleep, sucks up to the 'whips', acts as if he were a 'whip' already, curries favour with the chaplain by confessing his 'dirty thoughts' and utters anti-Semitic remarks. There are blind opters-out like 'Peanuts', the scientist totally absorbed in his telescope and in looking out to the stars. When Mick hands him a bullet, he hands it back uncomprehendingly. There is the permanent outsider, Biles, persecuted and harassed and, in a chilling scene, hunted and hounded by the boys through the gym and finally tied, upside-down, with his head stuck down the lavatory. Finally, there are the three rebels, Mick Travis (Malcolm McDowell), Johnny Knightly (David Wood) and Wallace (Richard Warwick). Mick's nonconformity is established at the outset, when he returns to school in a broad-brimmed hat and muffled up in a long black scarf. In the privacy of his study he removes the scarf to reveal the moustache he has grown. He shaves it off but thereafter behaves with studied insolence to all in authority. He and his fellow rebels drink gin and smoke illegally, fantasize and dream of freedom ('When do we live?'). In one exhilarating sequence Mick and Johnny break bounds, go into town, steal a motorbike and race through the countryside. After all three have been beaten for their 'general attitude', they rebel, first turning their rifles on the cadet corps exercise and, in the explosive finale, bombing and machine-gunning the assembly of dignitaries, boys and parents at Founder's Day.

What the boys are rebelling against is essentially the repression and authoritarianism embodied by the 'whips' and endorsed by the headmaster. Sexual repression is represented by Denson's suppressed longing for Bobby Phillips, mirrored in a close shot of Denson's face as Bobby shaves him; the sequence of the dowdy and timorous Mrs Kemp wandering naked through the empty dormitories; the chaplain's enquiry into Stephans's 'dirty thoughts'. The rebels are sexual freedom incarnate. Mick encounters a waitress in a café; they romp together on the floor, imitating tigers, at first clothed and later naked. The Girl (Christine Noonan) joins the rebels in their final revolt, as does Bobby Phillips (Rupert Webster), Denson's fag, for he falls in love with Wallace, a process visually encapsulated in the beautifully conceived slow-motion sequence in which Bobby admiringly watches Wallace working out on the bars in the gym. Later Wallace and Bobby smoke a cigarette in the school armoury and are subsequently seen in bed together. Bobby is the fifth and last of the crusaders. Authoritarianism takes the form of the savage beating at the end of which Mick, broken and in tears, takes Rowntree's outstretched hand and says faintly: 'Thank you, Rowntree.' His acting out of the ritual confirms his submission. But the rebels fight back.

At Founder's Day, with parents, boys, staff and visiting VIPs assembled, General Denson, national hero and old boy, addresses the school in a speech that captures perfectly the public school ethos which the rebels have set themselves to oppose:

You're lucky. Yes — a lot of men would give their eyeteeth to be sitting where you are sitting now. You are privileged. Now, for heaven's sake, don't get me wrong. There's nothing the matter with privilege as long as we're ready to pay for it. It's a very sad thing, but today it is fashionable to belittle tradition. The old order that made our nation a living force are for the most part scorned by modern psychiatrists, priests, pundits of all sorts. But what have they got to put in their place? Oh, politicians talk a lot about freedom. Well, freedom is the heritage of every Englishman who speaks with the tongue that Shakespeare spoke. But, you know, we won't stay free unless we are ready to fight. And you won't be any good as fighters unless you know something about discipline. The habit of obedience, how to give orders and how to take them. Never mind the sneers of the cynics. Let us be true to honour . . . duty . . . national pride. We still need loyalty. . . . We still need tradition. If we look around us at the world today, what do we see? We see bloodshed, confusion, decay. I know the world has changed a great deal in the past fifty years. But England, our England, doesn't change so easily. And back here in college today I feel, and it makes me jolly proud, that there is still a tradition here, which has not changed and by God it isn't going to change.

During the ceremony two old men in Crusader armour parade, reciting meaningless Latin formulae. But as the film makes clear, the rebels are the real crusaders, launching an attack on the entrenched forces of privilege and authority. The film's original title, indeed, was *Crusaders*. But as the two sides exchange fire, the headmaster steps out between them, urging a ceasefire and appealing to the rebels: 'Trust me.' The Girl shoots him through the head, and the battle continues. The choice of the Girl is significant. She is the only working-class character in the rebel band, and she is the only woman. She stands for female equality, unrepressed sexuality and youthful revolt. But, even more significantly, as the film ends the school forces, rallied by the bishop and the general, counter-attack, and Mick turns his gun on the audience.

It is a very personal film for its director, Lindsay Anderson. Not only was it filmed on location at his old school, Cheltenham College, but much of the detail was, as he has admitted, drawn from his own experience. 'I put a lot of myself into *If . . .*,' he said in 1969, 'It is largely autobiographical.'[2] The authors, David Sherwin and John Howlett, were also at public school (Tonbridge), and it is this first-hand experience that makes the texture of the life reconstructed on screen so convincing. But Anderson was not simply seeking to make a documentary study. He made his intentions clear in very detailed interviews both during and after shooting of the film:

> Probably all my work, even when it has been very realistic, has struggled for a poetic quality — for larger implications than the surface realities may suggest. I think the most important challenge is to get beyond pure naturalism into poetry. Some people call this fantasy, but these terms are dangerous, because words always mean different things to different people. I would call *If . . .* a realistic film — not completely naturalistic but trying to penetrate the reality of its particular world. I think that Brecht said that realism didn't show what things look like but how they really are.[3]

It is no coincidence that the film-makers whom he most admires are John Ford and Humphrey Jennings, who both aimed at a poetic truth and who both, like Anderson, were profoundly romantic.

The truth that he sought to portray through the life and structures of the school was the truth about society. He was deeply dismayed when critics saw it merely as an attack on the public schools. In his introduction to the published version of the screenplay he wrote:

> Essentially the public school milieu of the film provides material for a metaphor. Even the coincidence of its making and release with the worldwide phenomenon of student revolt was fortuitous. The basic tensions, between hierarchy and anarchy, independence and tradition, liberty and law, are always with us. That is why we scrupulously avoided contemporary references (on a journalistic level) which would date the picture; and why it is completely unimportant whether its slang, its manners or its details or organization are true to the schools of this year or that. And this is why the film has been understood — recognized — by so many people, of so many ages and so many countries.[4]

Anderson, a former film critic, had been part of the 'free cinema' group, one of those energizing groups of artists that appeared in the late 1950s. Their object was to galvanize the cinema and to stimulate the production of films that were 'vital, illuminating, personal and refreshing'. Anderson's direction of documentaries (*Every Day Except Christmas, O Dreamland*), plays at the Royal Court Theatre (notably *The Long and the Short and the Tall* and *Serjeant Musgrave's Dance*) and a feature film (*This Sporting Life*, 1963) led to his being grouped with the 'new wave',[5] but he was always very much his own man ('No film can be too personal,' he wrote).[6] The critic John Russell Taylor, assessing his career in 1975, declared:

> Among the directors at present working in the British cinema, Lindsay Anderson is the only one, of any generation, who is truly an international figure, who is . . . undoubtedly and unarguably an *auteur*.[7]

If . . . can properly be seen, then, as a personal statement about the educational system, about Britain and about society. Anderson described *If . . .* as 'deeply anarchistic' and said:

> People persistently misunderstand the term anarchistic, and think it just means wildly chucking bombs about. But anarchy is a social and political philosophy which puts the highest possible value on responsibility. The film is not about responsibility against irresponsibility. It's about rival notions of responsibility and consequently well within a strong Puritan tradition.[8]

The evidence suggests that just as people misunderstand anarchy, according to Anderson, so also they misunderstood *If . . .*, a reaction that highlights the fact that audiences do not always take away from a film the message that the film-maker has intended to convey. Despite Anderson's explicit statements, many critics, particularly in the popular press, saw the film exclusively in terms of a critique of public schools. Felix Barker in the *Evening News* called it a 'savage attack on the public schools . . . witty, venomous, exaggerated but with a deadly underlying truth'.[9] Ernest Betts in the *People* saw it as a 'terrific swipe at the public school system'.[10] Madeleine Harmsworth in the *Sunday Mirror* regarded it as 'exploding a bomb under the English public school, blowing it to bits'.[11] Even Gavin Millar in *Sight and Sound* declared: 'No one has ever done such an effective hatchet job on the English public school.'[12]

Other critics, particularly those of the quality papers, saw beyond this and accepted Anderson's statement that he intended the school to be a metaphor. Patrick Gibbs in the *Daily Telegraph* wrote: 'Anderson uses, reasonably enough, satire on one aspect of the British educational system to attack the established order in general. It is an inventive, and well organized satire.'[13] Dilys Powell in the *Sunday Times* commented: '*If . . .* is not just about an imaginary public school. It is about the rigid ideas and the authoritarian society which Mr Anderson and his collaborators see rooted in the public school.'[14] John Russell Taylor in *The Times* called the film a 'rich, complex, obscure metaphor of the way we live now'.[15] Michael Walsh in the *Daily Express* called it a 'brilliant, merciless, indictment of the public school system and by inference of the Establishment'.[16] David Robinson in the *Financial Times* declared: 'the film offers a vivid metaphor for conflicts in contemporary society.'[17] Nina Hibbin in the *Morning Star* called it a 'devastating view . . . of the cruel traditions which go into the shaping of the ruling class'.[18]

Whatever the differences of opinion about its meaning, critics were almost totally united in praising the film's execution. Nina Hibbin in the *Morning Star* thought it the 'best and most significant film of the Sixties'.[19] Felix Barker in the *Evening News* called it 'superb'.[20] Ernest Betts in the *People* described it as 'brilliant and absorbing'.[21] Penelope Mortimer in the *Observer* proclaimed it a 'masterwork . . . a tremendous artistic success'.[22] Clive Hirschhorn in the *Sunday Express* declared it a 'masterpiece', as did Richard Roud in the *Guardian*.[23] Patrick Gibbs in the *Daily Telegraph* thought it 'superbly executed'.[24] Almost the only dissenting voice was that of Eric Rhode in the *Listener*. He called it the 'most hating film I know' and went on: 'You can't expect a spewing man to be articulate. . . . [His] films seemed to be working out personal grudges and resentments in terms of social conflict. . . . If the public schools had not existed, Anderson would have had to create something like them.'[25]

What is interesting about the critics' reaction to *If . . .* is that, by contrast with their response to *The Guinea Pig,* they did not on the whole engage with the issues on a personal level. Patrick Gibbs complained that the action looked like a parody of what went on around him at Oundle in the 1930s and did not present a contemporary view of the public school. But that was not Anderson's aim. Most people seem to have accepted Anderson's criticisms of the system at face value, indicating the success of several generations of literary conditioning.

Despite the film's critical success, it experienced considerable difficult in obtaining a general release. It had been a long time gestating. It had originally been scripted under the title *Crusaders* by David Sherwin and John Howlett between 1958 and 1960, while they were at Oxford. Five years later Seth Holt expressed an interest in filming it, but when other commitments turned up to occupy his attention he drew Lindsay Anderson's notice to it. Anderson and Sherwin reworked the script in 1967, and Anderson took it to Memorial Enterprises, the company founded by actor Albert Finney and headed by Michael Medwin. They agreed to produce it, but they were totally unable to find a British backer. The American television company CBS, which had just formed a film division, accepted it, but it withdrew six weeks before shooting was due to start. Paramount stepped in just in time to save the project, and the film was shot and released in 1968.[26] Initially it was shown only at the Paramount Cinema, Lower Regent Street, London. After determined lobbying, supported by the fact that the film had taken £40,000 since it opened just before Christmas 1968, the ABC circuit agreed in January 1969 to give it a national release.[27]

The film marked yet another milestone in the progressive liberalization of film censorship. For although the censors removed a few shots in which male genitalia were in evidence, they permitted the full frontal view of a nude female for the first time, in the sequence of Mrs Kemp wandering through the dormitories. John Trevelyan, Secretary of the British Board of Film Censors, was quoted as saying: 'There is nothing erotic in the scene. In the context there's nothing offensive about it.'[28]

It was, however, not just the content of the film that must have given distributors pause for thought. Its form was extremely unusual. David Robinson called it the 'first English poetic feature film', by which he meant that it 'juxtaposes elements to produce impressions greater than the sum of these elements'.[29] John Russell Taylor called it an 'extraordinary film, a film that virtually defies ordinary verbal description, because it works as only the cinema can, on the indistinct border between fantasy which has the solidity of tangible experience and reality which seems as remote and elsewhere as a dream'.[30] Anderson himself said:

> Stylistically I don't really think *If . . .* fits very closely into a contemporary picture of film-making, except in so far as developments in the last — what? — ten years have made it possible to work with much greater freedom in the cinema than before, and to be personal and not to be bound to the traditional and conventional ideas of narrative construction and narrative style. I think where it isn't contemporary is that its technique, I would say on the whole, is extremely sober. In fact this is both natural to me and the result of a quite conscious determination on my part. The more what we might call 'trendy', or eccentric, or showy technique has tended to become in the last few years, the more I have felt I wanted to try and make films with as much simplicity and as much directness as possible. . . . Qualities of rhythm and balance and composition inside a very straightforward and sober technique are the problems that interest me most.[31]

A viewing of the film bears out this claim. Anderson avoids fancy camerawork, tracks on movement, uses close-ups for emphasis and keeps his camera still in medium shot when there is a lot of action going on in the frame. What is unusual is the blending of fantasy and reality, the switching from colour to black and white and back again and the division of the film into eight chapters, which follow the school through the term from the first day to Founder's Day. It thus creates an overall picture of school life, into which the story of the rebels is woven.

The changes from colour to black and white were justified by Anderson as a Brechtian device:

> *If . . .* is not meant to be a film that excites or agitates but I hope that people understand it; this is why the division into chapters and, up to a certain point, the use of black and white and colour are what Brecht calls processes of distanciation which detach the spectator from his emotion.[32]

But there was a practical reason for it too:

> When Mirek [Ondricek] said that with our budget [for lamps] and our schedule he could not guarantee consistency of colour for the chapel

If . . .

In *If . . .* Lindsay Anderson explores life in a public school, using it as a metaphor for society at large. The school is ruled by an authoritarian prefectorial elite, the 'whips' (Peter Sproule, Michael Cadman and Hugh Thomas) (1). The school regime is sexually repressive — Matron (Mona Washbourne) conducts compulsory medical inspection (2). It also encourages cruelty by boys (3) and by masters (Geoffrey Chater and Sean Bury) (4).

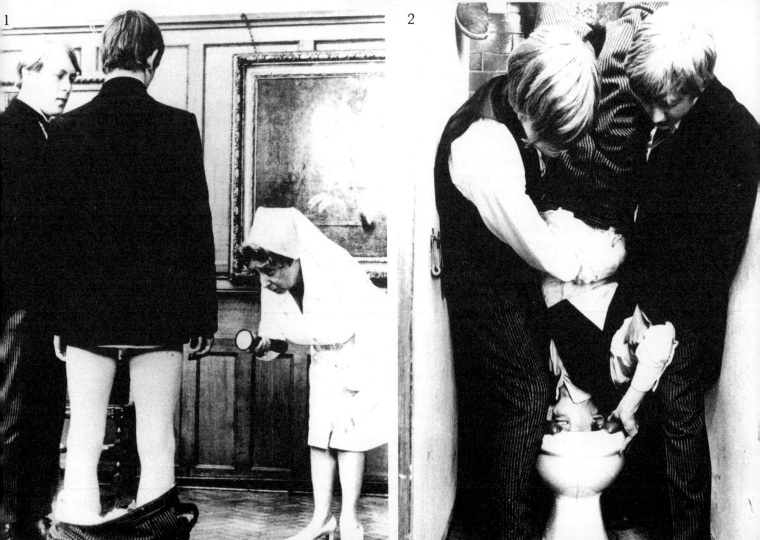

4

5

Johnny (David Wood), Wallace (Richard Warwick) and Mick (Malcolm McDowell) rebel against the system, at first by drinking illicitly (5) and then by declaring open war with the help of the Girl (Christine Noonan) (6).

In the light of this comment, it looks as if Anderson was making a Brechtian virtue out of a technical necessity. In fact, a number of interiors are in black and white, and Anderson said in his introduction to the screenplay:

> The important thing to realize is that there is no symbolism involved in the choice of sequences filmed in black and white, nothing expressionist or schematic.[34]

The problem with this is that many people have spent time trying to work out the justification for the black-and-white sequences. They have invariably ended up confused and frustrated.[35]

The division between fantasy and reality has posed another problem. Elizabeth Sussex sets the problem in perspective:

> The threshold between fantasy and reality in the film is then something that must vary according to how much reality the individual spectator can bear. And the film's supreme achievement is in enabling audiences to interpret it according to their own idea of what is real. Undoubtedly some people find a lot of fantasy in *If. . . .* For others, like Anderson himself, 'It's all real.'[36]

This is a sensible enough view. It could all be regarded as real, even the final rebellion. There had after all been the Great Marlborough Rebellion in 1851, when the boys, in protest against magisterial tyranny, starvation and beatings, arranged a great firework explosion for 5 November, a pyrotechnical precursor of *If . . .*:

> On the signal the school appeared to blow up. The court became ablaze with fireworks, and fireworks shot from every building. Mr Wilkinson, rushing out in a state of extreme agitation, had a bottle full of gunpowder exploded behind his back and rushed back. The other masters were equally powerless. Chaos reigned all night. The long corridors of B House echoed to ceaseless denotations. For two days the college reeked of gunpowder and smoke drifted through the smashed windows and broken doors. The authorities were paralysed.[37]

The rebellion was successful, and the cowed headmaster made immediate concessions.

However, there is one sequence in the film which disturbs this interpretation — the scene in which, after Mick has apparently bayoneted the chaplain, the headmaster produces him from a drawer in his office and gets the rebels to apologize to him. Up to that point none of the action has been intrinsically unlikely, but that sequence fatally dissipates the tension, compromising the finale. Anderson admitted of this scene: 'Harold Pinter got very upset about that moment. He thought it got very out of style. He may well be right.'[38] Of course, it could be yet another 'distanciation' device. If it is, it does as much to confuse viewers as the other devices.

Despite these problems, *If . . .* remains a magnificent piece of film-making, savagely funny, gripping, richly textured and extremely well acted by a then unknown young cast backed up by some distinguished British character actors giving beautifully judged performances. However personal a film Anderson thought it, and whatever his own interpretation, it will probably be remembered — and was certainly interpreted at the time — as highlighting two preoccupations of the 1960s.[39]

First, it completely demolished the public school as an educational institution. The fact that public schools had changed considerably since Anderson's schooldays and that uniforms, fagging, beating, athleticism, compulsory chapel and the cadet corps had all declined in importance, and in some cases had even disappeared, was irrelevant. The bulk of Anderson's audience had never been to public school, and his cinematic version merely confirmed the picture that had emerged from literature, particularly in the inter-war period, of the public school as a source of arrogance, elitism, constraint, cruelty and conformism.

Second, it appealed dramatically to the self-image of the 'Swinging Sixties', an image that combined youth, sex and rebellion, individual self-expression as opposed to authority, tradition, hierarchy and age. The poster advertising the film appealed directly to this youthful audience. It featured a set of stills from the film grouped in the shape of a hand grenade. Super-imposed on that were two pictures of Malcolm McDowell, one of him in school uniform carrying books and the other of him in leather jacket carrying a machine-gun, with the caption underneath: 'Which side will you be on?'[40]

In view of this, it is surely ingenuous of Anderson to claim:

> Essentially the heroes of If . . . are, without knowing it, old-fashioned boys. They are not anti-heroes, or drop-outs, or Marxist—Leninists or Maoists or readers of Marcuse. Their revolt is inevitable, not because of what they *think* but because of what they *are*. Mick plays a little at being an intellectual . . . but when he acts, it is instinctively because of his outraged dignity, his frustrated passion, his vital energy, his sense of fair play, if you like. . . . In this sense Mick and Johnny and Wallace and Bobby Phillips and the Girl are traditionalists.[41]

For even if Anderson feels this, it is not a view that communicates itself to the majority of his audiences. He points to the fencing match in the gym when the boys cry things like 'England, awake!' and 'Death to tyrants!' as evidence of their essentially old-fashioned romanticism. But it is not this, nor the swearing of blood brotherhood with the oath 'Death to the oppressor', that catches the attention of the audience. Anderson makes the crusaders sound rather like Stalky and Co., a trio of public schoolboys who also broke bounds, smoked illegally, despised games, were beaten for misbehaving — and were created by Kipling, whose spirit the film seems to be mockingly evoking in its title, which it shares with Kipling's most famous poem. But the difference is that while Stalky and Co. were genuine patriots, believed that the headmaster was right to beat them and went off to serve the Empire, Mick and Co. are identified with Third World resistance to the imperial powers. Mick pins up a picture of a black freedom fighter on the wall and says admiringly, 'Fantastic.' He declares: 'Violence and revolution are the only pure acts.' He listens constantly to the *Sanctus* from the Congolese *Missa Luba*, with its throbbing, exciting, primitive rhythm, speaking of the rebellion, vitality and youth of an emerging continent. It is no coincidence that sales of the *Sanctus* rocketed after the film's release. This was the aspect of Mick that appealed, not his putative traditionalism.

Similarly, when Anderson says of his final sequence, 'Its violence is so plainly metaphorical' he is again misjudging its effect.[42] Audiences saw this as the message. The only way to deal with the public school system and the society that it supports is to sweep them both away. When the headmaster, the voice of compromise and consensus, is shot through the head, when the old lady in a flowered hat grabs a machine gun and opens up on the rebels, screaming 'Bastards! Bastards!', when Mick turns his machine gun on the cinema audience to fire directly into camera, it is indeed, as Anderson says 'exhilarating, funny, a bit shocking, magnificent', but so are all revolutions and this is surely the beginning of the revolution. Audiences who interpreted the film as a clarion call arousing them from their complacency saw Mick and his friends precisely as Anderson says they were not to be seen — "as anti-heroes, dropouts, Marxist—Leninists."

In retrospect, *If . . .* can be regarded as almost encapsulating the rise and fall of the 1960s. In his brilliant analysis of that decade, *The Neophiliacs*, Christopher Booker sees the 1960s as essentially a creation of fantasy, which eventually self-destructed. Booker divides the growth of this fantasy into five stages: anticipation, rising excitement, frustration, nightmare and death-wish, followed by the explosion into reality. *If . . .*, the title itself redolent of fantasy, follows exactly this course: the anticipation of rebellion, the breaking of bounds, the beating, the shooting up of the corps and, finally, the rebellion. But at the end of the film the Establishment is fighting back. As Anderson observed in 1969: 'It doesn't look to me as though Mick can win. The world rallies, as it always will, and brings its overwhelming fire-power to bear on the man who says "No."' In reality too the Establishment was fighting back. In 1970 the years of Labour Government came to an end with the re-election of the Conservatives. The years of prosperity drew to a close, and recession set in.

Like *If . . .*, the British film industry itself conformed to Booker's thesis. The social and cultural revolution of the late 1950s had seen the renaissance of British film-making in the so-called 'new wave'. A new and talented generation of film directors brought to the screen the frustrations, limitations and aspirations of the working-class young in films like *Room at the Top* (1959), *Saturday Night and Sunday Morning* (1960), *A Taste of Honey* (1961), *A Kind of Loving* (1962) and *The Loneliness of the Long Distance Runner* (1962). All these films were shot in black and white on genuine North Country locations; all had melancholy and dissonant jazz scores; and all featured a new breed of working-class anti-hero, played by a new breed of working-class actors like Albert Finney, Tom Courtenay and Alan Bates. But by 1964 the 'new wave' had spent itself. 'Swinging London' had been born, an increasingly frenzied saturnalia whose cult was the new and the now, a world of colour supplements, pirate radio, glamorous television commercials, dolly birds, discos and boutiques. With the backing of the Hollywood giants, British film-makers set out to capture the glitter and the glamour. Sober realism and earnest social comment gave way to fantasy, extravaganza and escapism; black-and-white photography and Northern locations to colour and the lure of the metropolis; Puritanical self-discipline to hedonistic self-indulgence; plain, truthful settings to flamboyant, unrealistic decorativeness. Films became locked in a heady spiral of mounting extravagance, febrile excitement and faddish innovation. Seen from the depressed and sober vantage point of succeeding generations, these films seem akin to highly coloured ephemera from the last days of the Roman Empire, a madcap efflorescence preceding extinction.[43] If Tony Richardson was the key figure of the 'new wave', the celebrant of the 'Swinging London' style was Dick Lester. Lester's films, particularly *The Knack* and *Help*, were mercurial, modish mosaics, his style fragmented and breathtakingly fast-moving, an amalgam of influences from television commercials, cartoon strips and Goon Show surrealism. It was this style that Anderson resolutely eschewed.

Amidst all the fun and frenzy a few films looked honourably back to the 'new wave' and remained valiantly out of step with the mood of the times. Ken Loach's *Kes* (1969) notably kept the Orwellian flag flying amid the Byzantine excesses raging all around it. Anderson struck out on his own with *If . . . .* But the bubble of 'Swinging London' burst when a clutch of grossly self-indulgent and hopelessly uncommercial films failed at the box office. The Hollywood companies lost heavily and in 1969 pulled out virtually all together. With the 1970s came the cinema's exposure to reality. London stopped swinging. The butterfly culture of the 1960s flew away. The cold, harsh light of reality broke in on the tinsel world. The British film industry collapsed, and the historians reached for their pens to chart its rise and fall.

Notes

1 On the 1960s, see Arthur Marwick, *British Society since 1945,* Harmondsworth, 1982; Christopher Booker, *The Neophiliacs,* London, 1969; Bernard Levin, *The Pendulum Years,* London, 1970.
2 Elizabeth Sussex, *Lindsay Anderson,* London, 1969, p. 68.
3 ibid., p. 12.
4 Lindsay Anderson and David Sherwin, *If . . .*, Lorrimer Modern Film Scripts, London, 1969, p. 9.
5 For a detailed discussion of Anderson's career see Sussex, *Lindsay Anderson.*
6 ibid., p. 31.
7 John Russell Taylor, *Directors and Directions,* London, 1975, p. 69.
8 Sussex, *Lindsay Anderson,* p. 89.
9 *Evening News,* 19 December 1968.
10 *People,* 22 December 1968.
11 *Sunday Mirror,* 22 December 1968.
12 *Sight and Sound,* Winter 1968—69, p. 42.
13 *Daily Telegraph,* 20 December 1968.
14 *Sunday Times,* 22 December 1968.
15 *The Times,* 20 December 1968.
16 *Daily Express,* 19 December 1968.
17 *Financial Times,* 20 December 1968.
18 *Morning Star,* 20 December 1968.
19 ibid., 15 March 1969.
20 *Evening News,* 19 December 1968.
21 *People,* 22 December 1968.
22 *Observer,* 22 December 1968.
23 *Sunday Express,* 22 December 1968; *Guardian,* 19 December 1968.
24 *Daily Telegraph,* 20 December 1968.
25 *Listener,* 26 December 1968.
26 For details, see Sussex, *Lindsay Anderson,* pp. 68—70.
27 *Guardian,* 17 January 1969.
28 *Daily Mail,* 18 December 1968.
29 *Financial Times,* 20 December 1968.
30 Taylor, *Directors and Directions,* p. 91.
31 Sussex, *Lindsay Anderson,* pp. 89—90.
32 ibid., p. 75.
33 Anderson and Sherwin, *If . . .* p. 10.
34 ibid.

35 I base this observation on discussions with students after showings of the film over several years.
36 Sussex, *Lindsay Anderson,* pp. 83—4.
37 Jonathan Gathorne-Hardy, *The Public School Phenomenon,* Harmondsworth, 1979, pp. 115—16.
38 Sussex, *Lindsay Anderson,* p. 86.
39 *If . . .* was the official British entry at the Cannes Film Festival in 1969.
40 The poster is reproduced in Lindsay Anderson's article '*If . . .*', in *The Movie,* 64, 1981, pp. 1276—7.
41 Anderson and Sherwin, *If . . .,* p. 12.
42 *ibid.*
43 The period is discussed in detail in Alexander Walker, *Hollywood, England,* London, 1974.

Filmography

Sanders of the River (1935)

Production company: London Films
Distributors: United Artists
Director: Zoltan Korda
Producer: Alexander Korda
Screenplay: Lajos Biro and Jeffrey Dell (from the stories by Edgar Wallace)
Photographer: Georges Périnal
Editor: Charles Crichton
Art director: Vincent Korda
Music: Mischa Spoliansky
Cast: Leslie Banks (Commissioner Sanders), Paul Robeson (Bosambo), Nina Mae McKinney (Lilongo), Robert Cochran (Lt Tibbets), Martin Walker (Commissioner Ferguson), Richard Grey (Captain Hamilton), Tony Wane (King Mofalaba), Marquis de Portago (Farini), Eric Maturin (Smith), Allan Jeayes (Father O'Leary), Charles Carson (Governor)
Running time: 98 minutes
Available on 16 mm from Anthony Morris Film

South Riding (1938)

Production company: Victor Saville Productions for London Films
Distributors: United Artists
Director—producer: Victor Saville
Screenplay: Ian Dalrymple and Donald Bull (from the novel by Winifred Holtby)
Photographer: Harry Stradling
Editor: Hugh Stewart
Art director: Lazare Meerson
Music: Richard Addinsell
Cast: Ralph Richardson (Robert Carne), Edna Best (Sarah Burton), Edmund Gwenn (Alfred Huggins), Ann Todd (Madge Carne), Glynis Johns (Midge Carne), John Clements (Joe Astell), Marie Lohr (Mrs Beddows), Milton

Rosmer (Alderman Snaith), Joan Ellum (Lydia Holly), Herbert Lomas (Castle), Peggy Novak (Bessie Warbuckle), Gus McNaughton (Tadman), Lewis Casson (Lord Sedgmire), Felix Aylmer (Chairman of Council), Jean Cadell (Miss Dry), Edward Lexy (Mr Holly), Josephine Wilson (Mrs Holly), Skelton Knaggs (Reg Aythorne)
Running time: 91 minutes
Available on 16 mm from Harris Films

The Life and Death of Colonel Blimp (1943)

Production company: The Archers
Distributors: GFD
Director—producer—screenplay: Michael Powell and Emeric Pressburger
Photographer: Georges Périnal
Editor: John Seabourne
Production designer: Alfred Junge
Music: Allan Gray
Cast: Anton Walbrook (Theo Kretschmar-Schuldorff), Roger Livesey (Clive Candy), Deborah Kerr (Edith Hunter, Barbara Wynne, Angela 'Johnny' Cannon), Ursula Jeans (Frau von Kalteneck), Roland Culver (Colonel Betteridge), Albert Lieven (Von Ritter), John Laurie (Murdoch), Robert Harris (Embassy Secretary), Arthur Wontner (Embassy counsellor), Felix Aylmer (Bishop), Harry Welchman (Major Davis), David Hutcheson (Captain 'Hoppy' Hopwell), James McKechnie (Captain 'Spud' Wilson), Reginald Tate (Captain Van Zijl), Neville Mapp ('Stuffy' Graves), David Ward (Kaunitz), Eric Maturin (Colonel Goodhead), Muriel Aked (Aunt Margaret), Valentine Dyall (Von Schonborn), Frith Banbury ('Babyface' Fitzroy), A. E. Matthews (President), Carl Jaffe (Von Reumann), Dennis Arundell (Orchestra leader)
Running time: 163 minutes
Available on 16 mm from the British Film Institute

A Canterbury Tale (1944)

Production company: The Archers
Distributors: Eagle—Lion
Director—producer—screenplay: Michael Powell and Emeric Pressburger
Photgrapher: Erwin Hillier
Editor: John Seabourne
Production designer: Alfred Junge
Music: Allan Gray
Cast: Eric Portman (Thomas Colpeper), Sheila Sim (Alison Smith), Dennis Price (Sgt Peter Gibbs), Sgt John Sweet (Sgt Bob Johnson), Esmond Knight (Narrator, Seven Sisters soldier, Village idiot), Charles Hawtrey (Thomas Duckett), Hay Petrie (Woodcock), George Merritt (Ned Horton), Edward Rigby (Jim Horton), Freda Jackson (Prudence Honeywood), Betty Jardine (Fee Baker), Eliot Makeham (Organist), Harvey Golden (Sgt Roczinsky), Esma Cannon (Maid), John Slater (Len), Graham Moffatt (Stuffy), Anthony Holles (Sgt Bassett), Leonard Smith (Leslie), James Tamsitt (Terry), David Todd (David), Judith Furst (Dorothy Bird)
Running time: 124 minutes
Available on 16 mm from the British Film Institute

Fame is the Spur (1947)

Production company: Two Cities Films
Distributors: GFD
Director: Roy Boulting
Producer: John Boulting
Screenplay: Nigel Balchin (from the novel by Howard Spring)
Photographer: Gunther Krampf
Editor: Richard Best
Art director: John Howell
Music: John Wooldridge
Cast: Michael Redgrave (Hamer Radshaw), Rosamund John (Ann Radshaw), Bernard Miles (Tom Hannaway), Hugh Burden (Arnold Ryerson), Carla Lehmann (Lettice, Lady Liskeard), Marjorie Fielding (Lizzie Lightowler), Sir Seymour Hicks (Lord Lostwithiel), David Tomlinson (Lord Liskeard), Anthony Wager (Hamer as a child), Brian Weske (Arnold as a child), Gerald Fox (Tom as a child), Milton Rosmer (Magistrate), Wylie Watson (Pendleton)
Running time: 116 minutes

The Guinea Pig (1948)

Production company: Pilgrim Pictures
Distributors: Pathé
Director: Roy Boulting
Producer: John Boulting
Screenplay: Warren Chetham Strode, Bernard Miles and Roy Boulting (from the play by Warren Chetham Strode)
Photographer: Gilbert Taylor
Editor: Richard Best
Art Director: John Howell
Music: John Wooldridge
Cast: Richard Attenborough (Jack Read), Sheila Sim (Lynne Hartley), Bernard Miles (Mr Read), Cecil Trouncer (Lloyd Hartley), Robert Flemyng (Nigel Lorraine), Edith Sharpe (Mrs Hartley), Joan Hickson (Mrs Read), Tim Bateson (Ronald Tracey), Clive Baxter (Gregory), Basil Cunard (Buckton), John Forrest (Fitch), Maureen Glynne (Bessie), Brenda Hogan (Lorna Beckett), Herbert Lomas (Sir James Corfield), Anthony Newley (Miles Minor), Anthony Nicholls (Mr Stringer), Wally Patch (Uncle Percy), Hay Petrie (Peck), Oscar Quitak (David Tracey), Kynaston Reeves (Bishop), Peter Reynolds (Grimmett), Olive Sloane (Aunt Mabel), Anthony Wager (Bert), Percy Walsh (Alec Stevens), Norman Watson (Fanshaw)
Running time: 97 minutes
Available on 16 mm from Connoisseur Films

The Ladykillers (1955)

Production company: Ealing Studios
Distributors: Rank Film Distributors
Director: Alexander Mackendrick
Producer: Michael Balcon
Screenplay: William Rose

Photographer: Otto Heller
Editor: Jack Harris
Art director: Jim Morahan
Music: Tristram Cary
Cast: Katie Johnson (Mrs Louisa Wilberforce), Alec Guinness (Professor Marcus), Cecil Parker (Major Courtney), Herbert Lom (Louis), Peter Sellers (Harry), Danny Green ('One-Round'), Jack Warner (Superintendent), Philip Stainton (Police sergeant), Ewan Roberts (Police constable), Frankie Howerd (Barrow boy), Kenneth Connor (Taxi driver), Edie Martin (Lettice), Helen Burls (Hypatia), Evelyn Kerry (Amelia), Phoebe Hodgson (Fourth guest), Leonard Sharp (Pavement artist), Harold Goodwin (Parcels clerk), Stratford Johns (Security guard)
Running time: 97 minutes
Available on 16 mm from Columbia—EMI—Warner Ltd

I'm All Right Jack (1959)

Production company: Charter Films
Distributors: British Lion
Director: John Boulting
Producer: Roy Boulting
Screenplay: Frank Harvey and John Boulting with Alan Hackney (from the novel *Private Life* by Alan Hackney)
Photographer: Max Greene
Editor: Anthony Harvey
Art director: Bill Andrews
Music: Ken Hoare and Ron Goodwin
Cast: Ian Carmichael (Stanley Windrush), Terry-Thomas (Major Hitchcock), Peter Sellers (Fred Kite), Richard Attenborough (Sidney de Vere Cox), Margaret Rutherford (Aunt Dolly), Dennis Price (Bertram Tracepurcel), Irene Handl (Mrs Kite), Miles Malleson (Mr Windrush), Victor Maddern (Knowles), Liz Fraser (Cynthia Kite), John Le Mesurier (Waters), Marne Maitland (Mr Mohammed), Kenneth Griffith (Dai), Raymond Huntley (Magistrate), Cardew Robinson (Shop steward), Terry Scott (Crawley), Esma Cannon (Spencer), Ronnie Stevens (Hooper), Basil Dignam (Minister of Labour), Frank Phillips (BBC announcer), Harry Locke (TUC official), John Comer (Shop steward), Wally Patch (Old worker), Muriel Young (Announcer), Malcolm Muggeridge (Himself)
Running time: 105 minutes
Available on 16 mm from Rank Film Library

Saturday Night and Sunday Morning (1960)

Production company: Woodfall
Distributors: British Lion
Director: Karel Reisz
Producers: Harry Saltzman and Tony Richardson
Screenplay: Alan Sillitoe (from his own novel)
Photographer: Freddie Francis
Editor: Seth Holt
Art director: Ted Marshall
Music: Johnny Dankworth

Cast: Albert Finney (Arthur Seaton), Shirley Anne Field (Doreen Gretton), Rachel Roberts (Brenda), Hylda Baker (Aunt Ada), Norman Rossington (Bert), Bryan Pringle (Jack), Robert Cawdron (Robboe), Edna Morris (Mrs Bull), Elsie Wagstaffe (Mrs Seaton), Frank Pettitt (Mr Seaton), Avis Bunnage (Blowsy woman), Colin Blakeley (Loudmouth), Louise Dunn (Betty), Irene Raymond (Mrs Gretton), Anne Blake (Civil Defence officer), Peter Madden (Drunk)
Running time: 89 minutes
Available on 16 mm from Rank Film Distributors

If . . . (1968)

Production company: Memorial Enterprises Ltd
Distributors: Paramount Pictures
Director: Lindsay Anderson
Producers: Michael Medwin and Lindsay Anderson
Screenplay: David Sherwin and Lindsay Anderson (from an original script, *Crusaders,* by David Sherwin and John Howlett)
Photographer: Miroslav Ondricek
Editor: David Gladwell
Production designer: Jocelyn Herbert
Music: Marc Wilkinson
Cast: Malcolm McDowell (Mick Travis), David Wood (Johnny Knightly), Richard Warwick (Wallace), Christine Noonan (The Girl), Rupert Webster (Bobby Phillips), Robert Swann (Rowntree), Hugh Thomas (Denson), Michael Cadman (Fortinbras), Peter Sproule (Barnes), Peter Jeffrey (Headmaster), Anthony Nicholls (General Denson), Arthur Lowe (Mr Kemp), Mona Washbourne (Matron), Mary Macleod (Mrs Kemp), Geoffrey Chater (Chaplain), Ben Aris (John Thomas), Graham Crowden (History master), Charles Lloyd Pack (Classics master), John Garrie (Music master), Tommy Godfrey (School porter), Guy Ross (Stephans), Robin Askwith (Keating), Richard Everitt (Pussy Graves), Philip Bagenal ('Peanuts'), Nicholas Page (Cox), Robert Yetzes (Fisher), David Griffin (Willens), Graham Sharman (Van Eyssen), Richard Tombleson (Baird), Richard Davies (Machin), Brian Pettifer (Biles), Michael Newport (Brunning), Charles Sturridge (Markland), Sean Bury (Jute), Martin Beaumont (Hunter)
Running time: 111 minutes
Available on 16 mm from Rank Film Distributors

Index

The Gershwins'
Porgy and Bess

The Gershwins'
Porgy and Bess

A 75TH ANNIVERSARY CELEBRATION

Robin Thompson

AMADEUS
PRESS

An Imprint of Hal Leonard Corporation

Copyright © 2010 by Robin Thompson

Published in 2010 by Amadeus Press
An Imprint of Hal Leonard Corporation
7777 West Bluemound Road
Milwaukee, WI 53213

Trade Book Division Editorial Offices
33 Plymouth Street, Montclair, NJ 07042

Book design by Adam Fulrath
Photo credits:
Pages 3, 5, 13, 15, 33, 44, 55, 57, 60, 72, 71, 72, 80, 102, 128, 129, 130, 137–138, 140, 143, 145, 147, 149–155, 160, 168:
The George and Ira Gershwin Collection, Library of Congress
Pages 2, 5 (bottom), 8, 27, 114, 145, 148, 152, 154, 172, 185: The Ira and Leonore Gershwin Trusts
Pages x, 10, 100, 112: Photofest
Pages 158, 161: Getty Images
Pages 4, 5 (bottom), 11, 35, 36, 37, 67, 69, 75, 82, 83, 84, 86, 88, 90, 93, 98, 104, 106, 107, 111, 118, 132,
163–165, 170, 173–174, 176–177, 182, 184, 185: Author's collection
Pages 28, 50, 53, 42: New York Public Library
Color insert: The George and Ira Gershwin Collection, Library of Congress; The Ira and Leonore Gershwin Trusts;
Author's collection

Printed in the United States of America

Library of Congress Cataloging-in-Publication Data is available upon request.

ISBN 978-1-57467-191-9

www.amadeuspress.com

ACKNOWLEDGMENTS

For Lee Whelchel

I would like to express my gratitude to Gayletha Nichols and to Rusty Cutchin, my editor at Hal Leonard Performing Arts Publishing. His "call" on this project went far beyond any kind of "duty" I can think of.

I also owe debts of gratitude to John Cerullo, Group Publisher at Hal Leonard Performing Arts Publishing, Daniel Chilewich and Todd Gershwin of Premiere Media, and Marc Gershwin for his time, insights, and the foreword to this book. Equally helpful were Michael Strunsky and Michael Owen with the holdings at the Ira and Leonore Gershwin Trusts.

Thanks also go to Elizabeth Auman and Richard A. White in the Music Division and Alice Birney in the Manuscript Division of the Library of Congress; Marty Jacobs and Robbi Siegel at the Museum of the City of New York; Christina Schellepmann and Scott Guezielek at the Washington National Opera; Sarah Billinghurst at the Metropolitan Opera; Jeffrey Guimond, Abe Jacob, and Susan Woelzl at the New York City Opera; and Clare Avery and John Goberman at *Live From Lincoln Center*.

Thanks also to designer Adam Fulrath and copy editor Patty Hammond for their tireless efforts under very tight deadlines.

I am particularly grateful to my colleagues John DeMain, Cori Ellison, Sherwin M. Goldman, Sam Paul, Tazewell Thompson, and Francesca Zambello, all of whom have been more than generous in sharing their knowledge of, and direct experience with, *Porgy and Bess.* Special thanks are owed to Robert Benton, Karen Cooper, Lionel Larner, Stephen Lawless, Carol Rosegg, Allan Schwartz, and Karen Thompson, each of whom, in their own way, have helped to make this book possible.

—**Robin Thompson**
September 2010

CONTENTS

PART 3 A NEW ENTHUSIASM

FOREWORD

I first saw *Porgy and Bess* as a boy when one of the classic productions described in this book—the Leontyne Price–William Warfield version with Cab Calloway as Sportin' Life—was mounted in New York at the Ziegfeld Theater. Over the years, I've attended many productions of the work in many diverse locations throughout the world. Even though my uncles, George and Ira, created the opera with the originator of the book and play, DuBose Heyward, I experience the same thrill as do audience members everywhere when the orchestra launches into the "Introduction and Jasbo Brown" music, signaling the beginning of the score and the first scene in Catfish Row.

Porgy and Bess has endured for many reasons: there's the triumph of Porgy's goodness and humanity over the destructive forces of decadence and exploitation represented by Crown and Sportin' Life. There's the simple beauty of Clara's love for her child and the sacrifice she and her husband Jake must make. There's the communal bonding of the citizens of Catfish Row as they fight the twin overpowering forces—man made and natural—that challenge their existence every day.

But most of all, *Porgy and Bess* endures because of the compelling story created by DuBose Heyward and the music and lyrics of two brothers who, when writing, seemed to work as two halves of the same person rather than as two individuals. With Heyward, the Gershwin brothers created a work that confounded critics but proved to have universal appeal, with songs such as "Summertime," "I Got Plenty o' Nuttin," and "I Loves You, Porgy," becoming hit recordings for performers of all styles and the full opera continuing to gain new fans in a new century.

George Gershwin never heard another version of his opera after the original production. But Ira, who lived through decades of multiple interpretations of *Porgy*, would not be surprised that, 75 years after its premiere, his brother's dream has only grown in power and popularity. Today *Porgy and Bess* is universally accepted as a major American opera and is part of the repertoire of companies around the world. Its songs continue to be staples of the classical, pop, and even rock songbooks. Whether you call *Porgy and Bess* opera, musical, or something else, its power endures, and we in the family are proud that it and its creators are part of our heritage.

—Marc George Gershwin
Summer 2010

INTRODUCTION

Porgy and Bess, the American operatic masterpiece by George Gershwin, DuBose Heyward, and Ira Gershwin, reached its 75th anniversary in 2010. Its journey from novel to play to opera was as difficult and improbable as the one its hero contemplates at the opera's climax—an expedition from South Carolina to New York in a goat cart. For that alone, the opera's journey should be not only commemorated, but celebrated. First and foremost, however, *Porgy and Bess* should be celebrated as a groundbreaking work by a set of spectacularly gifted artists. It should be celebrated for what it has come to represent to so many—a work of art in music that has not only entertained but inspired listeners, provided opportunity to underrepresented performers, and challenged the status quo. It should be celebrated in a way that recognizes *Porgy and Bess* as having become part of the fabric of American life and acknowledges its status as a national treasure—one that fills the listener with joy as it touches on the complex nature of what it is to be an American.

A great deal has already been written about *Porgy and Bess*, the groundbreaking opera; *Porgy*, the hit play upon which it is based, and *Porgy*, the best-selling novel that started it all. The volume of material that is available in print and over the Internet is vast. The remarkable life stories and prolific artistic output of the Gershwin brothers have been the subject of books, documentaries, and spectacular musical tributes. *Porgy and Bess* itself has become standard repertory in opera houses worldwide. Attention also has been duly paid to producers, productions, and tours, as well as the conductors, stage directors, designers, singers, and dancers who have brought this work so vividly to life.

Todd Duncan and Anne Brown, the original Porgy and Bess.

My goal here is to distill the story of *Porgy and Bess* and its creators from the abundance of available literature and offer a new recounting that celebrates the first 75 years of this very special work. I'll also offer some thoughts about *Porgy's* future.

THE TIMES IN CONTEXT

Even a general survey of *Porgy and Bess* must come to grips with a catalogue of relevant changes in American life, the scope of which can be difficult to take in. In order to fully understand the true genius of George Gershwin and the lasting impact of *Porgy and Bess*, it is helpful to see their story in context.

In 1898 when Moishe and Rose Gershvin welcomed their second son, Jacob, into the world, life already included his older brother Israel but neither the movies, nor the radio, nor the airplane. During their youth and in the years leading up to *Porgy and Bess,* George and Ira would watch the movies grow up and learn to talk, George would host his own radio

George and Ira Gershwin.

show, and the two brothers would fly on Trans World Airlines from New York to Hollywood. There, in later years, they would write film scores for pictures like *Shall We Dance*, starring Fred Astaire, whom George had met and befriended when they were both teenagers, and Ginger Rogers.

In 1925, a little-known and struggling writer named DuBose Heyward published his first novel, *Porgy*. Its most remarkable feature was the author's sympathetic treatment of his story's African American protagonists as fully developed human beings, a radical choice for the time, and one that placed Heyward's work in the vanguard of contemporary Southern literature. His accomplishment is even more remarkable when placed into the context of history. By the mid-1920s, the second iteration of the Ku Klux Klan had exploded into a national movement that claimed to include 15 percent of the country's "eligible population"—by their count between 4 and 5 million men (and some women). Heyward was not a civil rights activist per se, but his choice of subject matter was deliberate and motivated by his own experiences with debunking racial stereotypes.

The first page of the *Porgy and Bess* score, in George Gershwin's hand.

A UNIQUELY AMERICAN HISTORY

In its journey from idea to cultural treasure, Porgy led a complicated but fascinating life, one that parallels major events in the history and social evolution of America. Competing bids to theatricalize the best-selling novel came from a variety of sources, including Cecil B. DeMille, a towering figure in the history of American film. DeMille purchased the silent-film rights, but the project was canceled for financial reasons. Producing the play Porgy on Broadway in the late 1920s required a talent pool of trained African American actors, which did not exist. The opera's gestation period was unusually long and spanned the latter part of the Roaring Twenties, the 1929 stock market crash, and the first years of the Great Depression. Once it had been composed, differences in opinion about how best to shape the opera presented themselves immediately and remain part of the opera's story today. Throughout the 75-year history of Porgy on stage, its performers have held widely divergent views of the opera's place in African American history.

It is true that Gershwin's opera in its original form was much longer than the standard versions performed today. He heard it played and sung from beginning to end with orchestra, cast, and chorus only once—and that was at a large pretryout rehearsal. The moment that particular rehearsal ended, the cuts began. Some of them were made for artistic reasons and others out of sheer practicality. Changes to the score continued throughout a week of tryout performances in Boston right up until the Broadway opening on October 10, 1935. From that point on, Gershwin did not make any further changes himself. His tragically early death in 1937 precluded future generations from knowing if, given the opportunity, he would have gone back to his opera to make changes for specific production circumstances or supervise a composer-approved edition of a fully restored score.

The 400-year-old history of opera suggests that he would have. From its earliest days, the practice of post-premiere tinkering has been a time-honored tradition in the world of opera. For role models in this practice, Gershwin had an all-star lineup consisting of some of opera's greatest composers. Monteverdi, Handel, Mozart, Beethoven, Bellini, Mussorgsky, Verdi, Wagner, Puccini, and Richard Strauss, all known to Gershwin, continued to reshape their operas after opening night. However, many feel, not without justification, that the version Gershwin heard at *Porgy's* opening night—and made no effort to change during his lifetime—is the definitive edition of the piece. Producers and directors who have taken the opposite approach have restored music that was eliminated along the way to the New York opening, or substituted spoken dialogue for sung recitative, or changed the order of how the musical numbers are performed, or any and all of the above. 1n 1959, André Previn adapted and conducted the opera's score for a film version produced by Samuel L. Goldwyn and directed by Otto Preminger.

But that debate pales in comparison to the disagreements over the work's artistic categorization and societal impact. From the very beginning of its performance history, producers, critics, and audiences alike struggled with tagging *Porgy and Bess* as an opera or a musical—or a hybrid of both. The relationships African Americans forged with *Porgy and Bess* were wide ranging and complex. *Porgy* was variously praised as a leap forward for black performers and vilified for its perpetuation of reviled stereotypes. Generations of African American artists have spoken to this topic in very different ways. Gershwin and Heyward were determined men with strongly held opinions who both formed lasting relationships with African Americans. Their views on art and race, particularly Heyward's, would evolve over time, but their first concern was always telling Porgy's story with authenticity and in a way that would be compelling for their audience. Although the composer and authors were unlikely catalysts for long-term social, artistic, and intellectual debate, their work prompted exactly that.

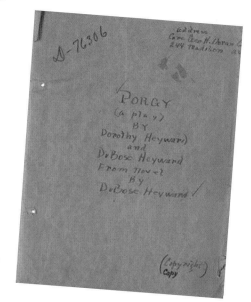

PORGY, THE NOVEL AND THE PLAY

DuBose Heyward's book, published in 1925, set the tone. Unconventional and daring for its time, it portrayed its African American protagonists as characters rather than caricatures. This artistic choice was all the more unexpected, coming as it did from the descendant of a long line of plantation-owning and slave-holding Southern aristocrats. The inspiration for the actual tale came from real life, but the motivation for telling it emanated from Heyward's search for artistic truth. This truth was to be reached by inhabiting the story's environment with precision, and creating its characters with honesty. His importance to our celebration of *Porgy's* 75th anniversary cannot be overestimated.

The novel's instant success led to an equally successful dramatization for Broadway, also called *Porgy,* coauthored by Dorothy Heyward and her husband. The play had the same unconventional and daring qualities as the novel, but bringing it to the New York stage demanded something that didn't exist at the time—a pool of trained African American actors large enough to cast a serious black drama on Broadway. During rehearsals, the Armenian émigré director Rouben Mamoulian had to painstakingly instruct his cast in the fundamental skills required for serious dramatic work in the spoken theater. While on the job, the cast had to learn to listen to each other

The cast of *Porgy*, the play.

on stage and perform in an ensemble, rather than attempting to stand out as a solo or group vaudeville act, as many had been trained to do. Conforming to the rehearsal and performance discipline of spoken theater was a sobering departure from their prior experience, working with a trained director and learning to motivate character were unfamiliar practices, and so on—the experience ran counter to everything they'd learned. Mastering the technical tools of their new trade was necessary to begin the hard separation from dead-end employment in pandering stand-alone vaudeville numbers or chorus work in uptown clubs. Although these were and still are basic techniques, the African American actor in the early 20th century generally had been neither required nor given the opportunity to learn them—but learn them they did. The play *Porgy*, which opened on October 27, 1927, and ran for an astonishing 367 performances, had given African American performers an entry into a previously forbidden theatrical world.

PORGY AND BESS, THE OPERA

The opera *Porgy and Bess* would prove to be unique in an even greater way. The period of its creation and its subsequent performance history have been unlike that of any other American opera. As far as George Gershwin was concerned, *Porgy and Bess* was an opera composed in the operatic tradition, rather than in the musical-comedy idiom of the mid-1930s. Like the book and play, it would break its own share of boundaries. Certainly, it would contradict the public's perception of what constituted opera at the time of its New York opening. *Porgy and Bess* examined American themes rather than those of European history, mythology, or Roman and Greek literature. It had the structure of opera, built from its customary musical forms of arias, duets, trios, choral ensembles, orchestral interludes and the like, but it was to be composed using the American musical idioms of jazz, "Negro" spirituals, and American popular song. "If I am successful," Gershwin wrote to a friend, "it will resemble a combination of the drama and romance of *Carmen* and the beauty of *Meistersinger,* if you can imagine that."

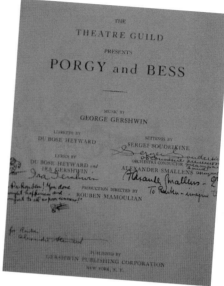

The printed libretto, with autographs by the Gershwins and director Rouben Mamoulian.

However, from its glittering opening on October 10, 1935, at Broadway's Alvin Theatre and for some years to come, the power to "imagine that" was somewhat lacking. Critics and audiences stationed themselves on either side of the great genre divide. If *Porgy and Bess* was an opera, then what was it doing in a Broadway theater? Since Gershwin himself called the solo musical numbers "songs" rather than "arias," didn't he mean us to understand the piece as a musical? Could American vernacular music really support the dramatic weight of larger-then-life operatic subject, and so forth. *Porgy* was confusing in a few ways. More than anything else it was confusing in its newness. Initially, *Porgy and Bess* did not have the long and successful run that its creators, producers, and cast had hoped for. However, it was far from a failure. Within a few short years, Gershwin's mix of traditional operatic form with American vernacular music came to be recognized as one of the work's principal glories rather than its central failing. Few now question the ultimate success of Gershwin's efforts.

The cast of *Porgy and Bess*, the opera.

AN AMERICAN WORK OF ART

Much of the criticism so often directed at *Porgy and Bess* is aimed precisely at the things that make it a prototypically American work of art. First, its creators did not fit the customary profiles of those historically associated with their roles. Most particularly, the composer was a product of the popular-music business rather than the classical music conservatory. This caused the musical establishment to criticize his work, some of them savagely. Whether they were right or wrong is for the listener to decide, but Gershwin's talent-driven perseverance, despite his lack of establishment approved credentials, operatic or otherwise, mirrored the enterprising spirit and boundless energy so indentified with Americans in the 20th century.

Second, its creators were, for the most part, first- or second-generation immigrants who had come to America for a life less fettered by the prejudices and hierarchies of the past. The composer and one of the librettists were American-born sons of Russian Jewish immigrants. The director was an Armenian immigrant who, while still a student in Moscow, fled the Bolshevik Revolution. The opera's premiere was conducted by a Russian-born Jew who also had fled intolerance. Their growth as artists was more or less guaranteed not to happen in their countries of origin, but in America they stood a chance—a chance at a better life and the possible realization of their artistic dreams.

Third, their work, *Porgy and Bess*, was something unprecedented and completely unexpected. Gershwin laid out the form of his opera along the well-known lines of traditional European opera, but he purposely composed its music in a new style not previously associated with the old form, that of American vernacular music. The result was something startling in its newness, and yet it was as organic to its time and place as *La Traviata* was to Verdi's. The musical language of *Porgy and Bess* is associated with the indigenous musical folklore of its creators' homeland in a way that is no less effective then the folkloric operas of Mussorgsky, Janacek, Dvorak, Smetana, and others.

Fourth, *Porgy and Bess* challenged existing social convention. DuBose Heyward, a white descendent of Thomas Heyward, Jr., a South Carolinian signer of the Declaration of Independence who was, in turn, a descendent of English emigrants himself. DuBose chose as his subject matter themes of love, death, betrayal, forgiveness, addiction, dignity, and community. He then wrote about their effect not on his own people but on the American descendents of African slaves. Before Heyward's novel, this had been unheard of. Dorothy Heyward's play then proved to white audiences that a group of black actors were capable of rising to the same artistic heights, and in the same way, as their white counterparts. And later still, the opera's realistic portrayal of the African American was enhanced by the depth of its musical characterization, something that was utterly new to the milieu of opera. By the time of the opera's opening night, exactly ten years after the opening night of the play,

Anne Brown recreates Bess in the movie *Rhapsody in Blue*.

Gershwin's original cast included graduates of America's finest music conservatories.

Lastly, the opera resisted categorization by genre. *Porgy and Bess* was challenging to theater audiences for being too much like opera, while opera patrons could fault the piece for being too much like musical theater. Indeed, it was something new. Given world events in the mid-1930s, the scope of *Porgy and Bess*'s achievements could only have happened in America.

OTHER PLAYERS

Rafts of other players figure prominently in the story of *Porgy and Bess*. Lawrence Langer and Theresa Helburn, founding managers of the Theatre Guild in New York, produced the premieres of both the play and the opera on Broadway.

Legendary producer Cheryl Crawford, who began as an assistant stage manager on the original production of the play, would later produce a more Broadway-friendly revival of the opera in 1942. It was one of *Porgy's* most successful runs. The indefatigable Robert Breen, with his financial partner Blevins Davis, produced the justifiably famous Everyman Opera tour of *Porgy* in the early 1950s. For four staggeringly successful years, Breen, who also directed the show with immense verve, brought the first all-black production of *Porgy and Bess* to the wider world. With the sponsorship of the U.S. State Department, Gershwin's opera could be seen and heard throughout Europe. Performances were given all across South and Central America, Mexico, Canada, the Middle East, and several Eastern Block countries. In a move that was unprecedented, Breen managed on his own, without State Department financial support, to take his company deep into the U.S.S.R. during the dangerously escalating Cold War. Truman Capote was to chronicle this leg of the journey in *The New Yorker*.

Ellen Gerber, the Everyman Opera's stage manager, went on to stage 21 productions of *Porgy and Bess* herself throughout the '60s and '70s. The larger-than-life movie mogul Samuel L. Goldwyn was intent on producing a film adaptation of *Porgy* that would be the high point of his long and notable career. The result was not what he had hoped. In 1975, the distinguished American conductor Lorin Maazel released a new recording of *Porgy* that became the benchmark against which all other recordings claiming to be "complete" would be judged. "Every bar of the 599 page vocal score is included," read the liner notes.

Porgy's legacy was advanced further by American

Theresa Helburn and Lawrence Langer of the Theatre Guild.

producers of our own time, like Sherwin M. Goldman, a tough businessman with the force of will and musical taste to bring *Porgy* back before the public as Gershwin intended it—as an opera with wide audience appeal. Goldman formed a partnership with the enterprising general director of the Houston Grand Opera, David Gockley, an impresario famously willing to think outside the box of operatic convention. As conducted by John DeMain and directed by Jack O'Brian, both in the early phases of what would prove to be brilliant careers in opera and theater, their award-winning production dominated the American theatrical and operatic landscape throughout the '70s and '80s.

The Metropolitan Opera came close to adding *Porgy and Bess* to its repertory a number of times, but it wasn't until the occasion of the opera's 50th anniversary in 1985 that a new production was presented in the house. On opening night, honored guests were Todd Duncan and Anne Brown, the originators of the roles of "Porgy" and "Bess." When England's Glyndebourne Festival Opera announced a new production for 1986, it seemed to give new definition to the term "out of context"—the rolling green hills of East Sussex being about as far away from Catfish Row as one could imagine. Gershwin's creation played alongside operas by Mozart and Verdi and was the success of the season. To this day, it remains a hallmark in the company's history. In 1987, David Gockley reunited with Sherwin M. Goldman to revive their production in a unique coproducing arrangement between 17 different American opera companies. This joint effort brought untold thousands of operagoers to *Porgy* for the first time and firmly established its place in the standard operatic repertory.

PORGY IN THE 21ST CENTURY

In 2000, Goldman, now executive producer of the New York City Opera, had the idea to revive the production to open the company's spring season. Paul Kellogg, the company's general and artistic director, was enthusiastic about bringing *Porgy and Bess* into the repertory of The People's Opera, as the company had been known historically. John DeMain, now a recognized, international authority on the score, was engaged to conduct, and the noted African American theater and opera director Tazewell Thompson

was brought in to restage the show from the ground up. The run of performances was a complete sellout and an artistic triumph for the company. In the spring of 2002, Goldman's production achieved another milestone in the history of Gershwin's opera. When PBS's *Live From Lincoln Center* telecast *Porgy* nationwide from the stage of the New York City Opera, Gershwin's opera could be enjoyed by an audience of millions.

In the middle of the new century's first decade, a large-scale American production was conceived and directed by Francesca Zambello and coproduced by opera companies in Washington, Los Angeles, Chicago, and San Francisco. Its interpretation of the material differed significantly

The set and cast of the original production.

from previous American productions in setting, tone, and effect. From the night of its premiere in 2005, Zambello's production has been regarded as a benchmark in *Porgy's* history. On November 4, 2008, the night that Barack Obama was elected President of the United States, the Zambello production of *Porgy* was in Chicago. The entire cast and staff flocked to Grant Park to hear the President-elect's acceptance speech.

PORGY AND RACE

Even a general survey of *Porgy and Bess* inevitably concerns itself with the issue of race. While the opera is not, strictly speaking, about race, the 75-year performance history of *Porgy and Bess* has paralleled a series of momentous events in the history of American race relations. The opera has been affected by race relations more than once. At times, it has even found itself on the front lines in the battle for advancement of equal rights in America. On the other hand, *Porgy* has also been vehemently criticized by black historians, social critics, and artists for its perceived stereotypes.

The fact that Heyward was audacious enough to write a realistic story about "Negroes" in the mid-1920s is stunning—as is the fact that the Heywards' coauthored adaptation for the stage became a groundbreaking theatrical event. It was the Heywards, two white Southerners, who made it a contractual condition that the play be cast with African American actors rather than white performers in blackface. Gershwin, having had his own artistically unsatisfying experience with performers in blackface, came to the same decision quite apart from the Heywards and before he read the novel. From the beginning he never even considered anything other than an all-black cast. That George Gershwin, by then a household name and a well-established composer, chose this material out of all the possible topics available to him, and then spent weeks on James Island, South Carolina, soaking up the language and music of Gullah blacks, speaks to the seriousness of his intent. That he painstakingly incorporated its essence into his opera and gave the material voice with such innovation and art, speaks volumes about his character and his gifts.

A WORK OF ART THAT CONTINUES TO THRIVE

Despite its many contradictions, or perhaps because of then, *Porgy and Bess* has not only endured, but also thrived. Never far from the public eye and ear, its iconic stature ensures that it is consistently performed. Its significance to a people inspires a unique depth of feeling in its performers, which translates into performances that can become, in the words of one critic, "a religious experience." In the end, however, it is the music of George Gershwin that keeps *Porgy and Bess* as moving, joyful, and alive as it was on October 10, 1935, and ensures its future for all people.

Join us in celebrating this 75th anniversary of *Porgy and Bess* by exploring the journey of this remarkable American creation. The story is a compelling one.

Gershwin, Mamoulian, Heyward, and the cast take their bows after the first preview in Boston, 1935.

PART 1
THE INVENTION
OF PORGY

CHAPTER 1

BEGINNINGS

Where did George Gershwin get the idea for *Porgy and Bess*? Is it a true story or folk tale? Was it an authentic creation of African Americans? Was there a real Catfish Row? Why do the performers express the words of the libretto in the theatrical anachronism once commonly known as "Negro dialect," singing *dem* for *them*, *yo* for *your*, and *mens* for *men*? What about strange words like *buckruh*? Are African Americans being parodied? These and many other questions usually rise to the surface when people, white or black, go to a live performance of *Porgy and Bess,* see it on TV, hear the opera on the radio, or listen to recordings of its songs by everyone from Leontyne Price, Frank Sinatra, and Billie Holliday to Nina Simone, Janis Joplin, and Peter Gabriel, among scores of others.

Porgy and Bess did not originate with George Gershwin. It is Gershwin's music that has allowed the story of Porgy to remain within earshot for 75 years and counting, but he found the inspiration from another source. Pivotal parts of Porgy were inspired by events that took place in Charleston, South Carolina. Many of the opera's characters were inspired by people the author knew or observed in real life. With a keen eye for character and the lyric skill of a poet, the author wove together real and imagined elements into a story so effective and so lifelike that the moment Gershwin read it, he knew that he had found the subject he sought. Yet the author who so realistically captured the details of this life was not himself African American.

Porgy's story can be traced back to an early 20th-century novel written by a white Southerner named DuBose Heyward. The *idea* of *Porgy* was entirely his. As a boy, Heyward lived

DuBose
Heyward.

19

during a time when everything around him was in a bewildering state of constant change. In the aftermath of the Civil War, one way of life in the South had given way to another on a scale—

Thomas Heyward, Jr., signer of the Declaration of Independence and DuBose Heyward's great-great-grandfather.

and at a pace—that was unprecedented. As a young man, Heyward was, in a very real way, a continuation of the traditions and values of the "Old South." This was not only encouraged by those around him, it was expected. However, through his writing he developed into a man less governed by the past and more attuned to the present. His break with that past was measured, but it was substantial.

A look at Heyward's ancestry, the events of his time, and the people with whom he lived helps us understand his perspective—one very different from our own. From our early-21st century perch, his world is a slow-moving and inconvenient one, missing all of our modern technology and most of our social constructs. We can easily regard much of the time in which he lived and wrote as shockingly devoid of civil rights. But it would be wrong to regard his life, or Gershwin's for that matter, through the lens of our own time. His concerns were not ours. To Heyward, he was living at the dawn of a modern

Dock workers in Charleston at the end of the Civil War.

age. When he wrote the novel *Porgy*, his main concern was to tell a story, of course. Yet in choosing the story that he did, one that treated its African Americans characters as fully developed human beings, he did something completely new. Heyward was not a civil-rights activist as we understand the phrase today, but neither was he unaware of the effect that *Porgy* would have on its readers. As the man who invented the character of "Porgy," Heyward is the progenitor of the story, and his world is the natural place for us to begin our journey into the story of Gershwin's opera.

SCION OF CHARLESTON ARISTOCRACY

Edwin DuBose Heyward was born into the frayed remains of Charleston, South Carolina, aristocracy on August 31, 1885.

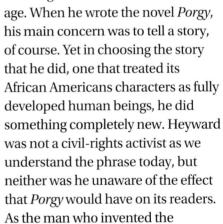

His family name had been distinguished by his great-great-grandfather Thomas Heyward, Jr., who, as representative of South Carolina to the Continental Congress, had signed the Declaration of Independence. Among those who firmly held to the values of the Old South, something of a specialty in Charleston, young Heyward's breeding was impeccable.

Weighing bales of cotton for shipment on the Charleston wharves.

For generations, the socially prominent Heyward family had owned large and prosperous plantations that had made them wealthy. Their principal crop was rice, grown in fields tended by African slaves bought at auction in Charleston. Heyward's grandparents lived during the height of the antebellum period when Charleston was the shipping, banking and cultural epicenter of the Coastal South. It was also the center of the slave trade. Nearly half of the African slaves reaching America passed through the port of Charleston. Those brought by boat from the West Coast of Africa, in a barbaric journey that would become known as the "Middle Passage", were particularly sought after by the plantation owners of the low country. In Charleston, these slaves would become known as "Gullahs."

EDWIN AND JANE

When DuBose Heyward's young parents, Edwin Watkins Heyward and Jane Screven DuBose, were married in November, 1884, the Civil War had been over for 19 years. Reconstruction had officially come and gone but much of Charleston still lay in ruin. The DuBose family, also plantation owners, had been as prosperous as the Heywards had, but by the war's end, both families had lost everything. Edwin, who had begun life as the scion of a plantation-owning family that grew rice, now worked as a laborer in the mill that processed it. Despite this and many other stories of cataclysmic reversals in fortune, mythologizing the city's antebellum past had become a way of life for Charleston's shadow aristocracy. In their world, Ned and Janie's identity could only be sustained by adhering to the social customs of an era that had slipped through their gloved fingers. This meant that above all else, at least the *appearance* of gentility had to be maintained. Appropriate to the idea of who they were rather than the harsh reality of what they had become, their wedding was a lavish occasion calculated to invoke a glorious past.

In 1888, when his son was only two years old, Edwin was tragically killed in an accident at the mill. Jane, who had been brought up to believe that a suitable husband was not only desirable but a necessity for the future, was left to care for DuBose and his newborn sister alone. With no family plantation to return to, there were few acceptable options for a woman of Jane's social standing. Fragile and consumed with anxiety for her family, at first she took in boarders. As she regained her footing, she began to write short poems as therapeutic way of dealing with her grief and fear. Her poetry led her to writing articles about local history that began to appear in Charleston's papers. As a child, Jane had been tended to by a "Mauma," the Gullah word describing an African American woman who would oversee the proper raising of white children. From her Mauma, Jane had learned the Gullah language and much of their oral storytelling traditions. Before the war, she had given lectures on the Gullah at private "ladies' functions," but in this new reality, she began to see there was a market for her expertise.

Soon, she had a modest income from leading tours around Charleston for Northerners who had become fascinated by Southern culture. As her confidence grew, she also continued with her writing. In 1895, when DuBose was ten years old, she published her own book of verse, *Wild Roses*.

EDWIN DUBOSE HEYWARD

Jane's son, who would always be called by his middle name, had been a sickly child from birth. A series of strange maladies kept him home and in bed for long periods of time. It was during one of these early bouts with illness that DuBose began to pass the time by drawing figures and writing simple poems. These two artistic aptitudes emerged early in the boy, but they did little to help him with his academic studies. Never able to sustain concentration long enough to be a good student, he dropped out of high school at age 14. DuBose chose to announce this news after the fact, telling his mother he'd already left school and taken a full-time job in a hardware store. Chivalrously, he wanted to help make ends meet.

Despite the family's misfortunes, and his own continuing and serious physical maladies of various sorts, DuBose was by all accounts a happy young man. He was well liked, exemplified the courtly manners of the Old South, and had a good sense of humor. He took to his often physically strenuous work at the hardware store unloading shipments, lugging up stock from the basement storage, and waiting on customers. But he returned home exhausted every night, something that may have contributed to what lay ahead. At age 18, he became mysteriously and gravely ill. Headaches and a debilitating numbness in his arms, particularly the left one, the one with which he wrote, began to keep him home again. His doctors were unable to determine the cause. After months had passed without any signs of recovery, a cousin was able to take him to a specialist in Philadelphia. There he received the correct diagnosis—polio. It wasn't a lethal case, but the pace of recovery was slow and painful—but he did recover. The fact that he recovered at all was something of a miracle in 1903, but the illness had taken its toll. DuBose would give the impression of physical frailness for the rest of his life.

A HEATHENISH PLACE

In 1905, DuBose was now 20 and healthy enough to go back to work, as long as it was not too physically demanding. Because he'd had no formal education, the usual route for a young Southern men with an aristocratic background (usually, law or medicine) would have required the kind of remedial school time than he didn't feel he had. Adding to the pressure, his mother's fledgling efforts on the lecture circuit did not bring in much income. He needed a job, any kind of job. That fall, in a move that would prove prophetic, he took a job on the Charleston waterfront as a cotton checker for a steamship line. The area that had once been the frenetic hub of Charleston's busy port had long ago fallen into disrepair, a casualty of the Civil War and shifting industries. The run down and largely abandoned buildings now provided a haven for the various enterprises—bordellos and saloons—that thrived in an unfashionable and out-of-the-way location. At night, warehousemen, riverboat sailors, and seamen would careen through the streets on the arms of the prostitutes who worked the area. Geographically this was not that far from where DuBose lived, but it was a separate universe from the decorum-bound Charleston he knew. The area pulsed with its own wild and flagrant life, much of which he would recall and use in his writing. Additional theatrics were provided by the regular visits of Baptist preachers who'd come to save the sinners from themselves. "A heathenish place," they called

The Charleston cotton wharfs at the turn of the 20th century, where Heyward would later meet the stevedores and denizens upon whom he would base the characters in his novel.

it. DuBose noticed that their crusades had little lasting effect upon the "heathens."

It was here on the Charleston waterfront that DuBose would come into close, daily contact with the Gullah men who were employed as stevedores on the docks. Never having had contact with African Americans other than his own Mauma and the other black household servants and field hands he knew as a boy, these men immediately struck him as something apart. He was amazed by their strength and virility, which in his imagination took on a mythic quality. DuBose made an effort to befriend the stevedores and gain their trust. DuBose didn't know what to make of their seemingly carefree and lively behavior. Frank Duran, an early biographer of Heyward, wrote, "The Negro on the waterfront was a savage, removed from the soil to the underworld of the city—alien, exotic, childlike, fierce and intensely human." Looking past Duran's now awkward terminology, we can see that what DuBose was responding to was the Gullah stevedores' direct connection to their African American heritage. To DuBose they *were* "alien and exotic." It seemed as though the debilitating effects of slavery had bypassed them altogether. Certainly, their "fierce and intensely human" qualities were a world apart from Charleston's anemic white culture, sustained as it was by the aura of genteel poverty and a romanticized version of the past. Heyward himself said that he was transfixed "by the color, mystery and movement of Negro life ... Negros in long lines trucking cotton on the wharves; dim figures in a deserted warehouse squatting over a crap game; spirituals bringing me up short to listen against the wall of a dilapidated church that I had to pass by on the way to work."[1]

Like his mother before him, DuBose had learned to speak Gullah before he had learned English, something that greatly impressed the stevedores. They, in turn, offered him the kind masculine presence that the fatherless boy had lacked in his own life. By delving into this new world, he was able to escape, at least temporarily, the heavy weight of history that, as a Heyward, required him to follow in the footsteps of his forbearers. That year spent in the company of these Gullah men made a deep and abiding impression on DuBose.

INSURANCE AND POETRY

The cotton business was moving westward toward the Deep South states of Alabama and Mississippi. As a result, the steamship company failed within a year. The 21-year-old Heyward once more found himself in need of employment. When a young friend proposed that he and Heyward go into the insurance business together, DuBose reluctantly agreed. Despite the fact that neither one of them had any experience in insurance, the business prospered. The prestigious Heyward name coupled with a natural charm soon made DuBose a sought-after member of Charleston society. Even so, serious illness continued to sidetrack DuBose for months and even years at a time. Before he was fully recovered from the polio, he contracted typhoid. In 1906, he contracted pleurisy and was forced to spend 18 months recovering in Arizona. After returning to his business and making a success of it for 11 years, he was once more

King Street, looking north, Charleston, South Carolina, between 1910 and 1920.

diagnosed with pleurisy. The year was 1917. As America moved ever closer to entering World War I, DuBose again retreated to the North Carolina mountains to try to regain his health. This time the long recovery period would mark a turning point.

Since early childhood, Heyward had an interest in artistic expression, something he had inherited from his mother. While recuperating, he became determined to find a way of expressing himself through an artistic medium. At first, he tried painting, but this eventually gave way to serious thoughts of making his way as a writer. He found that the isolation of the mountains helped him to write, and so he bought property in Hendersonville, North Carolina, and built a cottage in which he planned to write. Between 1917 and 1920, he would return to Hendersonville whenever he could get away from the insurance business without jeopardizing the support that allowed him to continue writing. The cottage was devoid of basic creature comforts, like running water or electricity, but it offered the undisturbed solitude he found conducive to writing. It was there in the peace of the Smoky Mountains that he wrote his first short stories and poems. At this point in his development as a writer, John Bennett, an older and more established South Carolina author, took the younger man on as a protégé. Together, the two men would form the Poetry Society of South Carolina, an organization that has been credited with initiating the1920s' literary renaissance in the South. However, Heyward's real breakthrough came in 1922 when he and Hervey Allen, a fellow poet and Society member, pooled their work to jointly publish a collection of poetry titled *Carolina Chansons: Legends of the Low Country.* Heyward's best poems in the collection would turn out to be inspired by his year working around the Gullah on the Charleston docks.

The coastal areas of the southeastern United States, home to the Gullah, or Geechie, peoples.

Heyward has by now keenly aware of the life and culture of Charleston's Gullah blacks. Two of the poems in this collection, "Modern Philosopher" and "Gamesters All," reflected this interest. The narrative of the latter revolves around a group of Gullah men playing craps and an ensuing altercation with the police that ends in a tragic death. These are all things that Heyward could have witnessed while working on the waterfront. Stanzas from the poem would be quoted verbatim in the *Porgy and Bess* libretto DuBose would write for George Gershwin some 13 years later.

DOROTHY HARTZELL KUHNS

In 1923, Heyward would be invited to spend the summer at the Edward MacDowell Colony, a retreat in Peterborough, Vermont, dedicated to providing an environment conducive to the creation of art by all types of artists. Living quarters were spread throughout the woods, isolated one from the other in order to provide a tranquil atmosphere in which to write, compose, paint, sculpt, and so on. That it did, and more. It was at MacDowell that he would first meet an attractive young writer who would later become his wife and writing partner for the stage version of *Porgy*.

Dorothy Hartzell Kuhns—smart, petite, and pretty—was an aspiring playwright who was slightly more advanced in her career than her future husband. After a youth spent in Canton, Ohio, Dorothy had been admitted to New York's Columbia University to study drama and persue a career in the theater. After a brief collision with being a chorus girl, she turned to playwriting. One of her early efforts was good enough to have gotten her a fellowship at MacDowell. Dorothy and DuBose soon found each other, and before long DuBose, in his quiet way, was smitten. Each day they would meet each other for lunch in the woods, halfway between their respective cottages. By then, Dorothy had come to realize that she felt the same way about DuBose as he felt about her. A fellow writer at MacDowell said, "They looked like Hansel and Gretel lost in a wood, perhaps of their own making."

DUBOSE AND DOROTHY HEYWARD

The couple kept romance at bay that summer because of their work—DuBose on his poems and stories, and Dorothy on her new play. After almost a year apart, they both returned to MacDowell in the summer of 1923. This time, Southern decorum was not on Mr. Heyward's mind. Within hours of their mutual arrival, he proposed, and Dorothy accepted. That very same day, a telegram arrived at the Colony for Dorothy. She had submitted the play she had been working on the previous summer, *Nancy Ann,* to a competition at Harvard University. The unexpected telegram was to tell Dorothy that *Nancy Ann* was the winner of that year's Harvard Prize for Drama. The much-coveted prize consisted of a cash award and the guarantee of a Broadway production for the winning play. For the future Mrs. Heyward, it had been a banner day. In another break from Southern tradition, that of a lengthy engagement, DuBose and Dorothy were married a few weeks later at the Little Church Around the Corner in New York City.

CHAPTER 2

INSPIRATION

After their first few months together in Charleston, Dorothy had to return to New York. *Nancy Ann* began rehearsals in mid February, 1924, so she went North to do her authorial duty. While she was away, DuBose would interrupt his usual walk to the insurance-company office for breakfast at his sister Jeannie's. It was on one of these mornings that a small item in the *Charleston News and Courier* caught his eye.

Cripple Accused of Firing at Woman.

Samuel Smalls, who is a cripple and is familiar to King Street, with his goat and cart, was held for the June term of court of sessions on an aggravated assault charge. It is alleged that on Saturday night he attempted to shoot Maggie Barnes at number four Romney Street. His shots went wide the mark. Smalls was up on a similar charge some months ago and was given a suspended sentence. Smalls had attempted to escape in his wagon, and had been run down and captured by the police patrol." *Charleston News and Courier*, March 25, 1924.[1]

Heyward had become so familiar with African American life in Charleston that this minor police report, something that would go unnoticed by most readers, had an immediate effect on him. He remembered having seen Smalls, who was

Maria points out the source of Porgy's troubles in the original production of the play, *Porgy*.

A Virginia child in a goat cart, soon to play an important role in the characterization of Porgy.

The grave of "Goat Cart" Sam, the inspiration for Porgy.

known on the street as "Goat Cart Sammy," being pulled by a goat through town on a cart begging for money or selling vegetables. He looked up at his sister and said, "Just think of that old wreck having enough manhood left to do a thing like that. I think it has great dramatic possibilities. Do you mind if I cut it out?"[2] Like most everyone who passed by Sammy, he had never thought the beggar's life would have included anything other than the daily peddling and begging, but here was something unexpectedly revealing. Reflecting on the moment, Heyward later wrote, "And yet this crushed, seriocomic figure, over on the other side of the color wall, had known not only one but two tremendous moments. Into the brief paragraph, one could read passion, hate, [and] despair."[3] The haunting image of Smalls, and an intense curiosity to learn more of his story, began to take root in Heyward's dramatic imagination.

MYSTERIOUS FORCE

Heyward's reading about Sammy's arrest coincided with his desire to write something about the Gullah on a scale larger than that of his short stories and poems. Now his imagination had been fired. Sammy's brush with the law mixed with his fascination with the Gullah and soon became an obsession. "What," Heyward asked himself, "was the unique characteristic ... that endowed them with the power to stir me suddenly and inexplicably to tears or laughter? What was the mysterious force that for generations had resisted the pressure of our civilization and underlaid the apparently haphazard existence of the Negro with a fundamental unity? What was the quality in spiritual sung in the secrecy of some back room that bought the chance listener up short against the outer wall with a contraction of the solar plexus ... that he was powerless to control?"[4]

Things would begin to move quickly now. *Nancy Ann* opened in New York on March 31, 1924, but was not a success. "I flopped it," Dorothy said.[5] The play sputtered on through 40 performances, but Dorothy returned to Charleston immediately. The strain of the entire experience—so different from the solitary work of a writer— sent Dorothy into a significant depression. It also made her realize that having to deal with actors' egos, temperamental directors, and printed potshots from New York theater critics was not for her. She returned to South Carolina completely shattered. Following the advice of her doctor, DuBose prepared to take Dorothy to Hendersonville for a rest cure. Meanwhile, DuBose had already made preliminary character sketches for what he thought might be a new novel. Chief among them was the protagonist, whom he first called Porgo. In May, DuBose wrote to his mentor John Bennett, "Excuse this scribble which should be a real letter, but just too busy doing things now to tell about them. I have fixed my plans to quit insurance and take the plunge. Very exciting, but a long story. When I am in the God given quiet of the mountains will tell you all about it."[6]

CONFLUENCE

The story of Samuel Smalls had sparked a transformation in Heyward, one that would set off a confluence of memory and experience that would in turn propel his writing. For a man of his background to enter into this rushing stream of unprecedented ideas required an even greater break with the past. The rational questions of income and family support were subsumed in a burst of activity. His desire to be a full-time, serious writer had long been waiting in the wings. His mother's reinvention of herself as an authority on the Gullah had made a lasting impression on DuBose as a boy. His near-mystical first encounter with the Gullah stevedores had allowed him to open his mind to the idea that these people had their own history and fully developed culture, and enviable ones at that.

Heyward was now 38 and a well-established presence within his community. In the 18 years since working with the Gullah stevedores, he had thought deeply about the status of African Americans in his immediate world. He had done so not out of any sense of social activism that we might be tempted to attribute to him today, but simply because he thought of them as complete human beings. He found the sanctimonious white crusaders determined to save these people from themselves, in either a religious or behavioral way, to be fundamentally wrong. What others saw as base and dangerous, Heyward now saw as strangely alluring, exotic, and infinitely human. He could see that what the practice of slavery had tried to eradicate in others was still vibrantly alive in the Gullah: namely, a deep connection with their identity as a people. Their desirability as slaves for the rice fields in the South Carolina lowland had largely kept them from being scattered throughout the slave-holding states. He understood that their having colonized on the relatively isolated outer banks, undesirable territory to most Charlestonians, had insulated them from the main battles of the Civil War. These quirks of fate had allowed them to retain their African heritage through an unbroken stream of what he would term *racial memory*.

HELL-BENT

In June, 1924, Heyward and Dorothy returned for their third summer at the MacDowell Colony. One evening, DuBose decided to reveal his loosely sketched ideas for the new novel to his wife. The idea of a novel with a black protagonist was something of a jolt for Dorothy. All along, she had encouraged her husband's poetry on African American themes, so there was no sense of disapproval—far from it. As he read, she heard in his characters the making of a powerful new play, an idea she kept to herself for the time being.

In July, Heyward wrote to Bennett that he was "hell-bent on the Negro novel. It is still so experimental. I am just feeling it out."[7] By August he followed up with another letter to Bennett: "John, I am almost sure that I have closed my hands about something alive in my *Porgo*. The spirit of God has been perched upon the studio gable for a month and where the stuff came from I can't imagine ... I might be all

DuBose Heyward

RESPITE.

To The MacDowell Colony.

We have come out quite suddenly together
Under the dizzy arches of a dream.
These steeps of glittering weather,
This grass, and stream,
The slackened pull of time's deep undertow
About our hastening feet:
These for a moment we may touch and know,
Who only knew the street.

We must not speak; we must not even wonder.
Or presently the deafening wall of sound
That stopped our ears with thunder
May rim this ground.

Dreamers have been who ached with listening
Until at last they heard,
In this far spot, a deep-toned silence sing
God's timid word.

The Heywards wrote a poem in tribute to the MacDowell Colony, the artists' retreat where they met and fell in love.

wrong. I am pretty drunk over it now ... it is nearly done right up to the last final copying and I'll not do more on it now."[8] After she'd read the first draft, Dorothy thought the timing right to bring up her instinct about the dramatic potential of the book, but DuBose dismissed the idea, thinking that Broadway would not be interested in a serious drama about African Americans. He wasn't wrong about the risk, but his real motive was to protect his wife. DuBose was not anxious for Dorothy to return to an environment that, for her, had been so debilitating.

By November, Heyward had changed the name of his novel to *Porgy*, perhaps after the type of blackfish caught along the Southern Coast, though the exact derivation is not clear. He sent the completed manuscript off to Charleston.

His friend, poet Herve Allen, had worried that his friend's prose work might "fall into the error of writing from the undiluted, unchanged point of view of the defensive Southerner," but when Bennett read the manuscript, he was "instantly struck by its novelty ... by the absolutely unexampled newness of its outlook. There had never been anything like it."[9] Within a month's time, Bennett had given the manuscript to John Farrar of the publishing house George H. Doran Company. Farrar was already familiar with Heyward's poetry, which he admired, so he read the manuscript quickly. Excited by the groundbreaking nature of the book, and sensing its potential success, Farrar quickly offered to publish *Porgy*. In January, 1925 Heyward signed the contract.

PORGY, A NOVEL

Porgy was published in September, 1925, and was an instant success. Generally recognized as the first psychologically true representation of African American life, Northern or Southern, by a white man, it quickly became a national best seller. Most critics were rhapsodic in their reaction to the story of Porgy, the crippled beggar whose quest was no different than any man's; Bess, the sultry but conflicted woman torn between two ways of life; Crown, the belligerent sexual bully who holds society's rules in contempt; Serena, the religious scold whose faith is made more humane by tragedy; and Sportin' Life, the wily and manipulative survivor whose every move is calculated to insure his success in the North.

Reaction from the press was swift and near unanimous in its praise. "No more beautiful nor authentic novel has been published in a decade," wrote the critic from the *Virginia Quarterly Review*, adding that Heyward had created a story about "a real Negro, not a black-faced white man."[10] The *Chicago Daily News* called *Porgy* "The best novel of the season by an American author."[11] In his column, "It Seems to Me," the often caustic Heywood Broun wrote that he was, "fully prepared for another of those condescending books about fine old black mammies." However, after reading *Porgy*, he wrote, "a literary advance in the South must be acknowledged when writers of that land come to realize, as Heyward does, the incredibly rich material in Negro life which so far has been neglected. He leads the way with a magnificent novel." Broun wondered how African Americans would respond to Heyward's portrayal of "the people of *Porgy* as savage aliens," but went on to defend the choice, saying "[by] recognizing an alien quality in the Negros of his story, Mr. Heyward takes a step beyond the usual attitude of white writers in the South who deal with Negro life." Where other writers have found there evidence proving their view of racial inferiority, Heyward has found "Negro life more colorful and spirited and vital than the life of the white community. If the two cultures don't readily mix, it may be the Nordic who lags."[12] Overnight, the ever-courtly and socially reticent Southerner had become the newest celebrity amongst the literati elite of New York. Even so, nothing in their experience could have prepared the Heywards of South Carolina for the series of remarkable events that would now start to unfold.

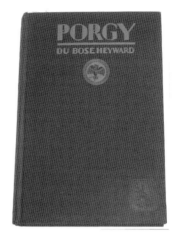

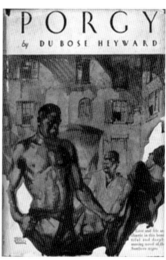

Unbeknownst to them, a prepublication galley of the book had found its way to Cecil B. DeMille's office at the newly formed Producer's Distributing Corporation. DeMille was not in New York at the time, but the property was thought to be hot enough that one of his lieutenants contacted him about it immediately. A long-distance telephone call, still something of a novelty in 1925, was placed. After hearing the gist of *Porgy's* plot, DeMille considered *the big picture*, a term he helped popularize. "It sounds like it's got problems, but it's a challenge for us," he responded. "Buy it—but $7,500 is the absolute limit."[13] The lieutenant lowballed his first offer and was able to strike a deal for $4,500, a bonus as far as DuBose was concerned. The great American bass-baritone Paul Robson was signed to play Porgy (ironic, considering that the movie would be a silent picture) for $250 a week. However, it was not to be. The moneymen at DeMille's studio killed the project on the grounds that they would not be able to release the picture across the South. The numbers didn't add up. They Heywards were disappointed, but their "bonus," which had arrived before the film's abandonment, paid for a new house in the Smoky Mountains—this time with indoor plumbing.

By 1926, Heyward had become one of America's most talked about novelists. Over the course of the ten or so months since *Porgy* had been published, DuBose received no less than three inquiries for the rights to turn his novel into a play. Even though the *New York Herald Tribune's* review of the novel had said, "Porgy falls into almost dramatic scenes

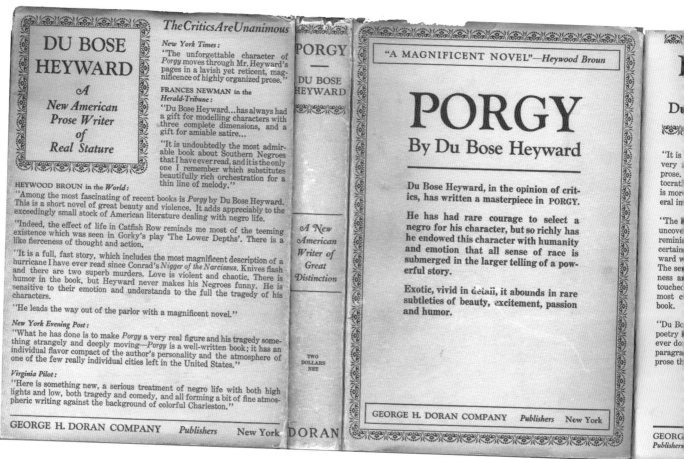

The Critics Are Unanimous

DU BOSE HEYWARD

A New American Prose Writer of Real Stature

New York Times :
"The unforgettable character of *Porgy* moves through Mr. Heyward's pages in a lavish yet reticent, magnificence of highly organized prose."

FRANCES NEWMAN in the *Herald-Tribune :*
"Du Bose Heyward...has always had a gift for modelling characters with three complete dimensions, and a gift for amiable satire...

"It is undoubtedly the most admirable book about Southern Negroes that I have ever read, and it is the only one I remember which substitutes beautifully rich orchestration for a thin line of melody."

HEYWOOD BROUN in the *World :*
"Among the most fascinating of recent books is *Porgy* by Du Bose Heyward. This is a short novel of great beauty and violence. It adds appreciably to the exceedingly small stock of American literature dealing with negro life.

"Indeed, the effect of life in Catfish Row reminds me most of the teeming existence which was seen in Gorky's play 'The Lower Depths'. There is a like fierceness of thought and action.

"It is a full, fast story, which includes the most magnificent description of a hurricane I have ever read since Conrad's *Nigger of the Narcissus*. Knives flash and there are two superb murders. Love is violent and chaotic. There is humor in the book, but Heyward never makes his Negroes funny. He is sensitive to their emotion and understands to the full the tragedy of his characters.

"He leads the way out of the parlor with a magnificent novel."

New York Evening Post :
"What he has done is to make *Porgy* a very real figure and his tragedy something strangely and deeply moving—*Porgy* is a well-written book; it has an individual flavor compact of the author's personality and the atmosphere of one of the few really individual cities left in the United States."

Virginia Pilot :
"Here is something new, a serious treatment of negro life with both high lights and low, both tragedy and comedy, and all forming a bit of fine atmospheric writing against the background of colorful Charleston."

GEORGE H. DORAN COMPANY   *Publishers*   New York

PORGY
—
DU BOSE HEYWARD

A New American Writer of Great Distinction

TWO
DOLLARS
NET

DORAN

"A MAGNIFICENT NOVEL"—*Heywood Broun*

PORGY
By Du Bose Heyward

Du Bose Heyward, in the opinion of critics, has written a masterpiece in PORGY.

He has had rare courage to select a negro for his character, but so richly has he endowed this character with humanity and emotion that all sense of race is submerged in the larger telling of a powerful story.

Exotic, vivid in detail, it abounds in rare subtleties of beauty, excitement, passion and humor.

GEORGE H. DORAN COMPANY   *Publishers*   New York

A promotional cover for the second edition of the novel.

which would suggest that DuBose Heyward was born for the theater," to him it was still not good material for the stage.[14] Early that summer, he received a letter that would change his mind for good.

GERSHWIN, BRIEFLY

George Gershwin, by that time a household name, picked up *Porgy* late one night when his recurrent insomnia kept him from sleep. Once he started he became so enthralled that he read it straight through in one sitting. That same night he wrote to Heyward suggesting they work together on an opera based on his book. "Of course, DuBose was delighted," Dorothy later recalled, "but when Gershwin came into the picture I had to come out into the open."[15] She asked her husband to listen to something she had written and began reading her work on the play. Despite his prior lack of faith and worry about his wife's health, he was deeply moved by what she had done. He was also amazed by how much he liked the idea once he heard it. Genuinely won over, he offered to help her in writing the dramatic treatment but insisted that it would be her play. (This is why her name is always billed before his in the play's credits.) Still, this onslaught of opportunity put DuBose in a tricky spot. The chance to work with George Gershwin on an operatic version was enticing for all the obvious reasons, and DuBose also believed Gershwin's music to be absolutely perfect for this American story. Dorothy later said, "He was torn between the prospect of the play and the opera. We both thought of it as 'either, or.'"[16] DuBose wrote back to Gershwin with his regrets, telling him that a play based on the novel was already in the works. To the Heywards' surprise, Gershwin replied that a spoken play of *Porgy* would not, in his view, interfere with plans for their opera. Despite being 12 years Heyward's junior, Gershwin had the benefit of hands-on theatrical experience. He understood that creating an opera libretto from a play would put them a step ahead of starting from something as diffuse as a novel.

PORGY, A PLAY

Dorothy and DuBose were delighted and began working as a team on their play immediately. Once at work, Dorothy's experience with the craft of playwriting paid off. She had a feeling for dialogue that her husband lacked. They worked well together, avoiding the egoist jousting match so often associated with a husband and wife team. The Gullah dialect presented a problem at first. If it was as authentic as it had been in the novel, it would not be understood in the theater. For many of the individual lines, DuBose would translate them into Gullah and then Dorothy would adjust each passage until they felt they had found a good middle ground of intelligibility.

It was Dorothy who, in a stroke of brilliance, came up with the idea of ending the play differently from the novel. DuBose had chosen to end his novel in stillness and heartbreak. Porgy is last seen in the light of an elegiac yet ironic sunrise, accepting with poetic resignation Bess's having been lured away to Savannah by Sportin' Life.

Dorothy's intuitive sense as a dramatist told her that more theatrical impact would be gained by Sportin' Life taking Bess to the North—to New York. And that rather than accepting this, Porgy would gather himself up and follow her on his goat cart. She felt that the counterpoint between his unconditional love for Bess and the unlikely nature of his heroic journey would bring tremendous pathos to the final stage picture. DuBose loved the idea. They gave their play the working title of *Catfish Row* and finished it by the end of the summer. Dorothy typed up copies, sent them off to three New York producers, and then they waited. Once more, *Porgy* was to exceed expectations.

THE THEATRE GUILD

New York's most distinguished producer of new plays, The Theatre Guild, accepted *Catfish Row* within a week. Lawrence Langer and Theresa Helburn, the Theatre Guild's creative leaders, convinced the other members of the Guild's board of managers that the time was right for a realistic Broadway play about African American life instead of another derivative revue or low farce. But as often happens in the theater, the artistic choice to stage the Heywards' play was driven by a practical reason as well. The Theatre Guild had made a name for itself by producing a string of successful new plays by English and European playwrights, but had recently come under fire for "ignoring" American playwrights. The *Catfish Row* manuscript arrived at the very moment that their dilemma had reached a crisis point. They were desperate to get a new American play into a season and soon. *Catfish Row* had arrived like manna from the mailman, but a major drawback to choosing it would be the abnormally high costs incurred by its large cast. An even bigger challenge for the Guild lay in a condition that the Heywards, to their unending credit, had attached to their submission. As Heyward described it, "It was obvious to both of us that, in spite of the many difficulties, the play would [require] the interpretation of the story by the race with which it was concerned. Our first resolution was that we would stand or fall with a Negro cast. That if no such cast was yet available we would hold the play indefinitely rather than resort to the use of disguised white actors."[17] There were African Americans performing on Broadway—Paul Robeson for one—but in singular rolls within a white company. Up to

The Guild Theatre, which eventually became the August Wilson, as it appeared when the play *Porgy* opened there in 1928.

this point, there had never been an all-black cast appearing in a serious drama on Broadway. By accepting the Heywards' casting demand, the Guild's managers risked losing their subscribers and going broke. On the other hand, in taking the risk they were fulfilling their institutional mission and creating a sense of excitement by doing something entirely new. In the end, Langer and Helburn made the case for *Porgy* effectively enough for the other managing board members to agree. Helburn contacted the playwrights, gave them the exciting news, and asked them to come North for meetings and auditions.

The Heywards traveled to New York in September of 1926,[18] expecting a straightforward process of choosing actors who closely resembled their characters as described in the book or as revised by the play manuscript. When they arrived, they were in for a rude awakening. The Guild had dutifully announced auditions in advance, but few turned up and none were chosen. Next, the Guild's chosen director, Robert Milton, was so disinterested that he left the project. The Heywards had come to New York hoping to get *Catfish Row* produced in 1926-27 season, but with no director on board and no cast in sight, they had to accept that this seemed impossible. Even so, Theresa Helburn suggested many revisions to their manuscript. (One that proved to be particularly astute was to enlarge the role of Bess.) If that weren't enough, the press office asked that the play's title be changed to *Porgy* to capitalize on the success of the novel. With the box office take in mind, their wish was granted. Discouraged, the Heywards left New York for a few days of quiet during the off-season in Atlantic City, and the one bright spot of their time in the North.

ON THE BOARDWALK

In a prearranged meeting that fall in Atlantic City, DuBose and Dorothy met George and Ira Gershwin for the first time. The Gershwin brothers had taken the train from Philadelphia, where they were supervising out-of-town tryouts for their new musical *Oh, Kay!* George and DuBose walked along the boardwalk deep in discussion while Ira and Dorothy trailed from a discrete distance. As he listened, Heyward was surprised to learn that Gershwin had been thinking of the opera as a project for sometime in the future rather than as his next composition. Not only was he fully booked for several seasons, Gershwin didn't think he was technically ready to tackle something as ambitious as a full-scale opera. He had already taken his maiden voyage onto the rough waters of opera with a 20-minute "Vaudeville opera" called *Blue Monday*. It had not gone well. It had only been Gershwin's first attempt to meld the form of opera with the content of American vernacular music. Not all the critics hated it, but Gershwin, always able to assess his strengths and weaknesses with equal clarity, knew that a ful-length opera was a massive undertaking. It would require him to become familiar with exactly how the great masters of the genre had composed and orchestrated their most successful works. Gershwin was as enthusiastic as ever about the operatic potential for *Porgy*, but before starting he wanted to spend more time in Europe attending opera and conferring with as many of the Continent's leading composers as he could.

Although this was not the news Heyward wanted, he had been as impressed by Gershwin as were all who met him. Heyward would vividly recall his first impression of "a young man of enormous physical and emotional vitality, who possessed the faculty of seeing himself impersonally and realistically, and knew exactly what he wanted and where he was going. This characteristic put him beyond both modesty and conceit. About himself he would merely mention certain facts, aspirations, failings." As they continued their animated stroll, Gershwin reiterated his view that a spoken dramatization of the novel occurring before they started working on the opera would only improve their chances. Besides, "it would be a number of years" before he thought he "would be prepared technically to compose an opera." Gershwin's comment, coming from a man whose fame had already landed him on the cover of *Time* magazine, fairly stunned Heyward. "It was extraordinary," he remarked, "in view of a success that might have dazzled any man, he could appraise his talent with such complete detachment." For the time being, George and Ira returned to Philadelphia and *Oh, Kay!* With no further developments in New York, DuBose and Dorothy returned to North Carolina to wait it out. In the spring of 1927, they set sail for England where they would spend the summer in a seaside cottage working on other projects and waiting for news from the Theatre Guild.

The Gershwins met the Heywards before the play *Porgy* reached the Guild Theatre stage, but it would be several more years before DuBose and Ira collaborated on song lyrics.

CHAPTER 3

A NEW PLAY

Back in New York, Theresa Helburn had encountered great difficulty in finding a replacement director for *Porgy*. The general outcome of her search was that none of the directors the Guild found suitable were willing to risk the negative career exposure they thought would come from this surefire disaster. At that time, theater directors were wary of working with black actors, because of rumored difficulties in the areas of technique and discipline. To most directors, a dramatic play requiring performances of depth from its leading players and unified support from a large ensemble was a familiar challenge, but attempting that with an all-black cast was unheard of. Yet for the right person, it was not only an opportunity, but potentially the career move of a lifetime. As it happened, Langer had been for the last year or so relentlessly pestered for work by Rouben Mamoulian, a young Russian-Armenian director who had recently emigrated from Europe. The thought of considering a fledgling director for *Porgy*, a project that Langer knew would test the most experienced of directors, never entered his mind. This was no time for a beginner.

ROUBEN MAMOULIAN

Rouben Mamoulian's cultural acumen and artistic gifts were staggering. He was born in 1898 in Tiflis, the capital of what we now know as the Republic of Georgia, into an Armenian-Russian family of privilege and sophistication. His Armenian father was a successful banker, and his Russian mother was president of the Armenian theater in town and directed many of its productions—not quite "born in a trunk," but

The cast of *Porgy*, the play, reaches up to Heaven.

he did spend his early years backstage. When he was still a young child, the family moved to Paris where Rouben quickly learned French and became an avid reader of the weekly serial *Les Aventures de Buffalo Bill.* Mamoulian himself would later say this was the beginning of his fascination with America.

When he was of age, his father shipped him off to law school in Moscow. Once there, Rouben spent more time at the famous Moscow Art Theater learning Constantine Stanislavsky's acting and directing techniques (what we in America would come to call "The Method") than he did with his law books. In 1916, Imperial Russia was teetering on the brink of revolution. Anti-Tsarist rhetoric boiled over into every corner of Moscow, including the halls of Stanislavsky's theater. Unlike most of his fellow students, art for political or social purposes was of no interest to Mamoulian. Perhaps

because of this, Rouben sensed that a Russian future under the Bolshevik's could be dangerous. Life outside his work in a theater (or later, a movie studio) made no sense to him, so he made little attempt to remember it. For this reason the factual details of his early life remain vague and conflicting. In his excellent study of Rouben Mamoulian, Mark Spergel writes "He conveyed an impression of having missed the revolution altogether. The only impact ... he admitted to was the termination of his allowance."[1] We know the one thing he did not miss was the chance to get out. He managed to obtain a visa to visit his sister in London before the Bolshevik Revolution began. Once he was there, he turned his back on the East and faced ever westward for the rest of his life. Rouben Mamoulian was 21 years old.

After directing a play in London during the 1922 season, he was offered a position in Paris as one of the three directors of the Theatre de Champs Elysees. He was all of 25 but had already proved himself as a man of talent, intelligence, and ambition. However, when he returned to his Parisian hotel that night, Mamoulian faced an enticing and life-changing dilemma. A telegram had arrived from George Eastman (of

Eastman Kodak fame) offering him a position at the Eastman
School of Music at the University of Rochester. Mamoulian
had never heard of either. Eastman was determined to add
a vocal department to the school and a professional opera
company to the town. The American Opera Company, as it
would be called, would perform in English, with an emphasis
on dramatic viability. As it turned out, a Russian musician
already teaching at Eastman knew Mamoulian from London.
He had so enthusiastically recommended him to Eastman
that the telegram Mamoulian held in his hand offered him,
sight unseen, the codirectorship of both the opera department
and the professional company. At the time, Mamoulian had
thoroughly studied the violin and so was a musician, but he
had no expertise in opera at all. What he did have in abundance
was confidence, so he accepted the offer immediately. In short
order, the Theatre de Champs Elysees was bid a hasty adieu, the
history and literature of opera was given a bit of intensive study,
and he sailed to New York. He was now 26, and this was his
first time in the United States. When he was later asked what
prompted such a gamble, not to mention leaving a prestigious
position in Paris for a teaching job in Rochester, Mamoulian
said he'd been predisposed to America by his childhood
memories of *Les Aventures de Buffalo Bill.*

COINCIDENCE AND OPPORTUNITY

While serving as a managing director at the Theatre Guild
and simultaneously nurturing his own career as a playwright,
Lawrence Langer had somehow managed to find the time
to heed the old theatrical adage about keeping a day job.

Langer was engaged as a full-time patent attorney, and at least twice a year his law practice took him to Rochester. In a coincidence worthy of one of the Hollywood films Rouben Mamoulian would later direct, Lawrence Langer during one such trip would attend a student production that happened to be directed by Mamoulian. Langer was so impressed by the dramatic aspect of what he saw, that he offered Mamoulian a teaching position at a new training school the Theatre Guild was planning. After three years of directing at the Eastman School, Mamoulian moved to New York City in 1926.

Gifted, driven, disciplined, intelligent, confident, and charming when necessary, Rouben Mamoulian would become well known for living in his own demanding artistic world. His sense of reality was anchored in the rules of the theater and not the haphazard chaos of life outside. His work with the students in Rochester had been impressive and it had gotten him to New York. Now he wanted what he knew he was meant for, his own Broadway production. In Langer's words, "soon after he arrived in New York, he began to pester the Guild in the most efficiently irritating manner."[2] Now that Robert Milton had pulled out of *Porgy* and Helburn had run out of other options, Mamoulian saw his chance. Even thought his only American credits had been plays, operettas, and operas at a fledgling music school in Rochester, plus some equally impressive work for the Guild's training program, the managing directors eventually agreed to hire him for the play *Porgy*.

Characteristically, Mamoulian catapulted himself into the job and had a lot to do with early alterations to the scrip. Overall, his contributions to the growth and development of *Porgy* in all its theatrical forms (he would later be Gershwin's choice for his opera) would prove to be central to their success. It's doubtful that the Guild's managers knew this when they hired him for the Heywards' play, but his heritage, intense training, steady discipline, and unerring instinct for the right look for a scene—in short everything he had done up to this point—prepared him for the momentous challenges that lay ahead. Soon, the Heywards received a letter from Helburn at their summer retreat. She wrote in the glowing terms of a practiced press agent about the exciting young director for their play, which was something of a comfort to the Heywards who, of course, had never heard of Rouben Mamoulian. She also let them know that rehearsals would begin in September and that their play was set to open the Theatre Guild's season on October 10, 1927.

FINDING PORGY

While the Heywards were still in England, Mamoulian and his American designer Cleon Throckmorton traveled to Charleston for inspiration and atmosphere. With John Bennett as their guide, they studied the look of the city and saw the outer banks where they learned about the Gullah and heard their spirituals. Bennett took them to hear street vendors selling their wares (one such vignette: the "Honey Man" was already in the play). Throckmorton was able to see firsthand the Sunday clothes worn by the local African Americans who were on their way to church or to a picnic, all wildly colorful and festooned with bows, military-style sashes, regimental badges, and shined up old Civil War medals. While visiting the Jenkins Orphanage, Mamoulian was so taken by their famous band that he persuaded them to come to New York to appear in the play.

In early September, casting sessions began with the Heywards in New York. Mamoulian had spent a great deal of time earlier in the year combing Harlem revues, theater groups, and cabarets for prospective cast members. More auditionees turned up than the last time around, but again the theater

In Charleston, Mamoulian recruited the Jenkins Orphanage Band, already gaining attention far beyond South Carolina, to appear in *Porgy*.

encountered a general lack of black actors and actresses from which to choose. Heyward looked back on this experience in his essay, "The American Negro in Art," which he later wrote as the introduction to the published version of the play. "Unfortunately, America has not yet had an opportunity of developing a Negro theater with its proven performers. Our only procedure was to use a drag-net, and bring in every available actor of the least promise." He and Dorothy were dismayed by the eventual choices, because none of the actors cast in the leading roles remotely resembled the characters that had been described on the printed page. "We found this painful at first," Heyward wrote. "The Bess of my novel had been a gaunt, tragic figure such as I had often seen on the Charleston waterfront. The part was given to Evelyn Ellis, young, slender, and immediately noticeable for a certain radiant charm." Frank Wilson, also trim and young but an actor they'd admired in *Abraham's Bosom*, one of the

few other plays featuring black actors, "was equally far from our idea of what Porgy should look like in the flesh." At least Heyward agreed with some of the casting, particularly Georgette Harvey, whom he found "the reincarnation of Black Maria." Harvey would be the only actress cast in the play that would go on to repeat her role in Gershwin's opera.

The Heywards may not have found these actors right as types, but at least those hired for the leading roles had some experience. Casting the ensemble that would fill out the full cast of 35 was another story. Heyward recalled that it really had amounted to hiring whoever showed up! Nonetheless, a full cast was finally hired and rehearsals were ready to begin.

LIKE BREAKING MOUNTAINS OF ICE

In 1927, few black performers had professional experience in anything other than comic vaudeville routines or uptown nightclub revues. For them, success meant standing out

The lead actors in the play *Porgy*: Frank Wilson (Porgy), Evelyn Ellis (Bess), and Percy Verwayne (Sporting Life).

and being noticed. They had no experience working within an ensemble cast that was focused as a group on a single dramatic event or theme. Indeed, for these African American men and women, presenting themselves in anything resembling naturalistic style would have been career suicide. Most of them knew what white audiences expected to see and to hear, so in order to work *at all* they had to honor that expectation. Their theatrical persona was an exaggerated stereotype, which they wore as survival technique. It was neither realistic on the stage nor a reflection of who they were in real life.

As to that, at the opposite end of the spectrum there lay a different dilemma. The idea of acting like poor Southern blacks on a Broadway stage was abhorrent to them. It ran counter to the "high hat" personas many of them had perfected for life on the streets of New York and particularly in Harlem, where the relatively sophisticated Northerners were anxious to avoid being associated with their country cousins from the rural South. This personality type, assumed from the outside, was the opposite of what Mamoulian sought for *Porgy*. He wanted character that emanated from the inside—from the heart, gut, and soul. Among the less experienced cast members (that is to say most of them) there was stunned disbelief and outright resistance at first. They simply had no idea how to accomplish what Mamoulian was asking, nor did it make any sense to them.

As a director, Mamoulian believed that there was a musicality inherent in every spoken scene, and that discovery of that musical undercurrent was what brought a

The *Porgy* cast in Catfish Row.

scene to life. To find this pulse, each scene had to be broken down into "acting beats," like beats of music. Those had to be discovered first by various means: study, improvisation, discussion, and so on. The text was voiced *on top* of the inner beats of the scene. This work created a complete life and existence for each character, whether the actor was in the front of a scene or watching in the background.

Not surprisingly, this was gibberish to the *Porgy* cast. "They had no conception, at first, of the importance of their work," Mamoulian said. "They showed little interest in the play. They would arrive an hour late at rehearsal, would forget their lines, and after I had told them several times how to do a scene, they would do it again the wrong way.[3] But Mamoulian would not be deterred. He knew where the acting beats were in each scene and knew that every member of the cast understood music. They had to in order to be able to sing the spirituals that peppered the play. The Gullah-inflected text of the play was itself musical. *Porgy* was nothing but music. Mamoulian understood this when his cast did not. "I think that at the time even the Guild had very little idea of the extent of their good fortune in making this choice," Heyward so acutely observed. "That he had already done brilliant work we were aware, but of his power to observe and assimilate new material, and his genius for rhythm, we had yet to learn."

First, he would explain the beats of each scene in minute detail and to every participant. Then, as they rehearsed each scene he would call out the beats, as Mark Spergel describes it, "direct with the script propped up on a music stand, keeping time with a conductor's baton, a metronome, and a whistle." He would address his black cast as "children," although his own 30th birthday nearly coincided with the opening of Porgy, and, Spergel adds, "most of the cast members were close to his age or older."[4]

In 1926 this method of preparing a scene was fairly new to America. But if the *Porgy* cast could count out the beats of a spiritual, then they could count out the beats of a spoken scene. The work was difficult and extremely repetitious. As Mamoulian himself said, it was "like breaking mountains of ice." But once the beats became second nature and internal, the external scene came to life. "Many of our people had been trained for the vaudeville stage," Heyward observed, "and what they had learned had to be laboriously broken down before they could start out correctly. It was then we realized what a tremendous asset we had in our director."

To the cast the process was a revelation. Every step they

The cast of the play onstage at the Guild Theatre, 1927.

took with their director was into completely new territory. "Rouben Mamoulian was not merely a director; he was a creative instructor as well," Heyward wrote. "In the Negro cast he had wonderfully plastic material. They liked him." Mamoulian held none of the barriers or preconceived notions about blacks shared by most mid-1920s Americans— even the liberal ones. His own mixed ethnic background had made him in youth an outsider in his own country. Although he would deny it, this clearly gave him insight into the psychological barriers that plagued his cast members. Being fiercely professional, he had no intention of letting

Frank Wilson in the goat-drawn cart. The goat cart would be integral to productions of the play and the opera until the 1960s.

anyone in his cast give anything less that he was putting into the effort himself. His ability to teach and gain their trust was unparalleled. "Mamoulian has been superhuman," Heyward wrote to his mother as rehearsals continued.[5] Soon, these men and women, most of whom had never been offered this kind of opportunity, responded with new willingness and complete devotion. Mamoulian literally created the very first *Porgy* company. It was a watershed event for all concerned.

A TURNING POINT

Despite the progress, the dress rehearsal went badly. An invitation-only event, Langer and Helburn had filled the house and the audience seemed genuinely moved, that is up until the play's final moments. As scripted by the Heywards and staged by Mamoulian, Porgy makes his final exit on his goat cart through Catfish Row's gate and off to his hero's journey. This time the goat went on his own journey, pulling Porgy right into a wall of the set missing the gate entirely. The audience, primed for pathos, roared with laughter instead. The poor goat turned straight downstage to the footlights, where it stared at the audience. Amid even louder howls, the Heywards sank lower into their seats.

Monday October 10, 1927, was *Porgy's* official opening night. Neither George nor Ira Gershwin was able to attend, because they were knee-deep in out-of-town tryouts for their newest musical, *Funny Face*. At that time theater critics customarily attended the opening night. At stake that night was much more than just the future of a single play. The investment and reputation of the Theatre Guild and the professional futures of Mamoulian, the Heywards, and the play's all-black cast were on the line. Curiosity ran high. Fortunately for all concerned, the performance went well. The goat was now firmly in the hands of a cast member, who led it off stage at just the right moment. But the first and arguably most important review, by Brooks Atkinson of *The New York Times*, sent a chill throughout the Theatre Guild offices. It read, in part, "The dramatization of *Porgy* turns out to be steadily interesting in the best tradition of the Guild," wrote Atkinson, but "transformed into a play it is not crisp and only spasmodically vivid." Hardly a pan, but certainly not a rave. A few other reviews that immediately followed were more supportive, but none were unquestioningly positive. The Heywards were called in by Langer, who asked for rewrites. The Heywards dutifully retreated to their hotel suite to work on even more rewrites. Toward the end of the week, they closed themselves off from the outside world, frantically working though changes for three solid days.

During their self-imposed embargo, the other reviews started pouring in. Everyone had been waiting for the worst from another important critic, Alexander Woollcott, but he had given them a rave, calling the opening night, "An evening of new experience, extraordinary interest, and high, startling beauty. In a dozen years of first nights I have not seen in the American theater an example of more resourceful and more outstanding direction." Woollcott also took pains to praise the Guild for avoiding white actors in blackface. In another glowing report, the *Herald*

Georgette Harvey, shown here in an undated drawing, was the only cast member to appear in both *Porgy*, the play, and *Porgy and Bess*, the opera.

Tribune's drama critic singled out Mamoulian, writing, "To his vivid direction must be ascribed much of the play's popularity." Another critic was stunned by the use of authentic spirituals. "To hear the spirituals sung as they were is worth twice the price of a seat at the Guild Theater. There were the fervor, the hysteria, the emotionalism, and the curious abandon that must accompany such outbursts. They raised their voices, gesticulated and gyrated, as they joined in the volcanic choruses. It was something new to most of us—may I say to all of us."

On a gray and drizzly Monday morning, the Heywards, completely oblivious to all of this heady praise, forced themselves to make their way through the theater district to Langer's office. They were exhausted from the intense mental effort of trying to rewrite their play and depressed because they didn't think they had improved on the original. They were so downhearted that a long line at the Theatre Guild box office failed to register with them. When they reached Langer's office to deliver the revised script, he said, "You're crazy to want to change it, we're a hit!"

Something else had happened to turn the tide. In his weekly Sunday follow-up column, Atkinson, having had time for reflection (or wanting to jump on the bandwagon before it was too late), was more generous in his reaction. Now he wrote that *Porgy* was an "illuminating chronicle of American folklore. In producing it, the Guild keeps the faith with its subscribers ... for pioneering, modern drama." Important too, particularly for the African American cast, were the comments of James Weldon Johnson, an early leader in the NAACP. "In Porgy, the Negro removed all doubts as to his ability to do acting that requires thoughtful interpretation and intelligent skill." Black leaders lauded the Guild's having employed over 60 African American actors for the production, a Broadway first. They were, indeed, "a hit."

The praise came in the midst of a Broadway year that encompassed a volume of activity hard for us to imagine today—268 plays in a single season. It is also hard to imagine that before *Porgy* African American actors as a group within the legitimate theater did not exist. DuBose Heyward had set out to tell a story about African Americans as human beings. Dorothy Heyward recognized in this the stuff of compelling theater. The Theatre Guild took a chance and won. Two of Rouben Mamoulian's next contracts would be to direct the original Broadway Productions of *Oklahoma!* and *Carousel* for the Guild.

Porgy ran for an astonishing 367 performances, closing on October 12, 1928. The production then played His Majesty's Theater in London from April 10 to May 25, 1929. Cheryl Crawford, who would later produce one of the more successful productions of *Porgy and Bess*, was the stage manager. George Gershwin and Kay Swift attended a New York performance of *Porgy* in early 1928. Although Gershwin loved *Porgy*, he was at the time considering another operatic topic, *The Dybbuk*.

IRONY

In one of theater and film history's more ironic twists, *The Jazz Singer,* starring Al Jolson, opened in New York on October 6, just four days before *Porgy.* The immediate reaction was not as euphoric as legend would have us believe. Many regarded *The Jazz Singer* as a novelty that would soon fade, but of course the doubters would live to be proven wrong. Jolson had been obsessed with *Porgy* since he read the novel. He had even gotten permission from the Heywards for a short adaptation for radio. But now that there were lines around the block at the Theatre Guild, he smelled movie box-office gold. He offered the Heywards $30,000 for the rights to make a "talkie" out of *Porgy,* starring himself in blackface. The offer was hard to refuse, but the Heywards would end up holding out for Gershwin and his opera. None of them, including Gershwin, would have then predicted that it would be an eight-year wait—to the day— before Porgy sang to his Bess on Broadway.

George Gershwin had become a star overnight when Al Jolson made "Swanee" a hit.

PART 2
AN AMERICAN FOLK OPERA

CHAPTER 4

NEW YORK CITY

In the early 1890s, Moishe Gershowitz, a 19-year-old cutter of women's shoes, met Rosa Brushkin, the beautiful 15-year-old daughter of a St. Petersburg furrier. He was instantly smitten. Unfortunately for Moishe, Rosa's father, like more than 2 million other Russian Jews, would soon pack up his family and leave his increasingly anti-Semitic homeland for America. Shortly thereafter, Moishe followed his hoped-for bride, captivated enough to cross a continent and an ocean for her. In the Russia that they left behind, Nicholas had not yet married Alexandra, laws restricting the activities of Jews were becoming ever more repressive, and Vladimir Lenin was just a 20-year-old student but already under surveillance as a radical. When Moishe applied for American citizenship, he wrote August 14, 1890, as the date of his arrival and gave his first name as the more Americanized "Morris." His journey paid off. On July 21, 1985, around five years after having met in what they now referred to as "the old country," Morris Gershowitz married "Rose Bruskin." Morris's new wife had also Americanized her name, something that was very common among those emigrants anxious to forget the hardships they had left behind.

ON THE MOVE

A year later, on December 6, 1896, Rose would give birth to the first of their four children, a son they named Israel. He was born while they were living in the midst of the large community of Russian Jews on the Lower East Side of Manhattan. Morris liked to live near where he worked; when a new business venture beckoned, the family moved.

George Gershwin as a young man.

On this occasion, it was to the East New York section of Brooklyn. There, at 242 Sneidicker Avenue, their second son, Jacob, was born on September 26, 1898. However, the delivering physician wrote Jacob "Gershwine" on the baby's birth certificate. The details are clouded, but it is believed that at some point before Jacob's birth, Morris had changed the family name to "Gershvin." In New York's Russian and Eastern European Jewish community, Gershvin could easily have been pronounced as Gershwine, so it's assumed that the doctor wrote out Jacob's last name phonetically. Whatever the reason, the Gershowitz family was now known as Gershvin. From the moment of birth, Jacob was already beginning to challenge the status quo. Israel was called "Izzy" for short, and no one remembers Jacob ever being called anything other than "George." Within six week's time, Morris moved again, taking Rose, Izzy, and George Gershvin back into Manhattan. Morris's business ventures were wide ranging—he was variously a maker of ladies shoes, owner of a small chain of restaurants, proprietor of several Turkish baths, and owner of a bakery, cigar store, and even pool parlor. A stint as bookie at Belmont Park was short lived. As Ira later wrote, "We were always moving. When my father sold a business and started another, we would inevitably move to a new neighborhood. George and I once counted over 20 different flats and apartments we remember having lived in during those days."[1]

During this seminomadic period, a third son, Arthur, would come along on March 14, 1900, and the Gershvin family would be completed with the birth of a daughter, Frances, on Dec 26, 1906. During one period of his occupational odyssey, Morris would own a bakery. In one of her earliest memories, Frances recalled that during those days George was known around the neighborhood as "Cheesecake."

PARENTS AND CHILDREN

The Gershvins were not the kind of traditional close-knit Jewish family that one was likely to encounter on the Lower East Side. Neither Morris nor Rose was particularly religious; the daily rituals of Jewish life were not particularly observed around their household. Ira was the only son to be given a bar mitzvah. Both parents had their own preoccupations with business and their own, largely separate, social lives. Although they were far from neglectful, Rose and Morris more or less left their children on their own.

Rose was a contradictory but enormously influential figure in the lives of her children. She was at once authoritarian, grand, and self-centered, but, as Gershwin biographer Joan Peyser described her, Rose Gershvin "seems to have radiated a kind of mesmerizing charm."[2] Others have portrayed her as a pragmatic woman for whom things meant more than people. Edward Jablonski described her as "concerned but not affectionate."[3] She was candid and at times blunt—particularly in English. However, in some ways Rose was a traditional mother. Like many women at that time, she was the parent who managed the household and watched over the finances. She passionately believed in the same precept held by most American mothers, particularly the newly immigrated: if their children were well educated, success would follow. George Gershwin himself described his mother as "nervous, ambitious, and purposeful. She was never the doting type ... She was set on having us completely educated, the idea being that if everything else failed we could always become school teachers."[4] A less guarded observation came from Frances who said, "My mother made no relationship with any of us, not even George. She was not mean, just a very bad mother who did not give herself to anyone. Everyone always had to do for her."[5] As Jablonski wrote, "Mother's Day was not conceived with Rose Gershwin in mind."[6] Most tellingly, when Ira called her to say that George was dying and she should come to California, Rose answered, "What good could I do then?" When he did pass away, she never showed any emotion.[7]

Gershwin described his father Morris as "a very easygoing humorous philosopher who [took] things as they came."[8] Frances, who at the time was eight years younger then George, and ten years younger than Ira, remembers her father "mostly as my mother's chauffeur." He did whatever Rose wanted him

Morris and Rose Gershvin moved frequently to stay close to Morris's various businesses, exposing George to the music of many different cultures. They allowed him to take over the piano they originally had bought for Ira's lessons.

to do. Morris was preoccupied with his various businesses and tried to insure that they were successful, but he was not as obsessed by the outward appearances of wealth as was his wife. He was gregarious to a point, famous for his awkward malapropisms, and socially obtuse.

The Gershvin's first son, Ira, was an introverted, bookish, and earnest child who always took care of himself. "Izzy" seemed an unlikely name for the Gershvin family resident scholar, even to him. He had always assumed that it was short for "Isadore," but by the time he thought to ask his parents what his real name was, they reportedly couldn't remember. Years later when he applied for a passport, he finally learned his birth name was actually "Israel," something he said he found difficult to get used to. However, the discovery was largely anecdotal, because by then he had long since been known as "Ira." In demeanor and appearance, Ira was more like his father than his mother—short, stocky, and taciturn. The best-known description of Ira as a child comes from his childhood friend and classmate E.Y. "Yip" Harburg— the eventual lyricist of "Brother Can You Spare a Dime," "Somewhere Over The Rainbow," and "April In Paris." Harburg wrote, "Ira was the shyest most diffident boy we had

E. Y. (Yip) Harburg was a childhood friend of Ira's. He grew up to become a famous and successful lyricist, penning "Somewhere Over the Rainbow" with Harold Arlen and "April in Paris" with Vernon Duke.

ever known. In a class of Lower East Side rapscallions, his soft-spoken gentleness and low-key personality made him a loveable incongruity. He spoke in murmurs, hiding behind a pair of steel-rimmed spectacles." The role reversal between Ira, the first-born son in a Jewish family, and George, the second son, was significant in many ways. As George found his way into his passion for music, Ira was the one family member who was always there for him in an emotional sense. Their mother was too preoccupied, their father was too retiring, and the other children were too young. Ira's adulation of his younger brother and his undying belief in him would be George Gershwin's rock. Years later, when the brothers were together and at the height of their success, friends would jokingly introduce them by saying, "I'd like you to meet George Gershwin and his lovely wife Ira." The fact was that Ira was perfectly content being "the other Gershwin."

A NUISANCE

As to the second son, and her older brother, Frances also recalled George to be "a pretty wild boy. People used to say, 'Mrs. Gershwin has nice children, but that son of hers—she's going to have trouble with that son, George.' And they felt sorry for her."[9] Harburg remembered, not without irony, "Ira had a kid brother who was a source of embarrassment to him. He wore high still collars, shirts with cuffs and he went out with girls." It's hard to imagine Ira thinking of the brother to whom he was so devoted as an "embarrassment," but in his role as stand-in parent, Ira did have to step in many times to get George out of one jam or another.

Isaac Goldberg, American author, critic, and teacher, wrote the earliest biography of George Gershwin in 1931. Goldberg was the only biographer who was able to work with Gershwin in person, a fact that makes his writing uniquely valuable. There is no mention of *Porgy*, either the novel or the play (Gershwin was very familiar with both by this time), but the insights into Gershwin's early life and his thoughts about music are invaluable. In one of their interviews, when asked to elaborate on his early childhood, Gershwin answered, "There is nothing I can really tell you about my pre-piano days, except that music never really interested me, that I spent most of my time with the boys in the street, skating and, in general, making a nuisance of myself."[10] Of this period in Gershwin's life, Goldberg wrote, "George, as he himself will remind you, was a rough and ready, the muscular type and not one of your sad contemplative children. He was the athletic champion of his gang—and, even more, the pavements—of New York. His parents held no high hope for his future. He was, frankly, a bad child."[11]

MELODY ON 135th STREET

By the time George was ready to start school, Morris had moved his family back to Manhattan, this time to stay. For several years, they would actually stay put on West 126th Street. Gershwin told Goldberg that when he was six, he spent most of his time playing hooky and roller skating, barefoot and in overalls, around the neighborhood. He remembered that his earliest musical experience occurred during one of his skates across 125th Street, which was a busy avenue and considered the main street of Harlem. In Manhattan, 125th Street was one of only two locations that could boast a Nickelodeon, and 14th street was the other. (In 1905, the Nickelodeon, an early-20th-century form of movie theater, was a national craze.) These small theaters showed 10- to 20-minute reels of black-and-white silent movies with live musical accompaniment, usually piano or organ but sometimes augmented by a violin or two. The musicians would play whatever music they knew and thought appropriate for the reel that was being shown. Ragtime tunes were used for chase sequences, ominous chords would be played in tremolo during what came to be know as "Eliza-crossing-the-ice" moments, and a solo string tune would fill in for the love scenes. Gershwin told Goldberg that, from the street outside a Nickelodeon, he heard "an automatic piano leaping through Rubenstein's *Melody in F*. The peculiar jumps in the music held me rooted."[12]

MUSIC IN THE AIR

Gershwin has said that before taking up the piano, he had no particular interest in music, but his story of being rooted to the spot by *Melody in F* sends us a different message. He certainly wasn't making music before he had a piano, but there was plenty of it in the air. The music of Gershwin's boyhood was of many different types, some receding and others emerging, but it was all competing for his attention. He wouldn't publish his first song until 1916, "Rhapsody In Blue" wouldn't be composed until 1924, and *Porgy and Bess* was even further into the future, but his musical influences were all around him. Most of the music that Gershwin heard then still sounds familiar to us today, but the ways of hearing it were altogether different.

A major difference was the central role that music and music making played in the lives of most families at home. Piano ownership had come to symbolize the virtues of the middle-class Victorian life that most Americans aspired to—particularly the newly emigrated. "There is probably no country in the world where piano playing is so widespread as in the United States," musical historian Louis C. Elson wrote in 1904. "Almost every home," Elson continued, "even among the humble, possesses its instrument and some amount of piano music." Rose Gershwin made sure this was true of her home in 1910, and the effect this had on her second son would be dramatic. Moreover, the business of music had been undergoing a metamorphosis since the mid-1800s, transforming itself from a geographically scattered assemblage of disconnected parts into what soon would be recognized as an industry.

George M. Cohan was the dominant performer, songwriter, and producer in the early years of the 20th century.

A MODERN MIRACLE

In addition to the business of music, the science of it, meaning electronically reproduced sound, was fundamentally changing the way Americans could access music. Recordings were in their infancy but growing into a hugely influential business. The Victrola was introduced in 1905, when George Gershwin was six going on seven and careening around Manhattan on his roller skates. In 1913, when George was 14 going on 15, electric models were introduced that boosted sales to over 250,000 sets per year. By the time George was 18 and working professionally in the music business, sales had increased to over 500,000 sets per year. The recording industry was here to stay, and Gershwin would be at its forefront.

Theater music was everywhere when Gershwin was a boy. New York was littered with legit theaters, music halls, vaudeville houses, Nickelodeons—and even minstrel shows for a few more years. In 1910, as the decade grew to a close and Gershwin was 11 going on 12, musicals and revues were big business. To keep up with demand, the Theater District migrated to Times Square, where it had grown to about 40 fully operating theaters. And there were more to come.

The range of musical sound that Gershwin heard all around him, and which profoundly shaped his musical character, extended from the echo of mid-19th-century parlor songs to the emerging music called jazz. In 1856, New York City had ten full-time resident companies performing minstrel shows, and twice as many by 1866. As one historian explains it, at first, there was no

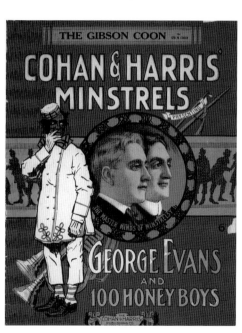

The minstrel shows of Cohan and Harris, as well as other producers, retained popularity until supplanted by the family entertainment of vaudeville.

Tin Pan Alley and the phonograph and radio were unknown. Minstrelsy gave those American songs nationwide exposure and repeated hearings so that they could catch on. At the same time, minstrelsy spurred the development of popular music in 19th-century America by being the first genre to commission songs specifically for use on the American stage. These commissions would be the basis for popular music publishing in America and, in turn, the Gershwins' eventual profession as songwriters. When George was 10 and Ira was 13 or so, the [George M.] Cohan and Harris Minstrels were still in full operation, even though they were the last of its type to play Broadway. However, minstrel traditions remained in use for decades of shows that included songs by major theater music composers like Cohan himself and even Irving Berlin. The most famous graduate of minstrelsy was Al Jolson, a man who would come to play a pivotal role in George Gershwin's career.

A REGRETTABLE PHENOMENON

A staple of minstrel shows was a type of American popular song that emerged out of the development of ragtime in the early 1880s. Regardless of their musical origins, the numbers, called "coon songs," presented a racist and stereotyped image of blacks that was intended to amuse white audiences. Hearing them would have been commonplace during Gershwin's life up until the mid-1920s, and they were big business for Tin Pan Alley, where he would work as a teenager. The national craze for coon songs perpetrated the racial stereotypes that Gershwin's *Porgy and Bess* would strive to discredit while still retaining the authenticity of its own time and place. By the turn of the century, the minstrel show was losing its popularity, but coon songs continued to be a mainstay of vaudeville. They were delivered by "coon shouters," who were typically white females appearing in blackface. Foremost among the coon shouters was May Irwin, whose signature number was the Charles Trevathan hit, "The Bully Song," introduced on Broadway in 1885 but continually performed until she retired in 1920. Her performances of this frankly racist number were sellouts and extremely influential in establishing the stereotype of the razor toting, jealously belligerent yet comically inept black male. (The character of "Crown" in *Porgy and Bess* would share some of these flaws, but in Gershwin and Heyward's hands, he would be neither comic nor inept.) Another well-

Al Jolson.

known coon shouter was Sophie Tucker, in reality a Russian-born Jew named Sonya Kalish, who immigrated to America at the same time as Morris Gershowitz. Billed as "The Last of the Red Hot Mamas," Tucker would make Gershwin's first Tin Pan Alley song, "When You Want 'Em You Can't Get 'Em, When You've Got 'Em You Don't Want 'Em," a hit novelty number. It is no coincidence that coon songs swept the country around the same time that Tin Pan Alley came into existence—1885. It's possible that one could have emerged without the other, but songs that sell in the millions of copies were financially attractive to both sides.

THE HEART OF AMERICAN SHOW BUSINESS

The rise of vaudeville overlapped with the decline of minstrel shows, and both Gershwin boys were teenagers during its heyday. At the heights of its popularity, vaudeville was known as "The Heart of American Show Business." Its success came from a simple premise: vaudeville was entertainment that everyone could enjoy, meaning not just men. Vaudeville generally offered an alternative to the bawdy shows of the time, and was deemed more appropriate for middle-class families. Other producers quickly saw how successful this formula was, and by the 1890s, vaudeville theater chains crisscrossed the country in what became known as "the circuit."

By the time George was 14, the capitol of "the big time" (a serious phrase for those who played the vaudeville circuit) was New York's Palace Theatre. The bills at "The Palace," as it was known to vaudevillians, were headlined by the era's

George Gershwin's first published song, "When You Want 'Em, You Can't Get 'Em, When You Got 'Em, You Don't Want 'Em."

biggest stars. It was there that a 16-year-old George Gershwin would meet a 15-year-old song-and-dance man in search of a new song for his duo, "Fred and Adele Astaire, the Youthful Brother and Sister." Gershwin remembered their meeting well, "It was at a time when Fred and Adele were doing a little vaudeville show of their own. Fred used to come in [to Remick's] to hear the new songs. I remember saying to him once, 'Wouldn't it be wonderful if one day I could write a show of my own and you and Adele could star in it?' We laughed then, but it came true."[13] The chance meeting on West 28th Street would begin lifelong friendships that eventually led to two Broadway shows and the Gershwin brothers' first Hollywood musical.

SOPHISTICATED GLAMOUR

In 1917, Fred and Adele Astaire would graduate from vaudeville to Broadway when they starred in *Over The Top*, a patriotic revue with music largely written by Sigmund Romberg. Revues were a more sophisticated (and expensive) type of entertainment than vaudeville. They appealed to an upscale audience for whom the social mores of middle-class America were of little concern—in other words, the opposite of Vaudeville. Revues material was almost exclusively musical: a sophisticated mix of romantic glamour and irreverent dissections of topical issues, all manner of public figures, and the latest fashionable activity or fad. For many, though, the primary attraction was to be found in the frank-for-the-times display of the female form. Florenz Ziegfeld, with his *Follies*, and George White, with his *Scandals*, would produce the epitome of the sophisticated New York revue. Importantly, Gershwin's Broadway debut would be in the style of a revue, and he would, at various times, work for both Ziegfeld and White on their productions.

Gershwin would start his Broadway career knowing that "interpolations," the practice of adding a song from a different source into a given show, was one of the rules of the game. He was grateful for the practice early on in his career, because it gave him opportunity for his material to be heard, something of real importance in the preradio days. Not long after his first successes, mixing and matching songs would be a practice he would leave behind, particularly after he started writing shows with Ira. Our modern idea of the book musical would find its bearings several years later with the 1927 opening of Ziegfeld's production of Jerome Kern and Oscar Hammerstein II's groundbreaking musical *Show Boat*.

CHAPTER 5

MUSICAL AWAKENINGS

There was so much music building up around George Gershwin that once lighting struck, the power of music would change his life. The family had moved back to New York's Lower East Side, where he was enrolled in P.S. 25. George was ten years old and up to his usual tricks, ditching a violin recital programmed to enrich the artistic sensibilities of the students. While he caroused in the schoolyard, an eight-year-old student named Max Rosensweig was playing violin for an auditorium assembly. (Rosensweig would go on to become Max Rosen, a world-renowned violinist.) As Rosensweig began to play, the music could be heard in the schoolyard below. Again, the music held Gershwin rooted, only this time it ignited his musical imagination. In a story he would often repeat, Gershwin said, "It was, to me, a flashing revelation of beauty."[1] Gershwin sought out the source of this beauty.

> "I found out where Maxie lived and, dripping wet as I was, trekked to his house, unceremoniously presenting myself as an admirer. Maxie, by this time, had left. His family were so amused, however, that they arranged a meeting. From the first moment, we became the closest of friends … we'd talk eternally about music—that is, when we weren't wrestling. I used to throw him every time, by the way."[2]

Gershwin in the early 1920s.

A GOOD BOY OUT OF A BAD ONE

The next and most fundamentally decisive step in Gershwin's musical awakening was organized by his mother. Rose's younger sister Kate had acquired a piano for her home, and Rose decided she needed one as well. In the late fall of 1910, a secondhand upright was purchased with the idea that 14-year-old Ira would be the one to study piano as part of his overall education. The family was now living on the second floor above a phonograph store (presumably Morris had gotten one by now) at 91 Second Avenue. As George described the scene, "No sooner had it come through the window and been backed up against the wall, than I was at the keys."[3]

What the family didn't know was that since having met Max Rosensweig, Gershwin had been secretly learning to play on another friend's piano. This was a relief to Ira, who knew he could now retreat from the threat of piano lessons and go back to his books. Rose, however, saw only opportunity. She decided George should have the piano lessons. The first lessons were with a neighbor, but George quickly outgrew his first teacher. Rose then took him to the local Hungarian bandleader who charged $1.50 an hour, a high fee that she regarded as an investment.

Maxie Rosenzweig with accompanist Claire Raphael Reis. The boy who inspired Gershwin's love of music would become the world-renowned violinist Max Rosen.

In the fall of 1913, when George was still 14, a friend introduced him to Charles Hambitzer, the man who would become his first real teacher. If Max Rosen "opened the world of music" to him, as Gershwin put it, Charles Hambitzer was "the first great musical influence in my life."[4] Hambitzer recognized his young pupil's abilities. In a letter to his sister, he wrote, "I have a pupil who will make his mark on music if anybody will. The boy is a genius without a doubt; he's just crazy about music and can't wait until it's time to take the lesson. He wants to go in for this modern stuff, jazz and what not. But I'm not going to let him for a while. I'll see that he gets a firm foundation in the standard music first."

The changes in Ira's "nuisance" of a kid brother were quick and profound—George changed before his family's eyes. Consumed by the world of music that had been all around him, he progressed so rapidly in his piano studies that even Morris and Rose began to think that he might have a future of some kind. Typically for Gershwin, his remembrance of his dramatic about-face was unsentimental and direct. "Studying the piano made a good boy out of a bad one. I was a changed person after I took it up."[5]

RAGTIME

For Morris and Rose, an unintended consequence of George's newfound immersion in the piano would be his dropping out of high school in May of 1914 to take a job pounding ragtime tunes on Tin Pan Alley. Ragtime, as a uniquely American genre of music, was still in its peak period of popularity. As Gershwin grew into musical awareness, ragtime would have been considered as something new, "the latest thing" in popular music, at least until jazz captured the public's imagination. As an adult composer, Gershwin would not be known for using rag rhythms in his work. but as a 15-year-old pianist with only three years of piano lessons under his belt, he was a good enough ragtime pianist to compete with seasoned professionals for a job in the heart of the American popular-song business. "He was probably the youngest piano pounder every employed on Tin Pan Alley," remembered Ira.

Scott Joplin was the foremost composer of ragtime tunes. The arrangements heavily influenced pianists like George Gershwin in the days before jazz emerged, partially as an outgrowth of ragtime.

Musicians generally identify ragtime's syncopated, or ragged, rhythm as its defining feature. Most musical historians agree that the root of this syncopation can be found in indigenous music carried by enslaved Africans to America. When later generations of African Americans began to hear the marches of John Philip Souza in 1886, what they called "the rag" developed as a synthesis of the two musical styles. Ragtime is thought to have begun in the late 1880s as dance music played on the piano throughout the red-light districts of St. Louis and New Orleans. This would have been around ten years before it appeared in Tin Pan Alley sheet music. Although he was not the first black musician to notate a rag, in 1899 Scott Joplin became the most famous when his "Maple Leaf Rag" was published. It was Joplin who called the effect of ragtime music "weird and intoxicating." Joplin may have even been the first musician to use the term swing while describing how to play a rag. "Play slowly until you catch the swing," was his advice.

TIN PAN ALLEY APPRENTICESHIP

Since the mid-1880s, popular-music publishing had been headquartered in New York. The publishers, anxious to be in the center of activity, clustered together in a single area around the legitimate theaters, vaudeville houses, burlesque palaces, and restaurants that offered entertainment as well as dining. West 14th Street was the first of these entertainment and publishing crossroads. Tin Pan Alley got its name around the turn of the 20th century, when the theater district moved north to 28th Street and the publishers followed. The term is attributed to a newspaper writer and part-time composer named Monroe Rosenfeld, who, after moving to New York from Ohio, coined the byline to symbolize the noise coming out of all the publishers' demonstration parlors. That cacophony of sound was created by dozens of "piano pounders," usually men, banging away on overused pianos, while almost as many "song pluggers," warbled the newest tune for sale. Sometimes the pounder did double duty as the plugger, as was often the case with Gershwin.

By the spring of 1914, George was eager to leave school and begin a music career. He heard of an opening at Jerome H. Remick & Company on West 28th Street and met the manager there. Gershwin was far younger than most of the other men working there, and he had no experience. However, his piano playing won him the job. Gershwin had been taking lessons seriously for only three or four years, but already he was as good as, and likely better than, most of the players at Remick's. Although the experience—and the salary—was beneficial, Gershwin did not remember the period fondly. "Every day at nine I was there at the piano, playing popular tunes for anyone who came along. Chorus ladies used to breathe down my neck, and some customers even treated me like dirt."[6] New York's theater district would gravitate north, leaving W. 28th Street behind and finally centering itself around 42nd Street and the surrounding blocks. The new theater district would be where the former Tin Pan alley piano pounder would have his greatest success.

When Gershwin was 16, he stopped his regular piano lessons, because Hambitzer couldn't tolerate his playing ragtime and theater tunes for a living. Coincidentally, he wrote his first song around the same time with a young lyricist named Murray Roth. Remick's didn't like its employees hawking their own tunes, so Gershwin and Roth signed a contract with a rival publisher, Harry Von Tilzer. Their contract for "When You Want 'Em You Can't Get 'Em, When You've Got 'Em You Don't Want 'Em," paid them an advance of one dollar against royalties and a quarter of a cent per copy sold after that. Roth was the savvier businessman and was able to squeeze an advance of $15 for himself out of Von Tilzer, but Gershwin decided to wait until there was more in the pot. Later, when he was tight for money, he approached Von Tilzer "and asked him for a little cash on the song. "He handed me five dollars," said Gershwin, "and I never got a cent more from him."[7] Sophie Tucker, a hugely popular singer who billed herself as "The Last of the Red Hot Mamas," convinced Von Tilzer to publish the song and then used it in her act until she retired in the early 1960s.

The 28th Street offices of music publisher Jerome H. Remick on Tin Pan Alley, where George Gershwin's first worked as a pianist for song pluggers.

PIANO ROLLS

To supplement his weekly salary at Remick's, in 1915 Gershwin began to cut music rolls for player pianos. He was hired by the Standard Music Roll Company in East Orange, New Jersey. The rolls have survived and are now available in modern recording formats. All of these early rolls (Gershwin made acoustically better ones later on, including one of *Rhapsody in Blue*) are of Tin Pan Alley tunes and give a pretty good idea of what Gershwin did all day as a piano plugger. ("When You Want 'Em, You Can't Get 'Em," is on one of the rolls.) Standard wanted to make it seem as though they employed more pianists than they did, so Gershwin recorded under several different pseudonyms: James Baker, Fred Murtha, and Bert Wynne, after the comedian Ed Wynn.

In 1915, Gershwin changed the last syllable of his name from "vin" to "win," an idea which may have originated in his thinking up pseudonyms. The rest of the family quickly followed suit.

Gershwin's piano-roll performances have been recorded and issued on several collections.

The daily grind of Tin Pan Alley and the popular music business, "a racket," as Gershwin later called it, "began to definitely get on my nerves. Its tunes began to offend me," he complained. "Or perhaps my ears were becoming attuned to better harmonies. I decided to leave after having been with them for over two years." He went on to say, "[Jerome] Kern was the first composer who made me conscious that most popular music was of inferior quality, and that musical-comedy music was made of better material." With this realization, but no new job in the offing, the 18-year-old Gershwin left Remick's on March 17, 1917.

"THESE BOYS WILL BE EATEN ALIVE!"

Gershwin wouldn't have to wait long before opportunity knocked. Word got out that Victor Herbert and Jerome Kern needed a rehearsal pianist for their new show *Miss 1917*. Gershwin beat out the competition and spent July through November in the company of these two musical-theater giants. He was working hard on his own songs, too, one of which would be written to lyrics by 21-year-old Irving Caesar. In December, he and Caesar signed a contract with Remick to publish "Yoo-oo, Just You" for an upcoming revue called *Hitchy-Koo of 1918*. When they had pitched the song to Remick's (Caesar plugged and Gershwin pounded), the manager, John Belcher, had asked, "Well, boys, how about $250?"

"We were speechless," said Caesar. "We both thought he was telling us we would have to pay him that to see the song in print. Belcher took our silence to mean we were not satisfied. He said, 'OK, I'll give you $500.'" The two "kids" were so excited that they hurried uptown to where the Gershwins were then living. "Many years have passed since that day," admitted Caesar, "but I have never forgotten what Rose said: 'Morris,' she told her husband, 'Send a lawyer to help them. These boys will be eaten alive.'"[8]

When the revue opened in June the following year, "Yoo-oo" would be George Gershwin's first song on Broadway. That same December would bring another step forward in the careers of both the Gershwins; George and Ira would work on their very first collaboration, a song called "You Are Not the Girl."

Despite the flush of his biggest advance to date, Gershwin still needed a job if he was going to continue to contribute to expenses at home, as he was expected to do. Before the remarkably productive month of December of 1917 was up, the manager of *Miss 1917* arranged for Gershwin to meet the legendary music publisher, Max Dreyfus of T.B. Harms Company. Dreyfus was a formidable presence in the world of theater music publishing. He also was unusual in that he could read music—a distinct rarity in the world of music publishing. He had heard about Gershwin in advance, and after listening to the songs he had in his portfolio (including "You Are Not the Girl"), Dreyfus offered him $35 a week just to write songs. Neither plugging nor pounding were required.

A TUNE BOOK AND AMBITION

On February 10, 1918, 19-year-old George Gershwin reported for work at the T.B. Harms Company on West 45th Street. He was in good company. Max Dreyfus's track record included scouting out Jerome Kern in 1903 and hiring him when he was still an 18-year-old music student. By the time Gershwin started at Harms, Kern and his librettists were in their 30s and well known. They had a string of hits to their credit and were developing a reputation for creating shows that incorporated a more theatrically unified approach to musicals. Just ten days before Gershwin started at Harms, Kern and his current team, including the book writer Guy Bolton and lyricist P.G. Wodehouse, had opened their latest show, *Oh, Lady! Lady!* to rapturous reviews. Writing in *Vanity Fair*, no less of a

Irving Caesar in the 1930s.

critic than Dorothy Parker put it, "Bolton and Wodehouse and Kern are my favorite indoor sport. I like the way they go about a musical comedy ... I like the way the action slides casually into the songs ... I like the deft rhyming of the song that is always sung in the last act by two comedians and a comedienne. And oh, how I do like Jerome Kern's music."

Jerome Kern in the 1930s.

At Harms, Gershwin now found himself in the center of a heady atmosphere of success mingled with artistic intent. His ambitions were fired, and he had come a long way from the days of "chorus ladies" breathing down his neck at Remick's.

Two years earlier, Gershwin began to keep what he called his "tune book," jotting down melodies as they occurred to him. What he didn't keep was a diary. Fortunately, his brother Ira did. In an entry written around the same time George left Tin Pan Alley, Ira mentions that his brother's reason for leaving Remick's was to find time to study. The reference is revealing. Relieved of having to plug tunes all day, Gershwin used the relative freedom allowed by his job at Harms to begin serious, private study in harmony and orchestration with Edward Kilenyi. Their work together would continue through 1921, but there would be other teachers, too. Long before he started writing *Porgy and Bess*, Gershwin would find various ways to study the history of music, the technical aspects of composition, the craft of orchestration, and the art of conducting.

DINNER AT DINTY'S

A month after starting at Harms, Gershwin met his friend and collaborator Irving Caesar for dinner at Dinty Moore's, a Times Square restaurant famous for its bar, its Irish stew, and a hungry theater crowd known for digging into both. As Caesar tells the story, on the way to Dinty's, he mentioned the runaway success of "Hindustan," a one-step dance tune that was capitalizing on the fad du jour for exotic locations and, as in other hits like "China Town, My Chinatown," a kind of ersatz Orientalism. Knowing that "Hindustan" was about as exotically Oriental as Oliver G. Wallace and Harold T. Weeks, the Tin Pan Alley team that wrote it, Caesar brought up the topic again over dinner. "Why don't we write our own one-step, George?" They both knew that the Orientalism fad would soon fade, but there still would be a market for one-steps. It was Caesar's idea for them to write a one-step with an American locale. Gershwin, doubtlessly with Stephen Foster's "Old Folks at Home" and its opening line, "Way down upon the Swanee River," playing in his head, suggested the South and the river for a location. They left the restaurant and, while riding the bus to the Gershwin family apartment, sketched out the basic structure of the lyrics with some idea of a tune. Once they were in front of the family piano, they banged away at both the lyrics and the tune, heedless of shouted complaints coming from Morri's poker pals in the next room. According to Caesar, "Swanee" took them 15 minutes to complete. Once they had completed their work, Morris joined the boys and played along on a tissue-wrapped comb as they belted out their new creation.[9]

That same spring, Gershwin had gotten permission from Dreyfus to work as pianist for the *Ziegfeld Follies of 1918*. Most of the score was by Louis Hirsch and Dave Stamper, but, as with all revues large or small, there were a number of interpolated tunes by other composers. While the show was still in rehearsal, Caesar stopped by for a look, but just as he arrived, the director, Ned Wayburn, called a break. Caesar watched as Gershwin took advantage of the moment and jumped at the chance to play "Swanee" for the chorus girls who, as always, were huddled around him at the piano. They went crazy for it, something that did not go unnoticed by Wayburn. Right away, the director promised to include "Swanee" in the new revue he was producing for the opening of the Capitol Theater in 1919.

While this would push "Swanee's" Broadway debut further into the future than the eager Gershwin would have liked, the year 1918 still held four important milestones in store for him. In June, *Hitchy-Koo of 1918* opened with a score that included "You-oo, Just You," the song he'd already written with Caesar. This was the first George Gershwin melody heard on Broadway. In September, his first song for Harms was published, "Some Wonderful Sort of Someone," with lyrics by Schuyler Green. In October, the revue *Ladies First* opened with a score that included an interpolated Gershwin tune called "The Real American Folk Song (Is a Rag)." It was the first Broadway musical to include a song with music by George and lyrics by Ira (working under the pseudonym "Arthur

Frances" for now). Most important of all, on November 11, Germany's surrender brought World War I to a close before either brother's draft number was called.

LA LA LUCILLE!

"Every career needs a lucky break to start it on its way," Gershwin told a radio audience during an interview years later, "and my lucky break came in 1919 when I was brought to Alex Aarons, a dapper young man who had made some money selling smart clothes and wanted to have a fling at producing a show. I was 20 years old at the time, and Arthur Jackson, the lyric writer, was the man who brought us together." Two of the 26 songs Gershwin played during rehearsals for the *Ziegfeld Follies of 1918* were written by the team of B.G. "Buddy" DeSylva and Arthur Jackson. Both men, along with Aarons, played important roles in Gershwin's career advancement.

"The Real American Folk Song (Is a Rag)" was the first song with music by George and lyrics by Ira (working under the pseudonym "Arthur Frances") to appear in a Broadway musical.

DeSylva, a songwriter on his way up, had dropped out of college to come to New York after Al Jolson heard him sing some of his material in a Los Angeles nightclub. Jolson liked DeSylva's work well enough to buy partial ownership in some of his material and encourage him to come to New York. Jackson had made the introduction to Alex Aarons, who was producing the show *La La Lucille!*, which was to have music by the composer Victor Herbert. Alex had heard some of Gershwin's work and preferred its contemporary sound to that of Herbert's operetta-based songs. In short order, Aarons hired Gershwin to write his first full score for a Broadway show, adding Jackson and DeSylva as colyricists. After previews in Boston, La La Lucille! opened in New York on May 26, 1919, and ran until an actors strike shut down the theaters on August 19. The show did not set the world, nor Gershwin's career, on fire, but he now had a full score to his credit, and he had made a few connections that were about to pay off handsomely.

THE WORLD'S GREATEST ENTERTAINER

In August of 1919, construction of the Capitol Theater was finally completed. From the beginning, it had been designed as a theater that would alternate premiere silent films with musical revues. Ned Wayburn lived up to his word, and "Swanee" was given a production number in his revue. The show opened on October 24, 1919. When it came time for "Swanee," Muriel DeForrest performed the number while 50 dancers appeared on stage with small electric lights in their dance shoes. Even with that kind of visual razzmatazz, "Swanee" didn't generate much of a reaction. Gershwin and Caesar even stood in the lobby selling copies of the sheet music to boost sales, but the song was more or less ignored. That is, until Buddy DeSylva returned to New York. Al Jolson had interpolated one of DeSylva's songs into his current hit show, *Sinbad*, while it was out on the road. With DeSylva in tow, Jolson had returned to New York for a few days to make an appearance at one of his famous Sunday Night Concerts at the Winter Garden Theater and make some recordings. DeSylva took Gershwin with him to the concert, and then to a party that Jolson was hosting in Harlem.

It was well known among the Tin Pan Alley composers that Jolson's magic touch had been responsible for making Irving Berlin's 1911 song, "Alexander's Ragtime Band," a mammoth hit. Once they arrived at Al Jolson's party, DeSylva invited Gershwin to play. Gershwin saw an opportunity and took it. Mixed in with a few other songs was "Swanee," which he proceeded to plug just as he had done at Remick's. Jolson reacted to Gershwin's energetic playing and singing just as he thought he might—"Swanee" was a perfect fit. When Jolson returned to *Sinbad,* he interpolated the song into the show immediately, never mind that he was ostensibly portraying a porter in "old Bagdad," a long way from the Swanee river. In the show's setup for musical numbers, the porter meets a series of characters from the *Arabian*

Gershwin's *La La Lucille* featured a song, "Swannee," that didn't make much of a splash, until it was recorded by Al Jolson, creating a hit that changed Gershwin's life.

Nights, including Sinbad himself, who transports him to various exotic settings, all of which was concocted as a vehicle for Jolson and to take advantage of the momentary fad for musicals set in exotic locations. His performing "Swanee" made no dramatic sense in the show, but it wasn't expected to. What it did prove was that Irving Caesar and George Gershwin were right: the musical hunger for the exotic was fading, and it was perfect timing for a new American one-step.

"THE FOUR CORNERS OF THE EARTH"

Al Jolson recorded "Swanee" for Columbia records on January 8, 1920. "After that," said Gershwin, "'Swanee' penetrated the four corners of the earth."[10] It was the No. 1 song in America for nine weeks and on the list of top sellers for another nine. It sold a million copies in sheet music and an estimated 2 million records. "Swanee" would prove to be Gershwin's first hit and the biggest-selling song of his career. He reportedly earned $10,000 in royalty income within the

Al Jolson performing in *The Jazz Singer* (1927). Opposite page: Performing for troops in Korea 25 years later.

first year of the song's release, money that would allow him to concentrate on theater work and films. Above all, his name became a household word overnight, and his career as a composer was launched.

Of course, Gershwin was not the only young man with talent living in New York in the Roaring Twenties. The city was overflowing with young men and women who were full of "Jazz Age" ambition; the years were defined by it. However, unlike most of them, George Gershwin's ambition was matched, if not exceeded, by a talent of such magnitude that one quality alternately propelled the other toward a realization that was inevitable.

CHAPTER 6

JAZZ OPERA AND A BLUE NOTE RHAPSODY

When Gershwin was the rehearsal pianist on *Miss 1917*, one of the show's dancers happened to be a young man named George White. By 1919 White had hung up his dancing shoes in favor of producing revues intended to rival the *Ziegfeld Follies*. His first season, *George White's Scandals of 1919,* had been a moderate success, but White wanted more. He suspected that the music had been at fault, and word quickly got around that he was in the market for a new composer. Gershwin heard this and, at the height of "Swanee"'s popularity, took a train to Chicago where White was conducting auditions for the *Scandals of 1920.* He introduced himself to White and then wasted no time in proposing himself for the job. In a wise business decision, White agreed, and an important partnership was formed. Over the next five years, Gershwin would write scores for the *Scandals* that turned White's productions into a serious rival to the *Follies.* Buddy DeSylva was Gershwin's lyricist for the *Scandals of 1922.* The two men had also become friends, and DeSylva knew about Gershwin's aspirations

Gershwin, the composer.

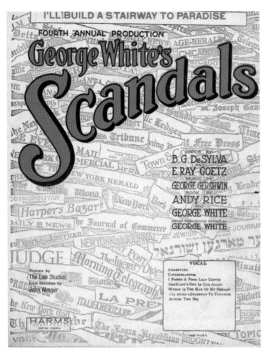

Former dancer George White mounted a challenge to Ziegfeld's dominance of the revue form and gave Gershwin his important Broadway assignments after "Swanee."

to compose serious music for the concert hall and opera house. DeSylva also knew about New York and kept his fingers on the pulse of the city's musical scene. DeSylva brought up the idea of working on a short "vaudeville opera," something that could pick up on the musical themes and ideas coming out of the "New Negro Movement" up in Harlem. What DeSylva referred to would become more widely known as the Harlem Renaissance, a period of unprecedented creativity that would make that part of New York the epicenter of the Jazz Age.

HARLEM'S RENAISSANCE

The seeds of the Harlem Renaissance were sown around 1900 by a combination of failed real-estate speculation and mass migration. Up until 1880, Harlem had remained a village surrounded by farmland estates. Manhattan's center of economic and social gravity was below 14th Street. The extension of elevated railroads into Harlem around 1880, combined with announced plans for a subway that would connect the area with Wall Street, fueled a ten-year boom in building and real-estate speculation. In 1889, Oscar Hammerstein I opened the Harlem Opera House on W. 125th Street, built expressly to cater to wealthy Germans moving into the area.

Harlem in the 1920s, during a rally for the United Negro Improvement Association (UNIA) in support of the "new Negro."

But delays in the subway extension and economic downturns led to a glut of buildings, and an African American developer named Philip Payton began buying up property at low prices. For years, since the postbellum Great Migration from the rural South to the urban North, New York had received a large influx of African Americans, resulting in overcrowding and racially motivated crime from neighboring whites in several sections of the city. With Payton as a prospective landlord, a black migration to Harlem from less hospitable parts of the city began.

With the return in 1918 of African American soldiers who had survived World War I, residents of Harlem began to challenge the stereotypes of blackface entertainment that had been prevalent among whites since the mid-1880s. Theater, literature, and poetry by black writers now boldly began to express the realities of contemporary African American life. In Harlem, the intellectual and artistic leaders, many of whom had attained the highest levels of education both here and abroad, proclaimed that it would be the "New Negro" who would, through intellect and the creation of literature, art, and music, set an example that could effectively challenge the country's pervading racism. If the "Old Negro" was represented by the corrupted view of African Americans as seen in minstrel shows and heard in Tin Pan Alley's coon songs, the New Negro would be represented by admirable achievement and racial pride.

Four artists associated with the Harlem Renaissance (counterclockwise from upper right): The poet and dramatist Langston Hughes; the writer Claude McKay, author of the defiant poem, "If We Must Die"; the jazz legend Duke Ellington, who would later disparage *Porgy and Bess*; and the team of Noble Sissell and Eubie Blake, creators of the first hit Broadway revue authored by an African American writing team, *Shuffle Along*.

Another characteristic of the Harlem Renaissance was a newfound interested on the part of liberal-minded whites in so-called primitive cultures. We know this to be true of DuBose Heyward, who was so riveted by what he called the "savage and alien" culture of the Gullah. African musical influences that had survived the middle passage and given birth to forms a diverse as ragtime and spirituals were now spinning off early forms of the new musical styles of jazz and the blues. Simultaneously, African Americans began to merge with whites into the world of musical composition. As Langston Hughes dryly observed, "The Negro is in vogue."

Buddy DeSylva's motives in suggesting a short opera on Harlemesque themes probably were not as noble an idea as the intermingling of cultural influences. He also knew about the success of Broadway's first all-black musical, *Shuffle Along*, by Eubie Blake and Noble Sissle. It had just closed after 484 sold-out performances. Because *Shuffle Along* was the first commercially successful show on Broadway to beproduced, directed, conducted, and performed completely by African Americans, it had been heralded as a major advancement for blacks in the theater. This is true to a point. *Shuffle Along* did have a plot of sorts, but it was primarily a revue. With numbers titled, " If You Haven't Been Vamped by a Brownskin, You Haven't Been Vamped at All," "Uncle Tom and Old Black Joe," "Bandana Days," and "Sing Me to Sleep, Dear Mammy," *Shuffle Along* seemed to rely more on the Old Negro than the New. As the show ended, one character explained that the lighter an African American woman's skin was, the more desirable she was. However, the show was a step forward for black producers and performers. It had a major hit in "I'm Just Wild About Harry," and the show opened with a statement, in a song "I'm Simply Full of Jazz," as performed by Ruth Little and Syncopation Steppers. The Jazz Age had set up shop on Broadway.

OLD JAZZ FOR NEW JAZZ

As a genre of music, jazz originated in the American South, principally in the city of New Orleans, where it was developed mainly by black musicians. Jazz and ragtime share a common ancestry, but as a new and different form, jazz began to distinguish itself from ragtime around 1910. The term *jazz* came into general use between 1913 and 1915. The legend is that the name came about when many of the prostitutes in New Orleans started wearing a perfume called Jasmine. Because most of the young jazz musicians made their new music in the New Orleans brothels, people referred to the new sound as "jasmine music," which soon was shortened to "jass" and ultimately "jazz." George Gershwin called it the New Jazz

If the "old jazz" was Ragtime, the New Jazz was something altogether different. Rather than the musician having to closely follow the notes on the page, as in ragtime, jazz encouraged improvisation while staying within the general outlines of the piece. This allowed musicians and singers a degree of freedom to express their own musical personalities. In praising a singer he was working with in the early '20s, Gershwin wrote, "She sings jazz better, I believe, than any other great singer on our concert or opera stage today, because she interprets with fidelity and enthusiasm, not merely the notes, but the spirit and rhythm of the music."[1] More important, jazz just *sounded* different from ragtime. The sonorities of jazz often emphasized what is known as the "blue note." In jazz and blues, a blue note (sometimes called a "bent" or "worried" note) is sung or played at a slightly lower pitch than the notes in a major scale. That lower sound is used by the musician to express a wider range of emotion. In popular jazz standards, Gershwin's "The Man I Love" is a good example of how blue notes can get across the quality of longing. Gershwin's *Rhapsody in Blue* derives its name from the blue note. In *Porgy and Bess*, "What You Want Wid Bess?" is a great example of a blue sound within the opera. In other words, the blue note is used to create sound that's very different from the jaunty and largely bright sound of Scott Joplin's "Maple Leaf Rag," or Tin Pan Alley tunes like "Swanee," or Gershwin's later show tunes like "I Got Rhythm." In his essay, "The Negro Artist and the Racial Mountain," Langston Hughes wrote, "... jazz to me is one of the inherent expressions of Negro life in America; the eternal tom-tom beating in the Negro soul ..."

GERSHWIN AND BLACK MUSIC

Gershwin had the great good fortune to be coming into his own musically at the dawn of the Harlem Renaissance, the lifeblood of which was the new sound of jazz. As Hollis Alpert writes in his wonderfully exhaustive survey, *The Life and Times of Porgy and Bess*, "Harlem was where Gershwin, as a boy, first heard the jazz that entranced him so, gave sparkle and the blue note to his music, and led him on the path to *Porgy and Bess*."[2] Morris had relocated the family to neighborhoods that were close to Harlem several times, so it was easy for the teenage Gershwin to slip into hot spots like Barron Wilkin's Nightclub at 135th Street and Seventh Avenue. There he would have heard James Reese Europe conducting his "Society Orchestra," or pianistic giants like James P. Johnson and Luckey Roberts. Johnson had grown up listening to the music of Scott Joplin and by the time he was a teenager had become known as one of the best ragtime pianists on the Eastern seaboard. He and Gershwin had met when they were both recording piano rolls in Aeolian Hall. "He [Gershwin] had written "Swanee," remembered Johnson, "and was interested in rhythm and blues. Like myself he wanted to write them on a higher level. We had lots of talks about our ambitions to do great music on American themes."[3] Luckey Roberts started playing piano as a child and acting professionally in traveling Negro minstrel shows. As an adult, he had been one of the leading pianists in Harlem since1910. American actress and jazz legend Ethel Waters once said, "Men like James P. Johnson, Willie the Lion Smith, and Charley Johnson could make you sing until your tonsils fell out. They stirred you into joy and wild ecstasy. They could make you cry. And you'd do anything and work until you dropped for these musicians. The master of them all, though, was Luckey Roberts."[4] Johnson and Roberts were particularly known for the evolution of ragtime piano into the earliest form of piano jazz called "Harlem Stride." The name "stride" comes from the left-hand movement "striding" rapidly and effortlessly up and down the keyboard in a highly rhythmic and somewhat percussive manner. James P. Johnson would come to be known the "Father of Stride."

Eubie Blake started playing piano in James Reese Europe's orchestra when he was 25. In an interview with jazz writer John Wilson, Blake remembered having heard of Gershwin when he first moved from Baltimore to New York. "James P. Johnson and Luckey Roberts told me of this very talented 'ofay' piano player at Remick's." ("Ofey" is Pig Latin for "foe." As a code word, it was used by black musicians when they talked about white musicians who they felt were getting the benefits from the music that was rightly theirs.) "They said he was as good enough to learn some of those terribly difficult tricks that only a few of us could master."[5] There was no animosity for Gershwin, however, because according to Roberts, Gershwin had come to his apartment to watch him play.[6] Given Gershwin's kinetic style as a pianist and his phenomenal ability in the left hand, this is an easy story to believe.

Stride pianist extraordinaire Luckey Roberts.

BLUE MONDAY

The vaudeville opera that DeSylva suggested would become known as *Blue Monday Blues*, a twenty minute piece on Harlem themes that would open Act II of *George White's Scandals of 1922*. "It was the hey-day of the new jazz," wrote Goldberg in his Gershwin biography, so

The Eubie Blake hit from *Shuffle Along*, "I'm Just Wild About Harry."

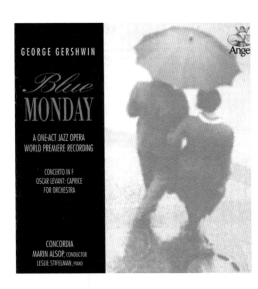

Blue Monday, Gershwin's first attempt at an American operatic piece, occupied a segment within *George White's Scandals of 1922*. It was quickly pulled from the show.

the timing seemed right. They brought the idea to White, who at first agreed, but then production problems changed his mind. It was assumed by everyone that white singers would sing all the roles in blackface, something that was still common in the theater. When White realized that changing out of the heavy makeup would slow down the show's pace, he changed his mind. However, three weeks before opening night, White announced that he'd reversed his decision and was willing to give *Blue Monday Blues* a try. Gershwin and DeSylva finished the 20-minute piece in five days and nights. Gershwin would date the beginning of a recurring condition he called "composer's stomach," a combination of indigestion, anxiety and physical pain, to the opening night of *Blue Monday Blues* during the show's tryout in New Haven.

George White's Scandal's of 1922 featuring the Paul Whiteman Orchestra opened on August 22, 1922. In general the show was a success but as the first number in Act II, *Blue Monday Blues* was a failure. The majority of the reviews were negative with one going so far as to call *Blue Monday Blues*, "the most dismal, stupid and incredible blackface sketch that has probably ever been perpetrated." White found the piece too downbeat for his clientele and removed it from the show after a single performance. Doubtless, the blackface makeup probably wreaked havoc with fast costume changes between numbers in Act II. However, as a forerunner of *Porgy and Bess*, *Blue Monday Blues* is important. It was Gershwin's first attempt to write a theater piece that employed the structure of opera and using contemporary music. A critic who was favorably impressed by *Blue Monday Blues*, wrote, "... the first real American opera ... set to music in the popular vein, using jazz at only the right moments, the sentimental song, the blues, and, above all, a new and free ragtime recitative. True, there were crudities, but in it we see the first gleam of a new American musical art." In retrospect, we have the luxury of knowing how accurate these observations were.

George Gershwin's "folk opera" *Porgy and Bess* was inspired by DuBose Heyward's novel *Porgy*. Heyward became the librettist of the opera and colyricist of the songs with Ira Gershwin.

Gershwin's red "tune book" was the repository for ideas that culminated in the creation of *A Rhapsody in Blue*, *An American in Paris*, and *Porgy and Bess*. Members of the original cast are visible on the album cover at bottom. A sketchbook by designer Sergey Soudeikin is at lower left. The bottom of the following page shows handwritten notes specifying which composer wrote which lyrics for the songs in *Porgy and Bess*.

George Gershwin & DuBose Heyward's

PORGY and **BESS**

Gershwin portraits: George Gershwin, upper left (artist unknown), painted his own likeness and those of others frequently, including DuBose Heyward, his collaborator on *Porgy and Bess* (lower left). Ira Gershwin (lower right) also painted a self-portrait.

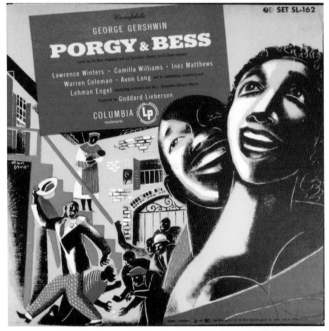

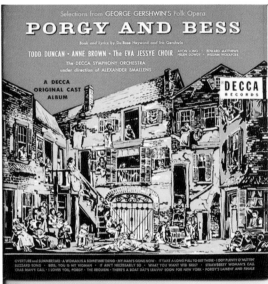

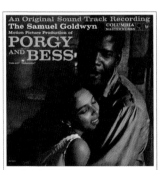

The music of *Porgy and Bess* has been recorded by many different artists in many genres. Opposite page: A film version starring Sidney Poitier, Dorothy Dandridge, and Sammy Davis, Jr., was beset by problems.

SAMUEL GOLDWYN
PRESENTS
THE MOTION PICTURE PRODUCTION

PORGY
and
BESS

SIDNEY POITIER · DOROTHY DANDRIDGE · SAMMY DAVIS, JR. · PEARL BAILEY

OTTO PREMINGER

SAMUEL GOLDWYNS
FILMPRODUKTION

Porgy und Bess

Prädikat:
BESONDERS WERTVOLL

SIDNEY POITIER · DOROTHY DANDRIDGE
SAMMY DAVIS, JR. · PEARL BAILEY

MUSIK VON GEORGE GERSHWIN · LIBRETTO VON DuBOSE HEYWARD

REGIE: OTTO PREMINGER

IM VERLEIH DER COLUMBIA · CinemaScope · TECHNICOLOR · STEREO-TON

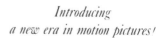

*Introducing
a new era in motion pictures!*

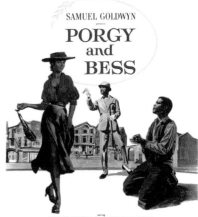

SAMUEL GOLDWYN
presents

**PORGY
and
BESS**

SIDNEY POITIER · DOROTHY DANDRIDGE
SAMMY DAVIS, JR. · PEARL BAILEY

Music by GEORGE GERSHWIN

Directed by OTTO PREMINGER · Distributed by COLUMBIA PICTURES

TODD-AO · TECHNICOLOR · STEREOPHONIC SOUND

Scenes from *Porgy and Bess* in various productions around the world.

TOWARD EUROPE AND THE CLASSICS

It's likely that Gershwin was a bit thrown by *Blue Monday* and his first serious drubbing from the critics, because his next show, *Our Nell*, didn't go up until December, and he was not the sole composer. In January he traveled to London and Paris before returning to New York in late April for work on *George White's Scandal's of 1923* and other revues throughout the year. Gershwin resumed studying in earnest, but a series of lessons in harmony with noted teacher Rubin Goldmark ended after a few weeks.

But George kept a musical scrapbook of reviews, news articles, and programs from all the concerts of classical music he attended at Carnegie Hall, Aeolian Hall, and other venues. There were also portraits of famous classical musicians like Richard Wagner; Jules Massanet, the prolific French lyric opera composer; Franz Liszt; Jósef Hofmann; and many others. Gershwin's appetite for this music was voracious, something that mystified those who knew him only from his days at Remick's or as the songwriter who hit it big with "Swanee." Going back to the moment he had been captivated by *Melody in F* and *Humoresque*, Gershwin's musical heart had always been divided. His facility for song tunes came to him easily and naturally, but in writing the songs he often added a deeper dimension that reflected his higher goals as a composer.

AN EXPERIMENT IN MODERN MUSIC

Paul Whiteman was a successful dance-band leader whose "orchestra" had played for the *Scandals of 1922*. Whiteman and the band specialized in a sound that blended popular music with a symphonic sound that turned their recordings for Victor into a string of nationwide hits. At the height of his popularity, he was billed as the "The King of Jazz," and his group was the orchestra of choice for high society functions from New York to Chicago. Toward the end of 1923, he and his band had moved from the *Scandals* to the more prestigious *Ziegfeld Follies*, but his true ambition was to be known as more than just a dance-band leader. Despite *Blue Monday Blues* having been yanked from the *Scandals of 1922*, Whiteman had been impressed by what he detected as a

Paul Whiteman was an enormously popular dance-band leader in the 1920s who became known as the King of Jazz, though his music had little to do with jazz as we now know it. He made possible the debut of Gershwin's *Rhapsody in Blue* by presenting the concert "An Experiment in Modern Music."

move toward a fuller, more concert-like sound in Gershwin's music. After the opera's performance, he spoke in general terms to Gershwin about collaborating on a concert piece in the jazz idiom that his orchestra might premiere. But Gershwin did not expect what he learned while playing a game of pool with DeSylva at a billiard parlor as Ira read that day's *New York Tribune.* In it, he noticed a small byline titled, "Whiteman Judges Named; Committee Will Decide 'What Is American Music?'" The last sentence of the press release read, "George Gershwin is at work on a jazz concerto, Irving Berlin is writing a syncopated tone poem and Victor Herbert is working on an American suite." It also noted that the concert was to take place at the Aeolian Hall and was scheduled for the afternoon of February 12, 1924—39 days from that moment.

Gershwin called Whiteman the next morning to say he was too busy with rehearsals for his current show to participate, but Whiteman convinced him that it was still possible. Eventually Gershwin agreed, not to a formally structured concerto, but rather a piece in a freer format that could be less complicated to compose and orchestrate. By the end of their conversation Gershwin envisioned something along the lines of a fantasia or a rhapsody. Using a fragment he found in his tune book, Gershwin began to compose what he initially called *American Rhapsody* . He worked feverishly at an upright piano in a back room of the Gershwin family home. Each day Whiteman's pianist, Ferde

Grofe, who was also hard at work orchestrating the piece, stopped at the Gershwin's home to pick up whatever had been composed the day before. Gershwin completed a two-piano version on January 25, 21 days after the newspaper story. Along the way, Ira suggested the title change to *Rhapsody in Blue* after having attended an exhibition at the Metropolitan Museum of Art where he saw two Whistler paintings, "Nocturne in Black and Gold" and "Arrangement in Gray and Black," the latter known more informally as "Whistler's Mother."

The "Experiment in Modern Music, a Program of Semi-Symphonic Arrangements of Popular Melodies," as Whiteman had named his concert, took place on a snowy afternoon at Aeolian Hall in midtown Manhattan. From the clarinetist's opening glissando, rising quickly at first and then holding back before spiraling down into the opening theme from Gershwin's tune book, the music galvanized listeners' attention. What no one knew was that the version of *Rhapsody in Blue* heard that day would never be heard again. The scores from which Whiteman conducted and that the individual orchestra members played had several large blank spots in them. At the first of those blank spots, Whiteman's score had the handwritten direction, "Wait for nod." In the best tradition of jazz, one of the elements that had distinguished it from ragtime, Gershwin was going to improvise all of his cadenzas. No one knew what he was going to play, probably not even him. He played what he felt.

In the audience for the world premiere of *Rhapsody in Blue* was the conductor Leopold Stokowski; Metropolitan Opera stars Alma Gluck and Mary Garden, the famous violinist Fritz Kreisler, and the composer Sergi Rachmaninoff. "It was a strange audience," Whiteman later wrote, "vaudevillians, concert managers come to have a look at the novelty, Tin Pan Alleyites, composers, symphony and opera stars, flappers, cake-eaters, all mixed up higgledy-piggledy."[7] Musical history was made that afternoon and no one, particularly the classical music audience and critics, would ever have to ask who George Gershwin was again. He had taken the tonality of European classical music as it had descended to us in a direct line from Bach, Handel, Hayden, Mozart, Beethoven, Wagner, and Verdi and filtered it through American popular music's affinity for melody. Most of all, he had taken a purely American musical form, one that had its roots in Western Africa but that had undergone a profound metamorphosis into ragtime and jazz, and

A handbill for the concert that featured the debut of *Rhapsody in Blue*, and a program for a separate classical concert at Aeolian Hall.

infused *Rhapsody in Blue* with its strong rhythm. Gershwin had found his compositional voice. His desire to go further and write an American opera that would follow this model of stylistic synthesis would only intensify. On April 21, 1924, the Paul Whiteman Orchestra premiered *Rhapsody in Blue* at Carnegie Hall with Gershwin at the piano. A four-city American tour followed, ending with an abridged recording of the *Rhapsody* on June 10 in New York.

AT AN EVER ACCELERATING PACE

The pace of George Gershwin's life for the next few years is one of breakneck speed and dazzling accomplishment. Twenty days after returning from the tour with Whiteman, George White's *Scandals of 1924* opened on June 30 at the Apollo Theater and ran for 196 performances. For the second time he traveled to London where the revue *Primrose* opened at the Winter Garden Theater in September. Back in New York, *Lady Be Good* starring Gertrude Lawrence opened on December 1 at the Liberty Theater for a run of 330 performances. It was the first full show written by George and Ira Gershwin together with no other collaborators. On July 20, 1925 Gershwin appears on the cover of *Time* magazine, the first American composer to be so honored.

In the fall of 1925, he began work on his second major composition for piano and orchestra, the *Concerto in F*. Walter Damrosch conducted the premiere performance at Carnegie Hall On December 3 with Gershwin at the piano.

A scant three weeks later, his next show *Tip-Toes* opened at the Liberty on December 28 and ran for 194 performances. The next day, December 29, Paul Whiteman conducts a concert of *Blue Monday*, which has now been retitled *135th Street,* on the bill of his "Second Experiment in Modern Music," this time at Carnegie Hall. On December 30, *Song of the Flame,* a pastiche of musical, opera, and revue with music by Gershwin and Herbert Stothart, with lyrics by Otto Harbach and Oscar Hammerstein II, opens at the 44th Street Theater and runs for 219 performances.

A revised version of *Lady Be Good* (with three new songs) opened on April 14, 1926, at the Empire Theater in London. Later that month Gershwin recorded the piece with the full and original cast for Columbia Records. Gershwin spent the summer in Paris, where he conceived the idea for his symphonic poem, *An American in Paris*. In August he returned to London, where *Tip-Toes* opens at the Winter Garden Theater on August 31. Shortly thereafter Gershwin was back in New York. In September, he and Ira began work on a new musical for Gertrude Lawrence to be called *Oh, Kay!*

However, on September 14, Ira would take time out to marry Leonore Strunsky, the daughter of a real estate developer he had met earlier that year. George would serve as his brother's best man in a traditional Jewish wedding ceremony that took place in the Gershwin's home, now on 103rd Street. In the same month, Leonore's sister, Emily Strunsky Paley, a member of Gershwin's inner circle for several years, sends George a small gift that would inspire the first great and truly American opera. It was a copy of DuBose Heyward's first novel, *Porgy*.

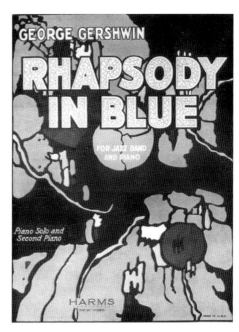

The published sheet music cover for *Rhapsody in Blue*.

George and Ira, at work in the early 1930s.

CHAPTER 7

A SENSATION, AN INNOVATION, AND A LABOR OF LOVE

Shortly after "Swanee" brought fame and fortune his way, Gershwin outlined his musical goals for the future in an interview for *Edison Musical Magazine* in October of 1920. "Operettas that represent the life and spirit of this country are decidedly my aim. After that may come opera, but I want all my work to have the one element of appealing to the great majority of our people."

At the time, Gershwin may have considered operetta a loftier musical goal than the mix and match type Tin Pan Alley shows that defined Broadway's brand of musical entertainment. Ethan Mordden sums this up neatly in *Make Believe: The Broadway Musical in the 1920s.* He writes, "The 1920s as a whole saw the form so refine and transform itself that, by the decade's finish, the "Tee-Oodle-Um-Bum-Bo" chorus line, the Bubble Dances, the nineteenth-century comedy, and the unmotivated star shot would be virtually extinct, unknown to the better writers and unpopular even with second raters." Gershwin's remarks about operetta may have been motivated by their popularity at the box office. Sigmund

Gershwin, the conductor.

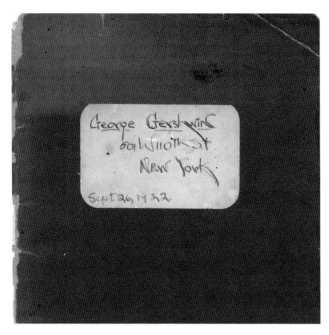

A portion of the cover of George Gershwin's "tune book," in which he jotted down musical ideas—from his days as a song plugger's accompanist to his brief tenure as opera composer.

Romberg's 1917 operetta *Maytime* had a healthy run of 492 performances, something of which Gershwin would have been well aware.

Two years later, his musical ambitions had turned from operetta to opera. We'll never know if *Blue Monday Blues* would have achieved success with the public, because George White removed it from his *Scandals of 1922* after a single performance. Of far greater importance was that for Gershwin, as a first attempt at composing in operatic form, *Blue Monday Blues* was a critically valuable experience. In *George Gershwin, His Life and Work*, Howard Pollack writes, "The work provided him an opportunity to shape song, recitative, pantomime, dance, and melodrama into a compelling whole."[1] Gershwin himself referred to *Blue Monday Blues*, along with other early works, as "experiments—aboratory work in American music."[2]

Three years after *Blue Monday*, an interview in the April, 1925, edition of *Musical America* demonstrates how Gershwin's ideas about opera had gained a sharper focus. "I think it should be a Negro opera, almost a Negro 'Scheherazade.' Negro, because it is not incongruous for a Negro to live jazz. It would not be absurd on stage. The mood could change from ecstasy to lyricism, plausibly because the Negro has so much of both in his nature ... I would like to see it put on with a Negro cast. Artists trained in the old tradition could not sing such music, but Negro singers could. It would be a sensation as well as an innovation."

Heyward's *Porgy* had been published three months before the *Musical America* interview appeared in print. It would be another year before Gershwin would find his way to reading the novel.

A PERFECT FIT

Late one evening in the summer of 1926, Gershwin returned to his home from rehearsals for his new show *Oh, Kay!* Too keyed up to sleep, he thought reading might help him to relax and picked up a copy of Heyward's novel, which had been sent to him by a friend. Everything about Porgy must have had an uncanny and exhilarating resonance for Gershwin. To the composer of *Blue Monday Blues*, the themes in Heyward's *Porgy* were strikingly familiar. Gambling—crap games, no less—figure as a background for death in both works. In *Blue Monday*, the character Vi's irrational jealousy and flash-point anger cause her to commit murder. In *Porgy*, the same emotions drive Porgy and Crown to kill. In *Blue Monday*, Tom is an arrogant bully who attempts to use his sexual power as a means of controlling Vi. Crown is equally brutish in *Porgy*, but his sexual manipulation of Bess is successful to the point of tragedy. But even more than the outward similarities, Porgy's poetic references to music and the novel's use of spirituals as a device for storytelling and characterization would have been exhilarating for Gershwin. For example, an early scene in the novel demonstrates its inherent musicality as it describes the funeral of Serena's husband Robbins, who has been brutally murdered by Crown.

The mourners gathered close about the grave.

'Death, ain't yuh gots no shame,' called a clear, high, soprano voice; and immediately the immortal embodiment of infinite sorrow broke and swayed about the grave in the funeral chant. Three times the line swung its curve of song, shrill, keen, and agonizing; then it fell away to a heart-wrenching minor on the burden:

'Take dis man an' gone—gone.

Death, aint's yuh gots no shame?'

When the singing ceased, the burial service commenced, the preacher extemporizing fluently. Taking his rhythm from the hymn, he poured his words along its interminable reiteration until the cumulative effect rocked the entire company."

On page after page, Heyward similarly evokes the life of his Gullah-inspired characters through music. The singing of spirituals is central to the story, and Heyward's prose style

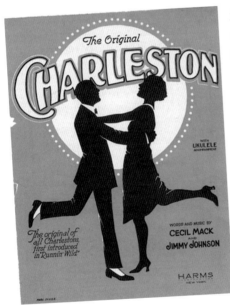

Runnin' Wild, with music by the stride-piano legend James P. Johnson (billed here as Jimmy Johnson) featured the iconic '20s song and dance, "Charleston." The show was another step forward for African Americans in musical theater, and its composer became a friend of Gershwin's.

was rich in musical reference and detail.

In his *Musical America* interview, Gershwin's mention of *Scheherazade*, the ancient Persian tale of a nobleman's daughter who uses learning and the power of storytelling to stay her execution, was in reference to a symphonic suite on the subject by the Russian composer Nikolai Rimsky-Korsakov. This was no accident. With its large orchestration full of exotic sound colors and attention-getting effects, it was a piece that Gershwin, an avid concertgoer, would have known. In the 1920s, exoticism also was a trend in popular music. Certainly, it helped make "Swanee," Gershwin and Caesar's answer to popular Tin Pan Alley rags set in foreign locales, a career-making hit. Attuned as Gershwin was to the idea of exoticism, reading this strange tale set among the Gullah, whom Heyward himself described as "removed from the soil to the underworld of the city—alien, exotic, fierce and intensely human," clearly struck a chord.

Several of Gershwin's remarks reflect prevailing racial attitudes in the 1920s. It was correct for Gershwin to say that, at that time, the "type of opera" he had in mind could not be performed at the Metropolitan Opera. The Met was an all-white company then and would remain so until the great contralto Marian Anderson sang there in 1955. Even if the Met had agreed to integrate its casting for the sake of Gershwin's "Negro opera," the cost of engaging what would have amounted to a second company of black artists for only a few performances, would have been prohibitive. No, if he was to write an opera on African American themes using African American singers, he needed a different producing organization.

As to the use of jazz in depicting African American life on stage, Gershwin was able to say it would "not be incongruous," because of his personal experiences within African American life. He had been going to hear jazz musicians in Harlem since his teens. He was on a first-name basis with some of the greatest jazz musicians of the age. He also understood that jazz, in the sense that it had originated with black musicians, was "their music." Its most authentic onstage performances would come from African Americans and, in turn, jazz would be the most authentic way to portray their life on stage. The fact that two jazz-infused musicals, *Shuffle Along* (1921) and *Runnin' Wild* (1923), had been very recent box-office hits performed by all-black casts had not escaped his notice.

As to assembling a cast, Gershwin's belief that "artists trained in the old tradition could not sing such music," meaning jazz, was based on what was accepted performance practice in the mid-1920s. The dividing line between those who sang opera and those who sang popular tunes and in musical shows was much more distinct than today. For a singer to have success in both, what we now call a "crossover" artist, was very rare indeed. In terms of portraying a character on stage, acting as we know it today was not expected in the opera house. Opera singers who were able to galvanize audiences through physical and vocal characterization were the exception to the rule. In the end, it was the voice that counted, not the way an opera singer looked or moved on stage. This was part of the "old tradition." Ironically, the opera he'd eventually compose would actually require its leads to be thoroughly trained in the old traditions of vocal technique in order to meet the score's musical demands. *Porgy and Bess* is not easy music. It requires stamina, experience, and a thorough knowledge of the voice and how it works. Because of this, the first *Porgy* cast would include graduates of some of America's finest musical conservatories.

A PARTNERSHIP BEGINS

When he finished reading *Porgy* at 4 a.m., Gershwin immediately wrote a note to Heyward suggesting they collaborate on an operatic version of his novel. The letter asked Heyward to call him so they might have an initial conversation about the idea. But when Heyward did call, Gershwin thought it best to be purposefully vague and sidestepped any definite commitment. Perhaps in the cold light of day, his euphoria had cooled a bit—not out of diminished interest in Porgy but from, among other things, his lineup of other commitments left him with no time to compose an opera. Gershwin soon received a follow-up letter from Heyward, who again expressed his great enthusiasm for the idea of an opera, but told the composer he'd committed to a stage version of the novel. Gershwin's response was that a play seen in New York first would not prevent an opera coming later. If fact, it would make it easier. From Gershwin's point of view, the hard work of condensing an entire novel into dialogue for the stage would have been done. This indicated Gershwin's growing theatrical savvy. His last experience with opera had been rushed. The words and music for *Blue Monday* were created more or less simultaneously and Gershwin had learned from this experience. *Porgy* was the right material for an opera, but for the time being, he had other things on his mind.

The Gershwin musical *Oh, Kay!* with its enduring classic, "Someone to Watch Over Me," premiered in November of 1926.

First was the completion of *Oh, Kay!* Gershwin met with Heyward in Atlantic City during the Philadelphia tryouts. The show opened in New York on November 8, 1926, and was a hit, running a total of 256 performances. Less than a month after the opening, Gershwin accompanied a friend, the contralto Marguerite d'Alvarez, in a recital given in the Hotel Roosevelt in New York City. It was also the occasion for the premiere of his latest composition, *Five Piano Preludes*.

In July of 1927, Gershwin would begin a ten-year association with the summer concert series in the Levisohn Stadium, a 6,000-seat sports stadium on the campus of New York University. Between 1927 and 1937, the music of George Gershwin would be featured for seven seasons, with Gershwin being present for all but one of those seasons. At Lewisohn, he would play his piano concertos or conduct the orchestra in his purely symphonic works. Howard Pollack wrote, "These concerts included two all-Gershwin concerts: the first of its kind (and the first time the Philharmonic ever devoted an entire program to a living composer) on August 16, 1932." Pollack continues, "And another on July 9, 1936, that featured selections from *Porgy and Bess* in addition to various instrumental works. All-Gershwin events— 'Gershwin Nights'—remained a staple at Lewisohn Stadium, as at the Hollywood Bowl, for decades after the composer's death."[3]

The fall season in 1927 was less kind. It would bring a disappointing failure when Gershwin's newest show, losed

Strike Up the Band, closed after two weeks of out-of-town previews. Prospects for their next project, the musical *Funny Face,* looked equally grim when the first preview performance, announced for October 10, 1927, in Philadelphia, had to be postponed for a night. The show was, in the words of one of its stars, Fred Astaire, "a mess. We were awful."[4] It was working on *Funny Face* that prevented Gershwin from attending the opening night of Heyward's *Porgy*— also scheduled for October 10, 1927. (Gershwin did see the play later in its successful run.) After six more weeks of previews, *Funny Face* eventually came together. It opened at the Alvin Theatre (now the Neil Simon Theatre) on November 22 and was a hit that ran for 250 performances.

Two other notable events that season would change the future of their respective art forms. Warner Brother's *The Jazz Singer,* starring Al Jolson, introduced synchronized sound to the movies on October 6. The world's first "talkie" changed the motion picture business forever. Within three years, George Gershwin would be writing a movie musical for 20th Century Fox.

The other game changer was the December 27 premiere of *Show Boat,* by Jerome Kern and Oscar Hammerstein

Just Another Big Hit !

ALEX. A. AARONS & VINTON FREEDLEY
present
FRED & ADELE
ASTAIRE
WILLIAM   VICTOR   ALLEN
KENT   MOORE   KEARNS
in
GAY *and* TUNEFUL

"FUNNY FACE"

GLORIOUS
GEORGE
GERSHWIN
MUSIC

Book by
FRED THOMPSON
&
PAUL GERARD
SMITH
Lyrics by
IRA GERSHWIN

With All That You Can Expect in a
PERFECT MUSICAL COMEDY

Funny Face marked the high point of the Gershwins' long association with Fred Astaire, first with his sister Adele and later in the movies with Ginger Rogers.

The Jazz Singer opened in 1927, heralding a revolution in filmed entertainment by adding sound to movies even as it perpetuated the stereotypes associated with minstrelsy.

II. *Show Boat* is widely recognized as the first completely successful integration of music, lyric and spoken dialogue in a musical play. And it included African Americans in both individual singing roles and a complete chorus of male and female singers. Hugely successful with press and public alike, it ran for 572 performances at the Ziegfeld Theater on Sixth Avenue and 54th Street, the same theater in which Leontyne Price and William Warfield would sing *Porgy and Bess* in 1952.

AN AMERICAN IN PARIS, AND IN LONDON AND VIENNA

For his entire career, there would be a tension between the parallel paths of George Gershwin's musical ambitions. On one hand, he was a populist whose facility for writing hit tunes and musicals was as prodigious as it was innate. On the other hand, he longed to be taken seriously as a composer of orchestral and operatic works in the European tradition. In this, he was often dismissed by other composers and attacked, sometimes viciously, by the music critics.

To some degree, Gershwin himself was aware of his need for further study. And he did study, fitfully but without abandoning the idea, until his death. On his own, he read copiously and always had a score by Bach, Mozart, Beethoven, Brahms, Wagner, Stravinsky, or one of the other great masters, at hand. He wrote hundreds of expressive personal letters and several well-written essays on musical topics that were published in leading newspapers and magazines. His popular songs and musicals, with brother Ira's sophisticated and witty lyrics, gave him an instant entrée into New York's café society. His having played his two concertos, *Rhapsody in Blue* and *Concerto in F* at Carnegie Hall, the latter with the New York Symphony (a precursor to the New York Philharmonic) under the baton of Walter Damrosch, gave him credibility among New York's elite circle of powerful businessmen, philanthropists, and their socialite wives. He acquired a certain intellectual and social polish that was not afforded him growing up, but he still did not consider himself fully prepared to tackle his most formidable musical goal, grand opera.

The year of 1928 began with *Rosalie*, a musical with songs by Gershwin and Sigmund Romberg that became

Gershwin's third most successful musical after *Lady Be Good!* and *Of Thee I Sing.* With two hits running on Broadway simultaneously (*Funny Face* and *Rosalie*), Gershwin decided to take an extended break. Gershwin met the French composer Maurice Ravel at a dinner party in New York. Ravel asked for tickets to *Funny Face* and Gershwin took the 53-year-old Frenchman to Harlem to hear authentic jazz. Gershwin told Ravel that he would like to study with him. He was politely refused. Ravel was afraid that their working together would cause Gershwin to "write bad Ravel" and "lose his gift of melody and spontaneity."[5] Instead, Ravel offered to write a letter of introduction to the most acclaimed and sought-after teacher of the time, Nadia Boulanger.

On March 10, Gershwin sailed for continental Europe with nine pages of initial sketches for what would become *An American in Paris* in tow. In an interview by Hyman Sandow appearing in *Musical America* just before his departure, Gershwin explained that the three-and-a-half-month journey was "to benefit my technic [sic] as much as possible from a study of European orchestral methods." Sandow continued, "I asked Mr. Gershwin if it were true that he might soon undertake to compose an American opera. He said he did not contemplate any such work, just now, nor did he expect to attempt so arduous a task until he could devote at least two years entirely to it." Whether he avoided the subject of *Porgy* on purpose is hard to tell, but Gershwin's estimation of how long he would need to compose an opera was fairly exact. With the exception of hosting 30 minutes of weekly radio programming each week for two seasons lasting three months each, Gershwin would devote a full 20 months to *Porgy and Bess.* During this period, he would not take on any other composing projects.

The legendary French teacher Nadia Boulanger told Gershwin, "What I could teach you wouldn't help you much."

After a stop in London, Gershwin attended the Paris premieres of *Rhapsody in Blue* and *Concerto in F.* Both pieces were very well received, and Gershwin became the toast of Paris. When he did meet with the formidable Boulanger, who had been impressed by Ravel's recommendation, she asked him to play some of his work for her. She too refused to take him on as a student, more or less seconding Ravel's opinion that subjecting such a tremendous natural gift to a strict regimen of lessons would do more harm than good. Many interpreted this rejection as a sign of Boulanger's having thought Gershwin unworthy of her tutelage. This would not have been out of character for her.

Some years later, Ira wrote about this episode:

> "What does bother me is when I see phrases like 'naïve orchestration' or 'structural ignorance' as though my brother were just a terribly talented fellow (which they grant) who somehow stumbled into the concert hall, was impudent enough to take advantage of it, put on a high pressure sales talk – and got away with it. With these critics there is an utter disregard of the facts that George from the age of 13 or 14 never let up his studies of so-called classical foundations and that by the time he was 30 or so could be considered a musicologist (dreadful word) of the first degree besides being a composer. When, in 1928 he went to see Nadia Boulanger in Paris about studying with her she turned him down on the grounds that there was nothing she could teach him. And she wasn't kidding because she was quoted in *Time* on the matter."[6]

Boulanger's exact quote on the subject appeared in the February 28, 1938, edition of *Time* and read, "I had nothing to offer him. He was already quite well known when he came to my house, and I suggested that he was doing all right and should continue. I told him what I could teach him wouldn't help him much … and he agreed. Never have I regretted the outcome. He died famous." Before leaving Paris, Gershwin was taken by his friend Mable Schirmer to several Parisian auto-parts dealerships, where he bought the French taxi horns that would be used to great effect in *An American in Paris*.

In Vienna, Gershwin would attend performances at the Vienna State Opera and meet with Franz Lehar, the composer of *The Merry Widow*, along with Alban Berg, a leading composer of the Second Viennese School, a group of composers who wrote modern atonal music. Gershwin and Berg, two composers who couldn't have been more dissimilar in their approach to melody, nonetheless enjoyed a warm and cordial first meeting. Two days later, Gershwin was invited to a small concert where a quartet played Berg's string quartet in the presence of the composer. "Gershwin was asked to play and Berg was delighted," wrote Edward Jablonski. "But then suddenly Gershwin stopped; he felt uncomfortable playing show tunes, even *Rhapsody*, after Berg's cerebral quartet. Berg encouraged him to continue playing, reassuring him with, 'Mr. Gershwin, music is music.'"[7]

A recording of *An American in Paris* by the Victor Symphony Orchestra with George Gershwin.

Having left in March with nine pages of initial sketches for *An American in Paris*, Gershwin returned to New York in June with the piece fully outlined. He completed the two-piano version on August 1 and the orchestrations on November 18. The piece received its world premiere at Carnegie Hall on December 13, 1928. The critical reaction was again mixed, but it became a repertory staple for orchestras across the country and remains one of Gershwin's most popular symphonic works.

CRASHES AND COMMISSIONS

Since reading *Porgy* in 1926, Gershwin thought regularly of writing an opera. After all, taking on the composition of a grand opera was one of his reasons for having just spent several months in Europe. But twice in 1928, he publically disavowed any plans to write opera and never mentioned *Porgy*. On September 30, 1929, Gershwin signed a contract with Guilio Gatti-Casazza, the general manager of the Metropolitan Opera, for an opera based on Szymon Ansky's Yiddish play *The Dybbuk*. The contract listed April 1, 1931, as the date by which the competed full score was to be delivered, and it guaranteed four performances of the opera. He had already written a few melodic fragments in his tune book. Within a few days, a headline in the *Morning World*

An American in Paris inspired an Academy Award-winning film almost a quarter century after the work was first performed.

screamed out, "Gershwin Shelves Jazz to do Opera." Other dailies followed; "Gershwin Attuned to Write an Opera," was the title of a byline in the October 16 *New York Evening Post*; and "Gershwin to Quit Jazz for Opera," ran in the *Los Angeles Examiner*, on October 17, 1929. To the surprised press, who thought of Gershwin as a jazzman and Broadway composer, Gershwin explained, "It was a great thing for me. *The Dybbuk*, a somber and mystical play, would not by any means be a jazz opera, and the fact that it would be different from any [of my] previous works one of its attractions." Whether Heyward heard of Gershwin's new plan is not

George Gershwin backstage with a very young, pre-Hollywood Ginger Rogers and his star, Ethel Merman, during the run of Girl Crazy.

revealed in their communication, nor do we know if it would have precluded *Porgy*.

American financial markets were teetering on the brink in the weeks that followed Gershwin signing his Met contract. The Great Crash of 1929 reached a tipping point on October 24, or "Black Thursday," and the market slid into its greatest loss in history on "Black Tuesday," October 29, 1929. Within weeks Gershwin encountered two major disappointments: in December the Metropolitan Opera learned that an obscure Italian composer already owned the operatic rights for *The Dybbuk,* and the project was abandoned. Then, *Strike Up the Band* opened on January 14, 1930, to a generally negative critical response. It closed after only 111 performances.

TWO HITS AT HOME AND A *SECOND RHAPSODY*

Following a brief excursion to Hollywood for the movie *Delicious,* George made his third appearance at the Lewisohn Stadium, this time playing *Rhapsody in Blue* and *Concerto in F,* followed by conducting *An American in Paris.* After the disappointing reception given their last three shows, the brothers started the fall, 1930, theater season with a solid hit, *Girl Crazy,* starring Ginger Rogers and Ethel Merman. For most of 1931, George refined the themes he'd used in the film *Delicious* for the *Second Rhapsody* and worked with Ira on their new show, *Of Thee I Sing.* The show opened on December 26 and was the biggest hit of the Gershwins' career. *The Second Rhapsody* premiered in Boston on January 29, 1931. Critical reception was mixed. In February, 1932, George traveled to Cuba for a long-overdue holiday.

CHAPTER 8

COMING BACK TO PORGY

eturning from his Cuban holiday, Gershwin felt renewed enthusiasm for *Porgy*. On March 29, 1932, he wrote to Heyward, "In thinking of ideas for new compositions, I came back to one that I had several years ago—namely, *Porgy*—and the thought of setting it to music. It is still the most outstanding play I know about the colored people."[1] Gershwin asked Heyward to call him as soon as possible. After his experience with *The Dybbuk*, the first thing Gershwin wanted to know was if the rights were still available. In their phone call, Heyward confirmed that the rights were available and plunged immediately into new ideas for the libretto that had been incubating since their last contact. In a follow-up letter, Heyward wrote, "I want to tell you again how pleased I am that you have returned to your original idea of doing a musical setting of Porgy. I would be tremendously interested in working on the book with you."

"I have some new material," Heyward continued, "that might be introduced, and once I got your ideas as to the general form suitable for the musical version I am sure that I could do you a satisfactory story."[2] Champing at the bit to get started, Heyward began to think out loud. "As to the lyrics I am not so sure until I know more definitely what you have in mind. Perhaps your brother Ira would want to do them, or maybe we could do them together?" He closed this burst of pent-up enthusiasm, writing, "I want you to feel that I would be happy to do what you want me to do." [3]

Gershwin at Folly Beach, South Carolina.

GEORGE GERSHWIN
33 RIVERSIDE DRIVE
New York, New York

March 29 - 1932

My dear Mr. Heyward:

I am about to go abroad in a little over a week, and in
thinking of ideas for new compositions, I came back
to one that I had several years ago - namely, PORGY -
and the thought of setting it to music. It is still
the most outstanding play that I know, about the
colored people.

I should like very much to talk with you before I leave
for Europe, and the only way that I imagine that
would be possible would be by telephone. So if
you will be good enough to either telephone me
collect at Trafalgar 7-0727 - or send me your
telephone number by telegram, I will be glad to call
you.

Is there any chance of your being abroad in the next
couple of months?

I hope this letter finds you and your wife in the best
of health, and hoping to hear from you soon, I am

Sincerely yours,

George Gershwin

DuBose Heyward
Dawn Hill
Hendersonville, North Carolina

GEORGE GERSHWIN
33 RIVERSIDE DRIVE
New York, New York

May 20th, 1932.

Dear Mr. Heyward:

I was very glad to have your letter telling me that
the operatic rights to " Porgy " are free and clear.

Of course there is no possibility of the operatic
version's being written before January 1933. I
shall be around here most of the summer and will
read the book several times to see what ideas I
can evolve as to how it should be done. Any notions
I get I shall forward to you. I think it would be
wise for us to meet - either here or where you are -
several times, before any real start is made.

GG/eb

Sept.3rd.1932.

My dear Gershwin:

I attach a letter just received from my old Porgy
agents.I cannot see brother Jolson as Porgy,but I have heard that
he was casting about for something more artistic than his usual
Sonny Boy line,and what his real potentialities are,I have very
little idea.

Of course, this does not shake me in my desire to
work with you on the story, only it reminds me that I evidently
have an asset in Porgy,and in these trying times that has to be
considered. Therefore, before I turn this down flat, I think that
we should execute the customary agreement with your producer,with
whom,I presume, you have been already discussing the matter. With
this attended to I will withdraw the rights from the Century Play
Co, and will also withdraw from sale the picture rights,which are
at present on the market. It seems to me that this is very important for both of us,as certainly neither of us would wish to put
our time on it without this protection.

Will you please at earliest possible moment wire
me whether your associates are prepared to enter into a definite
agreement at this time,so that I may know how to handle the Jolson
matter.I will then leave promptly for New York so that we may
get that settled,and also have our first conference on the rewriting
of the book.

Please do not construe this letter as an attempt to
force a decision upon you in the matter. I understand perfectly
that you want to do the play.So do I. It is however,very important
for me to have some definiteness as to dates, and that would be the
principal value of a contract to me. I am always having a hard
time adjusting my work to my time.. Perhaps you have not yet taken
the matter up with a producer. All that I would ask then would be
your definite assurance that you would plan for production either
this spring or early next fall.

Would it be possible to use Jolson,and arrange
some sort of agreement with him, or is that too preposterous ?

Please let me hear from you at you very earliest
possible convenience,and I must act at once in this Jolson matter.

All good wishes,

Sincerely,

GEORGE GERSHWIN
33 RIVERSIDE DRIVE
New York, New York

September 9th, 1932.

My dear Heyward:

I have just returned from a short vacation in the Adirondacks
and found your letter.

I think it is very interesting that Al Jolson would like to
play the part of Porgy, but I really don't know how he would
be in it. Of course he is a very big star, who certainly
knows how to put over a song, and it might mean more to you
financially if he should do it - provided that the rest of
the production were well done. The sort of thing that I
should have in mind for PORGY is a much more serious thing
than Jolson could ever do.

Of course I would not attempt to write music to your play until
I had all the themes and musical devices worked out for such
an undertaking. It would be more a labor of love than any -
thing else.

If you can see your way to making some ready money from Jolson's
version I don't know that it would hurt a later version done by
an all-colored cast.

If you are planning to come north I shall be most anxious to see
you to discuss various aspects of the Opera. I expect to be here
until February. I have not planned with any producers yet as I
should like to write the work first and then see who would be the
best one to do it. I know that Shumlin, the producer of GRAND
HOTEL, is very much interested in the idea.

I hope that you and Mrs. Hayward are well.

Best wishes,

George Gershwin

Oct.17th.1932.

Dear George:

Miss Wood of the Century Play Company writes that Jolson has been hot on her trail for the Porgy book, and that in a 'phone conversation with you, she was advised by you that his use of the story for his particular sort of a musical play would not necessarily kill it for an eventual opera.

As a matter of fact, upon my return here after my talk with you I learned of circumstances that have put me in a fairly tight spot financially, and that, and that alone, has prompted me to write to Miss Wood as per enclosed carbon. Of course what I would like to be able to afford would be to wait indefinitely for your operatic version, and to work with you myself without the least thought of the commercial angle.

It is not my idea to work in any way upon a possible Jolson musical, but merely to sell the story. Later I shall hope to work with you as we outlined in our recent conversation.

Please let me tell you that I think your attitude in this matter is simply splendid. It makes me all the more eager to work with you some day, some time, before we wake up and find ourselves in our dotage.

Please feel free to call Miss Wood and insist upon conditions in the contract which will assure the proper release of the book for your use.

With all good wishes,

Sincerely,

GEORGE GERSHWIN
33 RIVERSIDE DRIVE
NEW YORK, NEW YORK

Dear DuBose:

I had a telephone call this morning from Miss Wood telling me that Al Jolson was is town and had telephoned her. She wanted to know from me what to do concerning him. I told her that if Jolson wanted to do the play right away and that it meant some money for you I saw no objection to it in view of the fact that Jolson couldn't do an operatic version of it anyway. His version would undoubtedly be the play as you wrote it with the addition of perhaps a few songs.

I really don't think that Jolson would consider doing an operatic version as I am quite sure that he would consider that out of his line. I have taken this attitude because I wouldn't want to stand in the way of your making some money with your property at the present time, and also because I don't believe that it would hurt a serious operatic version in any way. If anything further develops concerning Jolson I shall be happy to let you know.

It was indeed a pleasure to see you on this trip to New York and I am looking forward to seeing you again.

Best regards,

George Gershwin

14th October, 1932.

On May 3, Ira Gershwin, George S. Kaufmann, and Morrie Ryskind were announced as that season's winner of a Pulitzer Prize for *Of Thee I Sing,* in the category of Best American Play. At that time, there was no Pulitzer for music, so the committee did not include the show's composer. Ira was upset by this, of course, but George took it in stride and was proud of his brother. Gershwin wrote Heyward that he was "very glad" to know "that the operatic rights to *Porgy* are free and clear," but Heyward should understand that there was "no possibility of the operatic version's being written before January, 1933." Gershwin let Heyward know that he planned to "read the book several times to see what ideas I can evolve as to how it should be done. Any notions I get I shall forward to you."

COMPETING BIDS

That summer, Heyward would find himself in a dilemma of a different sort. Al Jolson *also* had returned to the idea of *Porgy* and had simultaneously approached the Theatre Guild for the rights to turn the play into a stage musical. Jolson's

While George contemplated his plans to write music for *Porgy and Bess*, Ira picked up a Pulitzer Prize for his work with George S. Kaufman and Morrie Ryskind for the musical *Of Thee I Sing*. George was not included, because composers were not eligible for the prize at the time.

pitch included the powerful lure of a Jerome Kern score set to lyrics by Oscar Hammerstein II. Jolson would star as Porgy, a role he intended to play in blackface. Sensing a ready-made hit, the Theatre Guild, which owned part of the rights to the play, urged Dorothy and DuBose to accept. While the Heywards preferred an opera by Gershwin, their investments had lost most of their value in the crash so they were not in a position to dismiss Jolson's inquiry out of hand. On September 3, 1932, DuBose wrote what Dorothy called his "Madison Avenue letter" to Gershwin. In it he wrote, "I can not see brother Jolson as Porgy," but he realized he "had an asset in *Porgy*, and in these trying times that has to be considered." Heyward made the assumption that Gershwin already had a producer for their opera lined up and that he'd be ready for a premiere in the fall of 1933. If Gershwin could sign a contract now, Heyward would be able to put Jolson off. Or, Heyward suggested, "Would it be possible to use Jolson [in the opera] and arrange some sort of agreement with him, or is that too preposterous?"[4]

In Gershwin's September 9 response, he wrote, "I think it is very interesting that Al Jolson would like to play the part of Porgy, but I really don't know how he would be in it. Of course he is a very big star, who certainly knows how to put over a song, and it might mean more to you financially if he should do it—providing that the rest of the production were well done." Gershwin added, "The sort of thing I should have in mind for Porgy is a much more serious thing than Jolson could ever do." Gershwin made other points about not wanting to start on the opera until he had "all the themes worked out for such an undertaking," adding that writing the opera "would be more of a labor of love than anything else." This was an important point for Gershwin to be making. He, too, would be sacrificing income by putting lucrative new work on hold while he wrote an opera. However, he was sympathetic to Heyward's financial problems and thought that if he could see his way to "making some ready money from Jolson's version," then Heyward should take advantage of the offer. Gershwin had respect for Kern and Hammerstein, but he didn't think Jolson in a blackface musical would threaten the success of their opera, which was to be authentically cast with all African Americans.

Heyward traveled to New York in early October of 1932 to meet with his agent and spend time talking through ideas for *Porgy* with Gershwin. When he returned to North Carolina, Heyward wrote a follow-up letter confirming that circumstances had absolutely put him "in a tight spot financially" so he was forced to proceed with selling the musical rights to Jolson. "Of course I would like to be able to wait indefinitely for your operatic version," wrote Heyward, "and to work with you myself without the least thought of a commercial angle." He told Gershwin that he did not intend to actually work on the Kern-Hammerstein-Jolson musical, only give them permission to go it alone. "Please let me tell you," he concluded, "that I think your attitude in this matter is simply splendid. It makes me all the more eager to work with you someday."

Around this same time, two conflicting events brought Porgy to a halt once more. Kaufmann and Ryskind submitted an idea to the Gershwins for a musical called *Let 'Em Eat Cake*. As a follow-up to their hit *Of Thee I Sing*, the idea was to bring it to Broadway in 1933. Taking it on would inevitably lead to a further delay for the Porgy opera, but to the Gershwins the outline for *Cake* was too good to refuse. For Heyward, the worst of it would be the news that Jolson's bid to take on *Porgy* had fallen through for a second time. Kern and Hammerstein were busy with their own show, *Music in the Air*, which would open at the end of November of 1932. Now came the news that they had both decided to take on other projects in 1933 that would make then unavailable through the spring of 1934. Without his star composer and lyricist, Jolson had lost two-thirds of his bargaining power. He was forced to abandon his plan for a musical of *Porgy*, and Heyward was back in the financial soup.

THE DESK IS CLEARED

By the summer of 1933, Heyward had begun to despair about ever having a Gershwin opera of his *Porgy*. They were now months past Gershwin's own projected start date of January. However, that same summer Gershwin called Heyward to tell him he was "clearing his desk" of all other projects to begin work on *Porgy* as soon as he and Ira finished *Let 'Em Eat Cake* in the fall. Heyward was not happy about the further delay but had little choice. *Let 'Em Eat Cake* opened at the Imperial on October 22. The bad news was that the show closed after only 90 performances. The good news was that the Theatre Guild had decided to produce Gershwin and Heyward's opera— the Guild's first. On October 26, 1933, just four days after the failed opening of *Cake*, contracts between the Theatre Guild, George Gershwin, and DuBose Heyward for an opera based on the play *Porgy* were finally signed.

Not wasting a moment, Heyward began working on the libretto immediately after returning to Hendersonville. His first task was to reduce the play's dialogue by about 40 percent and restructure the story into a scenario that would suggest vocal numbers and instrumental episodes to Gershwin. His work proceeded quickly, and on November 12, 1933, Heyward sent the libretto for Act I, Scene 1, to New York. Still, Gershwin would not be rushed. In his response, he told Heyward that he had a trip to Palm Beach planned for the holidays and asked if he might stop in Charleston "to see the town and hear some spirituals and perhaps go to a colored café or two if there are any." Returning to the subject of the libretto, Gershwin, who genuinely liked what Heyward was doing, added, "I have been reading through the first scene which you sent and think you have done a swell job, especially with the new lyrics." So that Heyward wouldn't expect too much, Gershwin added, "On account of the many things I have to do at the present I haven't started composing. I want to do a great deal of thinking about the thing and the gathering of thematic material before the actual writing begins. So, after my tour is ended [an early 1934 series of concerts celebrating the tenth anniversary of *Rhapsody in Blue*] I don't expect that I will have much finished, but after that I shall devote all my time to *Porgy*."

A ROAD TRIP SOUTH

On December 2, 1933, Gershwin drove down the East Coast to Charleston along with his Palm Beach host, Emil Mosbacher. Once they arrived, DuBose served as their guide to black Charleston. Never far from the watchful eye of the press, Gershwin's every move was chronicled by the local newspaper.

George Gershwin Arrives to Plan Opera on *Porgy*

George Gershwin, the outstanding composer of jazz music, is spending several days in Charleston obtaining atmosphere for an operatic version of DuBose Heyward's *Porgy*. "I felt that I should come to Charleston and see what it's like and study the Negroes as best I can," Mr. Gershwin said.

Opera is a new field for Mr. Gershwin, but he said he was glad to get the opportunity of putting music to *Porgy*. Yesterday afternoon he and Mr. Heyward went to a negro [sic] church and listened to the singing. "I'm sure that even Mr. Heyward was surprised by the primitiveness of this particular service and it gave me [lots] to think about," Mr. Gershwin said.

Mr. Heyward is going to conduct the composer around the city. They plan to arrange to hear as much negro music as possible and Mr. Gershwin is also anxious to listen in on some of the fish and vegetable hucksters.

But it is on the subject of jazz music that Mr. Gershwin becomes emphatic.

"There can be no question but that jazz [is] the first real American music," he said. He declared that jazz will live, probably with many variations, but always retaining its basic syncopation. "I have tried, myself, to do something more than just a song," he said. "I have tried to grasp the real spirit of our people. I have wanted to do something that would last. *Rhapsody in Blue* will celebrate its tenth anniversary soon, but I am looking for something more."

—*The Charleston News and Courier,* December 4, 1933

The service that Heyward had taken Gershwin to see and hear was in Charleston's Macedonia Church. Called an "experience service" by the members of the congregation, it was here that Gershwin first heard "Oh, Doctor Jesus," the spiritual that would serve as the inspiration for Serena's Act II supplication to God to bring Bess back to health. Howard Pollack wrote that years after Gershwin's death, when Kay Swift was visiting Charleston, a Macedonia church member told her Gershwin, "had come often to sing with them and that he always spoke to them when he came."[5]

WORKING LONG DISTANCE AND OTHER PURSUITS

One of the unique things about the Gershwin-Heyward collaboration is that they did so much of their work apart from one another—a very atypical arrangement for Gershwin. When he and his brother wrote a show, they worked very much together. Morrie Ryskind, a writer and director who worked with the Gershwins on *Of Thee I Sing*, wrote that he "especially remembered ... being amazed at the telepathy that existed between them. I've never seen anything even remotely like it with other songwriters."[6] But for *Porgy*, Gershwin's sole collaborator (at least at first) lived 600 miles due south and did not travel well. Heyward, who found his creative ability "practically paralyzed in a new environment," needed to be in his study at Dawn Hill, his home in Hendersonville, North Carolina, in order to be productive. Their many letters, written while *Porgy and Bess* was being created, give us a remarkably clear picture of how they worked apart, together, and ultimately with Ira as colyricist.

Heyward always was deferential to Gershwin, the lead creative force behind the opera, carefully labeling his ideas as "offerings" or "suggestions," but his ideas were concrete, well thought out, and theatrical. He had been living with this material since 1924 and, more important, had the practical experience of the play's being staged behind him. His sense for what would most effectively tell the *Porgy* story on stage was invaluable, and Gershwin was remarkably receptive to what he had to contribute. With each mailing of a completed a section of the libretto, Heyward included detailed explanations of his ideas for Gershwin to think about. It was Heyward's idea, for example, to open the opera not with the "riot of noise and color," as Mamoulian had done with the play (not to Heyward's liking), but "to let the scene, as I describe it, merge with the overture, almost in the sense of an illustration." Heyward continued, "I think it would be very effective to have the lights go out during the overture, so that the curtain rises in darkness, the first scene will begin to come up as the music takes up the theme of jazz from the dance hall piano." When completed, the full version of *Porgy and Bess* would open in exactly this way. The piano player would be called Jasbo (originally "Jazzbo") Brown, in reference to the legendary African American jazz musician and subject of a Heyward poem. The dance-hall setting would reference the countless African American pianists who developed early ragtime while playing in the bordellos of New Orleans.

In his desire for musical authenticity, as it related to *Porgy*, Gershwin often relied on Heyward for guidance. In one of his letters to Heyward he wrote, "I would like to write the song that opens the 2nd Act, sung by Jake with the fish nets, but I don't know the rhythm you had in mind—especially for the answers of the chorus, so I would appreciate it if you could put dots and dashes over the lyric and send it to me. Ira and I have worked on some words to music at the very opening, in Jazzbo [sic] Brown's room while the people are dancing, and I finish it up with a sort of African chant."[7] Heyward's self-effacing response read, "I have done my best to convey my own rather vague idea for the rhythm on the enclosed copy. If you will imagine yourself at an oar and write the music to conform to that rhythm that will give you a better idea than anything I can write."[8] In the end, there was never any doubt between the two men as to whose work *Porgy and Bess* was to be. They did have disagreements, but not of the heated variety. For example, in one of his letters, Heyward noted his "pretty definite feeling" that "all the dialog should be spoken ... this will give the opera speed and tempo."[9] Gershwin had already decided, however, that the dialogue would be sung in the manner of grand opera but with a contemporary approach. Gershwin knew what he wanted to do, but the composer's diplomatic response was, "There may be too much talk, but I can't tell until I start composing just how it will all work out."

While Gershwin was busy with his *Rhapsody in Blue* tour and its grueling schedule of 28 cities in 29 days, Heyward continued working on the Porgy libretto. Heyward begged Gershwin to find time to come South, "I can not urge you too strongly to plan to come to Charleston at the earliest convenience. You really haven't scratched the surface of the native material yet. This secular stuff, for instance."[10] What

Heyward didn't know about was Gershwin's new plan for financial stability during the long gestation period of their opera.

From early February of 1934 through October of 1935, Gershwin would devote all of his time and energy to composing his opera—that is, with the exception of programming and hosting Music by Gershwin, a weekly radio show on WJZ in New York. The program offered a substitute for fees from new compositions. It was sponsored by the laxative chewing gum Feen-A-Mint, and their offer of $2,000 a week for 15 weeks allowed Gershwin to put off composing anything other than Porgy. Preparation for the radio show was time-consuming and exhausting, but Gershwin plunged into the task with full enthusiasm. To his friend George Pallay, Gershwin wrote, "I am having a lot of fun doing my radio broadcasting," and urged him to tune in and "hear some Gershwin music and find out all about Feen-A-Mint laxatives—not that you need it, but maybe your [daughters] do!"[9] He was criticized by some for selling out to commercialism, an accusation that clearly annoyed him, and others made easy jokes about his sponsor. But in their book The Gershwins, Robert Kimball and Alfred Simon quote Gershwin as having said, "Without Feen-A-Mint I would not have been able to write Porgy and Bess."

On February 19, 1934, Heyward heard the premiere broadcast of Music by Gershwin on his local radio station and was alarmed by what he interpreted as another barrier to getting down to work on Porgy. A few days later he received a letter from Gershwin that allayed his fears. "Well, here I am back again after an arduous [tour] ... I received second act script and think it is fine," he wrote. Genuinely impressed with Heyward's work, Gershwin continued, "I really think you are doing a magnificent job with the new libretto and I hope I can match it musically." While this was reassuring, what was real music to Heyward's ears was Gershwin's adding, "I have begun composing ... and am starting with the songs and spirituals for Act I."

In early March, Heyward wrote to Gershwin that the "radio reception was so good it seemed as though you were in the room. In fact, the illusion was so perfect I could hardly keep from shouting at you, 'Swell show, George, but what the hell is the news about PORGY!!!'" Retracting a bit, Heyward quickly added, "It is a good show. You have managed to give it a charming informality, and, in spite of the brevity, a definite impress of your own personality. I am not criticizing your decision. I know well what an enormously advantageous arrangement the radio is … and I know … the broadcasts are rolling up publicity that will be good for us when the show opens, only I am disappointed. There is so much more here. Anyway, this can be offset to a great extent by my … availing myself of your invitation and stopping with you." He enclosed a copy of the libretto for Act II, Scene 3, which would start with their version of "Oh, Doctor Jesus," the spiritual they'd heard together in Charleston's Macedonia church, and end with the haunting "I Loves You Porgy."

EVOLVING A SYSTEM

Happy to hear that Heyward was coming North, Gershwin wrote back and mentioned that "Ira and I have worked on some of the words to the music at the very opening, in Jazzbo Brown's room while the people are dancing, and I finish it up with a sort of African chant." This was George's first mention of his brother's active participation in the process of creating *Porgy*.

Heyward traveled to New York in mid April. George installed his Southern friend in the guest quarters of his 14-room duplex and they got to work. As Ira described their process: "DuBose was a poet which I am not. He could do something like "Summertime," which is poetry. DuBose wasn't much good on a rhythm number, though, like "It Ain't Necessarily So." He would turn in his poetry and George would set it to music. With me it worked the other way. I cannot read music. I have to hear the tune before I can write the lyrics. My job was to sit and listen to the music that George created and then set lyrics to it."[12]

At one point during their work together, George suggested that "Porgy might sing something lighter and gayer than the melodies and recitatives he had been given in Act I."[13] As Ira recalled it, "He [George] went to the piano and began to improvise. A few preliminary chords, and in less than a minute, a well-rounded, cheerful melody." "Something like that," Gershwin said. Both Ira and DuBose jumped in with the same reaction, "That's it! Don't look any further!" "You really think so?" asked George.[14] When George played through the melody again, Ira recalled, "A title popped into my mind. (This was one out of only three or four times in my career that a possible title hit me on first hearing a tune. Usually I sweat for days.) 'I got plenty o' nuthin?' I said tentatively. And a moment later the obvious balance line, "An nuthin's plenty for me.' Both George and DuBose seemed delighted with it."[15] Ira said he'd work on the rest of the lyric later. But DuBose chimed in asking Ira if he'd mind if he gave it a try. "So far, everything I've done has been set by George and I've never written words to music," Heyward said. "If it's alright with you, I'd love to take the tune along with me to Charleston." Two weeks later Heyward sent them the first draft of "I Got Plenty O' Nuttin." Ira polished the lyric so the consonants and vowels were better placed for singing, and the song was set. Ira called it, "a 50/50 effort."[16] George later wrote that DuBose and Ira had "achieved a fine synchronization of diversified moods." Heyward wrote "most of the native material," as Gershwin explained it, and Ira "most of the sophisticated songs."[17]

Ira and DuBose would collaborate in the same manner on "Bess, You Is My Woman Now," but after a few productive weeks, Heyward returned to South Carolina. "The matter of effecting a happy union between words and music across a thousand miles of Atlantic seaboard baffle us for a moment," Heyward wrote. "The solution came quite naturally," he continued "when we associated Ira with us." "Presently we evolved a system by which, between my visits North, of George's dash to Charleston, I could send scenes and lyrics." By now Heyward knew how George and Ira would work through the material he sent North. "The brothers Gershwin, after their extraordinary fashion," he observed, "would get at the piano, pound, wrangle, swear, burst into weird snatches of song, and eventually emerge with a polished lyric."[18] In the end, Ira would set lyrics to his brother's tunes for "Oh, I Can't Sit Down," "I Ain't Got No Shame," "It Ain't Necessarily So," "Oh, Hev'nly Father," "A Red-Headed Woman," "There's a Boat Dat's Leavin' Soon for New York," and "Oh, Bess, Oh Where's My Bess." DuBose would provide George with the lyrics for everything else, plus scene settings and all the dialogue. Among Heyward's most notable contributions were "Summertime," "A Woman Is a Sometime Thing," "My Man's Gone Now, "I Loves You Porgy," "What You Want Wid Bess?" and "Oh Lawd, I'm on My Way." George would humorously claim credit for only one complete lyric in *Porgy and Bess*—the "sort of African chant," as he called it, heard in the opening Jasbo Brown scene: "Da-doo-da/Da-doo-da/Wa-wa,wa-wa/O-wa-de-wa …"[19]

The other unique thing about the Gershwin-Heyward-Gershwin working relationship is that it was such a happy one. The three men had deep respect for one another and shared a genuine affection between them. Heyward had only positive things to say about Gershwin after the eventual debut of *Porgy and Bess*. Gershwin's "self-appreciations were beyond modesty and beyond conceit," Heyward wrote. "He was incapable of insincerity; he didn't see why he should suppress a virtue or a talent just because it happened to belong to him. He was just plain dazzled by the spectacle of his own music and his own career; his unaffected delight in it was somewhat astonishing, but it was also amusing and refreshing."[20] Out of respect and kindness, Ira had wanted to share the lyricist credit for "It Ain't Necessarily So" with DuBose. This would give Heyward enough song credits to qualify for membership in the American Society of Composers, Authors, and Publishers (ASCAP), and therefore be able to collect future royalties. "You're very sweet, Ira," Heyward responded, "but no one will ever believe I had anything to do with that song."[21] Ultimately, Ira and DuBose agreed to split future royalties at 25 percent each with the remaining 50 percent going to George. After George's death, Ira wrote to DuBose, "George had, not only great respect for you, but also a deep affection and I assure you, though I believe you must have known, I felt the same way about you and considered it a great honor to be associated with you, however small my contribution."[22]

ON FOLLY ISLAND

The first season of *Music by Gershwin* ended on May 31, 1934. On June 16, Gershwin left New York by train for SouthCarolina with his cousin, the painter Henry Bodkin. Gershwin's all-around aide, Paul Mueller, drove down with all the heavy bags in advance. They converged on Folly Island, the outermost of the barrier islands ten miles southeast of Charleston, where Heyward had purchased a summer cottage. Close by, Gershwin rented a four-room plus sleeping-porch cottage that was Spartan by Gershwin's standards. His small room had an iron single bed, hooks on the walls for clothes, a washbasin, and a rented upright piano. Water jugs had to be brought in from town. "It looks like a battered, old South Sea Island," he wrote to Rose. "Imagine, there's not *one* telephone on the whole Island— public or private. The nearest telephone is about 10 miles away."

Nevertheless, Gershwin thought of the five-week expedition as an adventure and entered into the spirit of the place. On the first day or so of his stay, one writer arrived to interview Gershwin and found him nattily dressed in a linen coat and tie, the kind of suiting commonly worn in Palm Beach. When the same writer returned two weeks later, he reported that Gershwin was "black above the waist and habitually wearing only a two-inch beard and a pair of once white linen knickers."[23] To Emily Paley (the woman who had given him a copy of *Porgy* to read back in 1926), Gershwin wrote, "We go around with practically nothing on, shave only every other day (we do have visitors, you know) eat out on the porch not more than 30 feet away from the ocean at high tide, sit out at night gazing at the stars … and discuss our two favorite subjects, Hitler's Germany and God's women."[24]

Within a few days, word got around that Gershwin was out on Folly Island. Ashley Cooper, a reporter for the *Charleston News and Courier* was quickly sent out to Folly to interview Gershwin. After hunting him, Cooper finally found Gershwin "speeding along the beach in an open car, grinning like a kid. I waved him down and told him I was a reporter. 'Get in and ride, you can ask me questions' said he. To him Folly was nature in the raw, back to wilderness. It fascinated him, and he loved it. 'I've never ridden on a beach before' he beamed. 'It's exciting, eh?' Then he took me to the cottage where he was staying. I sampled some Hell Hole Swamp corn Whiskey, a Prohibition product. 'I've never lived in such a back-to-nature place' he said. 'At home I get up around noon. Here I get up every morning at 7:00—well, 7:30 anyway,' he admitted. He couldn't talk about music very long without wanting to play the piano. There was an old upright in the cottage on which he had been

Renderings of images from Folly Beach, South Carolina: The cottage Gershwin lived in. His silhouette is barely visible on steps at right (top); the composer at the piano inside (bottom).

composing, and he sat down and said, 'Here's a good one' [and started playing]. It was well after dark by the time I left. By that time 30 or 40 people—mostly servants from nearby cottages—were sitting out front. George kept playing and the people out front were swaying to the music. 'Don't know who that man is playing the piano,' said one of the listeners, 'but that man really can play!'"

Heyward and his family arrived a few days later. "Under the baking sun," he wrote later, "of [June and July] we established ourselves on Folly Island." Heyward continued, "James Island with its large population of Gullah Negros lay adjacent, and furnished us with a laboratory in which to test our theories, as well as an inexhaustible source of folk material."[25] During their time together on Folly Island, Gershwin composed in the morning and worked with Heyward on the libretto in the afternoon. As he walked the beaches of Folly, Gershwin met and befriended a local college student named Abe Dumas. He hired Dumas to be his driver and take him and Heyward to black churches on neighboring James Island. It was in this crucial phase of the opera's creation that Gershwin had the opportunity to listen to the Gullahs speak and sing spirituals or work songs. On one such outing, they attended a Gullah church meeting. "The Gullah Negro prides himself on what he calls 'shouting,' Heyward explained. "This is a complicated rhythmic pattern beaten out by feet and hands as an accompaniment to spirituals and is indubitably of African survival."

"I shall never forget the night," Heyward wrote, "when at a Negro meeting on a remote sea-island, George started 'shouting' with them. And evidentially, to their huge delight, stole the show from their champion 'shouter.'" Anne Brown, the first Bess, remembered Gershwin saying , "After it was over ... an old man clapped him on the back and said, 'By God you sure can beat out them rhythms, boy. I'm over 70 years old, and I ain't never seen no po' little white man take off and fly like you. You could be my own son.'"[26] As Heyward liked to say, "I think he is probably the only white man in America who could have done it."[27]

Gershwin's painting of the interior of the Folly Beach cottage, with modest bed, single-chain light,and piano (top); the piano today at the CharlestonMuseum (bottom).

Gershwin left Folly Island on July 22[28] and stopped in Hendersonville with Heyward for a few days on his way back to New York. While there, DuBose took George to a Negro Holy Rollers meeting in a makeshift mountain "praise house." "As we were about to enter," Heyward remembered, "George caught my arm and held me." To Heyward the sounds coming form these kinds of African American church services were ordinary in their familiarity. "But now," Heyward said, "Listening to it with him, and noticing his excitement, I began to catch its extraordinary quality. It consisted of perhaps a dozen voices raised in loud rhythmic prayer. While each had started at a different time, [and] upon a different theme, they formed a clearly defined rhythmic pattern, and that this, with the actual words lost, and the inevitable pounding of the rhythm, produced an effect almost terrifying in its primitive intensity. Inspired by the extraordinary effect, George wrote six simultaneous prayers producing a terrifying invocation to God in the face of [the Act II] hurricane."

CHAPTER 9

THE GREAT AMERICAN OPERA TAKES SHAPE

Notes from the creators of Porgy and Bess.

By September, Gershwin was back in New York. Even for someone who thrived on activity as much as he, the coming months would be extraordinarily demanding. Up to this point in the creation of their opera, the burden of productivity had been on Heyward. George and Ira needed his outline for *Porgy's* scenario and the first draft of the libretto in order to do their work. That phase of the creative process had been more or less completed, so moving *Porgy* forward was now in the hands of the Gershwins. For George, preoccupations were choosing the leading singers, finding an African American chorus, completing the piano score, and then beginning the massive job of orchestrating. The Theatre Guild was producing *Porgy*, but Gershwin had the final say in all of the creative areas. Choosing the conductor, director, and music staff was a negotiation between the two, but Gershwin's wishes were generally followed. In addition to *Porgy*, there was another series of *Music By Gershwin* broadcasts to produce. The first season had been such a success that Feen-A-Mint had ordered a second. The weekly broadcast of 30 minutes was to be heard live every Sunday night between September 30 and December 23. Far from being overwhelmed, Gershwin plunged into his fall schedule with contagious energy, verve, and good humor.

FINDING THE FIRST PORGY AND BESS

Gershwin had written to Heyward and asked him to make himself available for auditions starting in January of 1935. "I do hope you can come to New York for these auditions as your knowledge of certain types will be of great value in picking characters," he wrote. But before formal auditions started, Gershwin received an unexpected and urgent recommendation. Olin Downes, then the chief music critic for *The New York Times*, had been to a performance of *Cavalleria rusticana* (one of the operas that had inspired *Blue Monday Blues*) with an all African American cast. Downes was so impressed by a baritone in the cast named Todd Duncan that he wrote to Gershwin immediately.

At the time, Duncan was a Howard University professor of classical music, but he occasionally performed leading baritone roles on stage. Gershwin, who had wanted Paul Robeson to sing Porgy, was leery of a music professor's ability to pull off something as dramatically complex and vocally demanding as Porgy, but agreed to hear him. For his part, Duncan recalled, "I just wasn't very interested. I thought

Todd Duncan and Anne Brown, the first to play and sing the roles of Porgy and Bess.

of George Gershwin as being Tin Pan Alley and something beneath me." Nevertheless, Duncan arrived at Gershwin's apartment on December 17 ready to sing. He had brought with him a number of Italian art songs and German lieder but, unaware that it was customary for the singer to bring his own pianist, no one to play. Gershwin gamely said he'd play for Duncan, but when he saw the music, which he had neither heard nor played, he paused for a moment. Sensing the hesitation, Duncan said, "Well, can't you play?" Duncan volunteered to play himself but Gershwin jumped in saying, "Well, I play a little bit."

After Duncan had sung 12 bars, Gershwin stopped him and asked, "Do you know this by memory?" Defensively, Duncan answered, "Of course I know it by memory. I sing everything by memory." Completely unfazed, Gershwin asked Duncan to move around the piano and said, "Look straight into my eyes. Don't look anywhere else, look straight into my eyes." As they began again, Duncan remembered being astonished when he realized that, having already memorized it, Gershwin didn't need to look at the music, either. After singing a second 12 bars of music, Gershwin stopped again, but this time it was to ask, "Will you be my Porgy?" Duncan agreed and then went back to Washington. In the meantime, Gershwin dashed off an excited letter to Heyward letting him know that he may have found his Porgy.

During the Christmas week, Duncan returned, this time with his wife, Gladys. Assembled in George's townhouse were various officials from the Theatre Guild, all come to hear the possible answer to their casting prayers. After Duncan had sung a program of various songs for a full hour, the group had a meal while George and Ira talked about the opera. After supper, the Gershwins went to the piano to play and sing from *Porgy*. As Duncan remembered the scene,

> "He started out with the opening [imitating the trumpets with his voice], and I said to myself, 'Oh, my God. Gee, this is junk!' And then he segued into humming the orchestral opening of 'Summertime.' And Ira starts off with his rotten voice [horribly off pitch] 'Summertime, and the living is easy'. And [George] looked up at me and smiled. 'All this chopsticks,' I thought, and whispered to my wife, 'This stinks!' Then George sang, 'Fish

are jumpin,' with Ira finishing the verse, 'And the cotton is high.' Then George [now a raspy, guttural voice imitation worse than Ira's], 'Oh your daddy's ...' But when he got around to the second verse I could have wept. I said to myself, 'Well this is so beautiful. Where did this man get this from?' I just couldn't get over it. And then he went into the part where Porgy's theme enters. It was like the royal gates opened. And he had me hooked from then on."

Duncan later recalled, "Oh, he [Gershwin] loved to tell that story! He used to tell it at parties and he would say, 'I fell in love with that man then.' [George] was so honest and so true. That was the beginning of an exciting time in our lives."

Anne Wiggins Brown was a 20-year-old vocal major at the Juilliard School when she saw an announcement that George Gershwin was interviewing singers for his new all-black opera of *Porgy*. Originally from Baltimore, the daughter of a doctor, Brown wrote to Gershwin asking for an audition. Within a matter of days, she was called to sing for him at his apartment. Brown recalled,

"I found myself in the foyer of his apartment, bending over to look under the coat rack for a place to put my boots. 'What are you looking for?' he asked politely. I said without thinking, 'Your roller skates!' George Gershwin was quiet for a few moments and then he ... threw back his head and roared. 'How did you know about my roller skates?' he asked, still laughing. 'Well, I read, you know.' He laughed again. 'It's been many years,' he said, 'since I've had a pair of roller skates on my feet.' And then I told him about my own passion for roller skating—how many hours each week from the age of nine until I left my hometown of Baltimore, I skated."

Brown went on to sing for Gershwin that afternoon and was called back two more times, once for Ira and a third time with the Theatre Guild managing board in attendance. For weeks after that, Gershwin would call her and say, "Hey

Annie, I've just finished some music for Clara. I want you to come and sing it for me."

"This went on week after week," Brown said, "I'm a guinea pig … but I was happy to be that … we sang different songs and duets, and trios as soon as the ink was dry on the paper. And it was very good training for my sight-reading. And one day during this period, George Gershwin said, 'Annie, how would you like to sing the role of Bess?' I had suspected for some time he would say just that. Even so, it came as a surprise."

Brown was a beautiful and graceful woman: educated, intelligent, and light skinned. Very different from the Bess portrayed in the book or the play. "Bess is, in the original story, a very black woman," Gershwin explained to Brown, "But I can not see any reason why my Bess shouldn't have a *café au lait* complexion, can you?" In Brown's telling of the story, she immediately answered, "No, no!" and gave the composer a big hug. "What will you do if the Theatre Guild insists on engaging another [darker skinned] singer for the Bess role," she asked him. "They'll have to do it over my dead body," he said. "Don't worry, Annie, George Gershwin will have the last word."[1]

COMPLETING *PORGY'S* FIRST CAST

The role of Serena would be sung by Ruby Elzy, also a Juilliard graduate, who came recommended by Heyward. He had remembered her from a small role in the film of *The Emperor Jones*. Originally from rural Mississippi, she washed dishes to work her way through a Southern college, and then to Ohio State, and finally to Juilliard, where she learned acting skills to match her voice. By the time she auditioned for Gershwin, she was so impressive that he hired her after a single hearing.

Gershwin's first choice for Sportin' Life was John W. "Bubbles" Sublett, who along with his partner Floyd "Buck" Washington, were known as Buck and Bubbles. The two were popular vaudeville stars who headlined in the *Ziegfeld Follies of 1931* and were the first black artists to appear at the Radio City Music Hall. Known as the father of "rhythm tap," Sublett gave lessons in tap dancing to Fred Astaire, who considered Sublett the finest tap dancer of his generation. Bubbles was unable to read music, which caused problems during rehearsals.

The actress Georgette Harvey was the only performer to have appeared in the same role in both the play and the opera. Warren Coleman, an opera singer trained at the New

Clockwise (from top left): Ruby Elzy, John W. "Bubbles" Sublett, Abbie Mitchell, and Georgette Harvey.

England Conservatory in Boston, was cast as the first Crown. The role of Clara was created by Abbie Mitchell, a soprano who had studied in New York and Paris and also appeared in the *Cavalleria rusticana* production with Duncan. Edward Matthews, the baritone who created the role of Jake, had received his master's degree in music from Fisk University, where he also was a member of the famous Jubilee Singers. J. Rosamond Johnson, a composer friend of Heyward's and an authority on black music, was the first comically duplicitous Lawyer Frazier.

GERSHWIN ASSEMBLES HIS TEAM

Since directing the play of *Porgy* in 1927, Rouben Mamoulian had gone to Hollywood, where he had established himself as a major film director, with innovative films such as *City Streets* (1931), *Dr. Jekyll and Mr. Hyde* (1932), and *Love Me*

Tonight (1932), an early movie musical by Rodgers and Hart that starred Jeanette MacDonald and Maurice Chevalier.

Just before returning to New York to direct *Porgy and Bess*, Mamoulian directed the first Technicolor feature-length film, *Becky Sharp*, for RKO. There had been some tension between Heyward and Mamoulian during rehearsals for the play, so Heyward was not enthusiastic about the idea of Mamoulian directing the play But the Guild thought it best for someone who knew the play, had experience with opera, and understood how the theater worked to take the helm of such a massive project. Gershwin agreed and Heyward withdrew his objection. When the Guild offered Mamoulian *Porgy and Bess*, he accepted without hearing a note of the music. He had heard *Rhapsody in Blue* and other Gershwin works that had led him to recognize Gershwin's genius long before *Porgy and Bess*.

In the spring of 1935, Mamoulian came to New York to meet with George and Ira and hear music from *Porgy*. In his remembrances Mamoulian wrote, "All three of us were very excited. George and Ira were anxious for me to like the music. As for me, I was even more anxious." Mamoulian later wrote, "It was touching to see how Ira, while singing, would become so overwhelmed with admiration for his brother that he would look from him to me with half-open eyes and pantomime with a soft gesture of his hand, as if saying, 'He did it. Isn't it wonderful? Isn't *he* wonderful?'"[2] Deeply touched by the brothers' devotion to each other, Mamoulian was fond of saying, "In a way, it was the best performance of it I ever heard."[3]

Gershwin attended a performance of Virgil Thompson's *Four Saints in Three Acts*, which was very different from Porgy in every respect except one: it, too, had an all-black cast. Thompson's libretto was written by Gertrude Stein, and the opera opened on Broadway in February of 1934. Gershwin admired the work of the conductor, Alexander Smallens, and went backstage after the performance to ask Smallens to hear some of the music from *Porgy*. Smallens had immigrated from Russia and, in addition to conducting *Four Saints*, held the position of assistant conductor of the Philadelphia Orchestra.

Rouben Mamoulian

Edward Smallens

Eva Jessye

Smallens did meet with Gershwin and was invited to conduct the premiere. With *Porgy*, the two musicians began an association that would last until Gershwin's death.

Perhaps the hardest part of producing *Porgy* was finding an all-black, musically trained chorus. The chorus is the heart of *Porgy*, and Gershwin needed a group that could rise to the challenge. At that same performance of *Four Saints*, he heard the work of Eve Jessye and her choir. He could hear that the musical standards of the Eva Jessye Choir were high and he could see they were seasoned professionals. Gershwin asked her group of 20 singers to come to the Theatre Guild and sing an audition. When they sang the shout-style spiritual "Plenty Good Room," Gershwin jumped out of his seat and shouted, "That's it! That's what I want!" He then invited Jessye and her entire choir to his 72nd Street penthouse for a party.

A MILLION NOTES

In February, Gershwin went to his friend Emil Mosbacher's in Palm Beach and began orchestrating in earnest. While he was there, George wrote to Ira, "It goes slowly, there being a million notes."[4] "George was particularly keen to orchestrate the score by himself," remembered Mamoulian. "He worked very long and hard at it. He wrote me in a [March 1935] letter, 'I am orchestrating the opera at the present time and have about five month's work left. It really is a tremendous task scoring three hours of music.' It was and he did it. And his was such a beautiful looking manuscript!"

By July of 1935 Gershwin had completed the orchestration of Acts I and II and a battery of copyists (and friends like Kay Swift) had produced all the orchestra parts. On July 19, Gershwin's friend, William S. Paley, also the head of CBS, financed an orchestra of 43 pieces to play through the score, with Gershwin himself conducting.

Mamoulian and Gershwin outside the Guild Theatre.

Todd Duncan, Anne Brown, Abbie Mitchell, and Edward Matthews joined to sing through their roles for the first time with orchestra. Afterward, Gershwin began to tackle Act III, noting on the manuscript score that it was completed on July 22, 1935. He completed the orchestration of Act III by the end of August while staging rehearsals were already underway. The complete full score is marked in Gershwin's hand, "Orchestration begun late 1934—finished Sept. 2, 1935. For *George Gershwin*, a collection of reminiscences collected and edited by Merle Armitage, Ira wrote, "*Porgy and Bess*, his most ambitious work, was composed in eleven months and he did the orchestrating in nine; during this time he also did a good deal of broadcasting."

LIKE BREAKING MOUNTAINS OF ICE

Staging rehearsals had begun on August 26, 1935. "The first day of rehearsal is always difficult," wrote Rouben Mamoulian. "It is like breaking mountains of ice. The end of it leaves one completely exhausted and usually a little depressed. That's the way I felt after the first day of *Porgy and Bess*." What hit Mamoulian was the enormity of the job he had to do between August 26 and the projected Boston opening on September 30. "I lay in my bed ... indulging in rather melancholy thoughts. Suddenly the phone rang and George Gershwin was announced. This delighted me as I felt in need of encouragement and kind words. I picked up the receiver and said 'Hello' with eager anticipation. George's voice came glowing with enthusiasm: 'Rouben, I couldn't help calling you ... I am so thrilled and delighted over rehearsal today.' (My heart started warming up and I already began to feel better,) 'Of course,' he went on, 'I always knew that *Porgy and Bess* was wonderful, but I never thought I'd feel the way I feel now. I tell you, after listening to that rehearsal today, I think the music is so marvelous—I really don't believe I wrote it!'"

One crucial change had been made before rehearsals began. In August, the Guild's press department approached the creators of their season-opening production. Once they had seen the title *Porgy* on the marquee, they were concerned that theatergoers might think they were presenting a revival of the play. As Heyward and Gershwin searched for a solution, DuBose began to think out loud. He started to rattle off titles of other operas named after a male-female couple. "There has been, of course," Heyward said to Gershwin, "*Pelleas and Melisande, Samson and Delilah, Tristan and Isolde* ... and so ... why not *Porgy and Bess*?" Gershwin's immediate response was, "Of course, it's right in the operatic tradition."

IN REHEARSAL

The natural nervousness of Rouben Mamoulian notwithstanding, rehearsals were well underway by the end of August 1935. With previews a month away, vocal rehearsals, staging, and corrections to the libretto and score of a brand-new work had to be accomplished at an extraordinary pace.

"It was a wonderful cast," Todd Duncan said, "highly educated, highly trained. We never had the trouble casts do these days, you know, morale troubles. You know the last song, 'There's a Boat Dat's Leavin' Soon for New York,' when they [Sportin' Life and Bess] were sniffing that happy dust? Well, we didn't even know what it was! After the show we'd say, 'What's he talking about?' Of course, Bubbles knew what it was. He was a bit of a scoundrel, but a nice scoundrel; certainly a talented one."

Anne Brown remembered, "At the rehearsals George occasionally complained that many of the people in the cast had unfortunately been born in the North. Everyone laughed at this since many of us had never even *visited* the South! Some of us were college students and didn't know the dialect of the Southern Negro." Mamoulian had been to Charleston with his various designers several times, but never for more

Rouben Mamoulian, at center, directs the cast during rehearsals for the hurricane scene.

than a few days. Gershwin and Heyward were the only two people, save for perhaps Eva Jessye, who knew much about the Gullah at all. Alexander Seinert, the music coach working on *Porgy*, recalled that Gershwin, "often astonished the company by showing them how to interpret their parts authentically."[5]

Gershwin, Duncan, and Brown were all pleased with what Rouben Mamoulian was doing in rehearsal. Particularly Duncan, who said, "And then there was the work with Rouben Mamoulian. What an artist!"[6] Brown, who turned 23 during the rehearsals and was the youngest of the principals, had been trained as a classical singer but didn't have much stage experience. "Emotionally, of course, I had a lot to learn," she said, "and I did learn a great deal, especially from Rouben Mamoulian. He was such a brilliant man."[7] Brilliant, but also a pessimist and quite moody. Despite his having accepted, in principle, the Theatre Guild's invitation to direct *Porgy and Bess,* his contract negotiations with the Guild were difficult and protracted. According to Mark Spergel, it had made very clear during Mamoulian's contract negotiations that if there were "disagreements about his approach to the production, or if things did not go as he dictated, he would leave the show." But Gershwin knew the production needed Mamoulian's authoritarian approach to keep *Porgy and Bess* from jumping the track. Gershwin respected Mamoulian because of his directorial skills and did everything he could, as did Smallens and the Guild, to support the director. After opening night, Gershwin said about Rouben Mamoulian's work, "In my opinion he has left nothing to be desired in the direction."[8]

Alexander Smallens "was a fine conductor," said Anne Brown, " but, well, he wasn't a patient man, really. I always thought he played the score too fast, for the most part, and we made jokes about it because he lived in Connecticut and he had to take the train each night. 'Oh, he doesn't want to be late tonight!' And he would go through the score like a house afire! Gershwin would sometimes play for rehearsals and then the tempi were right. George's piano playing was simply spectacular."[9]

Gershwin attended rehearsals an hour or two each day. "He sat alone in the dark theater," remembered Brown, "wearing his hat and an old tweed sport jacket, and sometimes cracking and eating peanuts and occasionally smoking a thick cigar." Todd Duncan said, "George was very, very easygoing," but at the same time "highly critical." Brown too remembered

Gershwin as "a man of many faces."[10] According to Duncan, Gershwin would "write little things on a little pad of paper" and "After the rehearsal was over, he would come to me privately and just say, 'Todd, you did this, or sang this. Don't you think ...' and so forth."[11] As Jessye remembered it, "George didn't interfere with rehearsals; he let us do what we knew how to do." Jessye also remembered how he "would add things and allow changes in rehearsal constantly."[12]

Duncan said, "He could be enthusiastic when you did something interesting with his score." Duncan and Brown both vividly remembered the moment when Ruby Elzy was rehearsing "Oh, Doctor Jesus" and, as Brown described it, "embroidered her prayer with all sorts of ornamentation." Elzy captured Serena's character with such moving authenticity that she stopped the rehearsal in its tracks. In the stunned silence, Gershwin emerged from the back of the theater and walked down the isle. "He knew then," said Duncan, "that he had put down on paper accurately and truthfully something from the depth of the soul of a South Carolina Negro woman who feels the need of help and carries her troubles to her God." Brown remembered that Gershwin broke the tension with a smile and said, 'That's wonderful, keep keep [the improvised parts] in.'"[13] "Not only that," added Brown, "people who sang 'Summertime' in the jazz version—even back in the beginning—he never objected as long as you were singing *Gershwin* music."

On the other hand, some things drove him to distraction. "I never saw him lose his cool when something at a rehearsal would offend him," said Duncan, but "How quickly he would stop you if you sang a wrong note." Duncan added that Gershwin would be particularly disturbed "if you could not sense a rhythmic pattern or an off-beat ... he had so carefully calculated. That would draw him to the footlights like a ball from a canon." During particularly trying moments, Gershwin could be seen pacing back and forth in the back of the theater until he called his driver to come and pick him up. More than once, Todd Duncan was called in to assure the composer that he would see to it that the offending cast member would eventually get it right—every cast member, that is, except for Mr. John "Bubbles" Sublett ...

One thing that everyone agreed on was that there were problems with Bubbles. In rehearsal, Bubbles—a star vaudevillian—was unable or unwilling to conform to the musical and scheduling demands of a huge production like *Porgy*. He had received the score of *Porgy* in advance, but it

John "Bubbles" Sublett at work

baffled him. When he arrived for Smallen's music rehearsals, he knew neither the notes nor the rhythms of his role. Repeated coachings with Seinert seemed not to help. "He simply couldn't learn his part, and it was holding us all back," said Duncan.

Bubbles' repeated lateness angered Mamoulian and enraged Smallens. One day, while the entire cast stood around waiting for the overdue arrival of Bubbles, Smallens had enough. Erupting with anger, he threw down his conductor's baton and shouted out to Mamoulian, "I am sick of this waiting! We'll have to throw him out and get somebody else." This propelled Gershwin out of his seat and down the isle. "Throw him out?" Gershwin said, "You can't do that. Why, he's the black Toscanini!"

"He needed a lot of work," said Brown, "He smoked marijuana all the time and gave it to some of the girls in the chorus. He put the moves on me like all the others, but I just laughed at him. There was no question there. I was married at the time." But the production needed Bubbles. "I hated him," Duncan later admitted, "but he was an important entertainer, a big draw." After that, Duncan recalled, "Gershwin taught him to dance his part; taught him everything—all the notes, all the rhythms, all the cues—*with his feet*. It was brilliant. And when [Bubbles] learned to dance it, he never made a mistake after that. He was a genius on stage. Electric."

CHAPTER 10

THE FIRST 75 YEARS BEGINS

As the date of the first preview drew near, Alexander Smallens arranged for a full-scale run-through of the entire three-act opera with orchestra, principals, and chorus. The Theatre Guild had rented Carnegie Hall just for the occasion. The company was due to leave for Boston in a few days, but, as Ira recalled, "Until then only George knew what it would sound like."[1] There had been partial rehearsals of Acts I and II with orchestra in July, and three singers had been there, but it was true that only George Gershwin had a mental idea of what *Porgy and Bess* might sound like in its entirety. He had made a few changes while working on the orchestration, but the score heard at this rehearsal was the full score as Gershwin had conceived it, and before any substantive changes were made. The managing board of the Guild was there as well as family and friends of the company, but the rehearsal was closed to the public and the critics.

Most of the cast had only heard the score played on a piano in the rehearsal hall, and now they were singing with a 44-piece orchestra on the stage of Carnegie Hall. And the members of that orchestra were hearing the principals and the chorus for the first time. Emotions ran high. As Ira said, "The wonderful orchestra and the full chorus on the stage. I never realized it would be like that. I couldn't believe my ears. It was one of the great thrills of my life."

When the rehearsal was over, "We were—all of us—in tears," remembered Anne Brown, "it had been so moving. Todd Duncan turned to me and said, 'Do you realize, Annie, that we

Porgy (Todd Duncan) and Bess (Anne Brown).

are making history?' George Gershwin stood on the stage for a few minutes as if in a trance. Then, seeming to awaken, he said, "This music is so wonderful, so beautiful that I can hardly believe that I have written it myself."[2]

Gershwin's propensity for this kind of awestruck self-congratulation could—and did—elicit sharply negative reactions from strangers or casual acquaintances. The opposite was true for those that knew him, particularly people associated with *Porgy and Bess.* Gershwin and Heyward, through their work on their opera, had become devoted friends. Until his death, Heyward remained touchingly complimentary about Gershwin.[3] Rouben Mamoulian, who could be imperious and cutting when he wanted to be, had also grown to appreciate Gershwin's true nature. Mamoulian wrote, "George Gershwin's attitude about himself and his work was apt to be misunderstood by people who did not know him well. Because he liked his own music and praised himself, some thought he was conceited. [He] was so completely naïve and innocent in his liking his own work that it actually became one of the endearing qualities of his nature. Some little expressions that would seem arrogant coming from other men were touching and loveable when coming from George."[4]

Despite the love and respect Gershwin inspired, the pressure to make cuts in his opera began almost immediately. Lawrence Langer, codirector of the Theatre Guild, was already worried about production costs that had exceeded their budget for *Porgy and Bess.* Mamoulian's concerns were of a different sort. He was sure that cutting would tighten the drama. He also was afraid that a long evening would prompt many in the audience to leave after the second act. There was no love lost between Langer and Gershwin, so Mamoulian was delegated to speak to the elated Gershwin. His words were carefully chosen. "If you want to have success with your opera," Mamoulian said, "you may have to make some harsh cuts."[5]

BOSTON

The first out-of-town performance of *Porgy and Bess* took place at the Colonial theater in Boston on September 30, 1935. A major event for the cultural crown in Boston, the Colonial was filled to capacity. The normally staid Bostonians greeted Gershwin's new opera with cheers after each scene, and despite it being a long night, they remained enthusiastic throughout the performance. The first-nighters gave the

Porgy comes home, signaling the arrival of the show's protagonist and the beginning of a long road toward recognition as America's premiere opera.

entire company a rousing standing ovation at the evening's end. Gershwin's entrance for his curtain call initiated a 15-minute ovation. After the curtain came down, the cast surrounded Gershwin on stage, wrote J. Rosamond Johnson, the evening's Lawyer Frazier: "As he stood there on stage, I was amazed at the modest manner in which he received many warm and hearty congratulations. Finally, when I got a chance to grasp his hand, I whispered to him, 'George, you've done it—you're the Abraham Lincoln of Negro music.'"[6]

But despite the cuts made before they left New York, the first Boston performance had lasted over four hours. Almost 30 minutes of the total running time was taken up by interminable waits while Sergey Sudeikin's elaborate sets, greatly expanded from Cleon Throckmorton's 1927 design for the play, were changed. This problem would be solved for future productions, but with only one week left before a Broadway opening night in 1935, it was too late to rethink the physical production. Mamoulian and Gershwin knew cuts were needed. After the crowds had gone, Gershwin, Mamoulian, and Kay Swift talked until three in the morning arguing about further cuts. Dozens of small cuts were made throughout the score, and entire numbers were removed from the original Act II: Maria's only solo, "I Hates Your

Porgy in his shack; outside, the men of Catfish Row.

Strutting Style"; Porgy's tragic aria, "The Buzzard Song"; the chorus opening to the Kittiwah Island scene, "I Ain't Got No Shame"; and "Shame on All You Sinners," sung by Serena as she scolds the picnickers for being taken in by Sportin' Life's "It Ain't Necessarily So."

THE ALVIN THEATRE NEW YORK CITY

Porgy and Bess opened at the Alvin Theatre on October 10, 1935. Hollywood stars Leslie Howard, Joan Crawford, Norma Shearer, and Katharine Hepburn were in the audience as well as Metropolitan Opera stars Lily Pons and Kirsten Flagstad. World-renowned violinists Fritz Kreisler and Jascha Heifetz, popular bandleaders Paul Whiteman and Fred Waring, novelists Edna Ferber and J. B. Priestly, as well as publishers Harold Ross and Condé Nast were there. The New York audience endured the same waits for scene changes as did Boston patrons, but they greeted the opera, now breathlessly paced, with just as much enthusiasm. "George and Ira sat in the rear of the theater with Kay Swift," wrote Howard Pollack. "The house erupted into thunderous applause at various times throughout the evening, with 'I Got Plenty o' Nuttin', stopping the show."[7] As Kay Swift recalled, "The opening was great. During the intermission we went out into the alley on the side of the Alvin, and I remember Libby

The murder of Robbins.

Holman saying, 'Oh, George, it's so great I haven't stopped crying,' and she was sobbing right then. Everybody was. It was so moving."[8] With many in the audience in tears at the end of the show, Gershwin and Smallens were called back on stage for curtain calls. "The critics didn't know what hit them," added Swift, "They ate their words later."[9] While the critics receded into offices and bars to write their reviews, Condé Nast hosted the cast party in his cavernous Park Avenue apartment for 450 guests, including the full cast and chorus

Critical response to *Porgy* was decidedly mixed. The cast and production drew praise, but Gershwin's score perplexed many reviewers, who spent most of their columns debating whether *Porgy and Bess* was an opera or a musical. Brooks Atkinson, theater critic for *The New York Times*, wrote, "Let it be said at once that Mr. Gershwin has contributed something glorious to the spirit of Heyward's community legend. Whether or not Mr. Gershwin's score measures up to its intentions as American folk opera lies [with] Mr. Downes, who is beating his brow in the adjoining cubicle [where] there is an authoritative ring to his typewriter tonight. But to the ears of a theater critic, Mr. Gershwin's music gives a personal voice to Porgy's loneliness … that was inarticulate in the original play."

The town prepares for the picnic on Kittiwah, dancing to the music of a group portrayed by South Carolina's Jenkins Orphanage Band.

For his part, Olin Downes wrote in the *Times* that the premiere "vastly entertained last night's audience [and] has much to commend it from the musical standpoint, even if the work does not utilize all the resources of the operatic composer. [Gershwin's] native gifts won him success last night but ... the style is of one moment opera and another of operetta or sheer Broadway entertainment. The performance had much that was uncommonly interesting, particularly to the reviewer accustomed to the methods of the opera stage, [which are] usually out of date as the dodo. When it came to sheer acting last night, certain operatic functionaries should have been present. If the Met chorus could ever put one hair the action ... that the Negro cat put into the fight that followed the crap game, it would not be merely refreshing but miraculous."

One of the more balanced responses came form Lawrence Gilman, of the *New York Herald Tribune*. "Whether *Porgy and Bess* is or is not a blown-in-the-bottle opera seemed a matter of no concern at all to anyone last evening. But that is little reason why one should hesitate to call it that. Mr. Gershwin thinks it is, and the music critics present will surely agree with him. When last night's audience, at the close of Act II, broke into an outburst of applause elicited by the frenzy of the terrified gathering of the Negros shrinking from the storm

Crown subdues Bess after the picnic.

... it was evident that Mr. Gershwin, in the finest pages of the score, had given us something suspiciously like an authentic folk-opera in an unmistakably American vein."

There were negative reviews, too, and the first production of *Porgy and Bess* has come to be regarded as a near or complete failure. Considering that it ran for 124 consecutive performances, an unheard-of feat for any opera in any theater, *Porgy and Bess* was anything but a failure. It opened in 1935, one of the bleakest years in the Great Depression. The large chorus and orchestra made it expensive to run even when sales were strong. When sales did drop precipitously, the Theatre Guild could no longer afford to keep the show open. Running in the red, the production of *Porgy and Bess* closed on January 25, 1936. The songs, however, were well on their way to becoming American standards.

The coming storm.

PORGY'S FIRST TOUR

Shortly after closing in New York, *Porgy and Bess* went on its first tour. It opened in Philadelphia on January 27, 1936, Pittsburgh on February 10, Chicago on February 17, and Detroit on March 9. But at the final stop, the National Theatre in Washington, DC, Duncan and Brown refused to sing unless the theater's whites-only policy was rescinded. Brown recalled, "The minute I read the itinerary I said, 'Well, I'm not going to sing at the National Theatre … it's a segregated theater.'" When another cast member told her she couldn't refuse and that it would ruin her career, she answered, "I don't give a damn. I'll do something else. I'm not going to

The women of Catfish Row.

sing in Washington." Duncan took the same position simultaneously and even wrote letters to Eleanor Roosevelt and Ralph Bunche, the black political scientist and diplomat. When nervous theater officials offered the compromise of allowing blacks to sit in the balcony for Wednesday and Saturday matinees, Duncan refused. The offer was then adjusted to sitting in the rear balcony for every performance. "Nothing would do," said Duncan, "other than black people be allowed to buy tickets for any seat in the house." The National Theatre management did not want a scandal, so they conceded to Duncan and Brown's demands—for the week of *Porgy* performances beginning on March 16, 1936. Hundreds of African Americans

Porgy warns Sportin' Life
to stay away from Bess.

attended performances and took their seats throughout the theater without incident. This was a full three years before Marian Anderson, protesting segregated seating policy of Constitution Hall, would sing her famous Easter Sunday, 1939, concert on the steps of the Lincoln Memorial.

A TRAGIC LOSS

The Gershwins returned to California, where the brothers worked on three films: *Shall We Dance* and *A Damsel in Distress* for RKO, and *The Goldwyn Follies* for Samuel Goldwyn Studios. In February of 1937, the Los Angeles Symphony gave two all-Gershwin concerts. Gershwin played *Rhapsody in Blue* and *Concerto in F* with Smallens conducting. The concert closed with selections from *Porgy and Bess*. Oscar Levant, Gershwin's friend and pianist who had recorded both works was in the audience and noticed Gershwin making uncharacteristic mistakes in *Rhapsody* and leaving out several bars of the *Concerto* altogether. Backstage, Gershwin told Levant he was aware of the mistakes and complained of being constantly distracted by a strange burning smell and having occasional bouts of dizziness. As late as the last days of May, Gershwin was still writing to friends saying that all was going well in

Bess succumbs to temptation—and happy dust.

California but those who were with him began to notice an increased restlessness alternating with serious headaches and bouts of debilitating depression. By June, dizzy spells became a daily occurrence followed by extreme fatigue. He saw an internist on June 9. All of the tests were normal, but he was referred to a neurologist. He wrote to Rose finally admitting he had not been feeling well but told her not to worry, everything would be fine. On June 20, he saw the neurologist, who admitted him to Cedars of Lebanon Hospital for further tests on June 23. Results were still inconclusive. The doctors recommended a lumbar puncture to test for a brain tumor, but Gershwin, anxious about work, was against spending more time in the hospital. He was released on June 26. At home, his condition worsened, and on July 9, he fell into a coma. A spinal tap on July 10 showed evidence of a brain tumor. In the early morning hours of July 11, a University of California Medical School neurosurgeon named Howard Naffziger began a five-hour surgery. After several hours, a tumor was removed form Gershwin's right temporal lobe, and the family was sent home around 6 a.m. However, it was too late.

George Gershwin passed away at 10:35 a.m. on Sunday, July 11, 1937. He was two months shy of his 39th birthday. A funeral service was held in Temple Emmanu-El on Fifth Avenue in New York on a rainy July 15. Dr. Stephen Wise delivered the eulogy. Honorary pallbearers were Mayor Fiorello LaGuardia, Walter Damrosch, George M. Cohan, Vernon Duke, Al Jolson, and former mayor James J. Walker. Todd Duncan attended with his wife. He remembered, "When we came out of the synagogue, I saw a man walking down with his head down in the middle of Fifth Avenue. He was walking on the white line directly between the lanes of traffic that were beginning to move again at the conclusion of the service. It was Al Jolson. I watched him keep on walking, oblivious to all around him."[10]

PART 3
A NEW
ENTHUSIASM

William Warfield and Leontyne Price in the production that brought *Porgy and Bess* to audiences worldwide.

CHAPTER 11

A RENAISSANCE FOR CATFISH ROW

The first revival of *Porgy and Bess* was produced by Cheryl Crawford, who had been one of the original assistant stage managers on the 1927 production of *Porgy*, the play. The production was physically smaller than the original and employed a smaller chorus and orchestra. The other major difference from the original was that it was "streamlined" by the use of spoken dialogue instead of sung recitative. Originally intended to open for a limited run in a theater in Maplewood, New Jersey, the show turned out to be such a hit that it was picked up by the Schubert Organization. After three weeks in Boston, it opened at New York's Majestic Theatre on January 22, 1942. Many of the theater critics who had found *Porgy*'s more operatic features hard to take now gave the show raves. It played to packed houses until September, and then went on the road for 18 months.

Porgy's European debut came on March 27, 1943, in Copenhagen during the Nazi occupation of Denmark. The Danish Royal Opera was a repertory opera house with its own company of white artists who preformed the opera in blackface. The audience gave the performance a standing ovation every night, in part because they were overwhelmed by the opera, but also because their own national company had dared to do it in the face of likely Nazi threats. No attempt

A new set for the first revival in 1942, with Todd Duncan and Anne Brown reprising their roles.

In *Porgy and Bess*'s first European production, the actors (here Einor Norby and Else Brems) performed in blackface.

was made to disguise *Porgy's* being an American work about blacks written by three white men—two of whom were Jewish. After widespread critical praise in the Danish press—all subtly promoting the aspects of *Porgy* that were sure to offend Nazi sensibilities—occupying officials finally caught on. The Nazis threatened the opera house management, but performances continued, running in repertory with plays presented by the Danish National Theatre, for 22 sold-out performances. When the theater received suspicious bomb threats, the Gestapo closed the entire house on April 25, 1944. The Nazis thought that would put an end to this black opera by Jews, but they had underestimated the Danes. One of the earlier performances had been broadcast over Danish radio and recorded. When Goebbels's propaganda machine used commandeered radio frequencies to trumpet Nazi victories, the Danish resistance figured out how to intercept and sabotage their propaganda with "It Ain't Necessarily So"—sung in Danish.

In the spring of 1950, Robert Breen, a classical actor turned theater executive, was in Europe for meetings about a tour he was producing for Ballet Theater, the first visit by an American ballet company to the continent. Breen was a savvy and highly cultured man whose enthusiasm for the role of the classical performing arts in civic life was infectious. Breen was struck by the Europeans' marked enthusiasm for tours featuring performing artists who were American. And there was something else; he kept hearing people on the street humming and whistling music from *Porgy and Bess*. He had never seen a production of Gershwin's opera himself, but he knew enough of the music to recognize it. He also knew about its breakthrough audience popularity from the producer Cheryl Crawford. Suddenly, he hit on an idea for his next project: the first performances of *Porgy and Bess* in Europe by an all African American cast. He was sure that the time was right for an American opera overseas, particularly by George Gershwin. But Breen knew that a tour of a full-scale production of *Porgy and Bess* to the major capitals of Europe would be more costly than that of the Ballet Theater. He would need to find sponsors to make it happen.

THE EVERYMAN OPERA *PORGY AND BESS*

Blevins Davis, a wealthy philanthropist who was at that time president of the Ballet Theater Foundation, shared Breen's high-minded enthusiasm for the performing arts. Davis also admired Breen's organizational abilities and optimism. For Breen, Blevins Davis was not only a potential underwriter, but also a link to the highest office in the land. Harry Truman was President, and Davis had grown up next door to the Truman home in Independence, Missouri. He was on a first-name basis with the President and the First Lady. If Truman saw the benefit of a State Department-sponsored tour of *Porgy* and its cast as good-will ambassadors for America, then Breen's idea would be possible. Breen shared his idea with Davis, who was immediately enthusiastic. For Davis, it was the right moment to counter anti-American propaganda streaming out of the communist countries of the Eastern European bloc—particularly the heated rhetoric coming from Moscow, which accused the American government of keeping its black citizens in a state of unofficial slavery. "From the very beginning," said Wilva Breen, her husband's associate in all his business endeavors, "Those factors were uppermost in their minds. It was an essential element of the project." Together, the two men started their own company, the Everyman Opera Corporation, for the sole purpose of bringing an all-black production of *Porgy and Bess* to Europe.

Ira Gershwin thought it best to ask Rouben Mamoulian to

Avon Long replaced John "Bubbles" in the 1942 revival and made several recordings as Sportin Life.

direct, even though he told Breen, "Whenever [Mamoulian] gets into a theater, he thinks he invented the stage and that he superseded the Greeks." Breen followed though and asked Mamoulian to direct a production specifically designed to tour. Mamoulian was willing, provided he could work it in around his film schedule. Breen pursued Jose Ferrer and Orson Welles as backup plans, but to no avail. At the last minute, Mamoulian cancelled because of film commitments. Not being able to find a director with the right amount of theatrical flare or a marquee name to suit him, Breen decided to direct the show himself. Auditions began immediately. Cheryl Crawford recommended the operatic baritone William Warfield for the role of Porgy. To play Bess, Breen made an offer to 24-year-old Leontyne Price, who was still a student and singing the role of Mistress Ford in Verdi's *Falstaff* at the Juilliard School. "I wasn't too excited," Price remembered, because she was going to Europe on a Fulbright scholarship anyway. "They talked with me, and I sang 'Summertime' and some other things from *Porgy*." Two days later, she signed a contract to sing Bess. Cab Calloway's career was on the skids when Breen asked him to audition for Sportin' Life.

Calloway's type of nightclub revue had faded from popularity after the War and he had lost a lot of money at racetracks. At first, he ignored the offers, but Breen convinced him to audition. "Cab had a lot of mixed feelings about it," said his wife, Nuffie. "He had been away from the stage since *Hot Chocolates* of 1929, and he didn't know if he could do it. Finally, he agreed to try. God bless Robert Breen. He was fantastic and he knew how to get the best out of Cab."

As a director, Breen liked to demonstrate exactly what he wanted to his cast rather than engaging in analysis or improvisation in search of character. "He was the kind of director that they invented tennis shoes for," said Warfield. "He was always on the move as he directed, leaping from the orchestra seats in the house up to the stage to show us as well as tell us what he wanted."[1] For Breen, Gershwin's score was at once celebratory, moving, sensual, and seductive. In Crown's Act II seduction of Bess, she tries to escape, but he holds her back. Bess sings "Take yo' hands off me, I say," but instead of letting her go, Crown runs his hands up and down her body until Bess gives in to the sensuality of the moment, sighing "Yo' hands … yo' hands … yo' hands." In staging the scene, Breen asked the Crown (John McCurry, a six-foot-six former army captain) to run his hands across Bess's breasts. Price shot Breen a look and said, "What would my Pappy think?"

One of Breen's biggest ambitions for the tour was to restore music that had been cut from the first production under pressure. In order to make this possible, he eliminated the long waits between scenes by having the designer create a set that rotated. This also allowed him to telescope scenes ,so that just as one was ending the next one would overlap creating a seamless musical and dramatic flow. The first to be added back was Gershwin's evocative music for Heyward's Jasbo Brown sequence right after the overture. Porgy's "Buzzard Song" also returned, as did some of the recitative cut from the Crawford production.

Cab Calloway as Sportin' Life.

WARFIELD AND PRICE—A LEGENDARY *PORGY AND BESS*

The Everyman Opera production of *Porgy and Bess*, as presented by the Dallas Opera, opened on June 9, 1952, in their large theater on the Texas State Fairgrounds. It was a resounding success, and the Dallas Opera counts it as one of their most unforgettable evenings. Writing in the *Saturday Review*, critic John Rosenfeld was complimentary about the production and overwhelmed by Leontyne Price. "A sumptuously sung *Porgy,* of which Leontyne Price has been a Dallas sensation. The voice, a bright and focused soprano, has great impact, but that is only the half of it. She brought a lively theatrical imagination to the role of Bess, limning the animal passion and the alternating goodness of Crown and Porgy's woman with such vivid detail that the first-night audience lost its composure when she took her final curtain call."[2] The production played two sold-out weeks in Dallas where it was heralded as "the box-office champion in the history of Dallas summer musical shows." So far, so good.

Success followed this production wherever it played. Three sold-out weeks at the Lyric Opera of Chicago were followed by an equally successful week in Pittsburgh. When the tour reached Washington, D.C., its last stop before leaving for Europe, it played in the newly dedicated National Theatre. President and Mrs. Truman attended the gala August 6, 1952, opening night, as did New York Society doyenne, Pearl Mesta. President Truman, a great champion of civil rights, had already been the driving force behind the desegregation of the American Armed Forces. He now made sure that the State Department officially sponsored the *Porgy* European tour, thanks in no small part to Blevins Davis's skillful behind-the-scenes promoting. The company was scheduled to fly from Washington to Vienna on September 1, but before they left William Warfield and Leontyne Price used their day off to get married in New York's Abyssinian Baptist Church.

IN THE CAPITALS OF EUROPE

The company's first European performance, in Vienna's Volksoper on September 7, 1952, left the audience stunned. Pandemonium broke out during the curtain calls. "They had never seen anything in the theater like it," said Elle Gerber, Breen's assistant director. At the postperformance gala, Warfield astonished the Viennese when he sang note-perfect renditions of several Schubert songs in flawless German. *Porgy* then traveled to Berlin where it received the same sort of wild response. Twenty-one curtain calls followed the performance. A critic wrote, "One doesn't know where to praise and where to stop

That night, the German radio audience was able to tune in to a live broadcast of the first Berlin performance of *Porgy and Bess*. At the end of the evening, the announcer was dumbfounded by Gershwin's opera and the reaction of the public. "One sits in the audience amazed and breathless," he said. (This performance has recently been made available on CD.) The critic for the German newspaper *Der Tag* wrote, "Tempo without pause, number after number, unbelievable precision, a feel for rhythm which borders on the fantastic, and voices—voices that take one's breath away in astonishment." And so it went. Performances in London's Stoll Theatre were scheduled to run for three weeks. The demand for tickets at the Stoll was so intense that the run was extended four months. The London run was forced to close on February 10, 1953, only because the presenters in Paris had lost patience waiting. *Porgy* opened at the theater de l'Empire on February 16, 1953, and played to what Leontyne Price remembered as, "the most enthusiastic audiences of all."

The Everyman tour of *Porgy* returned to New York to take up residence in the Ziegfeld Theater, where it sold out from March 10 to November 28, 1953. During the Ziegfeld run, Breen had the idea to divide the opera into two acts by eliminating one intermission and placing the remaining break after the second scene of Gershwin's Act II. The new second act now opened with the picnic on Kittiwah Island. The eliminated 15-minute intermission allowed Breen to restore even more of Gershwin's original score. After New York, the tour embarked on a yearlong series of engagements in 19 cities across the United States and Canada.

PORGY AT LA SCALA

It was during their 1954 summer weeks in San Francisco that a number of *Porgy* cast members went out on the town after their own performance to The Purple Onion, a well-known North Beach hangout for Beat Generation jazz. There they heard an unusual young singer known for her calypso style singing and dancing. Her name was Maya Angelou. After several fits and starts, Angelou would join the company of *Porgy and Bess* for its return to Europe.

Spanish (top) and French (bottom) and sheet music for "Summertime."

Angelou toured with the Breen production from September of 1954 to May of 1955. She danced the role of Ruby in Paris, Venice, Zagreb, and Belgrade before the company made its historic trip to the Middle East. In Egypt, they sang Gershwin's opera in Alexandria and Cairo before continuing on to Athens, Tel Aviv, and Casablanca. Returning to Europe, the company performed in Barcelona's magnificent Gran Teatro del Liceo and opulent theaters in Lausanne and Marseilles. Their performances were cheered in the historic Italian opera houses of Naples, Genoa, Florence, Turin, and Rome. But the most thrilling of all was their week of playing *Porgy and Bess* in Milan's famed La Scala, arguably the world's most famous opera house. *Porgy and Bess* was the first American opera ever heard in La Scala and the first by African Americans. Of that February 23, 1954, opening night, Maya Angelou recalled,

> "Famous white sopranos, tenors and baritones from the United States had soloed at Milan's renowned opera house; now an entire cast of Negro singers were nervously rehearsing on the legendary stage …

"The moment the curtain opened, the singers in concert pulled the elegant first-night audience into the harshness of Black Southern life. When Robbins was killed, the moans were real ... the entrance of the white policeman was met with real fear ... the love story unfolded with such tenderness that the singers wept visible tears. The first smiles of the evening were shared during our bows. We had sung gloriously. Although we faced the audience—which was on its feet, yelling and applauding—we bowed to compliment each other. We had performed *Porgy and Bess* as never before, and if the La Scala patrons loved us, it was only fitting because we certainly performed as if we were in love with one another."[3]

After three more engagements in Europe, the company had a week off before performing in 11 cities throughout South and Central America from July through October, ending their Latin America performances in Mexico City's famed Teatro Bellas Artes. The demand for *Porgy* in Europe was still strong, so they returned for a third time.

CATFISH ROW IN THE USSR

By May of 1955, The Everyman Opera production of *Porgy and Bess* had been giving performances on the road for essentially three years. While the company was performing in Rome, Breen learned that representatives from the Soviet Union had indicated an interest in *Porgy* performances in Russia. Breen would now pull off his greatest coup. Political leadership on both sides of the Cold War was shifting. A blunt and plainspoken Nikita Khrushchev had become the Soviet leader after the death of the brutal dictator Joseph Stalin. Khrushchev was on the verge of denouncing Stalin and his "cult of personality." On the American side, Dwight D. Eisenhower had succeeded Harry Truman as president and warned against the growth of an all-powerful military-industrial complex. When Breen learned of the Soviet's surprising but indirect interest in *Porgy*, the ink had just dried on the Warsaw Pact. The Soviet's interest in *Porgy* had been covert, because the Kremlin did not want to be embarrassed if the U.S. State Department refused to allow the tour, particularly at a time when their premier was on the verge of announcing a radical break with the USSR's immediate past.

Breen needed the State Department to pay for the trip but suspected politics was causing a needless delay. "*Porgy and Bess* has been a historic milestone in the history of American theater and culture," he said, "[It] has done what no other production has ever done and perhaps will ever do for another 20 or 25 years—mainly because there might not be anyone around as crazy as we are to plunge ahead into the almost impossible."[4]

Bypassing the bureaucracy on both sides, Breen made a direct call to the Russian ambassador in Washington, who assured him that the interest in *Porgy* remained strong at the highest levels of Soviet government. Meanwhile, the tour had returned to Europe for a third time, but with bookings only until the end of the year. It was now November and Breen was involved with several projects in addition to *Porgy,* so he dispatched his wife, who was with the company in Brussels, to Moscow to negotiate on his behalf. While the tour was playing to rapturous audiences and sold-out houses in Düsseldorf, Frankfurt, and Munich, negotiations continued. Finally, on December 3, 1955, the Everyman Opera, Inc., signed a contract with the ministry of culture of the USSR. This cast of George Gershwin's opera would be the first American theater group to perform in Russia since the 1917 Bolshevik revolution. Everyman stood to lose thousands of dollars each week, but Robert Breen was elated. "Suffice it to say that when we do close, we will close loaded with debt—but who cares! We've done what no one else in the world has, and it has brought glory not only to everyone concerned, but to the United States itself, and we are very proud of it."[5]

The *Porgy and Bess* company left communist East Berlin bound for St. Petersburg, then known as Leningrad, on December 19, 1953. The troupe had acquired its own entourage of VIPs for the occasion, and several members of the press. Leonard Lyons, a popular syndicated columnist whose daily banner "The Lyons Den" was a New York institution, was there to chronicle every step of this unprecedented journey. *The New Yorker* sent the outré young writer Truman Capote to write his observations of the equally unprecedented idea of an opera company of African Americans traveling behind the Iron Curtain. Robert Breen had thought this a good idea, assuming he would get a literate journal of what was sure to be a history-making event and which would appear in American's most literate periodical.

Wilva Breen was less sure. Just before leaving East Berlin,

Posters in Russia for *Porgy and Bess*.

Capote said to her, "It's so chic to be going to Russia." Later she recalled that Capote couldn't understand why, for such an occasion, America was sending such a lowbrow piece full of drunks, prostitutes, and beggars. "What would you prefer?" she asked him. *"Lady Windermere's Fan?"*

"Why, yes," was his response.

"The members of the company began to sense that he regarded them as 'Uncle Toms' for playing in a work about distressed slum Negros," wrote Hollis Alpert. "Among themselves they referred to him as 'Little Eva'. This may also have been due to his high, childish voice, his small stature, and the huge yellow cashmere scarf he wore over his head and bundled around his neck whenever he poked his head outdoors." Capote's piece, *The Muses Are Heard* (originally titled *Porgy and Bess in Russia*) first appeared serialized in *The New Yorker* in early 1956. It has subsequently been published in a compilation of the author's essays, entitled *Portraits and Observations.*

The essay concentrates on the long journey aboard the uncomfortable and dinning-car-free train and the company's arrival in Leningrad to gawking crowds unaccustomed to foreigners (let alone ones with dark skin). The piece supplies a hilarious account of their hotel accommodations, touching portraits of the performers (one of whom attends a dour Russian protestant church service which she livens up considerably by singing spirituals), and a description (but not a review) of the opening night in the cavernous Leningrad Palace of Culture. It makes for a very good read, one that Robert and Wilva Breen, Lee Gershwin, and a number of others on the trip would live to regret. *The Muses Are Heard* is quick to seize on the theatricality of theater people, and always at their expense. The tour continued on to Moscow but Mr. Capote, perhaps thinking that Russia had lost its chic, returned to New York.

In Moscow, the seven performances of *Porgy and Bess* were more favorably housed in the 1,500-seat Stanislavsky Theater. But Soviet commitment to across-the-board equality among comrades was on shaky ground throughout the run. Tickets were nowhere to be found, largely because the Ministry of Culture had carefully distributed them to high-ranking Communist Party officials, favored members of the diplomatic corps, and stars of the Russian opera, theater, and ballet. A small contingent of everyday workers who had demonstrated exceptional levels of productivity had been awarded strategically placed tickets at every performance. Opening night was a triumph. *Izvestia*, one of the leading daily newspapers in Russia, wrote, "Our American guests have shown that original art is understandable for people of all countries."

What was missing was a contingent of USSR brass. Assured that if the top-tear officials came at all, it would be only for part of the final performance, Robert and Wilva Breen headed off to the Bolshoi Ballet on their second night in Moscow. Much to the amazement of the Russians, at the last minute the government box had to be cleared for the arrival of the premier, Nikita Khrushchev; his defense minister, Nikolai Bulganin; Vyacheslav Molotov, the feared protégé of Stalin, after whom the Molotov cocktail had been named; and an entourage of 16. By the time word of their attendance reached Breen and he rushed from the Bolshoi to the Stanislavski, the dignitaries were gone; they had left after the second curtain call. When Breen asked the minister of culture about the surprise visit, he quipped, "He's maybe afraid he couldn't get tickets if he waited."

Leontyne Price, William Warfield, and Cab Calloway in the Breen-Davis production.

The Everyman Opera *Porgy and Bess* played 13 more engagements after their historic two-city tour of the Soviet Union. The final performance took place in Amsterdam on June 3, 1956— nearly four years to the day since they had begun on the State Fairgrounds in Dallas, Texas, on June 9, 1952. Eighty separate engagements, lasting from a few days to a full nine months, had been booked in 70 cities across five continents. Millions had heard George Gershwin's score. By any measure, *Porgy and Bess* was now the most successful American opera of all time.

CHAPTER 12

AT THE MOVIES

Since its premier in 1935, more than 90 film producers, including Hal Wallis, L.B. Mayer, and Dore Schary, had expressed interest in adapting *Porgy and Bess* for the silver screen.[1] The economic problem of widely distributing a mainstream movie with an all-black cast in the still-segregated United States kept any movie project on the shelf. As a supposed fix, Harry Cohn floated an all-white Porgy, done in blackface makeup, with Al Jolson, Rita Hayworth, and Gershwin pal Fred Astaire as Sportin' Life. Ira Gershwin did not take the offer seriously.[2] Hollywood and America itself would need over 20 years and a veritable revolution in racial attitudes before *Porgy* would become a viable project. In May 1957, three years after the Supreme Court had issued its landmark decision in the *Brown v. Board of Education* case, independent producer Samuel Goldwyn obtained the film rights for *Porgy and Bess*. Goldwyn had been so impressed with *Porgy and Bess* onstage in 1935 that he hired the Gershwins to write songs for his 1938 movie *The Goldwyn Follies* and had nursed the dream of a film version of *Porgy* ever since.

SAMUEL GOLDWYN PRESENTS

Born Schmuel Gelbfisz in August 1879 in Warsaw, Poland, Sam Goldwyn (with Cecil B. DeMille, Louis B. Mayer, Harry Cohn, and a few others) was one of the original moguls of Hollywood. His long career dated to Cecil B. DeMille's 1913 movie *The Squaw Man,* which he produced, and included being a founding partner in two early Hollywood studios—one of which was absorbed by Paramount and the other, Goldwyn

Sidney Poitier and Dorothy Dandridge in the ill-fated film version of *Porgy and Bess*.

Left to right: André Previn, Samuel Goldwyn, Ira Gershwin, and Sidney Poitier.

Pictures Corporation, became the G in MGM. By the 1950s, he was the most highly regarded independent producer in Hollywood. His projects included 1946's *The Best Years of Our Lives*, which won seven Oscars, including best picture. That year, Goldwyn was also awarded the Irving G. Thalberg Award for his body of work, which also includes classics like 1939's *Wuthering Heights* (with Merle Oberon and Laurence Oliver) and 1941's *The Little Foxes* (with Bette Davis). Goldwyn was also the author of several colorful turns of phrase, which became known in Hollywood as "Goldwynisms." "Include me out!" became so identified with him that during a parlor game at Elsa Maxwell's he told guests he wanted "Include me out!" on his tombstone. Other Goldwynisms that circulated in newspaper columns and Hollywood gatherings included "I've been laid up with intentional flu" along with "We are dealing in facts, not realities" and "Give me a couple of years, and I'll make that actress an overnight success."

STARS ONLY

With the film rights secured, Goldwyn went after the best talent available, signing N. Richard Nash, who had written the play and movie *The Rainmaker*, to write the screenplay, Rouben Mamoulian to direct, and Andre Previn to direct the music. Goldwyn approached Leontyne Price to be the voice of Bess. "No body, no voice," she famously responded.[3] Acquiring talent for in front of the camera proved to be more problematic. The list of black movie stars was short and sweet—and virtually identical to the cast list for Otto

Preminger's 1954 *Carmen Jones*, an updating of *Carmen* set at an all-black U.S. Army camp. *Carmen Jones* placed the bewitchingly beautiful Dorothy Dandridge (with the singing voice of Marilyn Horne) in front of the public eye as a black woman movie star and garnered her an Oscar nomination as best actress, the first for a black woman. Alas, Dandridge's "Jones" costar Harry Belafonte turned down the role of Porgy, causing Goldwyn to set his sights on the young and gifted Sidney Poitier.

Dorothy Dandridge.

At first Poitier, like Belafonte, did not want to have anything to do with the movie, telling his agent that *Porgy and Bess* is "an insult to black people."[4] Goldwyn, however, brought public and private pressure to bear, forcing Poitier to agree to a meeting at Goldwyn's home in Los Angeles. Poitier was unimpressed by Goldwyn's perspective on *Porgy and Bess*. "This is one of the greatest things that has ever happened for the black race!" Goldwyn exclaimed.[5] Poitier remained obdurate until it appeared Goldwyn might interfere with a project Poitier was enthusiastic to do, Stanley Kramer's *The Defiant Ones*. A quiet conversation with Kramer about Goldwyn's ability to stall not only *The Defiant Ones* but Poitier's Hollywood career as well convinced him to relent.

As Hollywood's only black leading lady, Dorothy Dandridge was the obvious first choice for the role of Bess. Although *Carmen Jones* had established her as the top black star in Hollywood, no other film project had materialized in the three years since. Dandridge was supporting herself as a nightclub entertainer, a profession she did not enjoy. Still, deciding to take the role of Bess, a character that in the opera Maria describes as, "that liquor-guzzling slut," was difficult. The parts of Bess and the denizens of Catfish Row presented too many opportunities to perpetuate negative stereotypes that Hollywood had been circulating since the beginning of the silent era—the same stereotypes that Dandridge had been struggling against in her personal and professional life. Her friend and costar, Harry Belafonte advised her to stay away from the project. Her *Carmen Jones* director Otto Preminger encouraged her to take the part. Mamoulian stepped in to assuage Dandridge's apprehension. He informed the press he was planning to make "an uplifting film about the nobility of life." Finally, as she explained to the still uncommitted Poitier "[Goldwyn's] going to do this picture with or without me. He's going to do it with or without you. Now the way I'm thinking, if I can help to bring some dignity to the role, maybe that is what it needs." Resignedly, but with grace Dandridge agreed to bring her trademark glamour and bearing to the film.

Carmen Jones veterans Pearl Bailey, Brock Peters, and Diahann Carroll came aboard to fill out the cast, leaving Sportin' Life as the only main character to be cast. Sammy Davis, Jr., had campaigned openly for the role, although he knew Cab Calloway was Goldwyn's first choice. Lee Gershwin and Goldwyn were unimpressed when Davis staged an informal audition by performing for them during a party at Judy Garland's house. "Swear on your life you will never use him," Lee Gershwin demanded of Goldwyn. Goldwyn agreed. Like Goldwyn, Sammy Davis knew how to exert pressure and recruited his rat pack buddy Frank Sinatra for a little help. When Cab Calloway proved unavailable, Goldwyn offered Davis the part saying, "The part is yours. Now will you get all these guys off my back?"[6]

CATFISH ROW ON STAGE 8

The cast assembled, Mamoulian and Goldwyn prepared for filming by building a giant Catfish Row set on Goldwyn's Studio on Stage 8. Incredibly, the night before shooting was to begin, Stage 8, one of the largest in Hollywood, burned to the ground, injuring no one. Although some blamed arson, the cause of the fire was never determined. On the morning of July 2, 1958, Goldwyn, Mamoulian, set designer Oliver Smith, art director Joe Wright and a crying costume designer, Irene Sharaff, stood surveying the smoldering ruin on the Goldwyn lot. A message from Cecil B. DeMille, as well as support from Goldwyn's Hollywood peers like Jack Warner, William Wyler and David O. Selznick, did much to encourage Goldwyn to press on. "Tell Sam," DeMille said, "The phoenix arose from the ashes of a great fire and so will you with your great strength."[7] The fire resulted in a six-week delay in shooting, during which

Sidney Poitier and friends.

Mamoulian and Goldwyn had a falling out and Mamoulian was fired. Enraged by his dismissal after eight months of work, Mamoulian enlisted the Director's Guild and a press agent to wage war on Goldwyn. When the dust settled Mamoulian was still out, with his $75,000 fee fully paid, and Otto Preminger was tapped as his successor. Mamoulian would never complete another picture. Goldwyn, relieved to be at the end of yet another *Porgy*-related ordeal remarked, "I'm the only one who's exhausted from not talking."

OTTO ON A GOOD DAY

Born in Austria, Otto Preminger had been an A-list director since he produced and directed the film noir classic *Laura* in 1944. Ironically, as *Laura*'s producer, Preminger had fired Mamoulian before taking over the directing reigns himself. He was also an iconoclast who was at the forefront of challenging the Hollywood Production Code, a set of rules describing banned subjects and activities in movies. Preminger's *The Moon Is Blue*, a comedy about premarital sex, was released in 1953 without Production Code-approval but with a tantalizing label, "For adults only." The film managed to earn both a profit and an Oscar nomination for its female lead, newcomer Maggie McNamara. His 1955 *The Man with the Golden Arm,* a drama about drug addiction, was also denied Production Code-approval, but still managed to earn millions and an Oscar nomination for its star, Frank Sinatra. Widely acknowledged to be one of Hollywood's authentic geniuses, Preminger also had a reputation for being difficult and belligerent. In 1953, Preminger had a star turn as the Nazi commandant of a POW camp in *Stalag 17*, directed by fellow Austrian Billy Wilder. Keir Dullea, who worked with Otto on *Bunny Lake Is Missing*, described the portrayal of the petty, vain, sadistic commandant as "Otto on a good day."[8]

Prior to shooting, Preminger tousled with Goldwyn over the unrealistic Hollywood perfection of the set and costumes. "Look," he said, "You have a two-dollar whore in a two-thousand-dollar dress!" he charged in his nasal accent.[9] Goldwyn's original concept for the movie had been to stay close to Mamoulian's Broadway staging. Preminger constantly pushed Goldwyn to allow him to open up the film and shoot more scenes on location. A compromise was reached whereby the opening scene, Diahann Carrol singing "Summertime," and the Kittiwah Island scenes were filmed on location, and the Catfish Row scenes on the sets

Mamoulian had built.

On the first day of filming Preminger told his cast, "I want you to know that I grew up in Europe. For me there is no difference between black and white people. So if you behave badly, I'll be just as tough with you as I would be with white actors."[10] He seemed particularly eager to demonstrate this toughness when directing Dorothy Dandridge. Although Preminger had been a mentor and possibly more to Dandridge during the filming of *Carmen Jones*, by the time cameras started to roll for *Porgy and Bess,* he seemed determined to demonstrate that any regard or affection he had for Dandridge was well in the past. "You call yourself an actress?" Poitier remembers Preminger asking Dandridge in an explosive rage. "You get paid to perform, not to do stupid things."[11]

Poitier and Sammy Davis, Jr., were the subject of similar rants, but each successfully dealt with Preminger in his own way—Poitier by quietly walking off the set and noting his receptivity to an apology from Otto; Davis by shouting right back, or taking Preminger along on Rat Pack nights out. Dandridge though, was never able to defend herself against a man she had probably been in love with. Eventually members of the ensemble stepped in, informing Otto that his treatment of Dandridge was demeaning to all of them. If it continued, they made clear, he was facing an on-set mutiny. Thenceforth, Otto moderated his tone.

Racial sensitivities infused every aspect of the production. Pearl Bailey, who had initially stipulated that she would not wear a kerchief tied in her hair as a part

Otto Preminger with Poitier and Dandridge.

of her costume, shut down shooting on the first day by declaring that no woman in the movie could wear a kerchief. A tense conference was held, during which it was agreed that only some of the women in the movie would wear a kerchief. Another issue of contention was the dialogue. Instead of using the recitative from the opera, spoken dialogue would come between the songs. Prior to filming, both Dandridge and Poitier had worried that the dialect to be used on

Catfish Row could promulgate further negative stereotypes. Dandridge had met with the creative team to express her concerns. According to Brock Peters, Poitier expressed his concerns not by expressing them, but by cleansing his lines of any language he felt demeaning. The rest of the cast followed suit.[11] Preminger apparently never objected or was unable to hear the difference in dialects.

IN THE CAN

Shooting for *Porgy and Bess* ended on December 16, 1958. Sam Goldwyn, who had been attacked from inside and out during the project, wrote the epitaph for *Porgy and Bess*, his final production. "The only thing left to go wrong with this picture, is for me to go to jail." Goldwyn premiered the movie on June 25, 1959, at New York's Warner Theater, where *The Jazz Singer* had premiered in 1927. The reception of the movie was mixed, and the film only earned about half of the 7 million dollars it cost to make.

The *Porgy and Bess* movie now remains out of distribution, with the Gershwin family retaining the distribution rights. The footage is in need of restoration if it is to be rereleased. Though flawed, it is a highly watchable and entertaining movie. The score underlines the romance and tragedy of Catfish Row and is silent when the alien whites intrude, emphasizing the gulf that lies between the races. Poitier perhaps portrays a more dutiful and less inspirational Porgy than one would like. Yet, some of his moments are deeply affecting. Dandridge, every inch the beauty Queen, is effective yet too restrained as the passionate and foolish Bess. It's not hard to imagine her emotionally straitjacketed by Preminger's between-take rages. Of the three, only Sammy Davis, Jr., retains his familiar *joie de vivre*, infusing his Sportin' Life with an energy and effortlessness that transcends the potential for any stereotyping. Perhaps because his big number was filmed early in the shoot and outdoors on location, rather than on the oppressive Catfish Row set, his Sportin' Life shows the true potential of a *Porgy and Bess* movie that is still unrealized.

Sammy Davis, Jr.'s turn as Sportin' Life won the highest praise of any performance in the film.

AT THE OPERA

S herwin M Goldman was a law student at Yale University when he attended a debate-style lecture given by Gershwin scholar Robert Kimball. The talk mixed standard lecture format with the procedures of debate, and audience members were encouraged to refute points made by the speaker. When Kimball brought up Gershwin's *Porgy and Bess*, Goldman refuted its being an opera. He was sure that it was group of songs recorded by jazz singer Mel Tormé—an album that he owned. Kimball excused Goldman's youthful enthusiasm, and the two became friends. It was from Robert Kimball that Sherwin Goldman would learn just about all there was to know about George Gershwin's opera.

AMERICA'S BICENTENNIAL PORGY AND BESS

Goldman would later become the executive producer for American Ballet Theater. As the American bicentennial approached, Goldman was meeting with his friend Göran Gentele, the recently appointed general director of the Metropolitan Opera. Gentele was Swedish and asked his American friend for advice about what the Met might produce to mark America's 200th birthday. *Porgy and Bess* was Goldman's immediate response. Gentele didn't know *Porgy,* but after Goldman's description, he thought it sounded like the right idea and began to make production plans. Tragically, Gentele and several members of his family were killed in an automobile accident while on holiday in July 1972. His successor, Schuyler Chapin, did not think *Porgy* was

Donnie Ray Albert and Clamma Dale in the Houston Grand Opera production of *Porgy and Bess*.

a true opera and abandoned the provisional plans.

The distinguished American conductor Lorin Maazel disagreed. In 1975, he led the Cleveland Orchestra and chorus and an assemblage of African American opera stars in a concert of the full version of *Porgy*. A recording was made that reflected what Gershwin heard before the first round of cuts were made to *Porgy and Bess*. Goldman, however, was determined to produce a full version of *Porgy* on stage and began making plans of his own. But like those before him, Goldman soon realized that producing *Porgy and Bess* in the commercial theater—as Gershwin had intended it, as an opera with popular appeal—was financially out of the question. He knew that the answer was probably in the world of nonprofit opera, at the time far less costly, but he didn't know anyone in the opera business. He phoned a friend at the opera in his home town of Dallas, Texas, who introduced him to a young man who had just taken over the small regional opera company the Houston Grand Opera.

AMERICAN OPERA EMBRACES AN AMERICAN OPERA

David Gockley was in the first few weeks of his tenure as HGO's general director when he met Sherwin Goldman. Gockley would soon develop a reputation as an innovative opera producer and turn his company into a powerhouse. He loved the idea of producing a new *Porgy and Bess,* and the two men struck a deal. Goldman knew of sets and costumes that had been created for an early West Coast tour that had been canceled. He was able to rent them cheaply. HGO's music director, John DeMain, was engaged to conduct. DeMain, who had decided on a career in opera but was equally at home in Broadway musicals, had already begun to raise the musical standards of the Houston company. He had just worked with an equally brilliant young stage director named Jack O'Brian on a production at the Juilliard School. He suggested O'Brian direct the production, and both Gockley and Goldman agreed. Kimball introduced Goldman to Kay Swift, whom he approached to guide them to Gershwin's original intentions for his opera. Since she had helped the composer through creating the original orchestrations and had been there through all the rehearsals, she was the ideal authority, and she agreed to participate. With Swift's input, and using Robert Breen's way of dividing

Ira Gershwin was the guardian of all things George for a half-century after his brother's death.

the opera into two acts, DeMain, O'Brian, and Goldman worked to restore as much of the opera as possible while staying within a three-hour running time. Goldman had arranged for Lee Gershwin to attend the opening on July 1, 1976. A sigh of relief was heard throughout the state of Texas when she reported to Ira that she approved of what she saw and heard. Ira then gave Goldman permission for additional bookings, which Goldman had already made hoping that the results in Houston would be positive.

As the tour was about to arrive for performances in Philadelphia, a truly bizarre disaster struck. The city was in the midst of America's bicentennial celebrations, of which *Porgy* was a central part, when a mysterious illness began to sicken guests at the Bellevue Stratford Hotel where the American Legion was holding their national convention and the *Porgy* company was booked to stay. On July 18, 1976, the cause was identified as airborne bacteria traveling through the air-conditioning system of the hotel. In a panic over what would come to be known as Legionnaires' disease, central Philadelphia essentially shut down. While the company found other accommodations, no one came to the Academy of Music—across the street from the Bellevue Hotel—for *Porgy*. Goldman had to put up his house as collateral for a loan and pull in financial favors from friends in order to keep the company together. He made it, and the

Playbill from Goldman production.

company went on to sold-out runs at Wolftrap outside Washington, DC, and in Ottawa, Toronto, and Boston, where Goldman had arranged for the same seats Swift and George Gershwin had on September 30, 1935. *Porgy* as Gershwin had intended it had now proven itself as a box office success, and Goldman was able to book the production into the Uris Theater in New York. The production opened in New York on September 26, 1976, at the Uris and later moved to the Mark Hellinger. It was an enormous success, and *Porgy* was before the New York public again for ten weeks. RCA made a landmark recording of the production in November of 1976. In 1977, it was awarded a Tony Award for the Most Innovative Revival of a Musical work.

FROM RADIO CITY TO THE METROPOLITAN AND ACROSS AMERICA

For the next 20 years, a series of productions kept *Porgy* before the public. In March 1982, Radio City Music Hall Productions invited Goldman to create a brand-new production for the 5,882-seat theater. John DeMain conducted and Jack O'Brian directed, with new sets by Douglas Schmidt and costumes by Nancy Potts. The production was brilliantly lit by Gilbert Hemsley. It opened in 1983 playing 22 previews and 45 performances. A tour followed. To mark the 50th anniversary of *Porgy and Bess*, the Metropolitan Opera finally added Gershwin to its repertory in 1985. A new production was cast with opera singers and a full chorus. James Levine conducted the Met orchestra in a performance version that was virtually uncut. Todd Duncan and Anne Brown were honored guests. In 1987, Gockley negotiated an unprecedented agreement between 17 American Opera companies for a tour of Goldman's new production. The American Opera Company production achieved an unprecedented level of cooperation between opera houses. The effort firmly established *Porgy and Bess* as an opera-house repertory staple. The venture proved so successful that in the mid-1990s Gockley initiated a new co-production between a smaller number of opera companies.

LIVE FROM LINCOLN CENTER

In November 1995, Sherwin M. Goldman became executive producer of New York City Opera. The company had first produced Porgy and Bess in 1961 using the two-act version modeled on what Robert Breen had pioneered in the early 1950s. The production was a new one directed by William Ball, who would later become artistic director of the American Conservatory Theater in San Francisco. This New York opera company premiere was conducted by Julius Rudel, a Viennese musician who, in five years, would lead the company from City Center on W. 55th Street to Lincoln Center and its first Golden Age. Goldman suggested *Porgy* as the opening night of City Opera's Spring 2000 season, and the company's general director, Paul Kellogg, was happy to agree. Goldman's 1983 production was retrieved from storage and refurbished. African American director and theater artistic director Tazewell Thompson was engaged to completely restage the show. John DeMain, by now a recognized authority on Gershwin's score, plus a sought after conductor and opera company artistic director in his own right, was engaged to conduct. The first run proved so successful at the box office (the first run sold out before it opened) that the company brought it back two seasons later. On March 20, 2002, New York City Opera telecast its production on *Live From Lincoln Center* to PBS affiliates all across the company—a first for *Porgy and Bess*. Thompson's vivid staging, DeMain's incisive musical direction, and a superb American cast were captured for the camera by Kirk Browning, an acknowledged master in the genre of classical programming for television.

A RETURN TO OUR NATION'S CAPITOL

To mark the occasion of its 50th anniversary in 2005, Placido Domingo, then the Washington National Opera's general director, commissioned American opera and theater director Francesca Zambello to create an entirely new staging of *Porgy and Bess*. British conductor Wayne Marshall conducted. From the onset of planning, Zambello sought to "free *Porgy* of stereotype" by putting unusually strong emphasis on the characters of the men and women of Catfish Row; strong individuals who have an even stronger sense of community.

Alvy Powell as Porgy and
Marquita Lister as Bess
in the 2002 New York City
Opera production.

Their bond has been forged by their shared nature of their African cultural heritage, the collective memory of enslavement, and the conflict between the promise of life in America and the reality of Jim Crow laws. For Zambello, *Porgy* is the only American opera that "approaches race and class in the same way that Mozart and Verdi did in their time."

The debate about whether *Porgy* is an opera or a musical was unimportant to Zambello, but addressing the work's acquired cultural issues, unintended by its creators, was critical. She was convinced that at its core *Porgy* was a dark parable about, "drugs, abuse, crime, violence, and all the things that continue to plague our culture because of poverty and prejudice." As a director, she was equally convinced that the way to reach a contemporary audience in a deeper way was to address these underlying issues, rather than glossing over them in a picturesque way. This meant that the decision about the time period of the production was important.

The novel sets Porgy's story in "the Golden Age ... when men, not yet old, were boys in an ancient, beautiful city that time had forgotten before it destroyed," which in this case means the early 20th century. The play is more specifically set, "in the present," which meant 1927. The opera's 1935 premiere program also gave the period as "the present," but a random glance through programs from the last 75 years reveals everything from "mid-1920s," to "the 1930s—after slavery but before freedom" to just "the past." An individual's application of a learned stereotype begins in the eye before it is conceived in the mind. Zambello and her team felt that their goal of "freeing Porgy of stereotype" had to begin by removing the production from a literal, picturesque mid-1930s setting—one that bore more resemblance to the late 1890s than anything else. This new production made the setting less specific as to time, purpose, and detail. It also adopted costumes that referenced the 1950s without being literal re-creations of the era's fashions. Dark colors were used for the clothes of all characters except Bess, who wore vivid coral and pastel yellow. The treatment of Bess was a hallmark of this show. Rather than a conventional "liquor-guzzling slut," as Maria calls her, Bess is portrayed as a fully aware woman who, not unlike Violetta in Verdi's *La Traviata*, learns to survive in her male-dominated world. But whereas Violetta sacrifices herself for the benefit of her beloved and finds the strength to sustain her decision, Bess is unable to fight her tragic flaw. She is deeply conflicted between addiction (to cocaine and Crown) and an honest love (for Porgy). In the end, addiction wins.

The Zambello production in San Francisco.

In the mid-1920s, Gershwin's self-described musical aim was to create "operettas that represents the life and spirit of this country"[1] and have "the element of appealing to the great majority of our people."[2] By the early 1930s, his musical goals had matured. When he began composing *Porgy and Bess*, he wrote, "The production will be a serious attempt to put into operatic form a purely American theme."[3]

This particular production of *Porgy and Bess* has enjoyed acclaim from audiences and critics alike in Los Angeles, Chicago, and San Francisco. It made a successful return to the Washington National Opera in 2010. In each city, many ticket holders were attending their first performance of *Porgy and Bess,* which doubled as their first experience with opera. The success of this *Porgy and Bess*, the first large-scale new American production of the 21st century, has given testament to the enduring appeal of this great American opera.

NOTES

Chapter 1
1. Alpert 1990, 22.

Chapter 2
1. Alpert 1990, 17.
2. Durham 1954, 47.
3. Wyatt and Johnson 2004, 28.
4. Hutchisson 2000, 54.
5. Alpert 1990, 34–35.
6. Durham 1994, 44.
7. Durham 1994, 46.
8. Durham 1994, 48.
9. Hutchisson 2000, 54.
10. Hutchisson 2000, 61.
11. Alpert 1990, 39.
12. Alpert 1990, 39.
13. Alpert 1990, 40.
14. Alpert 1990, 19.
15. Alpert 1990, 45.
16. Alpert 1990, 45.
17. Wyatt and Johnson 2004, 29.
18. Hutchisson 2000, 76.

Chapter 3
1. Spergel 1993, 56.
2. Alpert 1990, 57–58.
3. Spergel 1993, 63.
4. Hutchisson 2000, 77.

Chapter 4
1. Peyser 2006, 24.
2. Peyser 2006, 18.
3. Jablonski and Stewart 1973, 4.
4. Jablonski and Stewart 1973, 4.
5. Peyser 2006, 18.
6. Jablonski and Stewart 1973, 4.
7. Peyser 2006, 21-22.
8. Jablonski and Stewart 1973, 4.
9. Jablonski 1992, 6.
10. Jablonski and Stewart 1973, 3.
11. Jablonski 1992, 6.
12. Alpert 1990, 25.
13. Jablonski and Stewart 1973, 124.

Chapter 5
1. Jablonski and Stewart 1973, 7.
2. Jablonski and Stewart 1973, 7.
3. Alpert 1990, 26
4. Jablonski and Stewart 1973, 10.
5. Peyser 2006, 26.
6. Alpert 1990, 26.
7. Jablonski and Stewart 1973, 19.
8. Peyser 2006, 48.
9. Jablonski and Stewart 1973, 30.
10. Rosenberg 1991, 39.

Chapter 6
1. Wyatt and Johnson 2004, 97.
2. Alpert 1990, 7.
3. Peyser 2006, 59.
4. Peyser 2006, 41.
5. Peyser 2006, 41–41.
6. Peyser 2006, 40.
7. Alpert 1990, 14.

Chapter 7
1. Pollack 2006, 271.
2. Jablonski and Stewart 1973, 53.
3. Pollack 2006, 125.
4. Pollack 2006, 407.
5. Jablonski and Stewart 1973, 154.
6. Jablonski and Stewart 1973, 158.
7. Jablonski and Stewart 1973, 167.

Chapter 8
1. Wyatt and Johnson 2004, 202.

2. Jablonski and Stewart 1973, 255.
3. Jablonski 1992, 95.
4. Jablonski and Stewart 1973, 256.
5. Pollack 2006, 577.
6. Pollack 2006, 187.
7. Wyatt and Johnson 2004, 209.
8. Jablonski and Stewart 1973, 270.
9. Wyatt and Johnson 2004, 204.
10. Jablonski and Stewart 1973, 276.
11. Jablonski and Stewart 1973, 261.
12. Alpert 1990, 82.
13. Furla 1996, 109.
14. Hutchisson 2000, 149.
15. Pollack 2006, 577.
16. Hutchisson 2000, 150.
17. Hutchisson, 2000, 149
18. Hutchisson 2000, 149.
19. Jablonski and Stewart 1973, 270.
20. Hutchisson 2000, 150.
21. Alpert 1990, 91.
22. Pollack 2006, 577.
23. Jablonski and Stewart 1973, 275.
24. Jablonski and Stewart 1973, 275.
25. Jablonski and Stewart 1973, 273.
26. Wyatt and Johnson 2004, 235.
27. Jablonski 1992, 99.
28. Jablonski and Stewart 1973, 275.

Chapter 9
1. Wyatt and Johnson 2004, 229.
2. Peyser 2006, 240.
3. Alpert 1990, 100.
4. Alpert 1990, 89.
5. Pollack 2006, 596.
6. Wyatt and Johnson 2004, 226
7. Wyatt and Johnson 2004, 231
8. Alpert 1990, 107.
9. Wyatt and Johnson 2004, 231.
10. Wyatt and Johnson 2004, 230.
11. Kimball and Simon 1973, 181.
12. Kimball and Simon 1973, 184.
13. Wyatt and Johnson 2004, 223.

Chapter 10
1. Alpert 1990, 101.
2. Wyatt and Johnson 2004, 232.
3. Hutchisson 2000, 150.
4. Jablonski 1992, 71.
5. Alpert 1990, 110.
6. Alpert 1990, 111.
7. Pollack 2006, 603.
8. Kimball and Simon 1973, 188.
9. Kimball and Simon 1973, 188.
10. Kimball and Simon 1973, 277.

Chapter 11
1. Warfield 1991, 131.
2. Alpert 1990, 169.
3. Angelou 1976, 602.
4. Alpert 1990, 216.
5. Alpert 1990, 217.

Chapter 12
1. Berg 1989, 478.
2. Berg 1989, 478.
3. Berg 1989, 482.
4. Poitier 1980, 206.
5. Poitier 1980, 208
6. Hirsh 2007, 288.
7. Berg 1989, 483.
8. Hirsh 2007, 403.
9. Berg 1989, 486.
10. Berg 1989, 486.
11. Poitier 1980, 221.
12. Hirsh 2007, 293.

Chapter 13
1. Pollack 2006, 567.
2. Pollack 2006, 567.
3. Alpert 1990, 98.

BIBLIOGRAPHY

Alpert, Hollis. 1990. *The Life and Times of Porgy and Bess.* New York: Alfred A Knopf.

Alpert, Hollis. 1991. *Broadway! 125 Years of Musical Theater.* New York: Arcade Publishing Inc.

Armitage, Merle, ed. 1938. *George Gershwin.* Reprint. New York: Da Capo Press, 1995.

Angelou, Maya. 1976. *Singin' and Swingin' and Gettin' Merry Like Christmas.* New York: Random House.

Berg, Scott A. 1989. *Goldwyn: A Biography.* New York: Alfred A. Knopf.

Bernstein, Leonard. 1959. *The Joy of Music.* New York: Simon and Schuster.

Bogle, Donald. 1997. *Dorothy Dandridge: A Biography.* New York: Amistad Press.

Calloway, Cab. 1976. *Of Minnie the Moocher and Me.* New York: Thomas Y. Crowell Co.

Capote, Truman. 2008. The Muses Are Heard. In *The Essays of Truman Capote* New York: Modern Library.

Carnes, Mark, ed. 2002. *Invisible Giants: 50 Americans Who Shaped the Nation but Missed the History Books.* New York: Oxford University Press.

Crawford, Richard. 2005. *America's Musical Life: A History.* New York: W.W. Norton.

Crawford, Richard. Where Did Porgy and Bess Come From? *Journal of Interdisciplinary History,* xxx: 4 (spring, 2006), 697–734.

Durham, Frank. 1954. *DuBose Heyward: The Man Who Wrote Porgy.* Columbia, SC: University of South Carolina Press.

Elliot, Jeff, ed. 1989. *Conversations with Maya Angelou.* Jackson, MI: University Press of Mississippi.

Ewan, David. 1970. *George Gershwin: His Journey to Greatness.* Englewood Cliffs, NJ: Prentice-Hall, Inc.

Fordham, Damon L. 2008. *The True Stories of Black South Carolina.* Charleston, SC: The History Press.

Furla, Phillip. 1996. *Ira Gershwin: The Art of the Lyricist.* New York: Oxford University Press.

Geraty, Virginia Mixson. 1990. *Porgy: A Gullah Version.* Charleston, SC: Wyrick and Co.

Gioia, Ted. 1997. *The History of Jazz.* New York: Oxford University Press.

Goldberg, Isaac. 1931. *George Gershwin: A Study in American Music.* New York: Simon and Schuster.

Heyward, Dorothy and DuBose Heyward. 1928. *Porgy: A Play in Four Acts* New York: Doubleday.

Heyward, DuBose. 1925. *Porgy.* Reprint. Jackson MI: University of Mississippi Press, 2001.

Hirsh, Foster. 2007. *Otto Preminger: The Man Who Would Be King.* New York: Alfred A Knopf.

Hutchinson, James M., ed. 2003. *A Dubose Heyward Reader.* Athens, GA: University of Georgia Press.

Hutchinson, James M. 2000. *Dubose Heyward: A Charleston Gentleman and the World of Porgy and Bess.* Jackson, MI: University Press of Mississippi.

Jablonski, Edward and Lawrence D. Stewart. 1973. *The Gershwin Years.* New York: Doubleday.

BIBLIOGRAPHY

Jablonski, Edward. 1992. *Gershwin Remembered.* Portland, OR: Amadeus Press.

Jablonski, Edward.1987. *Gershwin: A Biography.* New York: Doubleday.

Kimball, Robert and Alfred Simon. 1973. *The Gershwins.* New York: Atheneum.

Lyon, Hugh Lee. 2006. *Leontyne Price: Highlights of a Prima Donna.* New York: Vantage Press, 1973. Reprint. Authors Choice Press

Martin, George. 1999. *Twentieth Century Opera: A Guide.* New York: Proscenium Publishers, Inc.

Mordden, Ethan. 1997. *Make Believe: The Broadway Musical in the 1920s.* New York: Oxford University Press.

Ohl, Vicki. 2004. *Fine and Dandy: The Life and Work of Kay Swift.* New Haven, CT: Yale University Press.

Parker, Adam. 2009. 'Porgy and Bess' Creation Revisited. *The Post and Courier.* Charleston, South Carolina.

Paton, Maureen. 2002. "Method in the Rhythm Madness." *Telegraph Media Group Limited* 2010

Peyser, Joan. 2006. *The Memory of all That: The Life of George Gershwin.* New York: Simon & Schuster, 1993. Reprint, Hal Leonard Corporation.

Poitier, Sidney. 1980. *This Life.* New York: Alfred A. Knopf.

Pollack, Howard. 2006. *George Gershwin: His Life and Work.* Berkeley, CA: University of California Press.

Roell, Craig H. 1989. *The Piano in America.* Chapel Hill, NC: University of North Carolina Press.

Rosenberg, Deena. 1991. *Fascinating Rhythm: The Collaboration of George and Ira Gershwin.* New York: Dutton.

Ross, Alex. 2007. *The Rest is Noise: Listening to the Twentieth Century.* New York: Farrar, Straus and Giroux.

Schmeling, Laurie Lynn. 1993. *Negotiating "Catfish Row": The Robert Breen Production of "Porgy and Bess," 1952–1956, and The Question of Cultural Hegemony.* MA Thesis, Ohio State University.

Seebohm, Caroline. 1982. *The Man Who Was Vogue: The Life and Times of Conde Nast.* New York: The Viking Press, Inc.

Spergel, Mark. 1993. *Reinventing Reality: The Art of Life of Rouben Mamoulian.* Metuchen, NJ: The Scarecrow Press, Inc.

Standifer, James. 1997. The Complicated Life of Porgy and Bess. *Humanities.* November/December, vol 18, no. 6.

Tommassini, Anthony. 1997. *Virgil Thomson: Composer on the Aisle.* New York: W.W. Norton and Co.

Wyatt, Robert and John Andrew Johnson, eds. 2004. *The George Gershwin Reader.* New York: Oxford University Press.

Yuhl, Stephanie. 2005. *A Golden Haze of Memory: The Making of Historic Charleston.* Chapel Hill, NC: The University of North Carolina Press.

INDEX

INDEX